Contents

Introduction

The pace of change in the wine world makes each revision of this little annual a more absorbing task. With more correspondents than ever this year I have been able to revise all the main sections in nit-picking depth. In particular I have added many more producers' names as the key to finding true character and quality in all areas. Some of the telegraphese required to fit this material into 200 pages reads rather tersely, I fear; but in this pocket book a fact matters more than a turn of phrase.

To new readers I should explain that this book is a continuing attempt to squeeze in as much up-to-date information about the wines of the world as possible. The information is gleaned from many sources through innumerable visits and tastings and via a perpetual spate of correspondence. The process of revision never stops, whether it involves a change of emphasis or fact or vintage or a new entry. There is a constant pressure by new producers for inclusion; newness itself, however, is not a qualification for entry . . . old producers also do newsworthy things.

The arrangement of the book is intended to be as helpful as possible when you are buying a bottle, whether you are on the nursery slopes or an old hand with a bad memory. You are faced with a list of wines or an array of bottles in a restaurant, wine merchant's or bottle store. Your mind goes blank. You fumble for your little book. All you need to establish is what country a wine comes from. Look up the principal words on the label in the appropriate country's section. You will find enough potted information to let you judge whether this is the wine you want.

Specifically, you will find information on the colour and type of wine, its status or prestige, whether it is usually particularly good value, which vintages are good and which are ready to drink – and often considerably more . . . about the quantity made, the grapes used, ownership and the rest. Hundreds of cross-references help you delve further.

HUGH JOHNSON'S

· POCKET ·
WINE BOOK

· 1991 ·

REVISED AND
UPDATED

MITCHELL BEAZLEY

KEY TO SYMBOLS

r.	red	⎫
p.	rosé	⎬ (in brackets) means relatively unimportant
w.	white	
br.	brown	⎭
sw.	sweet	
s/sw.	semi-sweet	
dr.	dry	
sp.	sparkling	
★	plain, everyday quality	
★★	above average	
★★★	well known. highly reputed	
★★★★	grand, prestigious, expensive	
▨	usually particularly good value in its class	
( )	provisional rating	
83 84 etc.	recommended years which may be currently available.	
82′ etc.	Vintage regarded as particularly successful for the property in question.	
80 etc.	years in **bold** should be ready for drinking (the others should be kept). Where both reds and whites are indicated the red is intended unless otherwise stated.	
N.B.	German vintages are codified by a different system. See note on p. 103.	
D.Y.A.	drink the youngest available	
NV	vintage not normally shown on label. In Champagne, means a blend of several vintages for continuity.	

Cross-references are in SMALL CAPS

See p. 5 for extra explanation

A quick-reference vintage chart for France and Germany appears on p.200.

© 1977 Mitchell Beazley Publishers
Text © Hugh Johnson 1977, 1978, 1979, 1980, 1981, 1982, 1983, 1984, 1985, 1986, 1987, 1988, 1989, 1990
First edition published 1977
Revised editions published 1978, 1979, 1980, 1981, 1982, 1983, 1984, 1985, 1986, 1987, 1988, 1989, 1990
© 1990 Mitchell Beazley Publishers

A CIP catalogue record for this book is available from the British Library.

ISBN 0 85533 795 8

The author and publishers will be grateful for any information which will assist them in keeping future editions up to date. Although all reasonable care has been taken in the preparation of this book, neither the publishers nor the author can accept any liability for any consequences arising from the use thereof, or from the information contained herein.

Mitchell Beazley International Ltd.
Artists House, 14–15 Manette Street,
London W1V 5LB

Managing Editor   Chris Foulkes
Assistant Editors   Alison Franks, Alessandra Perotto
Production   Barbara Hind
Filmsetting by Litho Link Ltd, Welshpool, Powys, Wales
Produced by Mandarin Offset
Printed in Malaysia

How to read an entry

The top line of most entries consists of the following information.
1. Which part of the country in question the wine comes from.
2. Whether it is red, rosé or white (or brown/amber), dry, sweet or sparkling, or several of these.
3. Its general standing as to quality: a necessarily rough and ready guide based principally on an ascending scale:

   * plain, everyday quality
   ** above average
   *** well known, highly reputed
   **** grand, prestigious, expensive

So much is more or less objective. Additionally there is a subjective rating: shading around the stars of any wine which in my experience is usually particularly good (which means good value) within its price range. There are good everyday wines as well as good luxury wines. The box system helps you find them.
4. Vintage information: which were the more successful of the recent vintages which *may* still be available. And of these which are ready to drink this year, and which will probably improve with keeping. Your first choice for current drinking should be one of the vintage years printed in **bold** type. Buy light-type years for further maturing. The German vintage information works on a different principle: see page 103.

Acknowledgements

This store of detailed recommendations comes partly from my own notes and partly from those of a great number of kind friends. Without the generous help and co-operation of every single member of the wine trade I have approached, I could not attempt it. I particularly want to thank the following for help with research or in the areas of their special knowledge.

Rodrigo Alvarado
Burton Anderson
Anthony Barton
Jean-Claude Berrouet
Tim Bleach
Bernhard Breuer
Michael Broadbent M.W.
Dr. Bruno Roncarati
Bertrand de Rivoyre
Terry Dunleavy
Len Evans
Dereck Foster
Chris Foulkes
Rosemary George M.W.
Garry Grosvenor
James Halliday
Phyllis Hands
Peter Hasslacher
Ian Jamieson M.W.
Nathaniel Johnston
Matt Kramer
Tony Laithwaite

Miles Lambert-Gócs
John Lipitch
Peter M.F. Sichel
Tim Marshall
Patrick Matthews
Vladimir Moskvan
Christian Moueix
David Peppercorn M.W.
Istvn Pusztai
Belle Rhodes
Dr. Bernard Rhodes
Phillipa Richardson
Etienne le Riche
James Ross
Steven Skelton
Serena Sutcliffe M.W.
Bob Thompson
Liz Turner
Peter Vinding-Diers
Manfred Völpel
Dr Kurt Weibel
David Wolfe

Grape varieties

The most basic of all differences between wines is the flavour (or lack of it) of the grapes they are made of. Centuries of selection have resulted in each of the long-established wine areas having its favourite single variety, or a group of varieties whose juice or wine is blended together. Red burgundy is made of one grape, the Pinot Noir; red Bordeaux of three or four: two kinds of Cabernet, Merlot, Malbec and sometimes others (the proportions at the discretion of the grower). The laws say which grapes must be used, so the labels do not mention them.

So in newer regions the choice of a grape is the grower's single most crucial decision. Where he is proud of it, and intends his wine to have the character of a particular grape, the variety is the first thing he puts on the label. Hence the originally Californian term "varietal wine" – meaning, in principle, *one* grape variety.

Familiarity with the principal quality grape varieties, then, is the single most helpful piece of knowledge in finding wines you will like wherever they are grown. At least seven – Cabernet, Pinot Noir, Riesling, Sauvignon Blanc, Chardonnay, Gewürztraminer and Muscat – have memorable tastes and smells distinct enough to form international categories of wine. To these you might add Merlot, Syrah, Sémillon, Chenin Blanc, Pinots Blanc and Gris, Sylvaner, Nebbiolo, Sangiovese, Tempranillo . . .

Further notes on grapes will be found in the sections on Germany, Italy, central and south-east Europe, South Africa, etc. The following are the best and/or commonest wine grapes.

Grapes for white wine

Aligoté Burgundy's second-rank white grape. Crisp (often sharp) wine, needs drinking in 1-3 years. Perfect for mixing with cassis (blackcurrant liqueur) to make a "Kir".

Arneis Traditional grape of Piemonte being revived for high-quality, rich-textured whites.

Blanc Fumé Another name for SAUVIGNON BLANC, referring to the reputedly "smoky" smell of the wine, particularly on the upper Loire (Sancerre and Pouilly). In California the name is often reversed (to Fumé Blanc).

Bual Makes top-quality sweet Madeira wines.

Chardonnay The white burgundy grape, one of the grapes of Champagne, and considered the best white grape of California and more recently Australia. Gives dry wine of rich complexity, especially when aged some months in new barrels. Italy, Spain, New Zealand, Bulgaria, Oregon, Washington, New York, Chile and S. Africa all also now make good Chardonnays. One sometimes wishes they would try something else for a change.

Chasselas A prolific and widely grown early-ripening grape with little aroma, also grown for eating. Best known as Fendant in Switzerland (where it is supreme), Gutedel in Germany. Perhaps the same as Hungary's Leanyka and Romania's Feteasca.

Chenin Blanc
The leading white grape of the middle Loire (Vouvray, Layon, etc.). Wine can be dry or sweet (or very sweet), but always retains plenty of acidity – hence its popularity in California, where it can make fine wine, but is rarely so used. See also Steen.

Clairette A dull neutral grape formerly widely used in the s. of France.

Fendant See CHASSELAS.

Folle Blanche

High acid and little flavour makes it ideal for brandy. Known as Gros Plant in Brittany, Picpoul in Armagnac. Respectable in California.

Furmint A grape of great character: the trade mark of Hungary both as the principal grape in Tokay and as vivid vigorous table wine with an appley flavour. Called Sipon in Yugoslavia.

Grecheto or Greco

Ancient grape of central and s. Italy with vitality and style.

Gewürztraminer (or Traminer)

One of the most pungent wine grapes, distinctively spicy to smell and taste, with flavours often identified as being like rose petals and grapefruit. Wines are often rich and soft, even when fully dry. Best in Alsace; also good in Germany, e. Europe, Australia, California, New Zealand.

Grüner Veltliner

An Austrian speciality. Round Vienna and in the Wachau and Weinviertel (also in Moravia) can be delicious: light but dry and lively. Drink young.

Italian Riesling

Grown in n. Italy and all over central eastern Europe. Much inferior to Rhine Riesling with lower acidity. Alias Wälschriesling, Olaszrizling (but no longer legally labelled simply "Riesling").

Kerner The most successful of a wide range of recent German varieties, largely made by crossing Riesling and Sylvaner (but in this case Riesling and [red] Trollinger). Early-ripening, flowery (but often too blatant) wine with good acidity. Popular in Rheinpfalz, Rheinhessen.

Malvasia Known as Malmsey in Madeira, Malvasia in Italy, Malvoisie in France. Alias Vermentino. Also grown in Greece, Spain, W. Australia, eastern Europe. Makes rich brown wines or soft whites ageing magnificently with superb potential, not often realized.

Marsanne Principal white grape (with Rousanne) of the northern Rhône (i.e. St-Joseph, St-Péray, Crozes-Hermitage). Also used to effect in Victoria and (as Ermitage Blanc) in the Valais.

Müller-Thurgau

Dominant variety in Germany's Rheinhessen and Rheinpfalz; a cross between Riesling and Sylvaner. Ripens early to make soft flowery wines to drink young. Makes good sweet wines but dull dry ones.

Muscadet (alias Melon de Bourgogne)

Makes light, very dry wines with a seaside tang round Nantes in Brittany. They should not be sharp, but faintly salty, savoury and v. refreshing.

Muscat (Many varieties; the best is Muscat blanc à petits grains.) Universally grown easily recognized pungent grapes, mostly made into perfumed sweet wines, often fortified (as in France's VIN DOUX NATURELS). Muscat d'Alsace is unusual in being dry.

Palomino Alias Listan. Makes all the best sherry but poor table wine.

Pedro Ximénez

Said to have come to s. Spain from Germany. Makes very strong wine in Montilla and Malaga. Used in blending sherry. Also grown in Australia, California, South Africa.

Pinot Blanc

A close relation of CHARDONNAY without its strength of character. Grown in Champagne, Alsace (increasingly), n. Italy (good sparkling wine), s. Germany, eastern Europe. Called Weisserburgunder in Germany. California's "Pinot Blanc" is apparently actually Muscadet.

Pinot Gris Makes rather heavy, even "thick", full-bodied whites with a certain spicy style. Known as Tokay in Alsace, Tocai in n.e. Italy and Yugoslavia, Ruländer in Germany. Almost extinct (but traditional) in Burgundy and Champagne.

Pinot Noir Superlative black grape (see under Grapes for red wine) used in Champagne and occasionally elsewhere (e.g. California) for making white wine, or a very pale pink "vin gris".

Riesling Germany's finest grape, and at the moment the world's most underrated. Wine of brilliant sweet/acid balance, flowery in youth but maturing to subtle oily scents and flavours. Successful in Alsace (for dry wine), Austria, parts of eastern Europe, Australia (where it is widely grown), California, South Africa. Often called White, Johannisberg or Rhine Riesling. Subject to "noble rot". Due for a major revival, since (unlike Chardonnay) it does not need high alcohol for character.

Sauvignon Blanc
    Makes very distinctive aromatic, herby and sometimes smoky scented wine; can be austere (on the upper Loire) or buxom (in Sauternes, where it is combined with SÉMILLON, and parts of California). Also called Fumé Blanc or vice versa. Recently a brilliant success in New Zealand.

Scheurebe Spicy-flavoured German Riesling x Sylvaner cross, very successful in Rheinpfalz, esp. for Ausleses. Can be rather weedy in dry wines.

Sémillon The grape contributing the lusciousness to great Sauternes; subject to "noble rot" in the right conditions but increasingly important for Graves and dry white Bordeaux too. Makes soft dry wine of great potential. Traditionally called "Riesling" in parts of Australia. Old Hunter Valley Sémillon can be great wine.

Sercial Makes the driest Madeira; where they claim it is really Riesling.

Seyval Blanc
    French-made hybrid between French and American vines. Very hardy and attractively fruity. Popular and reasonably successful in the eastern States and England.

Steen South Africa's most popular white grape: good, lively, fruity wine. Said to be the Chenin Blanc of the Loire.

Sylvaner (Silvaner)
    Germany's former workhorse grape: wine rarely better than pleasant except in Franconia where it is savoury, and ages admirably in the Rheinhessen, where it is enjoying a rennaisance. Good in the Italian Tyrol and useful in Alsace. V.g. (and powerful) as "Johannisberg" in the Valais, Switzerland.

Tokay See Pinot Gris. Also a table grape in California and a supposedly Hungarian grape in Australia. The wine Tokay is made of FURMINT.

Traminer See Gewürztraminer.

Trebbiano Important grape of central Italy, used in Orvieto, Chianti, Soave, etc. Also grown in s. France as Ugni Blanc, and Cognac as "St-Emilion". Thin, neutral wine, really needs blending.

Ugni Blanc See Trebbiano.

Verdejo The grape of Rueda in Castile, potentially fine and long-lived.

Verdelho Madeira grape making excellent medium-sweet wine.

Verdicchio Gives its name to good dry wine in central-eastern Italy.

Vermentino See Malvasia.

Vernaccia Grape grown in central and s. Italy and Sardinia for strong, smooth, lively wine, sometimes inclining towards sherry.

Viognier Rare but remarkable grape of the Rhône valley, grown at Condrieu to make very fine fragrant wine. A little in California.

Welschriesling (or Wälschriesling) See Italian Riesling.

Weisserburgunder See Pinot Blanc.

Grapes for red wine

Aleatico Dark muscat variety, alias Allianico, used the length of western Italy for fragrant sweet wines.

Barbera One of several productive grapes of n. Italy, esp. Piemonte, giving dark, fruity, often sharp wine. Useful in blends in California.

Brunello S. Tuscan form of SANGIOVESE, splendid at Montalcino.

Cabernet Franc
The lesser of two sorts of Cabernet grown in Bordeaux; the Cabernet of the Loire making Chinon, etc., and rosé.

Cabernet Sauvignon
Grape of great character; spicy, herby and tannic. The first grape of the Médoc, also makes the best Californian, Australian, South American and eastern European reds. Its red wine always needs ageing and usually benefits from blending with e.g. Merlot or Syrah. Makes v. aromatic rosé.

Carignan By far the commonest grape of France, covering hundreds of thousands of acres. Prolific with dull but harmless wine. Also common in North Africa, Spain and California.

Cinsaut Common bulk-producing grape of s. France; in S. Africa crossed with PINOT NOIR to make Pinotage.

Dolcetto Source of soft, seductive dry red in Piemonte.

Gamay The Beaujolais grape: light very fragrant wines at their best young. Makes even lighter wine on the Loire and in Switzerland and Savoie. Known as Napa Gamay in California.

Gamay Beaujolais
Not Gamay but a variety of PINOT NOIR grown in California.

Grenache (alias Garnacha)
Useful grape for strong and fruity but pale wine: good rosé. Grown in s. France, Spain, California. Usually blended.

Grignolino Makes one of the good cheap table wines of Piemonte.

Lambrusco Productive grape of the lower Po valley, giving quintessentially Italian, cheerful sweet and fizzy red.

Malbec (also called Cot)
Minor in Bordeaux, major in Cahors and Argentina. Dark, dense and tannic wine capable of real quality.

Merlot Adaptable grape making the great fragrant and rich wines of Pomerol and St-Emilion, an important element in Médoc reds, soft and strong in California, lighter but often good in n. Italy, Italian Switzerland, Yugoslavia, Argentina, etc.

Mourvèdre (alias Mataro)
Excellent, dark, aromatic, tannic grape used for blending in Provence (esp. in Bandol).

Nebbiolo (also called Spanna and Chiavennasca)
One of Italy's best red grapes, the grape of Barolo, Barbaresco, Gattinara and Valtellina. Intense, nobly fruity and perfumed wine but very tannic, taking years to mature.

Petit Verdot Excellent but awkward Médoc grape now largely superceded by CABERNET SAUVIGNON.

Pinot Noir The glory of Burgundy's Côte d'Or, with scent, flavour, texture and body unmatched anywhere. Less happy elsewhere; makes light wines of no great distinction in Germany, Switzerland, Austria, Hungary. The great challenge to the winemakers of California and Australia (and recently S. Africa). Shows great promise in Oregon.

Sangiovese The main red grape of Chianti and much of central Italy. See also Brunello.

Spätburgunder
German for PINOT NOIR, but a v. pale shadow of burgundy.

Syrah (alias Shiraz)
The best Rhône red grape, with tannic purple wine, which can mature superbly. Very important as "Shiraz" in Australia.

Tempranillo
The characteristic fine Rioja grape, called Ull de Lebre in Catalonia, Cencibel in La Mancha. Early ripening.

Zinfandel Fruity adaptable grape peculiar to California. Also makes "blush" white wine.

Wine & Food

Attitudes to matching wine and food vary from the slapdash to the near-neurotic. It is a subject that is provoking closer study than ever before. Few combinations can be dismissed outright as "wrong", but generations of experience have produced certain working conventions that certainly do no harm. The following is a list of ideas intended to help you make quick decisions. Any of the groups of recommended wines could be extended almost indefinitely, drawing on the whole world's wine list. In general I have stuck to the wines that are widely available, at the same time trying to ring the changes so that the same wines don't come up time and time again – as they tend to do in real life.

The stars refer to the rating system used throughout the book.

Before the meal – apéritifs

The conventional apéritif wines are either sparkling (epitomized by champagne) or fortified (epitomized by sherry). They are still the best, but *avoid peanuts* with them, they destroy wine flavours. Eat almonds or walnuts instead. A glass of white wine before eating is the current fashion. It calls for something light and stimulating, dry but not acid, with a degree of character, such as:

France:
> Alsace Pinot Blanc, Riesling or Sylvaner; Chablis; Muscadet; Sauvignon de Touraine; Graves Blanc; Mâcon Blanc; Crépy; Bugey, Haut-Poitou, Côtes de Gascogne.

Germany:
> Any Kabinett wine or QbA. Choose a "halbtrocken" – nearly dry. Or open a rare old Spätlese.

Italy:
> Soave; Orvieto Secco; Frascati; Gavi; Pinot Bianco; Montecarlo; Vernaccia; Tocai; Lugana; Albana di Romagna.

Spain:
> Rioja Blanco Marqués de Caceres or Faustino V, or Albariño. But fino sherry, Manzanilla or Montilla is far better.

Portugal:
> Any vinho verde; Bucelas.

Eastern Europe:
> Veltliner, Welschriesling, Riesling, Chardonnay, Tokay Szamarodni.

USA.:
> California "Chablis"; Chenin Blanc; Riesling; French Colombard; Fumé Blanc; Gewürztraminer, or a good "house blend"; Riesling from New York or Oregon, Sémillon from Washington.

Australia:
> Barossa or Coonawarra Riesling. Houghton's "White Burgundy".

South Africa:
> Steen is ideal. (The K.W.V. labels it Chenin Blanc).

England:
> Almost any English wine is ideal as an apéritif.

References to these wines will be found in national A-Z sections.

First courses

Aïoli A thirst-quencher is needed with so much garlic. ∗→∗∗ Rhône, or Provence rosé, or Frascati, or Verdicchio, and lots of mineral water.

Antipasto   See also Hors d'oeuvre.

   ★★ dry or medium white, Italian (e.g. Soave), or German, or Chenin Blanc, or light red, e.g. Bardolino or young ★ Bordeaux. Or fino sherry.

Artichoke   ★ red or rosé.

   vinaigrette   ★ young red, e.g. Bordeaux, Côtes-du-Rhône.

   hollandaise   ★ or ★★ full-bodied dry or medium white, e.g. Mâcon Blanc, Rheinpfalz, or a California "house blend".

Asparagus   A difficult flavour for wine, so the wine needs plenty of its own. ★★→★★★ white burgundy or Chardonnay, or Corsican rosé.

Assiette anglaise   (assorted cold meats)

   ★★ dry white, e.g. Chablis, Muscadet, Silvaner, Riesling; esp. Trocken wines from the Mosel-Saar-Ruwer.

Avocado

   with prawns, crab, etc.   ★★→★★★ dry to medium white, e.g. Rheingau or Rheinpfalz Kabinett, Graves, California or Australian Chardonnay or Sauvignon, Cape Steen, or dry rosé.

   vinaigrette   ★ light red, or Manzanilla sherry.

Bisques   ★★ dry white with plenty of body: Pinot Gris, Chardonnay. Fino or amontillado sherry, or Montilla.

Bouillabaisse

   ★→★★ very dry white: Muscadet, Alsace Sylvaner, Entre-Deux-Mers, Pouilly-Fumé, Cassis, Tuscan Trebbiano, Grechetto.

Carpaccio   Seems to work well with the flavour of most wines, including ★★★ reds. Top Tuscan vino da tavola is appropriate.

Caviar   ★★★ champagne or iced vodka (or both).

Ceviche   ★★ California or Australian Chardonnay.

Cheese fondue

   ★★ dry white: Fendant or Johannisberg du Valais, Grüner Veltliner, Alsace Riesling, NZ Sauvignon Blanc.

Chicken liver pâté

   Appetizing dry white, e.g. ★★ white Bordeaux, Pouilly-Fumé or Rheingau Spätlese Trocken, or light fruity red; Beaujolais, Gamay de Touraine, young Chianti or Valpolicella.

Clams and Chowders

   ★★ big-scale white, not necessarily bone dry: e.g. Pinot Gris, dry Sauternes, Napa Chardonnay. Or fino sherry.

Consommé   ★★→★★★ medium-dry sherry, dry Madeira, Marsala.

Crudités   ★→★★ light red or rosé, e.g. Côtes-du-Rhône, Beaujolais. Minervois, Chianti, Zinfandel, Fino sherry.

Eggs   (See also Soufflés)

   These present difficulties: they clash with most wines and spoil good ones. So ★→★★ of whatever is going. I can bear champagne with scrambled eggs as a last resort.

Empanadas   Red El Biergo, or ★→★★ Chilean or Argentine Cabernet, Zinfandel.

Escargots   White Mâcon-Villages, a dry California Chardonnay or Beaujolais-Villages; or ★★ red Rhône.

Fish terrine

   Rheingau Riesling Trocken, Chablis, Washington or Australian Semillon, Rioja Blanco Fino sherry.

Foie gras

   ★★★→★★★★ white. In Bordeaux they drink Sauternes. Others prefer vintage champagne or a late-harvest Gewürztraminer.

Gazpacho   A glass of Fino before – and after.

Grapefruit   If you must start a meal with grapefruit try port, Madeira or sweet sherry with (or in) it.

Gravlax   Akvavit, or Grand Cru Chablis, or ★★★ Californian or Australian Chardonnay. Or vintage champagne.

Haddock, smoked mousse of
>A wonderful dish for showing off any stylish full-bodied white.

Ham, raw or cured See also Proscuitto. A lively young Spanish or Italian red.

Herrings, raw or pickled
>Dutch gin (young, not aged) or Scandinavian akvavit, and cold beer.

Hors d'oeuvres (See also Antipasto)
>★→★★ clean fruity sharp white: Sancerre or any Sauvignon, Alsace Silvaner, Muscadet, Cape Steen – or young light red Bordeaux, Rhône or equivalent. Or fino sherry.

Mackerel, smoked
>An oily wine-destroyer. Manzanilla sherry, Schnapps or ★★★★!

Mayonnaise Adds richness that calls for a contrasting bite in the wine. Côte Chalonnaise whites (e.g. Rully) are good. Try NZ Sauvignon Blanc or Yugoslavian Zilavka.

Melon Needs a strong sweet wine (if any) ★★ Port, Bual Madeira, Muscat, Oloroso sherry or Vin Doux Naturel.

Minestrone ★ red: Grignolino, Chianti, Zinfandel, Shiraz, etc. Or Fino.

Mushrooms à la Greque
>Robola from Cephalonia or any hefty dry white, or fresh young red.

Omelettes See under Eggs.

Onion/leek tart
>★→★★★ fruity, concentrated dry white, e.g. Alsace Pinot Gris or Riesling. Mâcon-Villages of good vintage, Jurançon, California or Australian Riesling. Or Beaujolais or Loire red.

Pasta ★→★★ red or white according to the sauce or trimmings, e.g.
>**with seafood sauce (vongole, etc.)** Verdicchio, Soave, Pomino, Sauvignon.
>**meat sauce** Chianti, Montepulciano d'Abruzzo, Montefalco d'Arquata.
>**tomato sauce** Barbera or Sicilian or Yugoslav red or Zinfandel.
>**cream sauce** Orvieto, Frascati or Italian Chardonnay.

Pâté According to constituents and quality e.g. chicken livers call for pungent white, a smooth red like a light Pomerol, or even amontillado sherry. For simple pâté – ★★ dry white: e.g. Mâcon-Villages, Graves, Fumé Blanc.

Peppers or aubergines (eggplant), stuffed
>★★ vigorous red: e.g. Chianti, Dolcetto, Zinfandel Bandol.

Pizza Any ★★ dry Italian red or a ★★ Rioja, Australian Shiraz or California Zinfandel. Or Corbières or Roussillon.

Prawns or shrimps
>★★→★★★ dry white: burgundy or Bordeaux, Chardonnay or Riesling. ("Cocktail sauce" kills any wine, and I suspect, in time, human beings.)

Prosciutto with melon
>★★→★★★ full-bodied dry or medium white: e.g. Orvieto or Frascati, Pomino, Fendant, Grüner Veltliner, Alsace or California Gewürztraminer, Australian Riesling.

Quenelles de brochet
>Best bottle of Pouilly Fumé, or Grand Cru Chablis, Alsace Pinot Gris, Hunter Valley Semillon.

Quiches ★→★★ dry white with body (Alsace, Graves, Sauvignon, Rheingau dry) or young red (e.g. Beaujolais-Villages), according to the ingredients. Never a fine wine dish. (A friend suggests sake.)

Ratatouille
>★★ vigorous young red, e.g. Chianti, Zinfandel, Bulgarian or young red Bordeaux or young Côtes du Rhône.

Salade niçoise
>★★ very dry not too light or flowery white or rosé, e.g. Rhône or Corsican, Catalan white, Dão California Sauvignon Blanc.

Salads As a first course, especially with blue cheese dressing, any dry and appetizing white wine. After a main course: no wine.

    N.B. Vinegar in salad dressings destroys the flavour of wine. If you want salad at a meal with fine wine, dress the salad with wine or a little lemon juice instead of vinegar.

Salami ★→★★ Very tasty red or rosé: e.g. Barbera, young Zinfandel, Tavel or Ajaccio rosé, young Bordeaux, Toro or Montepulciano d'Abruzzo.

Salmon, smoked

    A dry but pungent white, e.g. fino sherry, Alsace Pinot Gris, Chablis Grand Cru, Rheinpfalz Riesling Spätlese, vintage champagne.

Soufflés As show dishes these deserve ★★→★★★ wines.

    Fish Dry white, e.g. burgundy, Bordeaux, Alsace, Chard, etc.

    Cheese Red burgundy or Bordeaux, Cabernet Sauvignon, etc.

Taramasalata

    Calls for a rustic southern white of strong personality; not necessarily the Greek Retsina. Fino sherry works well.

Terrine As for pâté, or the equivalent red; e.g. Beaune, Mercurey, Beaujolais-Villages, fairly young ★★ St-Emilion, California Cabernet or Zinfandel, Bulgarian or Chilean Cabernet, etc.

Tomato sauce (on anything)

    The acidity of tomato sauce is no friend to fine wines. ★★ red will do. Try Chianti or a German wine with some sweetness.

Trout, smoked

    Sancerre, Pouilly-Fumé, or California or NZ Fumé Blanc. Or Rully.

Vegetable terrine

    Not a great help to fine wine, but Californian and Australian Chardonnays make a fashionable marriage.

Fish

Abalone ★★→★★★ dry or medium white: e.g. Sauvignon Blanc, Chardonnay, Pinot Grigio, Muscadet sur Lie.

Bass, striped

    Same wine as for sole.

Carpaccio of e.g. Salmon.

    Puligny-Montrachet or top-notch Australian Chard.

Cod A good neutral background for fine dry or medium whites, e.g. ★★→★★★ Chablis, Meursault, cru classé Graves, German Kabinett or dry Spätleses and their equivalents.

Coquilles St Jacques

    An inherently slightly sweet dish, best with medium-dry whites. **in cream sauces** ★★★ German Spätlese or a –Montrachet.

    grilled or fried Hermitage Blanc, Gewürztraminer, California Chenin Blanc, Riesling or champagne.

Crab, cold, with salad

    ★★★ California or Rheinpfalz Riesling Kabinett or Spätlese, or Viognier from Condrieu.

Crab, softshell

    ★★★ Chardonnay or top-quality German Riesling.

Eel, jellied

    NV champagne or a nice cup of tea.

    smoked Either strong or sharp wine, e.g. fino sherry or Bourgogne Aligoté. Or schnapps.

Fish and chips, fritto misto (or tempura)

    ★ white Bordeaux, Sauvignon Blanc, Torres' Waltraud, Montilla, Koshu, tea . . .

Haddock **→*** dry white with a certain richness: e.g. Meursault, California or Australian Chardonnay.

Herrings Need a white with some acidity to cut their richness. Burgundy Aligoté or Gros Plant from Brittany or dry Sauvignon Blanc.

Kippers A good cup of tea, preferably Ceylon (milk, no sugar).

Lamproie à la Bordelaise
  →* 5-y-o red Bordeaux, St-Emilion, Pomerol or Fronsac.

Lobster or Crab
  salad **→**** white. Non-vintage champagne, Alsace Riesling, Chablis Premier Cru, Condrieu, Mosel Spätlese.
  richly sauced Vintage champagne, fine white burgundy, cru classé Graves, California or Australian Chardonnay, Rheinpfalz Spätlese, Hermitage Blanc.

Mackerel ** hard or sharp white: Sauvignon Blanc from Bergerac or Touraine, Gros Plant, vinho verde, white Rioja. Or Guinness.

Mullet, red ** Mediterranean white, even Retsina, for the atmosphere. Reds go well, too.

Mussels *→** Gros Plant, Muscadet, California "Chablis".
  Stuffed with garlic – as for Escargots.

Oysters **→*** white. Champagne (non-vintage), Chablis or (better) Chablis Premier Cru, Muscadet, white Graves or Sancerre.

Salmon, fresh
  *** fine white burgundy: Puligny-or Chassagne-Montrachet, Meursault, Corton-Charlemagne, Chablis Grand Cru, California, Idaho or Australian Chardonnay, or Rheingau Kabinett or Spätlese, California Riesling or equivalent. Some (not me) like Beaujolais or a young ** red Bordeaux.

Sardines, fresh grilled
  *→** very dry white: e.g. vinho verde, Dão Muscadet.

Sashimi If you are prepared to forego the Wasabi, sparkling wines, incl. Californian, or California or Australian Chardonnay or Sauvignon. Chablis Grand Cru. Rheingau Riesling Halbtrocken. Otherwise, sake or beer.

Scallops See Coquilles St Jacques.

Shad **→*** white Graves or Meursault or Hunter Semillon.

Shellfish (general)
  Dry white with plain boiled shellfish, richer wines with richer sauces.

Shrimps, potted
  Fino sherry, Chablis, Gavi or New York Chardonnay.

Skate with black butter
  ** white with some pungency (e.g. Alsace Pinot Gris) or a clean straightforward one like Muscadet or Entre-Deux-Mers.

Sole, plaice, etc.
  plain, grilled or fried An ideal accompaniment for fine wines: * up to **** white burgundy, or its equivalent.
  with sauce Depending on the ingredients: sharp dry wine for tomato sauce, fairly rich for sole véronique, etc.

Sushi Hot wasabi is usually hidden in every piece. German QbA trocken wines or simple Chablis are good enough.

Swordfish ** dry white of whatever country you are in.

Tuna, grilled
  ** white or red (or rosé) of fairly fruity character. NZ Sauvignon Blanc or a top Côtes-du-Rhône would be fine.

Trout Delicate white wine, e.g. *** Mosel (esp. from the Saar).
  Smoked A full-flavoured **→*** white: Gewürztraminer, Alsace Pinot Gris, Rhine Spätlese, Pinot Blanc from Italy or Australian Hunter white.

Turbot Fine rich dry white, e.g. *** Meursault or its California, Australian or New Zealand equivalent. Viognier from Condrieu. Mature Rheingau, Mosel or Nahe Spätlese or Auslese.

Meat, poultry, etc.

Barbecues ★★ red with a slight rasp, therefore young, Shiraz, Chianti, Zinfandel, Turkish Buzbag. Bandol for a treat.

Beef, boiled
★★ red: e.g. Bordeaux (Bourg or Fronsac), Côtes-du-Rhône-Villages, Australian Shiraz. Or good Mâcon-Villages white.

Beef, roast
An ideal partner for fine red wine. ★★→★★★★ red of any kind.

Beef stew
★★→★★★ sturdy red, e.g. Pomerol or St-Emilion, Hermitage, Shiraz, California or Oregon Pinot Noir, Torres Sangre de Toro.

Beef Stroganoff
★★→★★★ suitably dramatic red: e.g. Barolo, Brunello, Valpolicella, Amarone, Hermitage, late-harvest Zinfandel – or even Georgian.

Cassoulet ★★ red from s.w. France, e.g. Madiran, Cahors or Corbières, or Barbera or Zinfandel or Shiraz.

Chicken or turkey, roast (or guinea fowl)
Virtually any wine, including your very best bottles of dry or medium white and finest old reds (esp. burgundy). The meat of fowl can be adapted with sauces to match almost any fine wine (e.g. coq au vin with red burgundy). Avoid tomato sauces for any good bottles.

Chili con carne
★→★★ young red: e.g. Bull's Blood, Chianti, Mountain Red.

Chinese food
Canton or Peking style ★★→★★★ dry to medium-dry white. Dry sparkling (esp. Cava) is good for cutting the oil. Eschew sweet/sour dishes and try an '83/'85 St-Emilion ★★ or St Estéphe cru bourgeois, or Châteauneuf with duck.
Szechuan style Very cold beer.

Choucroute Alsace Pinot Gris or Sylvaner.

Cold meats Generally taste better with full-flavoured white wine than red. Mosel Spätleses, Hochheimer are v.g.

Confit d'oie
★★→★★★ rather young and tannic red Bordeaux helps to cut the richness. Alsace Tokay or Gewürztraminer matches it.

Coq au vin ★★→★★★★ red burgundy. In an ideal world one bottle of Chambertin in the dish, two on the table.

Corned beef hash
★★ Zinfandel, Chianti, Côtes-du-Rhône red.

Couscous Young red with a bite; e.g. Shiraz, Corbiéres, Minervois, etc.

Curry ★→★★ medium-sweet white, very cold: e.g. Orvieto abboccato, California Chenin Blanc, Yugoslav Traminer, Indian "Champagne" or, as for Chinese food, deep-flavoured reds such as St-Emilion, Shiraz, Shiraz-Cabernet blends, Balbera, Valpolicella Amarone, but *no* sweet mango chutney.

Duck or goose
★★★ rather rich white, e.g. Rheinpfalz Spätlese or Alsace Réserve Exceptionelle, or ★★★ Bordeaux or burgundy.
With oranges or peaches, the Sauternais propose Sauternes.
Wild duck ★★★ big-scale red: e.g. Hermitage, Châteauneuf-du-Pape, Bandol, California. or S. African Cabernet, Australian Shiraz, Torres Gran Coronas.

Frankfurters
★→★★ German or Australian white, or Beaujolais. Or beer.

Game birds
Young birds plain roasted and not too well hung deserve the best red wine you can afford. With older birds in casseroles ★★→★★★ red, e.g. Gevrey-Chambertin, Pommard, Grand Cru St-Emilion, Napa Cab. With very high game, Hermitage, Châteauneuf-du-Pape, Vega Sicilia.

Game pie (Hot) ★★★ red wine. (Cold) Equivalent white.

Goulash ★★ strong young red: e.g. Zinfandel, Bulgarian Cabernet, Kadarka.

Grouse See Game birds – but push the boat out.

Ham ★★→★★★ fairly fresh red burgundy, e.g. Volnay, Savigny, Beaune, or red Loire, or a slightly sweet German white, e.g. a Rhine Spätlese, or a Tuscan red, or a lightish Cabernet (e.g. Chilean).

Hamburger ★→★★ young red: e.g. Beaujolais, Corbières or Minervois, Chianti, Zinfandel, Kadarka from Hungary.

Hare Jugged hare calls for ★★→★★★ red with plenty of flavour: not-too-old burgundy or Bordeaux, or Rhône; Gigondas e.g.; or Bandol or a fine Rioja Reserva. The same for saddle. Grange Hermitage would be an experience.

Kebabs ★★ vigorous red: e.g. Greek Demestica, Turkish Buzbag, Bulgarian or Chilean Cabernet, Zinfandel.

Kidneys ★★→★★★ red: Pomerol or St-Emilion, Rhône, Barbaresco, Rioja, California, Spanish or Australian Cabernet, Bairrada from Portugal.

Lamb cutlets or chops
As for roast lamb, but a little less grand.

Lamb, roast
One of the traditional and best partners for very good red Bordeaux – or its Cabernet equivalents from the New World. In Castile, the partner of the finest old Riojas.

Liver ★★→★★★ young red: Beaujolais-Villages, St-Joseph, Médoc, Italian Merlot, Zinfandel, Oregon Pinot Noir.

Meatballs ★★→★★★ red: e.g. Mercurey, Crozes-Hermitage, Madiran, Rubesco, Dão Bairrada, Zinfandel or Cabernet.

Mixed grill
A fairly light easily swallowable red; ★★ red Bordeaux from Bourg, Fronsac or Premières Côtes; Chianti; Bourgogne Passe-tout-grains, Chilean Cabernet, or a Cru Beaujolais such as Juliénas.

Moussaka ★→★★ red or rosé: e.g. Naoussa, Chianti, Corbières, Côtes de Provence, Ajaccio or Patrimonio, California Burgundy.

Oxtail ★★→★★★ rather rich red: e.g. St-Emilion or Pomerol, Burgundy, Barolo or Chianti Classico, Rioja Reserva, California or Coonawarra Cabernet or a dry Riesling Spätlese.

Paella ★★ Young Spanish r., dry w. or rosé, e.g. Penedés or Rioja.

Partridge, pheasant See under game birds.

Pigeons or squabs
★★→★★★★ red Bordeaux, Chianti Classico, California or Australian Cabernet. Silvaner Spätlese from Franconia.

Pork, roast
Pork is a good, rich, neutral background to a fairly light red or rich white. Portugal's famous sucking pig is eaten with Bairrada garrafeira.

Rabbit★→★★★ young red: Italian for preference. Or Rhône rosé.

Ris de veau See Sweetbreads.

Risotto Pinot Grigio from Friuli, Gavi, youngish Sémillon.

Sauerkraut Lager.

Sausages The British banger requires a 2½-year-old n.e. Italian Merlot. (A red wine, anyway.) See also salami.

Shepherd's Pie
★→★★ rough and ready red seems most appropriate, but no harm would come to a good one.

Steak and kidney pie or pudding
Red Rioja Reserva or mature ★★→★★★ Bordeaux.

Steaks
    Alligator Rum and coke?
    Au poivre A fairly young ★★★ Rhône red or Cabernet.

Tartare ★★ light young red: Beaujolais, Bergerac, Valpolicella.

Filet or Tournedos ★★★ red of any kind (but not old wines with Béarnaise sauce).

T-bone ★★→★★★ reds of similar bone-structure: e.g. Barolo, Hermitage, Australian Cabernet or Shiraz.

Fiorentina (bistecca) Chianti Classico Reserva or Brunello.

Ostrich South African Pinotage.

Stews and casseroles

A lusty full-flavoured red, e.g. young Côtes-du-Rhône, Cor-bières, Barbera, Shiraz, Zinfandel, etc.

Sweetbreads

These tend to be a grand dish, suggesting a grand wine, e.g. ★★★ Rhine Riesling or Franken Silvaner Spätlese, or well-matured Bordeaux or burgundy, depending on the sauce.

Tongue Ideal for favourite bottles of any red or white of abundant character, esp. Italian.

Tripe ★→★★ red: Corbières, Mâcon Rouge, etc., or rather sweet white, e.g. Liebfraumilch. Better: W. Australian "white burgundy".

Veal, roast

A good neutral background dish for any fine old red which may have faded with age (e.g. a Rioja Reserva) or a ★★★ German white.

Venison ★★★ big-scale red (Rhône, Bordeaux of a grand vintage) or rather rich white (Rheinpfalz Spätlese or Tokay d'Alsace).

Vitello tonnato

Light red (Valpolicella, Beaujolais) served cool.

Wiener Schnitzel

★★→★★★ light red from the Italian Tyrol (Alto Adige) or the Médoc: or Austrian Riesling, Grüner Veltliner or Gumpolds-kirchener. Or Czech Veltlinski.

Cheese

Very strong cheese completely masks the flavour of wine. Only serve fine wine with mild cheeses in peak condition.

Bleu de Bresse, Dolcelatte, Gorgonzola, Stilton, other English blue

Need emphatic accompaniment: young ★★ red wine (Barbera, Dolcetto, Moulin-â-Vent, etc.) or sweet white – or port.

Cream cheeses: Brie, Camembert, Bel Paese, Edam, etc.

In their mild state marry with any good wine, red or white.

Hard English (Scottish, Welsh and Irish) cheeses

Can be either mild or strong and acidic. The latter need sweet or strong wine.

Cheddar, Cheshire, Wensleydale, Gloucester, etc, etc. If mild, claret. If strong, ruby, tawny or vintage-character (not vintage) port, old dry oloroso sherry, or a very big red: Hermitage, Châteauneuf-du-Pape, Barolo, Barbaresco etc.

Goat cheeses

★★→★★★ white wine of marked character, either dry (e.g. Sancerre) or sweet (e.g. Monbazillac, Sauternes).

Hard Cheese, Parmesan, Gruyère, Emmenthal, old Gouda, Jarlsberg

Full-bodied dry whites, e.g. Tokay d'Alsace or Vernaccia, or fino or amontillado sherry. But it's worth experimenting with any fine wine: old Gouda and Jarlsberg have a sweetness that encourages fine old reds.

Roquefort, Danish Blue

Are so strong-flavoured that only the youngest, biggest or sweetest wines stand a chance. Old dry amontillado or oloroso sherries have the necessary horse-power.

Desserts

Apple pie, apple strudel
> ★★→★★★ sweet German, Austrian or Hungarian white.

Apples, Cox's Orange Pippins
> Vintage port (55, 60, 63, 66, 70, 75).

Bread and butter pudding
> 10-year-old Barsac from a good château.

Cakes Bual or Malmsey Madeira, Oloroso or cream sherry.

Cheesecake ★★→★★★ sweet white from Vouvray or Coteaux du Layon.

Chocolate cake, mousse, soufflés
> Bual Madeira, Huxelrebe Auslese or California orange muscat.

Christmas pudding, mince pies
> Tawny port, cream sherry – or Asti Spumante.

Creams and custards
> ★★→★★★ Sauternes, Loupiac, St Croix du Mont, or Monbazillac.

Crème brûlée
> The most luxurious dish, demanding ★★★→★★★★ Sauternes or Rhine Beerenauslese, or the best Madeira or Tokay.

Crêpes Suzette
> Sweet champagne or Asti Spumante.

Fruit, fresh
> Sweet Coteaux du Layon white, light sweet muscat (e.g. California).
> **Pears in red wine** A pause before the port.
> **Raspberries** (no cream, little sugar) Excellent with fine reds.
> **Rhubarb** Rhubarb wine, I suppose.

Fruit flans (i.e. peach, raspberry)
> ★★★ Sauternes, Monbazillac or sweet Vouvray or Anjou.

Fruit salads, orange salad
> No wine.

Nuts Oloroso sherry, Bual, Madeira, vintage or tawny port, Vinsanto.

Sorbets, ice-creams
> Asti Spumante, or better Moscato d'Asti Naturale.

Stewed fruits, i.e. apricots, pears, etc.
> Sweet Muscatel: e.g. Muscat de Beaumes de Venise, Moscato di Pantelleria or from Tarragona.

Strawberries and cream
> ★★★ Sauternes or similar sweet B'x, or Vouvray Moelleux.

Wild strawberries
> Serve with ★★★ red Bordeaux poured over them and in your glass (no cream).

Summer pudding
> Fairly young Sauternes of a good vintage (e.g. 82, 83, 85, 86).

Treacle tart
> Too sweet for any wine but a treacly Malmsey Madeira.

Trifle No wine: should be sufficiently vibrant with sherry.

Sweet soufflés
> Sauternes, sweet Vouvray or Coteaux du Layon. Sweet Champagne.

Walnuts Nature's match for finest port, madeira, oloroso.

Zabaglione Light gold Marsala.

Savouries

Generally highly seasoned, these are not ideal partners for the last glass of a fine wine. A Bual or Verdelho Madeira would come to no harm. But **cheese straws** make an admirable meal-ending with a final glass (or bottle) of any particularly good red wine.

A little learning . . .

The last fifteen years have seen a revolution in wine technology. They have also heard a revolution in wine-talk. Attempts to describe wine used to get no further than such vague terms as "fruity" and "full-bodied". Then came the demand for sterner, more scientific, stuff: the jargon of lab analysis. This hard-edge wine-talk is briefly explained below. For the trad. vocabulary see p.197.

The most frequent references are to the ripeness of grapes at picking; the resultant alcohol and sugar content of the wine; various measures of its acidity; the amount of sulphur dioxide used as a preservative, and the amount of "dry extract" – the sum of all the things that give wine its characteristic flavours.

The fashion today (French in origin) is for analogues with a quasi-poetic effect: "Scents of apricots, raspberries, leather; flavours of plum and truffle, shading to farmyard with a hint of fish-glue". Anybody can play. Few can play well.

The **sugar** in wine is mainly glucose and fructose, with traces of arabinose, xylose and other sugars that are not fermentable by yeast, but can be attacked by bacteria. Each country has its own system for measuring the sugar content or ripeness of grapes, known in English as the **"must-weight"**. The chart below relates the three principal ones (German, French and American) to each other, to specific gravity, and to the potential alcohol of the wine if all the sugar is fermented.

Sugar to alcohol: potential strength

Specific Gravity	°Oechsle	Baumé	Brix	% Potential Alcohol v/v
1.065	65	8.8	15.8	8.1
1.070	70	9.4	17.0	8.8
1.075	75	10.1	18.1	9.4
1.080	80	10.7	19.3	10.0
1.085	85	11.3	20.4	10.6
1.090	90	11.9	21.5	11.3
1.095	95	12.5	22.5	11.9
1.100	100	13.1	23.7	12.5
1.105	105	13.7	24.8	13.1
1.110	110	14.3	25.8	13.8
1.115	115	14.9	26.9	14.4
1.120	120	15.5	28.0	15.0

Residual sugar is the sugar left after fermentation has finished or been stopped, measured in grammes per litre.

Alcohol content (mainly ethyl alcohol) is expressed as a percentage by volume of the total liquid. (Also known as "degrees").

Acidity is both fixed and volatile. **Fixed acidity** consists principally of tartaric, malic and citric acids which are all found in the grape, and lactic and succinic acids, which are produced during fermentation. **Volatile acidity** consists mainly of acetic acid, which is rapidly formed by bacteria in the presence of oxygen. A small amount of volatile acidity is inevitable and attractive. With a larger amount the wine becomes "pricked" – i.e. starts to turn to vinegar.

Total acidity is fixed and volatile acidity combined. As a rule of thumb for a well-balanced wine it should be in the region of 1 gramme/thousand for each 10° Oechsle (see over).

pH is a measure of the strength of the acidity, rather than its volume. The lower the figure the more acid. Wine normally ranges in pH from 2.8 to 3.8. Winemakers in hot climates can have problems getting the pH low enough. Lower pH gives better colour, helps prevent bacterial spoilage, allows more of the SO_2 to be free and active as a preservative.

Sulphur dioxide (SO_2) is added to prevent oxidation and other accidents in wine-making. Some of it combines with sugars, etc., and is known as "bound". Only the "**free SO_2**" that remains in the wine is effective as a preservative. **Total SO_2** is controlled by law according to the level of residual sugar: the more sugar the more SO_2 needed.

Temperature

No single aspect of serving wine makes or mars it so easily as getting the temperature right. White wines almost invariably taste dull and insipid served warm and red wines have disappointingly little scent or flavour served cold. The chart below gives an indication of what is generally found to be the most satisfactory temperature for serving each class of wine.

	°F ● °C	
	68 ● 20	
Room	66 ● 19	
temperature		
	64 ● 18	Best red wines
	63 ● 17	especially Bordeaux
Red Burgundy	61 ● 16	
	59 ● 15	Chianti, Zinfandel
Best white Burgundy		Côtes-du-Rhône
Port, Madeira	57 ● 14	
	55 ● 13	Ordinaires
	54 ● 12	Lighter red wines
Ideal	Sherry	52 ● 11	e.g. Beaujolais
cellar	Fino sherry	50 ● 10	
	Most dry white wines	48 ● 9	Rosés
	Champagne	46 ● 8	Lambrusco
Domestic	45 ● 7	
fridge		
	43 ● 6	Most sweet white wines
	41 ● 5	Sparkling wines
	39 ● 4	
	37 ● 3	
	35 ● 2	
	33 ● 1	
	32 ● 0	

Is there an ideal wine glass?

Many of the traditional wine-growing regions of Europe have a design of glass considered ideal for enjoying their products. Some are based more on folklore than practicality. All good wine glasses are clear, thin, without cutting on the bowl, have a stem of moderate length and a relatively large bowl curving inwards towards the rim. The author is responsible for the design of the glasses illustrated. They constitute a matching set to do justice to all the main styles of wine.

Red Bordeaux   Champagne   Red burgundy

White wines   Sherry   Port

The 1989 vintage

1989 will easily be remembered by the inhabitants of northern Europe as the year of revolutions – and of the long hot summer. Bordeaux had its earliest vintage since 1893, of a quality that has brought comparisons with the famous 1982. Time will tell. All of France had the opportunity of making exceptional wine – the further north, the more exceptional. In Champagne, Alsace and the Loire it is considered one of the great vintages. Burgundy is less certain that superlatives are (or will be) justified – except in Chablis and Beaujolais – but the quality should unquestionably be high. Drought can prevent grapes from ripening to the full, however sweet they may be. This could be the problem with some Rhône and Midi wines as well as Burgundies in an otherwise excellent vintage.

The Germans had their second fine vintage running. All of central and eastern Europe was in the same happy position. The Mediterranean countries were rather less lucky, with only fair conditions for red wine through most of Italy except the north (Piemonte was lucky). Rioja and the Duero were happy: Penedès had problems with storms that appeared erratically at the end of the summer. The port country had a small but fine harvest.

Results in California were much more mixed, and in Australia they were almost the opposite of those in Europe: '89 will be a vintage to forget in most areas. New Zealand, on the other hand, had its best harvest yet. So the record of the '80s comes to a fitting finish. More good wine was made in the decade than ever before in history.

France

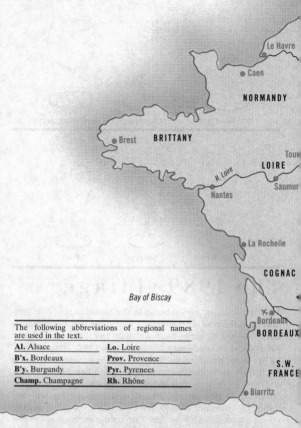

English Channel

Cala

Le Havre

Caen

NORMANDY

Brest　BRITTANY

Tou

LOIRE

R. Loire

Nantes

Saumur

La Rochelle

COGNAC

Bay of Biscay

Bordeaux

BORDEAUX

S.W.
FRANCE

Biarritz

Spain

The following abbreviations of regional names
are used in the text.

Al. Alsace	**Lo.** Loire
B'x. Bordeaux	**Prov.** Provence
B'y. Burgundy	**Pyr.** Pyrenees
Champ. Champagne	**Rh.** Rhône

Every year sees new challenges to France's pole position in the
wine world. Yet no-one has displaced her; and it is hard to
imagine that they ever will. Tens of thousands of properties
make wine of all complexions over a large part of her surface.
This is a guide to their names, types and producers: the essential
information in identifying what is authentic and good of its kind.

All France's best wine regions (producing about 30% of all her
wine) have Appellations Contrôlées, which may apply to a single
small vineyard or a whole large district. The system varies from
region to region. Burgundy on the whole has the smallest and
most precise appellations, grouped into larger units by compli-
cated formulae. Bordeaux has the widest and most general
appellations, in which it is the particular property (or "château")
that matters. In between lie an infinity of variations.

An Appellation Contrôlée is a guarantee of origin and of production method, of grape varieties and quantities produced, but only partially one of quality. All "AC" wines are officially tasted, but many of shoddy quality get through the net.

Appellations therefore are the first thing to look for on a label. But the next is the name of the maker. More recommended producers' names are included in this edition for this reason.

Wine regions without the overall quality and traditions required for an appellation can be ranked as Vins Délimités de Qualité Supérieure (VDQS). Most old VDQS areas have been promoted to AC as standards have improved. Now it is the turn of the third rank, the Vin de Pays, to prove its mettle. Vins de Pays are increasingly worth trying. They include some brilliant originals and often offer France's best value for money.

23

Recent vintages
of the French classics

Red Burgundy

Côte d'Or Côte de Beaune reds generally mature sooner than the bigger wines of the Côte de Nuits. Earliest drinking dates are for lighter commune wines: Volnay, Beaune, etc. latest for the biggest wines of Chambertin, Romanée, etc. Different growers make wines of different styles, for longer or shorter maturing, but even the best burgundies are much more attractive young than the equivalent red Bordeaux.

1989 All the omens are excellent, but this does not seem as fine a vintage as 1988.
1988 Exceptional quality; a great vintage.
1987 Small crop with promising ripe fruit flavours. Now-2010.
1986 A very mixed bag – generally lacks flesh. Now-2000.
1985 A great vintage. Concentrated wines will be splendid. Now-2000.
1984 Lacks natural ripeness; tends to be dry and/or watery. Now-'96.
1983 Powerful, vigorous, tannic and attractive vintage, compromised by rot. The best are splendid, but be careful. Now-2000.
1982 Big vintage, pale but round. Best in Côte de Beaune. Drink soon.
1981 A small crop, ripe but picked in rain. Some pleasant wines: Now.
1980 A late, wet year, but attractive wines from the best growers who avoided rot. Better in the Côte de Nuits. Keep (only) the best another year or two.
1979 Big generally good ripe vintage with weak spots. Drink up.
1978 A small vintage of outstanding quality. The best will live to 2000.
1977 Very wet summer. Better wine than expected, but drink up.
1976 Hot summer, excellent vintage. As usual great variations, but the best (esp. Côte de Beaune) tannic, rich and long-lived – to 1995.
1973 Light wines, but many fruity and delicate. Most are already too old.
1972 Firm and full of character, ageing well. Drink up.
1971 Very powerful and impressive wines, not as long-lasting as they first appeared. Drink.
Older fine vintages: '69, '66, '64, '62, '61, '59 (all mature).

Beaujolais 1989 was an outstanding vintage, both short and long-term. 1988 was v. attractive with Crus to keep. 1987 wines should be finished soon. 86s should be drunk. 1985 was a wonderful vintage, with Crus to keep still. Generally avoid older wines except possibly some Moulin à Vent.

White Burgundy

Côte de Beaune Well-made wines of good vintages with plenty of acidity as well as fruit will improve and gain depth and richness for some years – anything up to ten. Lesser wines from lighter years are ready for drinking after two or three years.

1989 Excellent omens, though some had hail damage. Fat wines, some low in acidity.
1988 Extremely good; some great wines – but others rather dilute. Now-2000.
1987 Mainly disappointing, though a few exceptions are emerging. Now-'98.
1986 Powerful wines with better acidity and balance than '85. Now-2000.
1985 Very ripe; many wines are too soft; be careful. Now-'95.
1984 Some well-balanced wines; most rather lean or hollow. Drink soon.
1983 Potent wines; some exaggerated, some faulty but the best splendid. -'95.
1982 Fat, tasty but delicate whites of low acidity, not for keeping.
1981 A sadly depleted crop with great promise. But time to drink up.
1980 A weak, but not bad, vintage. Should be finished.
1979 Big vintage. Overall good and useful, not great. Drink soon.
1978 Very good wines, firm and well-balanced. Keep only the best.
1977 Rather light; some well-balanced and good. Drink up.
1976 Hot summer, rather heavy wines; good but mostly passed it now.
1973 Very attractive, fruity, typical and plentiful. Drink up.
1972 High acidity, but plenty of character. All are now ready to drink.
1971 Great power and style. Top wines are now wonderful. Drink soon.

The white wines of the Mâconnais (Pouilly-Fuissé, St-Véran, Mâcon-Villages) follow a similar pattern, but do not last as long. They are more appreciated for their freshness than their richness.

Chablis Grand Cru Chablis of vintages with both strength and acidity can age superbly for up to ten years. Premiers Crus proportionately less, but too many growers are stressing quantity, which results in wines that fade away without ever achieving the classic Chablis flavour. Only buy Petit Chablis of ripe years, and drink it young.

1989 Excellent vintage of potent character.
1988 Almost a model: great pleasure in store. Now-'98.
1987 Rain at harvest but balanced wines for the short term. Drink soon.
1986 A splendid, big vintage. Now-1995.
1985 Good but often low-acid wines. The best Grands Crus will age to '95.
1984 A small vintage. Most too feeble to last long. Drink up.
1983 Superb vintage if not over-strong. The very best will improve until '93.
1982 Charming soft wines. Not to keep.
1981 Small, concentrated and fine harvest. Drink soon.
1980 More successful than the rest of burgundy. Drink up.
1979 Very big crop. Good easy wines, not for storing.
1978 Excellent wines now passing their peak.

Red Bordeaux

Médoc/red Graves For some wines bottle-age is optional: for these it is indispensable. Minor châteaux from light vintages need only two or three years, but even modest wines of great years can improve for 15 years or so, and the great châteaux of these years need double that time.

1989 Early spring and splendid summer. A great Cabernet vintage.
1988 Generally excellent; ripe, balanced, for long keeping. To 2020.
1987 Difficult; at best sound. Strict selection necessary. Not for long keeping.
1986 Another splendid (and huge) heatwave harvest. Superior to '85. In Pauillac and St-Julien.
1985 Very good vintage, in a heatwave. Some great wines. Now-2010.
1984 Only fair. Little Merlot but good ripe Cabernet. Originally overpriced. -'95?
1983 A classic vintage: abundant tannin with fruit to balance it. -2010.
1982 Made in a heatwave. Huge rich strong wines which promise a long life. Many Pomerols and St-Emilions and most petits châteaux are now rich and delicious. Keep the best.
1981 Admirable despite rain. Not rich, but balanced and fine. Now-'98.
1980 Small, late harvest, ripe but rained-on. Many delicious light wines. Drink up.
1979 Abundant harvest of above average quality. Now-'95.
1978 A miracle vintage: magnificent long warm autumn. Some superb wines. Now-2000.
1977 Pleasant light wine, many better than 1974. Now.
1976 Excessively hot, dry summer; rain just before vintage. Generally very good; now ready.
1975 A very fine vintage, with deep colour, high sugar content and (sometimes excessive) tannin. For long keeping but begin to drink: some may improve.
1974 Oceans of disappointing light wines. Be very careful.
1973 A huge vintage, attractive young and still give pleasure. Now or very soon.
1972 High acidity from unripe grapes. Now.
1971 Small crop. Less fruity than '70 and less consistent. All are ready to drink.
1970 Big excellent vintage with scarcely a failure. Now-'95.
1969/68 Avoid them both.
1967 Never seductive, but characterful in its maturity. Drink soon.
1966 A very fine vintage with depth, fruit and tannin. Now.
Older fine vintages: '62, '61, '59, '55, '53, '52, '50, '49, '48, '47, '45, '29, '28.

St-Emilion/Pomerol
1989 Large, ripe, early harvest, though Merlot may be not quite as great as the Cabernet wines.
1988 Generally excellent; ideal conditions.
1987 Some very adequate wines but for drinking soon.
1986 A prolific vintage; most wines need drinking soon.
1985 One of the great years, with a long future. -2010.
1984 A sad story. Most of the crop wiped out in spring. Avoid.
1983 Conditions were ideal. Some growers prefer this vintage to 1982.
1982 Enormously rich and concentrated wines, most excellent. Now-2000+.
1981 A very good vintage, if not as great as it first seemed. Now-'95+.
1980 A poor Merlot year; very variable quality. Choose carefully. Soon.
1979 A rival to '78, but not developing as well as hoped. Now-'95.
1978 Fine wines, but some lack flesh. Drink soon.
1977 Very wet summer. Mediocre with few exceptions. Drink up.
1976 Very hot, dry summer, but vintage rain. Some excellent. Drink soon.
1975 Most St-Emilions good, the best superb. Pomerol made splendid wine. Now-2000.
1974/73/72 All need drinking soon, if at all.
1971 On the whole better than Médocs but generally now ready.
1970 Beautiful wines with great fruit and strength. Very big crop. Now.
Older fine vintages: '67, '66, '64, '61, '59, '53, '52, '49, '47, '45.

Abel-Lepitre Brut NV, Cuvé 134 Blanc de Blancs **82** 83, Réserve Crémant 83, Rosé 83 Champagne house, founder of Les Grands Champagnes de Reims, also owning GOULET and St-Marceaux. Luxury Cuvée: Prince A. de Bourbon-Parme.

Abymes Savoie w. dr. ★ D.Y.A.
Hilly little area nr. Chambéry; light mild wine from Jacquère grape.

Ackerman-Laurance Champagne-method house of the Loire, at SAUMUR, said to be the first of the region. Fine CREMANT de Loire.

Ajaccio Corsica r. p. or w. dr. ★→★★★ **85' 86 87** 88 89'
The capital of Corsica. AC for some v. good SCIACARELLO reds.

Aligoté Second-rank burgundy white grape and its wine, often agreeably sharp and fruity and with considerable local character when young. BOUZERON (AC) makes the best, but don't hesitate to try others. Value.

Aloxe-Corton B'y. r. or w. ★★★ **69 71 76 78 79 80 82 83** 85 86 87 88' 89
Northernmost village of COTE DE BEAUNE famous for its two Grands Crus: CORTON (red) and CORTON-CHARLEMAGNE (white). Village wines (called Aloxe-Corton) are much lighter but can be good value.

Alsace Al. w. or (r.) ★★ **76 81 83' 85' 86 87** 88 89'
Aromatic, fruity, often strong white of rather Germanic character from eastern foothills of Vosges Mtns, bordering on the R. Rhine, increasingly made sweet (see Vendange Tardive). Normally sold by grape variety (RIESLING, GEWÜRZTRAMINER, etc.). Matures well up to 5, even 10, years; the next entry even longer.

Alsace Grand Cru ★★★ **71 76 79 81 82 83 85 86** 88 89'
Appellation restricted to about 45 of the best named v'yds.

Alsace Grand Vin or Réserve Wine with minimum 11° natural alcohol.

Ampeau, Robert Exceptional grower and specialist in MEURSAULT, POMMARD, etc; only releases matured bottles.

Anjou Lo. r. p. or w. (sw. dr. or sp.) ★→★★★ **76 78 82 83** 85' 86
Loire appellation embracing a wide spectrum of styles. Esp. good for red Anjou-Villages and luscious COTEAUX DU LAYON whites.

Anjou-Côteaux de la Loire AC for CHENIN BLANC whites, incl. the notable dry SAVENNIERES.

Appellation Contrôlée ("AC" or "AOC") Government control of origin and production of all the best French wines (see France Introduction).

Apremont Savoie w. dr. ★★ D.Y.A.
One of the best villages of SAVOIE for pale delicate whites, recently including some CHARDONNAY.

Arbin Savoie r. ★★ Drink at 1-2 years
Deep-coloured lively red of MONDEUSE grapes, rather like a good LOIRE Cabernet. Ideal après-ski wine.

Arbois Jura r. p. or w. (dr. sp.) ★★ On the whole, D.Y.A.
Various good and original light wines; speciality VIN JAUNE.

l'Ardèche, Coteaux de Central France r. (w. dr.) ★→★★★ D.Y.A.
Light country reds, the best made of SYRAH. A useful change from BEAUJOLAIS. Also powerful, almost burgundy-like CHARDONNAY from e.g. Louis LATOUR – a bargain.

Armagnac Region of s.w. France and its often excellent brandy, a fiery spirit of rustic character. The red wine of the area is MADIRAN.

Auxey-Duresses B'y. r. or w. ★★→★★★★ **76 78 79 82 83** 85 86 87 88' 89
Second-rank (but v. pretty) COTE DE BEAUNE village: has affinities with VOLNAY and MEURSAULT. Best estates: Duc de Magenta, Prunier, LEROY, Diconne, HOSPICES DE BEAUNE Cuvée Boillot.

Avize Champ. ★★★★
One of the best CHARDONNAY villages of CHAMPAGNE.

Ay Champ. ★★★★
One of the best black-grape villages of CHAMPAGNE.

Ayala NV "Château d'Ay" **75 76** 79 **82** 83, Grande Cuvée **82** 83 85 and Blanc de Blancs **79** 82 Once-famous Ay-based old-style champagne concern. Deserves more notice.

Bandol Prov. r. p. or (w.) ★★★ 76 78 **80 81 82 83 84** 85′ 86 87′ 88 89
Little coastal region near Toulon with Provence's best wines; vigorous reds from the Mourvèdre grape; esp. Ch Vannières, Domaine Tempier, Domaine Ott, Mas de la Rouvière, Domaine de Pibarnon, Ch Pradeaux.

Banyuls Pyr. br. sw. ★★ 75 78
One of the best VIN DOUX NATURELS (fortified sweet red wines) of the s. of France, made chiefly of GRENACHE. Technically a distant relation of port. Best wines from e.g. Domaine des Hospices, Dom. du Mas Blanc (★★★), at 10-15 yrs old. Also cheap NV wines.

Bar-sur-Aube Champ w. (p.) sp. ★★★
Important secondary Champagne region to the s. Some good lighter wines and excellent Rosé des RICEYS.

Barancourt Cramant NV, Cramant Grand Cru 76 78 79 80 **81**, Bouzy Brut, Bouzy **81**, Rosé NV Grower at Bouzy: full-bodied champagnes. Pricey.

Barsac B'x. w. sw. ★★→ ★★★★ 70 **71** 75 76′ 78 79′ **80 81 82 83′ 84** 85 86′ 88′ 89′ Neighbour of SAUTERNES with similar superb golden wines, generally less rich and more racy. Top ch'x: CLIMENS and COUTET.

Barton & Guestier Bordeaux shipper since c.18, now owned by Seagram's.

Bâtard-Montrachet B'y. w. dr. ★★★★ 71 78 79 **81 82 83 84 85** 86 87 88 89
Larger (55 acre) neighbour of MONTRACHET, the top white burgundy. Should be v. long-lived and intense in flavour. Top growers incl. LEFLAIVE, DROUHIN, LATOUR, BOUCHARD PÈRE, Gagnard, Morey, Niellon, CHARTRON & TREBUCHET, Lequin-Roussot, Ramonet, Sauzet.

Baumard, Domaine des Leading grower of ANJOU wine, especially SAVENNIERES and COTEAUX DU LAYON (Clos Ste Catherine).

Béarn s.w. France r. p. or w. dr. ★ D.Y.A.
Minor appellation of growing local (Basque country) interest, esp. wines from the coop of Sallies de Béarn-Bellocq.

Beaujolais B'y. r. (p. w.) ★ D.Y.A.
The simple appellation of the very big Beaujolais region: light short-lived fruity red of GAMAY grapes.

Confusingly, the best wines of the Beaujolais region are not identified as such on their labels by their appellations. They are known simply by the names of their "crus": Brouilly, Côte de Brouilly, Chénas, Chiroubles, Fleurie, Juliénas, Morgon, Moulin-à-Vent, Regnié, St-Amour. See entries for each of these. Since 1984 the Confrèrie des Compagnes du Beaujolais have offered a "Beaujolais Grumé" label to selected wines from the region, with ageing potential.

Beaujolais de l'année The Beaujolais of the latest vintage, until the next.

Beaujolais Primeur (or Nouveau) The same made in a hurry (often only 4-5 days fermenting) for release at midnight on the third Wednesday in November. Ideally soft, fruity and tempting but often crude, sharp and too alcoholic. BEAUJOLAIS-VILLAGES *should* be a better bet.

Beaujolais Supérieur B'y. r. (w.) ★ D.Y.A.
Beaujolais 1° of natural alcohol stronger than the 9⅓ minimum. Since sugar is almost always added this means little or nothing.

Beaujolais-Villages B'y. r. ★★ **88 89**
Wines from the better (northern) half of Beaujolais, should be much tastier than plain Beaujolais. The 10 (easily) best "villages" are the "crus": FLEURIE, BROUILLY, etc. (see note above). Of the 30 others the best lie around Beaujeu. The crus cannot be released "en primeur" before December 15th. They are best kept till spring (or longer).

Beaumes de Venise Rh. (r. p.) br. sw. ★★★ D.Y.A.
Generally France's best dessert wine MUSCAT, from the s. CÔTES-DU-RHONE; can be high-flavoured, subtle, lingering (e.g. Domaine de Coyeux, Domaine Durban, JABOULET). The red and rosé from Ch Redortier and the cooperative are also good.

Beaune B'y. r. or (w. dr.) ★★★ 76 78′ 82 83′ 85 86 87 88′ 89

Middle-rank classic burgundy. Many fine growers. Négociants' "CLOS" wines (usually "Premier Cru") are often best e.g. DROUHIN's superb "Clos des Mouches". "Beaune du Château" is a (good) brand of BOUCHARD PERE. Best v'yds incl: Grèves, Bressandes, Teurons, Marconnets, Fèves.

Becker, Caves J. Proud old family firm at Zellenberg, ALSACE.

Bégadan Leading village of the n. MEDOC (appellation Médoc). Ch'x incl. LA TOUR DE BY, VIEUX-CH-LANDON, GREYSAC, LAUJAC, PATACHE D'AUX. Often v.g. value. Also commendable coop (Cave St Jean).

Bellet Prov. p. r. w. dr. ★★★

Fashionable, much above average, local wine from near Nice. Ch'x de Bellet and Crémat are serious producers. But pricey.

Bergerac Dordogne r. or w. sw. or dr. ★★ 82 85 86 88 89

Lightweight, often tasty, Bordeaux-style. Drink young, the white very young. See also Pécharmant, Montravel, Monbazillac. Growers incl. CH DE PANISSEAU, JAUBERTIE, Courts-les-Muts, Tiregand.

Besserat de Bellefon Cuvée Blanc de Blancs, "B de B" NV, 75 79 82, Cuvée des Moines Brut and Rosé 79 82 Rising champagne house for light wines.

Beyer, Leon Ancient ALSACE family firm at Eguisheim making forceful dry wines that need ageing at least 2-3 yrs, esp. Comtes d'Eguisheim.

Bichot, Maison Albert One of BEAUNE's biggest grower and merchants. V'yds (Domaine du Clos Frantin is excellent) in CHAMBERTIN, CLOS DE VOUGEOT, RICHEBOURG, etc. and Domaine Long-Depaquit in CHABLIS, plus many other brand-names.

Billecart-Salmon NV, 75 76 78 79 82 83, Rosé NV, Bl. de Blancs 79 82 83

Good small champagne house. Fresh-flavoured wines incl. a very tasty rosé.

Bize, Simon Admirable red burgundy grower with 35 acres at SAVIGNY-LES-BEAUNE. Model wines, racy and elegant; fair prices.

Blagny B'y. r. or w. dr. ★★→★★★ 76 78 82 83 85 86 87 88′ 89

Hamlet between MEURSAULT and PULIGNY-MONTRACHET; affinities with both and VOLNAY for reds. Wines need age. Growers incl. LATOUR, AMPEAU, MATROT.

Blanc de Blancs Any white wine made from (only) white grapes, esp. CHAMPAGNE, which is usually made of both black and white. *Not* an indication of quality.

Blanc de Noirs White (or slightly pink or "blush") wine from black grapes.

Blanck, Marcel High-quality Alsace grower at Kientzheim, esp. for PINOT BLANC.

Blanquette de Limoux Midi w. dr. sp. ★★ normally NV

Good bargain sparkler from near Carcassonne made by a version of the METHODE CHAMPENOISE. Very dry and clean and increasingly tasty.

Blaye B'x. r. or w. dr. ★ 85 86 88 89

Your daily Bordeaux from e. of the Gironde. PREMIERES COTES DE BLAYE are better.

Boisset, Jean Claude Dynamic Burgundy merchant/grower at NUITS-ST-GEORGES, owns the houses of VIENOT, Bassot, Lionel Bruck and Pierre Ponnelle. High commercial standards.

Bollinger NV "Special Cuvée", Grande Année 69 70 73 75 76 79 82 83 85, Année Rare 73 75 83, Rosé 81 82 83 Top champagne house, at AY. Dry full-flavoured style. Luxury wines "RD" 73 75 76 79 and "Vieilles Vignes Françaises" 69 70 75 79 80 81 82 from ungrafted vines.

Bommes One of the five villages of SAUTERNES. Best ch'x: LATOUR-BLANCHE, LAFAURIE-PEYRAGUEY, etc.

Bonneau du Martray, Domaine Major grower (with 22 acres) of CORTON-CHARLEMAGNE of the highest quality; also red Grand Cru CORTON.

Bonnes Mares B'y. r. ★★★★ 66 69 71 76 78′ 79 80 82 83 85′ 86 87 88′ 89 37-acre Grand Cru between CHAMBOLLE-MUSIGNY and MOREY-SAINT-

Bonnezeaux Lo. w. sw. ★★★ **76 78 82** 85 86 88 89
Unusual rich, tangy wine from CHENIN BLANC grapes, the best of COTEAUX DU LAYON. Esp. Ch de Fesles, Domaine du Petit Val. Ages well.

Bordeaux B'x. r. or (p.) or w. ★ **85 86 88** 89 (for ch'x see p. 56)
Basic catch-all appellation for low-strength Bordeaux wine. Not to be despised. There is no more satisfactory daily drink.

Bordeaux Supérieur ★→→★
Ditto, with slightly more alcohol.

Bordeaux Côtes-de-Francs B'x. r. or w. dr. ★★ **82 83 85 86 88'** 89
Fringe Bordeaux from east of ST-EMILION, next door to CASTILLON. Increasingly attractive and tasty wines, esp. from Ch'x PUYGUERAUD, de Belcier, de France, la Prade, Lauriol.

Borie-Manoux Admirable Bordeaux shippers and château-owners, owned by the Castéja family. Ch'x incl. BATAILLEY, HAUT-BAGES MONPELOU, DOMAINE DE L'EGLISE, TROTTEVIEILLE, BEAU-SITE.

Bouchard Ainé Long-established burgundy shipper and grower with 62 acres in BEAUNE, MERCUREY, etc. Good, not top, quality.

Bouchard Père et Fils Important burgundy shipper (est. 1731) and grower with 209 acres of excellent v'yds, mainly in the COTE DE BEAUNE, and cellars at the Château de Beaune. Reliable quality, though whites tend to be too alcoholic.

Bourg B'x. r. or (w. dr.) ★★ **82 83 85 86 88'** 89
Un-fancy claret from e. of the Gironde. For ch'x see COTES DE BOURG.

Bourgogne B'y. r. (p.) or w. dr. ★★ **85 87 88'** 89
Catch-all appellation for Burgundy, but with theoretically higher standards than basic BORDEAUX. Light but often good flavour, best at 2-3 yrs. BEAUJOLAIS crus can also be labelled Bourgogne.

Bourgogne Grand Ordinaire B'y. r. (w.) ★ D.Y.A.
The lowest burgundy appellation for GAMAY wines. Rare.

Bourgogne Passe-tout-grains B'y. r. or (p.) ★ Age 1-2 years
Often enjoyable junior burgundy. ⅓ PINOT NOIR and ⅔ GAMAY grapes mixed in the vat. Not as "heady" as BEAUJOLAIS.

Bourgueil Lo. r. ★★★ **76' 81 82 83'** 85 86 88 89
Normally delicate fruity CABERNET red from Touraine. Deep-flavoured and long lasting in good years, ageing like Bordeaux. St Nicolas de Bourgueil is often lighter. Growers incl. Lamé-Delille-Boucard, Audebert, Cognard, Jamet, Billet, Druet.

Bouvet-Ladubay Major producer of sparkling SAUMUR, controlled by TAITTINGER. Excellent CREMANT de Loire. "Saphir" is vintage wine, "Trésor" the top grade.

Bouzeron Village of the COTE CHALONNAISE distinguished for the only single-village appellation ALIGOTE.

Bouzy Rouge Champ. r. ★★★ **82 83 85 86** 88 89
Still red wine from famous black-grape CHAMPAGNE village. Like light burgundy, ageing early but sometimes lasting well.

Brédif, Marc One of the most important growers and traders of VOUVRAY.

Bricout Small champagne house at AVIZE with good light wines. Brut **82** 85.

Brouilly B'y. r. ★★★ **88 89** 90
One of the 10 best CRUS of BEAUJOLAIS: fruity, round, refreshing. One year in bottle is usually enough. Ch de la Chaize is biggest estate.

Brut Term for the driest wines of CHAMPAGNE until recently, when some completely unsweetened wines have become available as "Brut Intégrale", "Brut non-dosé", "Brut zéro" etc.

Bugey Savoie w. dr. or sp. ★→ ★★ D.Y.A.
District with a variety of light sparkling, still or half-sparkling wines. Grapes incl. Roussette (or Roussanne) and good CHARD.

Buxy B'y. (r.) w. dr. ★★
Village in the AC MONTAGNY with a good coop.

Buzet s.w. France, r. or w. dr. ★★ **85 86 88** 89

Good Bordeaux-style wines from just s.e. of Bordeaux. Good-value area with well-run cooperative. Best wine: Cuvée Napoleon. Also Ch. Sauvagnéres.

Cabernet See Grapes for red wine.

Cabernet d'Anjou Lo. p. ★→★★ D.Y.A.

Delicate, grapey, often rather sweet rosé.

Cahors s.w. France r. ★→ ★★ **78 79 81 82 83 85** 86 88 89

Historically a hard "black" wine of Malbec grapes, now made more like Bordeaux, but can be full-bodied and increasingly distinct. Top growers: Baldès (esp. for "Prince Probus"), Jouffreau, Vigouroux (esp. Ch de Haute-Serre), Ch de Caix, Ch de Chambert, Ch Lagrezette, Ch St Didier, Clos la Coutale, Clos de Gamot, Dom. de Paillas, Dom Euganie. Lighter wines from the coop: Caves d'Olt.

Cairanne Rh. r. p. or w. dr. ★★ **83 84 85 86** 88 89

Village of cotes-du-rhone-villages. Good solid wines, esp. from Domaine Rabasse-Charavin, Dom. Brusset, Dom. l'Oratoire St-Martin.

Calvet Famous old shippers of Bordeaux and Burgundy, now owned by Whitbread. Some reliable standard wines, especially from Bordeaux.

Canard-Duchêne NV Brut, rosé and Charles VII NV, Vintage Charles VII and (sometimes) Coteaux Champenois. Medium-quality champagne house owned by veuve clicquot, hence Moët.

Canon-Fronsac B'x. r. ★★ →★★★ **70 75 78 79 81 82 83' 85 86** 88 89'

Full-flavoured reds of increasing quality and style from small area w. of pomerol. They generally need less age than formerly. Ch'x include Canon, Canon-Moueix, Canon-de-Brem, Coustolle, Junayme, Mazeris-Bellevue, Moulin-Pey-Labrie, Toumalin, Vraye-Canon-Boyer. See also Fronsac.

Cantenac B'x. r. ★★★

Village of the haut-medoc entitled to the appellation margaux. Top ch'x include palmer, brane-cantenac, etc.

Cap Corse Corsica w. dr. br. ★★→★★★

The wild north cape of the island. Splendid muscat and rare dry vermentino white. *Vaut le détour*, if not *le voyage*.

Caramany Pyr. r. (w. dr.) ★ **85 86 87 88** 89

New appellation for part of cotes de roussillon-villages.

Cassis Prov. (r. p.) w. dr. ★★ D.Y.A.

Seaside village e. of Marseille known for its lively dry white, exceptional for Provence (e.g. Domaine du Paternel). Not to be confused with cassis, a blackcurrant liqueur made in Dijon.

Castellane, de Long-established epernay champagne house. Very good, rather light wines incl. Maxim's house champagne.

Cave Cellar, or any wine establishment.

Cave coopérative Wine-growers' cooperative winery. Coops now account for 55% of all French production. 4 out of 10 of all French growers are coop members. Almost all coops are now well run, well equipped and making some of the best-value wine of their areas.

Cépage Variety of vine, e.g. chardonnay, merlot.

Cérons B'x. w. dr. or sw. ★★ **79 80 81 83 85 86** 88 89

Neighbour of sauternes with some good sweet-wine ch'x, e.g. Ch de Cérons et de Calvimont, Ch. Haura.

Chablis B'y. w. dr. ★★ **86** 88 89

Distinctive full-flavoured greeny-gold wine. Made only of chardonnay in n. Burgundy. Top growers incl. Raveneau, Dauvissat, laroche, Long-Depaquit, Michel, Droin, Pic, Fèvre, Vocoret etc. Simple unqualified "Chablis" may be thin: all the best Chablis is either Premier Cru or Grand Cru (see over). The modern growers coop, "La Chablisienne", has very high standards (and many different labels).

Chablis Grand Cru B'y. w. dr. ★★★★ 78 81 82 83 84 85 86 87 88 89
Strong, subtle and altogether splendid. Some of the greatest white burgundies, though less succulent than the top CÔTE DE BEAUNE. There are seven v'yds: Blanchots, Bougros, Clos, Grenouilles, Preuses, Valmur, Vaudésir. See also Moutonne.

Chablis Premier Cru B'y. w. dr. ★★★ 83 85 86 87 88 89
Second-rank but often excellent and more typical of Chablis than the Grands Crus. Best v'yds incl: Côte de Lechet, Fourchaume, Mont de Milieu, Montée de Tonnerre, Montmains, Vaillons.

Chai Building for storing and maturing wine, esp. in Bordeaux.

Chambertin B'y. r. ★★★★ 69 71 76 78 79 80 82 83 84 85 86 87 88 89
32-acre Grand Cru giving the meatiest, most enduring and sometimes the best red burgundy, 15 growers, incl. ROUSSEAU, DROUHIN, BOUCHARD PÈRE, Camus, Damoy, Tortochot, Rebourseau, Trapet, Ponsot.

Chambertin-Clos-de-Bèze B'y. r. ★★★★ 76 78 79 80 81 82 83 84 85 86 87 88 89
37-acre neighbour of CHAMBERTIN. Similarly splendid wine. 10 growers incl. CLAIR-DAU, DROUHIN, DROUHIN-LAROSE, FAIVELEY, JADOT, Trupet, Damoy, ROUSSEAU.

Chambolle-Musigny B'y. r. (w.) ★★★ 76 78 80 82 83 84 85 86 87 88' 89
420-acre CÔTE DE NUITS village with fabulously fragrant, complex, never heavy wine. Best v'yds: MUSIGNY, part of BONNES-MARES, Les Amoureuses, Les Charmes. Growers incl: DE VOGUE, DROUHIN, FAIVELEY, JADOT, Roumier, Moine-Hudelot, Mugnier, Hudelot-Noëllat, Mugneret, Serveau.

Champagne Sparkling wine of Pinots Noir and Meunier and/or Chardonnay from 60,000+ acres 90 miles e. of Paris, made by the MÉTHODE CHAMPENOISE. Wines from anywhere else, however good, cannot be Champagne. (See also names of brands.)

Champagne, Grande The appellation of the best area of COGNAC.

Champigny See Saumur.

Chandon de Briailles, Domaine Small burgundy estate at SAVIGNY. Makes wonderful CORTON and v.g. Pernand-Vergelesses.

Chanson Père et Fils Growers (with 110 acres) and négociants at BEAUNE.

Chantovent Major brand of VIN DE TABLE, largely from MINERVOIS.

Chapelle-Chambertin B'y. r. ★★★ 76 78 80 82 83' 85 86 87 88 89
13-acre neighbour of CHAMBERTIN. Wine more "nervous", not so meaty. Top producers: CLAIR-DAU, DROUHIN-LAROSE, LEROY, Trapet.

Chapoutier Long-established growers and traders of fine Rhône wines.

Charbaut, A. et Fils NV, Blanc de Blancs, Certificate Rosé NV, 73 76 79 82 85, Certificate Brut 82 85 ÉPERNAY champagne house. Very fine, clean light wines. Good Rosé.

Chardonnay See Grapes for white wine.

Charmes-Chambertin B'y. r. ★★★ 71 76 78 79 80 82 83 85 86 87 88 89
76-acre neighbour of CHAMBERTIN. Wine more "supple", rounder. Growers incl. Bachelet, Castagnier, DROUHIN, DUJAC, Roty, ROUSSEAU.

Chartron & Trebuchet Young company with delicate and harmonious white burgundies, esp. Domaine Chartron's PULIGNY-MONTRACHET, Clos de la Pucelle and BATARD and CHEVALIER-MONTRACHETS.

Chassagne-Montrachet B'y. r. or w. dr. ★★★→★★★★★ (reds ★★★) 76 78 80 (r.) 82 (r.) 83 84 85 86 87 88 89 750-acre CÔTE DE BEAUNE village with excellent rich dry whites and sterling hefty reds. The whites rarely have the exceptional finesse of PULIGNY-MONTRACHET next door. Best v'yds: MONTRACHET, BATARD-MONTRACHET, CRIOTS-BATARD-MONTRACHET, Ruchottes, Caillerets, Boudriottes (r. w.), Morgeot (r. w.), CLOS-ST-JEAN (r.). Growers incl. RAMONET-PRUDHON, Morey, MAGENTA, DELAGRANGE-BACHELET, Gagnard-Delagrange, Niellon, M. Colin-Deleger, J-N. Gagnard, Larny-Pillot, Bachelet-Ramonet.

Chasseloir, Domaine du The HQ of the firm of Chéreau-Carré, makers of several excellent domaine MUSCADETS, esp. Ch de Chasseloir, which are among the appellation's leaders.

Château An estate, big or small, good or indifferent, particularly in Bordeaux. In Burgundy the term "domaine" is used. For all Bordeaux châteaux see pp. 57-76.

Château-Chalon Jura w. dr. ★★★
Unique strong dry yellow wine, rather like a sharpish FINO sherry. Usually ready to drink when bottled (at about 6 years). A curiosity.

Château Corton-Grancey B'y. r. ★★★ 76 78 **81 82** 83 85 86 88 89
Famous estate at ALOXE-CORTON, the property of Louis LATOUR.

Château d'Arlay Major JURA estate; 160 acres in skilful hands.

Château de Beaucastel Rh. r. w. dr. ★★★ 78 **79 80 81 83 84 85** 86 87 88 89 One of the biggest (173 acres) and best-run estates of CHATEAUNEUF-DU-PAPE. Deep-hued wines intended for at least 10 yrs ageing. A small amount of wonderful white to keep 5-10 yrs. See Côtes du Ventoux, La Vielle Ferme.

Château de la Chaize B'y. r. ★★★ **88 89**
The best known estate of BROUILLY, with 200 acres.

Château de la Maltroye B'y. r. w. dr. ★★★
Very good 32-acre estate in CHASSAGNE-MONTRACHET and SANTENAY. Unpredictable wines.

Château de Meursault B'y. r. w. ★★★
100-acre estate owned by PATRIARCHE with good v'yds and v.g. wines in MEURSAULT, VOLNAY, POMMARD, BEAUNE. Splendid cellars open to the public for tasting. *Vaut le détour, mais? le prix.*

Château de Panisseau Dordogne r. p. w. dr. ★★ D.Y.A.
Well-known estate of BERGERAC: good dry SAUV BLANC and Sémillon.

Château de Selle Prov. r. p. or w. dr. ★★
100-acre estate of the OTT family near Cotignac, Var. Well-known and typical wines. "Cuvée Speciale" is largely CABERNET SAUVIGNON.

Château du Nozet Lo. w. dr. ★★★ 86 88 89
Biggest and best-known estate of Pouilly (FUMÉ) sur Loire. Top wine, Baron de L, can be wonderful (at a price).

Château Fortia Rh. r. (w. dr.) ★★★ 78 **81 83 84 85** 86 88 89
First-class property in CHATEAUNEUF-DU-PAPE. Traditional methods. The owner's father, Baron Le Roy, also fathered the APPELLATION CONTROLEE system in the 1920s.

Château-Grillet Rh. w. dr. ★★★★ 86 87 **88** 89
7½-acre v'yd with one of France's smallest appellations. Intense, fragrant, wildly over-expensive. Drink fairly young.

Châteaumeillant Lo. r. p. or w. dr. ★ D.Y.A.
Small VDQS area near SANCERRE. Light GAMAY and P NOIR.

Châteauneuf-du-Pape Rh. r. (w. dr.) ★★★ 78' 79 **81 83 84 85** 86 88 89
7,400 acres near Avignon with standards steadily rising. Best estate ("domaine") wines are dark, strong, exceptionally long-lived. Others may be light and/or disappointing. The white can be heavy: most now made to D.Y.A. Top growers incl. Ch'x FORTIA, RAYAS, Doms de BEAUCASTEL, VIEUX TELEGRAPH, Clos des Papes, Dom les Cailloux, etc.

Château Rayas Rh. r. (w. dr.) ★★★ 78' 81 **83** 85 86 87 88 89
Famous old-style property of only 38 acres in CHATEAUNEUF-DU-PAPE. Concentrated wines are entirely GRENACHE, yet can age superbly. "Pignan" is 2nd label. Also v.g. Ch. Fonsalette, CÔTES-DU-RHONE.

Château Simone Prov. r. p. or w. dr. ★★→★★★ Age 2-6 yrs.
Famous old property in Palette; the only one with a name in this appellation near Aix-en-Provence. The red is best: smooth but herby and spicy. Since '85 the white has been catching up.

Château Vignelaure Prov. r. ★★ **81 82 83' 84** 85 86 **87** 88 89
135-acre showpiece Provençal estate near Aix making exceptional, more-or-less Bordeaux-style wine with CABERNET, Syrah and Grenache grapes.

Chatillon-en-Diois Rh. r. p. or w. dr. ★ D.Y.A.

Small appellation e. of the Rhône near Die. Adequate GAMAY reds; white (some ALIGOTE) mostly made into CLAIRETTE DE DIE.

Chauvenet, F. Large commercial Burgundy firm linked with MARGNAT. Sound wines, esp. COTE DE BEAUNE whites.

Chave, Gérard To many the top grower of HERMITAGE, red, and white, recently promoted to superstar.

Chavignol Village of SANCERRE with famous v'yd, Les Monts Damnés. Chalky soil gives vivid wines that age 4-5 years.

Chénas B'y. r. ★★★ 85 86 87 88 89

Good BEAUJOLAIS CRU, neighbour to MOULIN-A-VENT and JULIENAS. One of the weightier Beaujolais. Growers incl. Ch. Chévres, Benon, Champagnon, Robin.

Chenin Blanc See Grapes for white wine.

Chevalier-Montrachet B'y. w. dr. ★★★★ 78 81 83 84 85 86 87 88 89

17-acre neighbour of MONTRACHET with similar luxurious wine, perhaps a little less powerful. Includes Les Demoiselles (LATOUR, JADOT). Other growers incl. BOUCHARD PÈRE, LEFLAIVE, Niellon, Prieur, CHARTRON & TREBUCHET, Deleger.

Cheverny Lo. r. p. or w. dr. (sp.) ★→★★★ D.Y.A.

Loire VDQS from near Chambord. Dry, crisp whites from Romorantin or SAUV BL; GAMAY, P NOIR or CAB reds; generally light but fresh and tasty.

Chevillon, R. Little 21-acre estate at NUITS; outstanding wine-making since 1980.

Chignin Savoie w. dr. ★ D.Y.A.

Light soft white of Jacquère grapes for Alpine summers. Chignin-Bergeron should be slightly better.

Chinon Lo. r. ★★★ 82 83′ 85 86 88

Juicy, variably rich CABERNET FRANC from TOURAINE. Drink cool when young. Exceptional vintages age like Bordeaux. Top growers: Baudry, Couly-Dutheil, Joguet, Raffault, Dom. de Roncée.

Chiroubles B'y. r. ★★★ 88 89

Good but tiny Beaujolais cru next to FLEURIE; freshly fruity silky wine for early drinking (at 1-2 years). Growers incl. Cheysson, Raousset, Passot, DUBOEUF, and the coop.

Chorey-lès-Beaune B'y. r. ★★ 83 85 86 87 88 89

Minor appellation on flat land n. of BEAUNE notable for one fine grower: TOLLOT-BEAUT.

Chusclan Rh. r. p. or w. dr. ★ 86 89

Village of COTE-DU-RHONE-VILLAGES. Middle-weight wines (rosé best) from the cooperative.

Cissac HAUT-MEDOC village just w. of PAUILLAC.

Clair, Bruno Recent little domaine at MARSANNAY. V.g. wines from FIXIN, MOREY-ST-DENIS, SAVIGNY.

Clair-Daü First-class 100-acre burgundy estate in northern COTE DE NUITS, with cellars at MARSANNAY. Bought in 1986 by (now sold as) JADOT.

Clairet Very light red wine, almost rosé.

Clairette Mediocre white grape of the s. of France. Gives neutral wine.

Clairette de Bellegarde Midi w. dr. ★ D.Y.A.

Plain neutral white from near Nîmes.

Clairette de Die Rh. w. dr. or s./sw. sp. ★★ NV

Popular dry or (better) semi-sweet rather MUSCAT-flavoured sparkling wine from the e. Rhône, or straight dry CLAIRETTE white, surprisingly ageing well 3-4 years. Worth trying.

Clairette du Languedoc Midi w. dr. ★ D.Y.A.

Plain neutral white from near Montpellier.

La Clape Midi r. p. or w. dr. ★→★★

Full-bodied VDQS wines from limestone hills between Narbonne and the sea. The (mainly CARIGNAN) red gains character after 2-3 years, the MALVASIA white even longer. V.g. rosé. Some experiments with CHARDONNAY N.B. Ch. Rouquette.

Claret Traditional English term for red BORDEAUX.

Climat Burgundian word for individual named v'yd, e.g. Beaune Grèves, Chambolle-Musigny les Amoureuses.

Clos A term carrying some prestige, reserved for distinct, usually walled, v'yds, often in one ownership. Frequent in Burgundy and Alsace. Les Clos is Chablis's Grandest Cru.

Clos-de-Bèze See Chambertin-Clos-de-Bèze.

Clos de la Roche B'y. r. ★★★ **71 76 78 80 82** 83 **84** 85' 86 87 88' 89
38-acre Grand Cru at MOREY-ST-DENIS. Powerful complex wine like CHAMBERTIN. Producers incl. BOUCHARD PERE, Bourée, Ponsot, DUJAC, ROUSSEAU, Rémy, Castagnier, Lignier.

The Confrèrie des Chevaliers du Tastevin is Burgundy's wine fraternity and the most famous of its kind in the world. It was founded in 1933 by a group of Burgundian patriots, headed by Camille Rodier and Georges Faiveley, to rescue their beloved Burgundy from a period of slump and despair by promoting its inimitable products. Today it regularly holds banquets with elaborate and sprightly ceremonial for 600 guests at its headquarters, the Cistercian château in the Clos de Vougeot. The Confrèrie has branches in many countries and members among lovers of wines all over the world. See also under Tastevin, p. 54.

Clos des Lambrays B'y. r. ★★★ **78 83 84** 85 86 87 88' 89
15-acre Grand Cru v'yd at MOREY-ST-DENIS. Changed hands in 1979 after a shaky period. Now looking good.

Clos des Mouches B'y. r. or w. dr. ★★★
Splendid Premier Cru v'yd of BEAUNE owned by DROUHIN. The unusual white made with Pinot Gris is particularly well-made and rewarding.

Clos de Tart B'y. r. ★★★ **71 76 78 79 80 82 83' 84** 85' 86 87 88' 89
18-acre Grand Cru at MOREY-ST-DENIS owned by MOMMESSIN. At best wonderfully fragrant, whether young or old.

Clos de Vougeot B'y. r. ★★★ **71 76 78 80 82 83** 85 86 87 88 89
124-acre COTE-DE-NUITS Grand Cru with many owners. Bewilderingly variable, occasionally sublime. Maturity depends on the grower's philosophy, technique and position on the hill. Top growers incl: DROUHIN, CLAIR-DAU, DROUHIN-LAROSE, FAIVELEY, Grivot, Hudelot-Noellat, Gros, JADOT, LEROY, Méo-Camuzet, Mugneret, Roumier, Tardy.

Clos du Roi B'y. r. ★★★
Part of the Grand Cru CORTON. Also a Premier Cru of BEAUNE.

Clos St Denis B'y. r. ★★★ 76 78 79 80 82 83' 84 85 86 87 88 89
16-acre Grand Cru at MOREY-ST-DENIS. Splendid sturdy wine. Growers incl. DUJAC, Lignier, Ponsot.

Clos St Jacques B'y. r. ★★★ **71 76 78 79 80 82 83 84** 85' 86 87 88' 89
17-acre Premier Cru of GEVREY-CHAMBERTIN. Excellent powerful velvety wine, often better (and dearer) than some of the CHAMBERTIN Grands Crus. Main grower: ROUSSEAU.

Clos St Jean B'y. r. ★★★ **78 79 80 82** 83' **84** 85 86 87
36-acre Premier Cru of CHASSAGNE-MONTRACHET. Very good red, more solid than subtle from e.g. CH DE LA MALTROYE.

Coche-Dury 16-acre MEURSAULT domaine (+1 acre CORTON-CHARLEMAGNE) with sky-high reputation for oak-perfumed wines. Also v.g. ALIGOTÉ.

Cognac Town and region of western France and its brandy.

Collioure Pyr. r. ★★ **80 81 82 83 84** 85 86 88 89
Strong dry red from BANYULS area. Small production. Top growers incl. Dom. du Mas Blanc, de Bailleury, Guy de Barheute.

Condrieu Rh. w. dr. ★★★★ D.Y.A.
Outstanding soft fragrant white of great character (and price) from only 35 acres of the Viognier grape. Top growers: Vernay, Ch du Rozay, Guigal, Pinchon, Dumazet, DELAS. CHATEAU GRILLET is similar.

Corbières Midi r. or (p.) or (w.) ★★★★ 85 86 87 88 89
Good vigorous bargain reds, steadily improving and now rewarded with AC. Rarely disappointing at their price. Best growers incl. Ch'x des Ollieux, Aiguilloux, de Quéribus, Dom de Villemajou, Coops de Embrès et Castelmaur, Paziols, St Laurent-Cabrerisse, etc.

Cordier, Ets D. Important Bordeaux shipper and château-owner, including Ch'x GRUAUD-LAROSE, TALBOT, CANTEMERLE, MEYNEY, LAFAURIE-PEYRAGUEY and also SANCERRE, Clos de la Poussie.

Cornas Rh. r. ★★→★★★ 78′ 79 80 81 83′ 84 85′ 86 88 89
Expanding 400-acre district S. of HERMITAGE. Typical sturdy Rhône wine of v.g. quality from the SYRAH grape. Needs 3-6 years ageing. Top growers incl. Clape, JABOULET, de Barjac, Verset, DELAS.

Corse The island of Corsica. Strong wines of all colours. Better appellations incl. PATRIMONIO, SARTÈNE, AJACCIO, CAP CORSE.

Corton B'y. r. ★★★★ 71 76′ 78′ 80 82 83 84 85′ 86′ 87 88 89
The only Grand Cru red of the COTE DE BEAUNE. 200 acres in ALOXE-CORTON incl. les Bressandes and CLOS DU ROI. Rich powerful wines should be long-lived. Many good growers.

Corton-Charlemagne B'y. w. dr. ★★★★ 78′ 79 81 82 83 84 85 86 87 88 89
The white corton (one-third) of CORTON. Rich, spicy, lingering wine. Behaves like a red wine and ages magnificently. Top growers: BONNEAU DU MARTRAY, LATOUR, JADOT, COCHE-DURY.

Costières de Nîmes Midi r. p. or w. dr. ★→★★ D.Y.A.
New AC of improving quality from the Rhône delta N.B. Ch de la Tuilerie.

Coteaux Champenois Champ r. (p.) or w. dr. ★★★ D.Y.A.
The appellation for non-sparkling champagne. Vintages (if mentioned) follow those for Champagne. Do not pay inflated prices.

Coteaux d'Aix-en-Provence Prov r. p. or w. dr. ★→★★★
An appellation on the move. The established CH VIGNELAURE is challenged by Ch'x Fonscolombe, de Beaulieu, Commanderie de la Bargemone. See also Coteaux des Baux-en-Provence.

Coteaux d'Ancenis Lo. r. p. w. dr. ★ D.Y.A.
Light CABERNET and GAMAY reds and pinks; sharpish whites from MUSCADET country.

Coteaux de la Loire Lo. w. dr. sw. ★★→★★★ 79 82 85 86 88′ 89
Forceful and fragrant CHENIN BLANC whites from Anjou. The best are in SAVENNIERES. Excellent as an apéritif.

Coteaux de l'Ardèche Central France r. (p. w. dr.) ★ D.Y.A
Flourishing vin de pays: bargain GAMAY, etc.

Coteaux de l'Aubance Lo. p. or w. dr./sw. ★★ D.Y.A.
Light and typical minor ANJOU wines. The best are MOELLEUX from Dom. Richou and Dom. des Rochettes.

Coteaux de Peyriac Midi r.p. ★ D.Y.A.
The most-used vin de pays name of the Aude. Huge quantities.

Coteaux de Pierrevert Rh. r. p. or w. dr. or sp. ★ D.Y.A.
Minor southern VDQS from nr. Manosque. Well-made coop wine mostly rosé, with fresh whites.

Coteaux de Saumur Lo. w. sw. ★★ D.Y.A.
Potentially fine semi-sweet CHENIN BLANC.

Coteaux des Baux-en-Provence Prov. r. p. or w. dr. ★→ ★★★
Neighbour of COTEAUX D'AIX, also gathering speed. N.B. The excellent Domaine de Trévallon (CABERNET and SYRAH).

Coteaux du Giennois Lo. r. p. w. dr. ★ D.Y.A.
Up-and-coming V.D.Q.S. Loire area n. of SANCERRE. Light GAMAY and PINOT NOIR, SAUVIGNON à la SANCERRE Top grower Balland-Chapuis.

Coteaux du Languedoc Midi r. p. or w. dr. ★→★★
Scattered well-above-ordinary Midi areas with AC status. The best reds, (e.g. FAUGÈRES, St Saturnin, LA CLAPE, ST CHINIAN, Quatourze, St-Georges-d'Orques, Cabrières) age for 2-3 years. Follow with interest.

Coteaux du Layon Lo. w. s./sw. or sw. ****** 79 82 85 86 88' 89'
The heart of ANJOU, centered on Rochefort, s. of Angers, making sweet CHENIN BLANC with admirable acidity: excellent aperitifs. "C. du L-Chaume" and BONNEZEAUX are top appellations.

Coteaux du Loir Lo. r. p. or w. dr./sw. ****** 78 82 83 85 86 88 89'
Small region n. of Tours. Occasionally excellent wines. Best v'yd: JASNIERES. The Loir is a tributary of the Loire.

Coteaux du Lyonnais Rh. r. p. (w. dr.) ***** D.Y.A.
Junior Beaujolais, and whites in keeping. Best EN PRIMEUR.

Coteaux du Tricastin Rh. r. p. or w. dr. ***** 85 86 88 89
Fringe COTES-DU-RHONE of increasing quality from s. of Valence. Pierre Labeye is the chief producer. Attractive PRIMEUR red.

Coteaux du Vendomois Lo. r. p. or w. dr. ***** D.Y.A.
Fringe Loire from n. of Blois. Mainly GAMAY.

Coteaux Varois Prov. r. p. w. dr. ***→****
Substantial new VDQS zone with one California-style property, Domaine de St Jean de Villecroze.

Côte(s) Means hillside; generally a superior vineyard to those on the plain. Many appellations start with either Côtes or Coteaux, which means the same thing. In ST-EMILION it distinguishes the valley slopes from the higher plateau.

Côte Chalonnaise B'y. r. w. dr. sp. ****→*****
Lesser-known v'yd area between BEAUNE and MACON. See Mercurey, Givry, Rully, Montagny, Buxy. Alias "Région de Mercurey".

Côte de Beaune B'y. r. or w. dr. ****→******
Used geographically: the southern half of the COTE D'OR. Applies as an appellation only to parts of BEAUNE.

Côte de Beaune-Villages B'y. r. or w. dr. ****** 83 85 86 87 88 89
Regional appellation for secondary wines of the classic area. They cannot be labelled "Côte de Beaune" without either "-Villages" or the village name.

Côte de Brouilly B'y. r. ******* 86 88 89
Fruity, rich, vigorous Beaujolais cru. One of the best. Leading estates: Ch Thivin, Domaine de Chavanne.

Côte de Nuits B'y. r. or (w. dr.) ****→******
The northern half of the COTE D'OR. Nearly all red wine.

Côte de Nuits-Villages B'y. r. (w.) ****** 85 86 87 88 89
A junior appellation, well worth investigating.

Côte d'Or Département name applied to the central and principal Burgundy v'yd slopes, consisting of the COTE DE BEAUNE and COTE DE NUITS. The name is not used on labels.

Côte Rôtie Rh. r. ******* 78 79 80 82 83' 84' 85' 86 88 89
Potentially the finest Rhône red, from just s. of Vienne; achieves complex, almost Bordeaux-like, delicacy with age. Top growers include JABOULET, CHAPOUTIER, VIDAL-FLEURY, Barge, Gentaz-Dervieux, Jasmin, Guigal, Jamet, Rostaing, Champet, DELAS.

Côtes d'Auvergne Central France r. p. or (w. dr.) ***** D.Y.A.
Flourishing small VDQS area near Clermont-Ferrand. Red (at best) like light BEAUJOLAIS. Chanturgues is the best known.

Côtes de Blaye B'x. w. dr. ***** D.Y.A.
Run-of-the-mill Bordeaux white from BLAYE. (Reds are called PREMIERES COTES DE BLAYE.)

Côtes de Bordeaux Saint-Macaire B'x. w. dr./sw. ***** D.Y.A.
Run-of-the-mill Bordeaux white from east of SAUTERNES.

Côtes de Bourg B'x. r. ***→***** 81 82 83 85 86 88 89
Appellation used for many of the better reds of BOURG. Ch'x incl. de Barbe, La Barde, du Bousquet, La Croix de Millorit, de la Grave, Grand-Jour, Font Guilhem, Guerry, Rousset, Lalibarde, La Grolet, Brûléscaille, Tayac, Lamothe, Mendoce, Falfas, Peychaud, de Thau.

Côtes de Castillon B'x. r. ![] ★→★★ **78 82 83 85 86 87** 88 89
Flourishing region just e. of St-Emilion. Similar wines, though a touch lighter. Ch'x incl. Beleier, Beau-Séjour, Parenchére, La Clariére, Fonds-Rondes, Haut-Tuquet, Lardit, PITRAY, Ste Colombe, Moulin-Rouge, Rocher-Bellevue.

Côtes de Duras Dordogne r. or w. dr. ![] **85 86 88** 89
Neighbour to BERGERAC, dominated by its v. competent coop. Similar light wines.

Côtes de Francs See Bordeaux – Côtes de Francs.

Côtes de Fronsac See Fronsac.

Côtes de Gascogne s.w. France (r.) w. dr. ![] D.Y.A.
Vin de pays gaining a name for deliciously floral whites in bountiful supply. Top growers: Grassa and the Coop de Plaimont.

Côtes de Montravel Dordogne w. dr./sw. ![] D.Y.A.
Part of BERGERAC; traditional medium-sw. wine, now often dry.

Côtes de Provence Prov. r. p. or w. dr. ★→★★★
The wine of Provence; still often with more alcohol than character, though standards are rapidly improving as new investors move in. Domaine OTT, Commanderie de Peyrassol, Dom. Gavoty, Dom. Richeaume are leaders. 60% is rosé, 30% red. See under Coteaux d'Aix, Bandol, etc.

Côtes de Saint-Mont s.w. France r. w. dr. p. ![]
Promising VDQS from the Gers, not unlike MADIRAN. The same coop as COTES DE GASCOGNE.

Côtes de Thongue Midi r. w. dr. ![] D.Y.A.
Above-average Vins de Pays from the HERAULT.

Côtes de Toul e. France r. p. or w. dr. ★ D.Y.A.
Very light wines from Lorraine; mainly VIN GRIS (rosé).

Côtes du Forez Central France r. or p. ![] D.Y.A.
Light Beaujolais-style red, can be good in warm years.

Côtes du Frontonnais s.w. France r. or p. ★→★★ D.Y.A.
The local wine of Toulouse, gaining admirers elsewhere. Ch Bellevue-la-Forét (250 acres) makes outstanding silky red.

Côtes du Haut-Roussillon s.w. France br. sw. ★→★★ NV
Area for VINS DOUX NATURELS n. of Perpignan.

Côtes du Jura Jura r. p. or w. dr. (sp.) ★ D.Y.A.
Various light tints and tastes. ARBOIS is theoretically better.

Côtes du Luberon Rh. r. p. or w. dr. sp. ★→★★
Improving country wines from northern Provence. The star is Ch Val-Joannis, with good largely SYRAH red, and whites as well. Others incl. a good coop, Ch de Mille Ch. de la Canorgue.

Côtes du Marmandais Dordogne r. p. or w. dr. ★ D.Y.A.
Light wines from s.e. of Bordeaux. The coop at Cocumont makes most of the best.

Côtes-du-Rhône Rh. r. p. or w. dr. ★→★★**88 89**
The basic appellation of the Rhôn valley. Best drunk young – even as PRIMEUR. Wide variations of quality due to grape ripeness, therefore tending to rise with alcohol %. See Côtes-du-Rhône-Villages.

Côtes-du-Rhône-Villages Rh. r. p. or w. dr. ★→ ![] **85 86 88** 89
The wine of the 17 best villages of the southern Rhône. Substantial and on the whole reliable. Sometimes delicious. See under Cairanne, Chusclan, Laudun, Rasteau etc.

Côtes du Roussillon Pyr. r. or w. dr. ![] ★→★★ **85 86 87** 88 89
Country wine of e. Pyrenees. The hefty reds are best and can be very tasty. Some whites are sharp VINS VERTS.

Côtes du Roussillon-Villages Pyr. r. ★★ **83 84 85 86 87** 88 89
The best reds of the region, incl. CARAMANY and LATOUR DE FRANCE.

Côtes du Ventoux Prov. r. (w. dr.) ![] **88** 89
Booming appellation for tasty reds between the Rhône and Provence. La Vieille Ferme, owned by CH DE BEAUCASTEL, is top producer.

Côtes du Vivarais Prov. r. p. or w. dr. ★ D.Y.A.
  Pleasant country wines from s. Massif Centrale. Like light COTES-DU-RHONE e.g. Domaine de Belvezet.

Côtes Roannaises Central France r. ❋ D.Y.A.
  Minor GAMAY region high up the LOIRE.

Coulée de Serrant Lo. w. dr./sw. ★★★ 76 78 79 81 82 83 85 86 88 89
  10-acre v'yd on n. bank of LOIRE at SAVENNIERES, Anjou. Intense strong fruity/sharp wine, good as an apéritif. Ages well.

Crémant In Champagne means "Creaming" – i.e. half-sparkling. Since 1975 an appellation for high-quality champagne-method sparkling wines from Alsace, the Loire and Bourgogne – often a notable bargain. e.g . . .

Crémant de Loire w. dr. sp. ★★ NV
  High-quality sparkling wine from ANJOU, TOURAINE, and Pays Nantais.

Crépy Savoie w. dr. ★★ D.Y.A.
  Light, soft, Swiss-style white from south shore of the Lake of Geneva. "Crépitant" has been coined for its faint fizz.

Criots-Bâtard-Montrachet B'y. w. ★★★ 78 79 81 83 85 86 88 89
  4-acre neighbour to BATARD-MONTRACHET. Similar wine.

Burgundy boasts one of the world's most famous and certainly its most beautiful hospital, the Hospices de Beaune, founded in 1443 by Nicolas Rolin, Chancellor to the Duke of Burgundy, and his wife Guigone de Salins. The hospital he built and endowed with vineyards for its income still operates in the same building and still thrives, tending the sick of Beaune without charge, on the sale of its wine. Many growers since have bequeathed their land to the Hospices. Today it owns 125 acres of prime land in Beaune, Pommard, Volnay, Meursault, Corton and Mazis-Chambertin. The wine is sold by public auction every year on the third Sunday in November.

Crozes-Hermitage Rh. r. or (w. dr.) ★★ 82 83 84 85 86 88 89
  Larger and less distinguished neighbour to HERMITAGE. Robust and often excellent reds, but choose carefully: e.g. Domaine de Thalabert of JABOULET.

Cru "Growth", as in "first-growth" – meaning vineyard. Also, in BEAU-JOLAIS, one of the top nine villages.

Cru Bourgeois General term for MEDOC châteaux below CRU CLASSE.

Cru Bourgeois Supérieur (Cru Grand Bourgeois) Official rank one better than the last. Must be aged in barrels.

Cru Classé Classed growth. One of the first five official quality classes of the Médoc, classified in 1855. Also any classed growth of another district (e.g. GRAVES, ST-EMILION, SAUTERNES).

Cru Grand Bourgeois Exceptionnel Official rank above CRU BOURGEOIS SUPERIEUR, immediately below CRU CLASSE. Several fine châteaux are unofficially acknowledged (and labelled) as Exceptionnel, which makes them on a par with many CRUS CLASSES.

Cruse et Fils Frères Long-established Bordeaux shipper. Owned by the Societe des Vins de France. Members of the Cruse family (not the company) own Ch d'ISSAN.

Cubzac, St.-André-de B'x. r. or w. dr. ★→ ★★ 82 83 85 86 88 89
  Town 15 miles n.e. of Bordeaux, centre of the minor Cubzaguais region. Sound reds have the appellation Bordeaux Supérieur. Estates include: Ch du Bouilh, Ch de TERREFORT-QUANCARD, Ch TIMBERLAY, Domaine de Beychevelle.

Cussac Village just s. of ST JULIEN. Appellation Haut-Médoc.

Cuve Close Short-cut method of making sparkling wine in a tank. The sparkle dies much quicker than with METHODE CHAMPENOISE wine.

Cuvée de la Commanderie Pleasant blends of MEDOC, GRAVES and (best) SAUTERNES made for the Commanderie du Bontemps, the ceremonial/promotional body of the Médoc and Graves.

Cuvée The quality of wine produced in a "cuve" or vat. Also a word of many uses, incl. "blend". In Burgundy interchangeable with "Cru". Often just refers to a "lot" of wine.

d'Angerville, Marquis Famous burgundy grower with immaculate 30-acre estate in VOLNAY. Top wines: Clos des Ducs and Champans.

Degré alcoolique Degrees of alcohol, i.e. percent by volume.

De Ladoucette Leading producer of POUILLY-FUMÉ, based at CH DE NOZET. Luxury brand "Baron de L". Also SANCERRE Comte Lafond.

Delas Frères Long-established and excellent firm of Rhône-wine specialists with v'yds at CÔTE RÔTIE, HERMITAGE, CONDRIEU, COLNAS. Top wines: Marquise de Tourette Hermitages (red and white); Condrieu. Owned by DEUTZ.

Delorme, André Leading merchants and growers of the CÔTE CHALONNAISE. Specialists in excellent sparkling wine and RULLY.

De Luze, A. & Fils Bordeaux shipper owned by Rémy-Martin of Cognac. Members of the De Luze family own CH PAVEIL DE LUZE.

Demi-Sec "Half-dry": in practice more than half sweet.

Depagneux, Jacques de Cie Well-regarded merchants of BEAUJOLAIS.

Deutz Brut NV and **75 76 79 81 82** 85, Rosé **82** 85, Blanc de Blancs **78 79 81 82** 85 One of the best of the smaller champagne houses. Full-flavoured wines. Luxury brand: Cuvée William Deutz (**75 79 82** 85).

Domaine Property, particularly in Burgundy.

Domaine de Coussergues Midi r.w.p dr. ★★
Large estate in notorious territory near Beziers. But amazing CHARDONNAY.

Domaine de l'Eglantière Important CHABLIS estate. See Durup.

Domaine du Vieux Télégraphe Rh. r. (w. dr.) ★★★ **78′ 79 81 83 84 85** 86 88 89 A leader in the smaller, vigorous, modern CHÂTEAUNEUF-DU-PAPE.

Dom Pérignon **70 71 73 75 76 78 80 82** and Rosé **75 78**
Luxury brand of MOËT & CHANDON, named after the legendary Abbey cellarmaster who "invented" champagne. The '82 is exceptional.

Dopff "au Moulin" Ancient and top-class family wine-house at Riquewihr, Alsace. Best wines: Riesling Schoenenbourg, Gewürztraminer Eichberg. Pioneers of sparkling wine in Alsace.

Dopff & Irion Another excellent Riquewihr (ALSACE) business. Best wines include Muscat les Amandiers, Riesling de Riquewihr.

Doudet-Naudin Burgundy merchant and grower at Savigny-lès-Beaune. V'yds incl. BEAUNE CLOS DU ROI. Unfashionably dark long-lived wines supplied to Berry Bros & Rudd of London.

Dourthe Frères Well-reputed Bordeaux merchant representing a wide range of ch'x, mainly good Crus Bourgeois, incl. Ch'x MAUCAILLOU, TRONQUOY-LALANDE, BELGRAVE. "Numero 1" is their well-made brand.

Doux Sweet.

Drouhin, J. & Cie Deservedly prestigious Burgundy grower (130 acres) and merchant with highest standards. Offices in BEAUNE, v'yds in BEAUNE, MUSIGNY, CLOS DE VOUGEOT, CHABLIS, etc. Drouhin also owns JAFFELIN et Cie and a v'yd in Oregon. Top wines incl. Beaune Clos de Mouches and Puligny-Montrachet Les Folatières.

Drouhin-Larose Prosperous little domaine in GEVREY-CHAMBERTIN, CLOS DE BÈZE, CLOS DE VOUGEOT, etc.

Duboeuf, Georges Top-class BEAUJOLAIS merchant at Romanèche-Thorin. The leader of the region in every sense, with a huge range of admirable wines, including many of the best Crus.

Dujac, Domaine Fashionable burgundy grower at MOREY-ST-DENIS with v'yds in that village, ECHEZAUX, BONNES-MARES, GEVREY-CHAMBERTIN, etc. His wines are splendidly vivid and long-lived.

Durup, Jean One of the biggest Chablis growers with 140 acres, including the DOMAINE DE L'EGLANTIÈRE and admirable Ch de Maligny.

Echézeaux B'y. r. ★★★ **76 78′ 79 80 82 83′ 84** 85 86 87 88 89
74-acre Grand Cru between VOSNE-ROMANÉE and CLOS DE VOUGEOT. Can

be superlative fragrant burgundy without great weight e.g. from Mugneret, Gouroux, DOM DE LA ROMANEE-CONTI, Jacqueline Jayer.

Edelzwicker Alsace w. ☀ D.Y.A.
Modest light white from mixture of grapes, often fruity and good.

Engel, R. Top grower of VOSNE-ROMANEE, CLOS VOUGEOT, ECHEZEAUX.

Entre-Deux-Mers B'x. w. dr. ☀ D.Y.A.
Standard dry white Bordeaux from between the Garonne and Dordogne rivers. Often a good buy, esp. "La Gamage", Ch'x ST BONNET, Gournin, Latour-Laguens, Launay, Thieuley.

Eschenauer, Louis Famous Bordeaux merchants, owners of Ch'x RAUSAN-SEGLA and SMITH-HAUT-LAFITTE, DE LAMOUROUX and LA GARDE in GRAVES. Controlled by John Holt, part of the Lonrho group.

L'Estandon The vin ordinaire of Nice (AC Côtes de Provence).

l'Etoile Jura w. dr./sw./sp. ★★
Sub-region of the Jura known for stylish whites, incl. VIN JAUNE similar to CHATEAU-CHALON and good sparkling.

Faiveley, J. Family-owned growers (with 182 acres) and merchants at NUITS-ST-GEORGES, with v'yds in CHAMBERTIN-CLOS-DE-BEZE, CHAMBOLLE-MUSIGNY, CORTON, NUITS, MERCUREY (150 acres). Consistent high quality. 1988 wines are models. Wines for serious ageing.

Faller, Théo Top ALSACE grower at the Domaine Weinbach, Kaysersberg. Concentrated firm wines need unusually long ageing.

Faugères Midi r. (p. or w. dr.) ▩▬▶▶▶▶ 86 87 88 89
Isolated village of the COTEAUX DU LANGUEDOC making above-average reds. Became Appellation Contrôlée in 1982.

Fessy, Sylvain Dynamic BEAUJOLAIS merchant with wide range.

Fèvre, William Conservative and excellent Chablis grower with the biggest Grand Cru holding (40 acres). His label is Domaine de la Maladière.

Fitou Midi r. ★★ **84 85 86** 88 89
Superior CORBIERES red; powerful and ages well. Mostly from coop at Tuchan. Recent popularity has not improved standards.

Fixin B'y. r. ▨▩ **78 80 83** 85 86 87 88 89
A worthy and under-valued neighbour to GEVREY-CHAMBERTIN. Often splendid reds. Best v'yds: Clos du Chapitre, Les Hervelets, Clos Napoléon. Top growers: Clair, Bertheau, Gelin, Gelin-Moulin, Berthaut, FAIVELEY.

Fleurie B'y. r. ★★★ **86 88** 89
The epitome of a BEAUJOLAIS cru: fruity, scented, silky, racy. Top wines from DUBOEUF, Ch. de Fleurie, Chignard, the cave coop etc.

Frais Fresh or cool.

Frappé Ice-cold.

Froid Cold.

Fronsac B'x. r. ▩▬▶▶▶▶ **75 78 79 81 82 83 85 86** 88 89′
Pretty, hilly area of increasingly good reds just w. of St-Emilion. Ch'x incl. Dalem, La Dauphine, Mayne-Vieil, la Rivière, de Carles, La Valade, Villars, La Vieille Cure. See also Canon-Fronsac.

Frontignan Midi br. sw. ☀ NV
Strong sweet and liquorous muscat wine of ancient repute.

Gagnard-Delagrange, Jacques Estimable small (13-acre) grower of CHASSAGNE-MONTRACHET, including some LE MONTRACHET.

Gaillac s.w. France r. p. or w. dr./sw. or sp. ▩▬▶▶▶
Ancient area showing signs of new life after generations of dullness. Slightly fizzy "Perlé" is good value. Reds can age well. Ch Larroze is the quality leader. The major coop at Labastide de Lévis has recently produced some lovely fruity wines esp. from local Manzac grapes.

Gallaire Bordeaux merchant house of Peter A. Sichel, much-respected owner of Ch D'ANGLUDET and part-owner of Ch PALMER.

Gamay See Grapes for red wine.

Geisweiler et Fils One of the bigger merchant-houses of Burgundy: cellars and 50 acres of v'yds at NUITS-ST-GEORGES. Also 150 acres at Bevy in the HAUTES COTES DE NUITS and 30 in the COTE CHALONNAISE.

Gevrey-Chambertin B'y. r. ★★★ 76 78 79 80 82 83 85 86 87 88 89
The village containing the great CHAMBERTIN and many other noble v'yds, as well as a considerable number more commonplace. Growers incl. Leclerc, DROUHIN, Damoy, Trapet, Boillot, DOM. DES VAROILLES, ROTY, ROUSSEAU, DROUHIN-LAROSE, FAIVELEY.

Gewürztraminer The speciality grape of ALSACE: perfumed and spicy, whether dry or sweet.

Gigondas Rh. r. or p. ★★ 78 80 81 83 84 85 86 88 89
Worthy neighbour to CHATEAUNEUF-DU-PAPE. Strong, full-bodied, sometimes peppery wine, e.g. Dom les Goubert, Dom du Cayron, Dom les Pallières, Dom Raspail-Ay, and wines from MEFFRE.

Gilbey, S.A. British firm long-established as Bordeaux growers and merchants at Ch LOUDENNE in the MEDOC. Now owned by Grand Met.

Gisselbrecht, Louis High-quality Alsace shippers at Dambach-la-Ville.

Givry B'y. r. or w. dr. ★★ 83 84 85 86 87 88 89
Underrated village of the COTE CHALONNAISE: light but tasty and typical burgundy from e.g. Baron Thénard, Clos Salomon, Dom Joblot.

Gosset NV, 73 75 76 78 79 80 81 82 83 85
"Grande Réserve" and Rosé NV Small, very old champagne house at Ay. Excellent full wines (esp. Grande Réserve). Now linked with Philipponnat.

Gouges, Henri Worthy burgundy grower of NUITS-ST-GEORGES. Good reds and very rare white "La Perrière".

Goulaine, Château de The ceremonial showplace of MUSCADET; a noble family estate and its appropriate wine.

Goulet, Georges NV, rosé 76 79 83 85, Crémant Blanc de Blancs 79 and 71 73 75 76 79 81 83 85 High-quality Reims champagne house linked with Abel Lepitre. Luxury brand: Cuvée du Centenaire 74 76 79 83 85.

Goût Taste, e.g. "goût anglais" – as the English like it (i.e. dry).

Grand Cru One of the top Burgundy v'yds with its own appellation contrôlée. Similar meaning in Alsace but more vague elsewhere. In ST-EMILION the third rank of château, numbering about 200.

Grand Roussillon Midi br. sw. ★★ NV
Broad appellation for muscat and other sweet fortified wines ("Vins Doux Naturels") of eastern Pyrenees.

Grands-Echézeaux B'y. r. ★★★★ 69 71 76 78 79 80 82 83 84 85 86 87 88 89 Superlative 22-acre Grand Cru next to CLOS DE VOUGEOT. Top growers: Dom de la ROMANEE-CONTI, ENGEL, Mongeard-Mugneret.

Gratien, Alfred and Gratien & Meyer Excellent smaller champagne house (fine, very dry, long-lasting wine 73 76 79 82 83) and its counterpart at SAUMUR on the Loire.

Graves B'x. r. or w. ★→★★★★
Large region s. of Bordeaux city. Most of its best wines are red, but the name is used chiefly for its dry whites.

Graves-Pessac-Léognan New AOC for part of n. Graves, incl. the area of most of the Grands Crus. Since 1987 "Pessac-Léognan" alone has been allowed, without the name Graves.

Graves de Vayres B'x. r. or w. ★
Part of ENTRE-DEUX-MERS; of no special character.

Les Gravières B'y. r. ★★★
Famous Premier Cru v'yd of SANTENAY. Incl. Clos des Tavannes.

Grivot, Jean 25-acre COTE DE NUITS domaine, in VOSNE-ROMANEE, CLOS DE VOUGEOT, etc. Top quality.

Griotte-Chambertin B'y. r. ★★★ 69 71 76 78' 79 80 83 84 85' 86 87 88 89 14-acre Grand Cru adjoining CHAMBERTIN. Similar wine, but less masculine and more "tender". Growers incl. DROUHIN, PONSOT.

Gros Plant du Pays Nantais Lo. w. ★ D.Y.A.

Junior cousin of MUSCADET, sharper and lighter; made of the COGNAC grape also known as Folle Blanche, Ugni Blanc etc.

Guigal, E and M Celebrated growers and merchants of CÔTE RÔTIE and CONDRIEU. Since 85 owners of VIDAL-FLEURY.

Haut-Benauge B'x. w. dr. ★ D.Y.A.

Appellation for a limited area within ENTRE-DEUX-MERS.

Hautes-Côtes de Beaune B'y. r. or w. dr. ★★ 85 86 87 88 89

Appellation for a dozen villages in the hills behind the CÔTE DE BEAUNE. Light wines, worth investigating.

Hautes-Côtes de Nuits B'y. r. or w. dr. ★★ 78 83 85 86 87 88

The same for the CÔTE DE NUITS. An area on the way up. Has a large coop in BEAUNE. Also good wines from GEISWEILER.

Haut-Médoc B'x. r. ★★→★★★ 70 75 76 78 79 80 81 82 83 84 85 86 88 89

Big appellation including all the best areas of the Médoc. Most of the zone has communal appellations (e.g. MARGAUX, PAUILLAC). Some excellent ch'x (e.g. LA LAGUNE) are simply AC Haut-Médoc.

Haut-Montravel Dordogne w. sw. ★ 85 86 88 89

Medium-sweet BERGERAC.

Haut Poitou Lo. (r.) w. d.r. ★→★★★ D.Y.A.

Up-and-coming VDQS area south of ANJOU. Cooperative makes v. good whites, incl. CHARDONNAY and SAUVIGNON BLANC.

Heidsieck, Charles NV, rosé 81 and 73 75 76 79 81 83

Major champagne house of Reims, now controlled by Rémy Martin; also includes Trouillard and de Venoge. Luxury brands: Cuvée Champagne Charlie 79 81 83. Fine quality recently, incl. the NV.

Heidsieck, Monopole NV, rosé and 73 75 76 79 82 83

Important champagne merchant and grower of Reims now owned by MUMM. V.g. luxury brand: Diamant Bleu (76 79), Diamant rosé 82 85.

Henriot NV, Blanc de Blancs Crémant Brut Souverain NV; Brut Rosé 81 83 85; Cuvée Baccarat 79; and 79 82 85 Old family champagne house now owned by VEUVE CLICQUOT. Very big dry style. Luxury brand: Réserve Baron Philippe de Rothschild.

Hérault Midi

The biggest v'yd département in France with 400,000 hectares of vines. Chiefly vin ordinaire but some good COTEAUX DU LANGUEDOC.

Hermitage Rh. r. or w. dr. ★★★ 71 72 78' 79 80 82 83' 84 85 86 88 89

The "manliest" wine of France. Dark, powerful and profound. Needs long ageing. The white is heady and golden; now usually made for early drinking, though the best wines mature for many years. Top makers: CHAVE, JABOULET, CHAPOUTIER, DELAS, Grippat.

Hospices de Beaune Historic hospital in BEAUNE, with excellent v'yds in MEURSAULT, POMMARD, VOLNAY, BEAUNE, CORTON, etc. See panel on p. 38.

Hugel Père & Fils The best-known ALSACE growers and merchants. Founded at Riquewihr in 1639 and still in the family. Best wines are sweet: Cuvées Exceptionnelles, Selections de Grains Nobles.

I'lle de Beauté Name given to VIN DU PAYS from CORSICA. Two-thirds is red.

Imperiale Bordeaux bottle holding 8½ normal bottles (6.4 litres).

Irancy ("Bourgogne Irancy") B'y. r. (or p.) ★★ 83 85 86 88 89

Good light red made near CHABLIS and PINOT NOIR and "César". The best vintages are long-lived and mature well. To watch.

Irouléguy s.w. France r. p. (or w. dr.) ★★ D.Y.A.

Agreeable local wines, mainly Tannat reds, of the Basque country.

Jaboulet, Paul Old family firm at Tain, leading growers of HERMITAGE (esp. "La Chapelle" ★★★★) and merchants in other RHÔNE wines.

Jaboulet-Vercherre & Cie Burgundy merchant-house with v'yds (34 acres) in POMMARD, etc, and cellars in Beaune. Middling wines.

Jadot, Louis Much-respected top-quality Burgundy merchant-house with v'yds (50 acres) in BEAUNE, CORTON, etc. Includes former estate of CLAIR-DAU.

Jaffelin   Independently-run high-quality négociant, owned by DROUHIN.

Jardin de la France   Name given to VINS DU PAYS of the LOIRE valley. The great majority is dry white.

Jasnières   Lo. (r.) (p.) or w. dr. ★★★ 76 78 79 82 83 85 86 88 89
Rare dry, rather VOUVRAY-like wine of n. Touraine.

Jaubertie, Domaine de la   Top BERGERAC estate of 114 acres, English-owned. Cuvée Mirabelle is a sumptuous luxury Sauvignon Blanc. The reserve red is equally fine.

Jayer, Henri   Tiny VOSNE-ROMANÉE domaine acknowledged even by rivals as superlative. (Monsieur J. retired in '88.)

Jeroboam   In Bordeaux a 6-bottle bottle (holding 4.5 litres), or triple magnum; in Champagne a double magnum.

Josmeyer   Family house at Wintzenheim, ALSACE. V.g. long-ageing wines, esp. GEWÜRZ and superb PINOT BLANC.

Juliénas   B'y. r. ★★★ 88 89
Leading cru of Beaujolais: vigorous fruity wine to keep 2-3 years. Growers incl. Ch de Juliénas, Ch du Bois de la Salle, Ch des Capitaus, Dom. Bottiére, and the Cave Coop.

Jura   See Côtes de Jura.

Jurançon   s.w. France w. sw. or dr. ★★   82 83 85 86 88 89
Unusual high-flavoured and long-lived speciality of Pau in the Pyrenean foothills. Both sweet and dry should age well for several years. Top growers: Barrère, Chigné, Guirouilh, Lamouroux, Ramonteu. Also the coop's "Grain Sauvage".

Kressman, E.S. & Cie   Bordeaux merchants and owners of Ch LATOUR-MARTILLAC in GRAVES. "Monopole Rouge" is a standard blend.

Kreydenweiss   Fine ALSACE grower at Andlau, esp. for PINOTS GRIS, BLANC and RIES.

Kriter   Popular low-price sparkling wine processed in Burgundy by PATRIARCHE.

Krug   "Grande Cuvée" (NV), 64 66 69 71 73 75 76 79 81 82 83, Rosé and Clos du Mesnil Blanc de Blancs 79 80 Small but very prestigious champagne house known for full-bodied very dry wines of superlative quality. Owned by Rémy Martin (but no-one would know).

Kuentz-Bas   Top-quality ALSACE grower and merchant at Husseren-les-Châteaux, esp. for GEWÜRZTRAMINER and Pinot Gris (Tokay d'Alsace).

Labarde   Village just s. of MARGAUX and included in that appellation. Best ch: GISCOURS.

Labouré-Gontard   Makes high-quality CREMANT de Bourgogne at NUITS.

Labouré-Roi   Very reliable merchant at NUITS-ST-GEORGES. Many domaine wines, esp. René Manuel's MEURSAULT and Lescure's NUITS.

Lafarge, Michel   23-acre CÔTE DE BEAUNE estate, mainly in VOLNAY and Meursault. Fine quality.

Lafon, Domaine des Comtes   31-acre top-quality Burgundy estate in VOLNAY, MEURSAULT and LE MONTRACHET.

Laguiche, Marquis de   Largest owner of LE MONTRACHET. Wines made by DROUHIN.

Lalande de Pomerol   B'x. r. ★★   75 78 81 82 83 85 86 88 89
Neighbour to POMEROL. Wines similar but considerably less fine. Top ch'x, Les Annereaux, Belles-Graves, La Croix-Bellevue, Les Hauts-Conseillants, Les Hauts-Tuileries, Moncets, Tournefeuille, Belair, Siaurac.

Langlois-Château   Producer of sparkling SAUMUR, controlled by BOLLINGER.

Langon   The principal town of the s. GRAVES/SAUTERNES district.

Lanson Père & Fils   Black Label NV, rosé NV, Red Label 75 76 79 81 82 83 85 Important Champagne house, cellars at Reims. Luxury brands: Noble Cuvée 81 85. Black Label is a reliable fresh NV.

Laroche   Important (238 acres) grower and dynamic merchant of CHABLIS, incl. Domaines Laroche, La Jouchère. Labels incl. Bacheroy-Josselin.

Latour, Louis Top Burgundy merchant and grower with v'yds. (120 acres) in CORTON, BEAUNE, etc. Among the best for white wines.

Latour de France r. (w. dr.) ★→★★ 85 86 87 88 89
New appellation in COTES DE ROUSSILLON-VILLAGES.

Latricières-Chambertin B'y. r. ★★★ 76 78 80 82 83 84 85' 86 87 88 89
17-acre Grand Cru neighbour of CHAMBERTIN. Similar wine, but lighter and "prettier" e.g. from FAIVELEY, Ponsot, Trapet.

Laudun Rh. r. p. or w. dr. ★
Village of COTES-DU-RHONE-VILLAGES. Attractive wines from the cooperative incl. fresh whites. But Dom. Pelaquié is better.

Laugel, Michel One of the biggest ALSACE merchant/merchants, at Marlenheim.

Laurent-Perrier NV, rosé brut and 71 73 75 76 78 79 81 82 85
Excellent and highly successful young champagne house at Tours-sur-Marne. Luxury brand: Cuvée Grande Siècle. Ultra Brut is best buy.

Leflaive, Domaine Perhaps the best of all white burgundy growers, at PULIGNY-MONTRACHET. Best v'yds: Clavoillons, Pucelles, Bienvenue-, Chevalier-Montrachet.

Leflaive, Olivier Négociant at Puligny-Montrachet since '84, nephew of the above. Excellent whites and reds, incl. less famous appellations.

Léognan B'x. r. w. dr. ★★★
Leading village of the GRAVES with its own AC: Pessac-Léognan. Best ch'x: DOMAINE DE CHEVALIER, MALARTIC-LAGRAVIÈRE and HAUT-BAILLY.

Leroy Important négociant-élèveur at AUXEY-DURESSES with a growing domaine and the finest stocks of old wines in Burgundy. Part-owners and distributors of the DOMAINE DE LA ROMANEE-CONTI. In 88 bought the 35-acre Noëllat estate in ROMANEE-ST-VIVANT, CLOS VOUGEOT, NUITS, SAVIGNY, etc.

Lichine, Alexis & Cie Post-war Bordeaux merchants, proprietors of Ch LASCOMBES. No connection with Château PRIEURE LICHINE.

Lie, sur "On the lees." Muscadet is often bottled straight from the vat, without "racking" or filtering, for maximum freshness.

Limoux Pyr. r. or w. dr. ★★ NV
The austerely dry non-sparkling version of BLANQUETTE DE LIMOUX (sometimes labelled Limoux Nature) and a good fresh claret-like red from the cooperative: Anne des Joyeuses.

Lirac Rh. r. p. or (w. dr.) ★★ 84 85 86 88 89
Neighbouring village to TAVEL. Similar wine; the red becoming more important than the rosé, esp. Dom St-Roch, Ch de Segriés, Dom. Maby.

Listel Midi r. p. w. dr. ★→★★★ D.Y.A.
Vast (4,000+ acres) historic estate on the sandy beaches of the Golfe du Lion. Owned by the giant Salins du Midi. Pleasant light "vins des sables" incl. sparkling. Dom. du Bosquet is a fruity red. Dom. de Villeroy is a fresh blanc de blancs "SUR LIE". Also fruity, almost non-alcoholic "Pétillant", and Ch de Malijay, Côtes-du-Rhône.

Listrac B'x. r. ★★→ ★★★
Village of HAUT-MEDOC next to MOULIS. Best ch'x: FOURCAS-HOSTEN, FOURCAS-DUPRE, CLARKE, Fonréaud.

Long-Depaquit V.g. CHABLIS domaine (esp. MOUTONNE), owned by BICHOT.

Lorentz Two small high-quality Alsace houses at Bergheim, Gustave L. and Jerome L, have the same management.

Loron & Fils Big-scale burgundy grower and merchant at Pontanevaux, specialist in BEAUJOLAIS and sound VINS DE TABLE.

Loupiac B'x. w. sw. ★★ 76 79 80 83 85 86 88 89
Across the R. Garonne from SAUTERNES. Top ch'x: Loupiac-Gaudiet, de Ricaud, Haut-Loupiac, Clos-Jean, Rondillon.

Ludon HAUT-MEDOC village s. of MARGAUX. Best ch: LA LAGUNE.

Lugny ("Macon-Lugny") B'y. r. w. dr. sp. ★★ **88** 89
Village next to VIRE with active and good cooperative. Wine of Les Genièvres v'yd is sold by Louis LATOUR.

Lupé-Cholet & Cie Merchants and growers at NUITS-ST-GEORGES controlled by BICHOT. Best estate wines: Château Gris and Clos de Lupé.

Lussac-Saint-Emilion B'x. r. ★★ **82 83 85** 86 88 89
N.e. neighbour to ST-EMILION. Top ch'x incl. Lyonnat, Tour de Grenat, Barbe-Blanche, Bel Air, Villadière. Coop (at PUISSEGUIN) makes "Roc de Lussac".

Macau HAUT-MEDOC village s. of MARGAUX. Best ch: CANTEMERLE.

Macération carbonique Traditional technique of fermentation with whole bunches of unbroken grapes in a closed vat. Fermentation inside each grape eventually bursts it, giving vivid and very fruity mild wine for quick consumption. Esp. in BEAUJOLAIS; now much used in the MIDI and elsewhere.

Machard de Gramont Burgundy family estate: cellars in NUITS and v'yds in NUITS, SAVIGNY, BEAUNE, POMMARD. Extremely well-made reds.

Mâcon B'y. r. (p.) or w. dr. ★★ **88** 89
Southern district of sound, usually unremarkable, reds and very tasty dry (CHARDONNAY) whites. Wine with a village name (e.g. Mâcon-Prissé) is better. POUILLY-FUISSE is best appellation of the region. See also Mâcon-Villages.

Mâcon-Lugny See Lugny.

Mâcon Supérieur The same but slightly better, from riper grapes.

Mâcon-Villages B'y. w. dr. ★★→★★★ **86 88 89**
Increasingly well-made and typical white burgundies. Mâcon-Prissé, MACON-VIRE, MACON-LUGNY, Mâcon-Clessé are examples.

Mâcon-Viré See Mâcon-Villages and Viré.

Madiran s.w. France r. ★★ **82 83 84** 85 86 88
Dark vigorous red from ARMAGNAC. Ages 5-10 years. Top growers: Chx d'Arricau-Bordes, Aydié, Montus, Peyros, Dom de Bouscassé, Laplace, Barréjat.

Magenta, Duc de Burgundy estate (30 acres) based at CHASSAGNE-MONTRACHET, managed by JADOT.

Magnum A double bottle (1.5 litres).

Mähler-Besse First-class Dutch wine-merchants in Bordeaux, with a share in Ch PALMER. Brands incl. Cheval Noir.

Maire, Henri The biggest grower/merchant of JURA wines. Not the best.

Maranges B'y r. ★★
New ('89) A.C. for 600-odd acres of s. COTE DE BEAUNE, ⅓ 1er Cru.

Marc Grape skins after pressing; also the strong-smelling brandy made from them (cf. Italian "Grappa").

Marcillac s.w. France r. p. ★ D.Y.A.
Good rustic VDQS from the coop, Cave de Valady.

Margaux B'x. r. ★★→★★★★ **66 70 75 76 78 79 81** 82 83' **84** 85 86 87 88
Village of the HAUT-MEDOC making the most "elegant" red Bordeaux. The appellation includes CANTENAC and several other villages as well. Top ch'x include MARGAUX, LASCOMBES, RAUSAN-SEGLA, etc.

Margnat Major producer of everyday VIN DE TABLE.

Marque déposée Trade mark.

Marsannay B'y. (r.) p. or w. dr. ★★★ **78 80 83** 85 86 87 (rosé D.Y.A.)
Village near Dijon with fine light red and delicate PINOT NOIR rosé. Growers incl. CLAIR, Quillardet, JADOT, Trapet.

Mas de Daumas Gassac Midi r. (w. dr) ★★★ **80 81 82 83 84** 85 86 87 88 89 The one "first-growth" estate of the MIDI, producing potent Bordeaux-like, largely CABERNET wines on apparently unique soil. Also "Rosé Frisant" and since 87 sumptuous white of CHARDONNAY and VIOGNIER. Sensational quality.

Maufoux, Prosper Family firm of burgundy merchants at SANTENAY. Reliable wines, esp. whites, keep well. Alias Marcel Amance.

Maury Pyr. r. sw. ★→→★ NV
Red VIN DOUX NATUREL from ROUSSILLON.

Mazis (or Mazy) Chambertin B'y. r. ★★★ 76 78 80 82 83 85 86 87 88 89
30-acre Grand Cru neighbour of CHAMBERTIN. Lighter wine. Best from LEROY, FAIVELEY, Roty.

Médoc B'x. r. ★★ 78 79 81 82 83 84 85 86 87 88 89
Appellation for reds of the less good (n.) part of Bordeaux's biggest and best district. Flavours tend to slight earthiness. HAUT-MÉDOC is better.

Meffre, Gabriel The biggest southern Rhône estate, based at GIGONDAS. Includes Ch de Vaudieu, CHATEAUNEUF-DU-PAPE. Variable quality.

Ménétou-Salon Lo. r. p. or w. dr. ★★ D.Y.A.
Attractive light wines from w. of SANCERRE. SAUVIGNON white; P NOIR red.

Mercier & Cie NV, Extra Rich and Rosé **80** 81 82 83 85 and **73** 75 76 **78 80 81 82** 83 85 One of the biggest champagne houses, at Epernay. Controlled by MOËT & CHANDON. Commercial quality. Belle d'Or is new (1988) NV.

Mercurey B'y. r. or w. dr ★★ 78 83 85 86 87 88 89
Leading red-wine village of the CÔTE CHALONNAISE. Good middle-rank burgundy. Growers incl. Ch de Chamirey, FAIVELEY, Chanzy.

Mercurey, Région de The up-to-date way of referring to the CÔTE CHALONNAISE.

Métaireau, Louis The ring-leader of a group of top Muscadet growers. Expensive well-finished wines.

Méthode champenoise The traditional laborious method of putting the bubbles in champagne by refermenting the wine in its bottle.

Meursault B'y. (r.) w. dr. ★★★→★★★★ 78 82 83 85 86 87 88 89
CÔTE DE BEAUNE village with some of the world's greatest whites: rich, savoury, dry but mellow. Best v'yds: Perrières, Genièvres, Charmes. Others v.g. incl. Goutte d'Or, Meursault-Blagny, Poruzots, Tillets. Top growers incl: AMPEAU, COCHE-DURY, Delagrange, Diconne, LAFON, LATOUR, MAGENTA, Matrot, Michelot-Buisson, CH DE MEURSAULT, P. Morey, G. ROULOT, Manuel, Jobard. See also Blagny.

Meursault-Blagny See Blagny.

Midi General term for the south of France. Dismal reputation, brilliant promise.

Minervois Midi r. or (p.) (w.) or br. sw. ★→★★ 85 86 88 89
Hilly area with some of the best wines of the Midi: lively and full of flavour esp. from Ch de Gourgazand, Dom. de Ste Eulalie and la Livinère. Also sweet MUSCAT de St Jean de M.

Mise en bouteilles au château, au domaine Bottled at the château, at the property or estate. N.B. dans nos caves (in our cellars) or dans la région de production (in the area of production) are often used, even by good producers, although they mean little.

Moelleux Mellow. Used of the sweet wines of VOUVRAY, etc.

Moët & Chandon NV, rosé **81 82**, Dry Imperial **75 76 78 80 81 82** 83 85 86 Much the biggest champagne merchant and grower, with cellars in Epernay and sparkling wine branches in Argentina, Brazil, Spain, Australia and California. Consistent quality. Luxury brand: DOM PERIGNON.

Moillard Big family firm of growers (Domaine Thomas-Moillard) and merchants in NUITS-ST-GEORGES, making dark and v.tasty wines, incl CLOS DE VOUGEOT, CORTON, CLOS DE ROI etc.

Mommessin, J. Major BEAUJOLAIS merchant. Owner of CLOS DE TART.

Monbazillac Dordogne w. sw. ★★ **71** 75 76 78 79 80 81 83 85 86 88 89
Golden SAUTERNES-style wine from BERGERAC. Can age well. Ch Monbazillac and Ch Septy are best known.

Mondeuse Savoie r. ██ ** D.Y.A.
Red grape of SAVOIE. Good, vigorous, deep-coloured wine.

Mongeard-Mugneret 40-acre VOSNE-ROMANEE estate. Fine ECHEZEAUX, VOUGEOT, etc.

Monopole Vineyard in single ownership.

Montagne-Saint-Emilion B'x. r. ██ ** **75 78 79 81 82 83 85** 86 88 89
North-east neighbour of ST-EMILION with similar wines, becoming more important with each year. Top ch'x: Calon, St-André-Corbin, Vieux-Ch-St-André, Roudier, Haut-Gillet, Teyssier, des Tours.

Montagny B'y. (r.) w. dr. **★★→★★★** **86 87** 88
COTE CHALONNAISE village between MACON and MEURSAULT, both geographically and gastronomically. A little red, too. Top producer: LATOUR.

Montée de Tonnerre B'y. w. dr. ██ *** **85 86** 88 89
Famous and excellent PREMIER CRU of CHABLIS.

Monthelie B'y. r. ██ *** **78 80 82 83 85 86** 87 88 89
Little-known neighbour and almost equal of VOLNAY. Excellent fragrant reds. Growers incl: Ch de Monthélie, Monthélie-Douhairet, DROUHIN, BOUCHARD PERE, de Suremain.

Montlouis Lo. w. sw./dr. (sp.) **★★ 75 76 78 82 83' 84 85 86** 88' 89
Neighbour of VOUVRAY. Similar sweet or dry long-lived wine.

Montrachet B'y. w. dr. **★★★★ 69 71 78 79 81 82 83 84** 85 86 87 88 89
19-acre Grand Cru v'yd in both PULIGNY and CHASSAGNE-MONTRACHET. Potentially the greatest white burgundy: strong, perfumed, intense, dry yet luscious. (Both "t"s are silent.) Top wines from RAMONET, LATOUR, REMOISSENET, DROUHIN.

Montravel See Côtes de Montravel.

Mont-Redon, Domaine de Rh. r. (w. dr.) **★★★ 81 83 85** 86 88 89
Outstanding 235-acre estate in CHATEAUNEUF-DU-PAPE. Reliable, fairly early-maturing wines.

Moreau et Fils CHABLIS merchant and grower with 175 acres. Also major table-wine producer. Best wine: Clos des Hospices (Grand Cru). Owned by Allied-Lyons-Hiram Walker.

Morey, Domaines 50 acres in CHASSAGNE-MONTRACHET. V.g. wines made by family members.

Morey-Saint-Denis B'y. r. ██ *** **71 76 78 79 80 82 83 84** 85 86 87 88
Small village with four Grands Crus between GEVREY-CHAMBERTIN and CHAMBOLLE-MUSIGNY. Glorious wine, often overlooked. Growers incl: Amiot, Catagnier, DUJAC, Groffier, Lignier, PONSOT, Serveau.

Morgon B'y. r. **★★★ 85 86 87** 88 89
The "firmest" cru of BEAUJOLAIS, needing time to develop its rich and savoury flavour. Growers incl: Janodet, Ancouer, Lapierre, Ch de Pizay.

Moueix, J-P et Cie The leading proprietor and merchant of St-Emilion, Pomerol and FRONSAC. Ch'x incl. MAGDELAINE, LAFLEUR-PETRUS, and part of PETRUS. Now also has a venture in California: see Dominus.

Moulin-à-Vent B'y. r. **★★★ 85 86 87 88** 89
The "biggest" and best wine of Beaujolais; powerful and long-lived, eventually tasting more like COTE D'OR wine. Many good growers.

Moulis B'x. r. **★★→★★★**
Village of the HAUT-MEDOC with its own appellation and several Crus Exceptionnels: CHASSE-SPLEEN, POUJEAUX-THEIL, MAUCAILLOU, etc. Wines are growing steadily finer.

Mousseux Sparkling.

Mouton Cadet Best-selling brand of blended red and white Bordeaux.

Moutonne CHABLIS GRAND CRU *honoris causa*, owned by BICHOT.

Mumm, G. H. & Cie NV "Cordon Rouge", rosé **79 82** 85, Crémant de Cramant (NV) and **69 71 73 75 76 79 82** 85 Major champagne grower and merchant owned by Seagram's. Luxury brand: René Lalou (**79 82** 85). The Cramant is superb. Cordon Rouge can be pretty tasteless.

Muscadet Lo. w. dr. ****** D.Y.A.

Popular, good-value, often delicious dry wine from round Nantes in s. Brittany. Should never be sharp but have an iodine tang. Perfect with fish. The best wines are bottled "sur lie" – on their lees.

Muscadet de Sèvre-et-Maine Wine from the central part of the area.

Muscat Distinctively perfumed grape and its (usually sweet) wine, often fortified as VDN. Made dry in ALSACE.

Muscat de Beaumes de Venise See Beaumes de Venise.

Muscat de Frontignan Midi br. sw. ****** D.Y.A.

Sweet Midi muscat. Quality improving.

Muscat de Lunel Midi br. sw. ****** NV

Ditto. A small area but good.

Muscat de Mireval Midi br. sw. ****** NV

Ditto, from near Montpellier.

Muscat de Rivesaltes Midi br. sw. ***** NV

Sweet muscat from a big zone near Perpignan.

Musigny B'y. r. (w. dr.) ****** 69 71 76 78 79 80 82 83 85** 86 87 88 89

25-acre Grand Cru in CHAMBOLLE-MUSIGNY. Can be the most beautiful, if not the most powerful, of all red burgundies (and a little white). Best growers: DE VOGUE, DROUHIN, LEROY, JADOT, Roumier, Mugnier.

Nature Natural or unprocessed, esp. of still champagne.

Néac Village n. of POMEROL. Wines sold as LALANDE-DE-POMEROL.

Négociant-éleveur Merchant who "brings up" (i.e. matures) the wine.

Nicolas, Ets. Paris-based wholesale and retail wine merchants controlled by Rémy-Martin. One of the biggest in France and one of the best.

Nuits-St-Georges r. ****→*** 69 71 76 78' 80 82** 83 85' 86 87 88 89

Important wine-town: wines of all qualities, typically sturdy and full-flavoured. Name can be shortened to "Nuits". Best v'yds incl. Les St-Georges, Vaucrains, Les Pruliers, Clos de Corvées, Les Cailles, etc. Many growers and merchants esp. FAIVELEY, LEROY, Chevillon, Bruck, MACHARD DE GRAMONT, JAYER, RION.

Oisly & Thesée, Vignerons de Go-ahead coop in e. TOURAINE (Loire), experimenting successfully with esp. SAUV BL, CAB, and (since '85) CHARD. Blended wines labelled Baronnie d'Aignan. Good value.

Orléanais, Vin d' Lo. r. p. w. dr. ***** D.Y.A.

Small VDQS area with light but fruity wines.

Ott, Domaine The most important producer of high-quality PROVENCE wines, incl. Ch de Selle and Clos Mireille. V.g. rosés.

Pacherenc-du-Vic-Bilh s.w. France w. sw. ***** NV

Rare minor speciality of the ARMAGNAC region.

Paillard, Bruno NV, Crémant Blanc de Blancs, Rosé, **75 76 79 81** 83 85

Small but prestigious young champagne house with excellent silky vintage and NV wines at fair prices.

Palette Prov. r. p. or w. dr. ******

Near Aix-en-Provence. Aromatic reds and good rosés from CH SIMONE.

Parigot-Richard Producer of v.g. CREMANT de Bourgogne at SAVIGNY.

Pasquier-Desvignes Very old firm of Beaujolais merchants nr. BROUILLY.

Patriarche One of the bigger firms of burgundy merchants. Cellars in Beaune; also owns CH DE MEURSAULT (100 acres), KRITER, etc.

Patrimonio Corsica r. w. dr. p ****→*****

Wide range from dramatic chalk hills in n. Corsica. Fragrant reds, crisp whites, fine VDN. Top grower: Gentile.

Pauillac B'x. r. ****→*** 66 70 75 76 78 79 81 82 83 84** 85 86 87 88 89

The only village in Bordeaux (HAUT-MEDOC) with three first-growths (Ch'x LAFITE, LATOUR, MOUTON) and many other fine ones, famous for high flavour; very various in style.

Pécharmant Dordogne r. **** 85 88** 89

Usually better-than-typical light BERGERAC red, with more "meat". Top estates: Ch de Tiregand, Dom. du Haut-Pécharmant. Coop wines not special.

Pelure d'oignon "Onion skin" – tawny tint of certain rosés.

Perlant or Perlé Very slightly sparkling.

Pernard-Vergelesses B'y. r. or (w. dr.) ★★★ 78 80 82 83 85 86 87 88 89 Village next to ALOXE-CORTON containing part of the great CORTON and CORTON-CHARLEMAGNE v'yds and one other top v'yd: Ile des Vergelesses. Growers incl. BONNEAU DE MARTRAY, Dubreuil-Fontaine, Rapet, Chandon, Delarche.

Perrier, Joseph NV, rosé and 71 73 75 76 79 82 83 85 Family-run champagne house with considerable v'yds at Chalon-sur-Marne. Consistent light and fruity style.

Perrier-Jouet NV, Blason de France, 71 73 75 76 79 82 85 Excellent champagne-growers and makers at Epernay now linked with MUMM. Luxury brands: Belle Epoque 79 82 83 85 (in a painted bottle), Blason de France (NV). Also Belle Epoque Rosé 79 82 85.

"Noble rot" (in French pourriture noble, in German Edelfäule, in Latin Botrytis cinerea) is a form of mould that attacks the skins of ripe grapes in certain vineyards in warm and misty autumn weather.

Its effect, instead of rotting the grapes, is to wither them. The skin grows soft and flaccid, the juice evaporates through it, and what is left is a super-sweet concentration of everything in the grape except its water content.

The world's best sweet table wines are all made of nobly rotten grapes. They occur in good vintages in Sauternes, the Rhine, the Mosel (where wine made from them is called Trockenbeerenauslese), in Tokaji in Hungary, in Burgenland in Austria, and occasionally elsewhere – California included. The danger is rain on pulpy grapes already far gone in noble rot. All too often, particularly in Sauternes, the grower's hopes are dashed by a break in the weather.

Pétillant Slightly sparkling.

Petit Chablis B'y. w. dr. ★★ D.Y.A. Wine from fourth-rank CHABLIS v'yds. Not much character.

Philipponnat NV, NV Rosé, Grand Blanc Vintage 76 81 82 85, Clos des Goisses 70 71 73 75 76 78 79 82 85 Small champagne house with well-structured wines, esp. the remarkable single v'yd Clos Goisses. Owned by GOSSET.

Piat Père & Fils Important merchants of BEAUJOLAIS and MACON wines at Mâcon, controlled by Grand Metropolitan. V'yds in MOULIN-A-VENT, also CLOS DE VOUGEOT. BEAUJOLAIS, MACON-VIRE in special Piat bottles maintain a fair standard. Piat d'Or is best-selling table wine.

Pic, Albert ine CHABLIS producer, controlled by DE LADOUCETTE.

Pineau de Charente Strong sweet apéritif made of white grape juice and Cognac.

Pinot See Grapes for white and red wine.

Piper-Heidsieck NV, Rosé 79 85, Vintage 71 73 75 76 79 82 85, Année Rare 76 79, Brut Sauvage 79 85 Champagne-makers of old repute at Reims.

Pol Roger NV, rosé 75 79 82 85, Blanc de Chardonnay 82 85 and 71 73 75 76 79 82 85 Excellent champagne house at Epernay. Particularly good non-vintage White Foil, Rosé, Réserve PR and Chardonnay. Luxury cuvée: "Sir Winston Churchill" 75 79 82 85.

Pomerol B'x. r. ★★ →★★★★ 70 71 75 76 78 79 81 82 83 85 86 88 89 Neighbour to ST-EMILION: similar but more "fleshy" wines, maturing sooner, reliable and delicious. Top ch PETRUS, TROTANOY, LA FLEUR-PETRUS, VIEUX-CH-CERTAN, LATOUR A POMEROL, etc . . .

Pommard B'y. r. ★★★ 69 71 76 78 80 82 83 84 85 86 87 88 89 The biggest and best-known COTE D'OR village. Few superlative wines, but many warmly appealing ones. Best v'yds: Rugiens, Epenots and HOSPICES DE BEAUNE cuvées. Growers incl: Courcel, Gaunoux, LEROY, Armand, Pothier-Rieusset, de Montille, Mussy, Machard de Gramont, Boillot.

Pommery & Greno NV, NV rosé and **71 73 75 76 78 79 80 81 82** 83
> Very big CHAMPAGNE growers and merchants at Reims. Wines are much improved. The luxury brand: Louise Pommery **80 81 82** is outstanding. Louise Pommery Rosé **82**

Pouilly-Fuissé B'y. w. dr. ★★→★★★ **88 89**
> The best white of the MACON area. At its best (e.g. Ch Fuissé Vieilles Vignes) excellent, but almost always over-priced.

Pouilly-Fumé Lo. w. dr. ★★→★★★ **86 88 89**
> "Gun-flinty", fruity, often sharp pale white from the upper Loire, next to SANCERRE. Grapes must be SAUVIGNON BLANC. Good vintages improve for 2-3 yrs. Top producers incl. LADOUCETTE, Bailly, Dagueneau, Redde, Saget, Renaud, Ch de Tracy.

Pouilly-Loché B'y. w. dr. ★★
> Neighbour of POUILLY-FUISSE. Similar wine but little of it.

Pouilly-sur-Loire Lo. w. dr. ★ D.Y.A.
> Inferior wine from the same v'yds as POUILLY-FUME, but different grapes (CHASSELAS). Rarely seen today.

Pouilly-Vinzelles B'y. w. dr. ★★ **88 89**
> Neighbour of POUILLY-FUISSE. Similar wine, worth looking for.

Pousse d'Or, Domaine de la 32-acre estate in POMMARD, SANTENAY and (esp.) VOLNAY, where its "monopoles", "Bousse d'Or" and "Clos des 60 Ouvrées" are tannic, austere, powerful and justly famous.

Premières Côtes de Blaye B'x. r. w. dr. ★→★★ **82 83 85 86** 88
> Restricted appellation for better reds of BLAYE. Ch'x include Barbé, Charron, Bourdieu, Haut-Sociondo, La Tonnelle, l'Escadre, Segonzac, Le Menaudat.

Premier Cru First-growth in Bordeaux (see p. 57), but the second rank of v'yds (after Grand Cru) in Burgundy.

Premières Côtes de Bordeaux B'x. r. (p.) or w. dr. or sw. ★→★★
> Large area east of GRAVES across the R. Garonne: a good bet for quality and value. Ch'x incl. Laffitte [*sic*], Gardera, Fayau, Haut-Brignon, REYNON, Tanesse. An area to watch.

Prieur, Domaine Jacques 35-acre estate all in top Burgundy sites, incl. Premier Cru MEURSAULT, VOLNAY, PULIGNY- and CHEVALIER-MONTRACHET. Disappointing in '80s. Now 50% owned by RODET. To watch.

Primeur "Early" wine for refreshment and uplift; esp. of BEAUJOLAIS.

Prissé See Mâcon-Villages.

Propriétaire-récoltant Owner-manager.

Provence See Côtes de Provence.

Puisseguin-Saint-Emilion B'x. r. ★★ **82 83 85** 86 88 89
> Eastern neighbour of ST-EMILION; wines similar – not so fine but often good value. Ch'x incl. Laurets, Vieux-Ch-Guibeau, Puisseguin, L Croix de Berny, Soleil, Teyssier. Also "Roc de Puisseguin" from coop.

Puligny-Montrachet B'y. w. dr. (r.) ★★★★ **78 81 82 83 85** 86 87 88
> Bigger neighbour of CHASSAGNE-MONTRACHET with even more glorious rich dry whites. Best v'yds: MONTRACHET, CHEVALIER-MONTRACHET, BATARD-MONTRACHET, Bienvenue-Bâtard-Montrachet, Les Combettes, Clavoillon, Pucelles, Champ-Canet, etc. Top growers incl: AMPEAU, DROUHIN, JADOT, Pernot, BOUCHARD PERE, CHARTRON, LEFLAIVE, SAUZET, L. Carillon.

Quarts de Chaume Lo. w. sw. ★★★ **75 76 78 79 82** 85 86 88 89
> Famous 120-acre plot in COTEAUX DU LAYON. CHENIN BLANC grapes. Long-lived, intense, rich golden wine, esp. Ch La Suronde, Dom. des Beaumard.

Quatourze Midi r. (p.) or w. dr. ★ **86 88** 89
> Minor VDQS area near Narbonne.

Quincy Lo. w. dr. ★★ **88 89**
> Small area making v. dry SANCERRE-style wine of SAUV BL. Worth trying.

Ramonet, Domaine Leading estate in CHASSAGNE-MONTRACHET with 34 acres, incl. some LE MONTRACHET. V.g. whites, and red Clos St-Jean.

Rancio Term for the tang of wood-aged fortified wine, esp. BANYULS and other VINS DOUX NATURELS. A fault in table wines.

Rasteau Rh. r. (p. w. dr.) or br. sw. **★★ 85' 86 88** 89
Village of s. Rhône valley. Very sound reds. Strong sweet dessert wine is the local speciality.

Ratafia de Champagne Sweet apéritif made in Champagne of ²⁄₃ grape juice and ⅓ brandy.

Récolte Crop or vintage.

Regnié Beaujolais village between MORGON and BROUILLY, promoted to "Cru" status in 1988. About 1,800 acres. Try DUBOEUF'S

Reine Pédauque, La Burgundy growers and merchants at ALOXE-CORTON.

Remoissenet Père & Fils Fine Burgundy merchants (esp. for white wines) with a tiny estate at BEAUNE.

Rémy Pannier Important Loire-wine merchants at SAUMUR.

Reuilly Lo. (r. p.) w. dr. **★★ 88** 89
Neighbour of QUINCY with similar wine; also good PINOT GRIS.

Riceys, Rosé des Champ. p. **★★★** D.Y.A.
Minute appellation in southern Champagne for a notable PINOT NOIR rosé. Principal producer; A. Bonnet.

Richebourg B'y. r. **★★★★ 69 71 76 78 79 80 82** 83 **84** 85 86 87 88 89
19-acre Grand Cru in VOSNE-ROMANÉE. Powerful, perfumed, fabulously expensive wine, among Burgundy's best. Top growers: DOM DE LA ROMANÉE-CONTI, GRIVOT, Gros, Méo-Camuzet.

Riesling See Grapes for white wine.

Rivesaltes Midi r. w. dr. br. sw. **★★** NV
Fortified sweet wine, some of it muscat-flavoured, from e. Pyrenees. An ancient tradition still very much alive, if struggling these days.

La Roche-aux-Moines Lo. w. dr./sw. **★★★ 75 76 78 79 82 83** 85 86 88 89
60-acre v'yd in Savennières, Anjou. Intense strong, fruity/sharp wine needs long ageing.

Rodet, Antonin Substantial Burgundy merchant with a large estate (375 acres), esp. in MERCUREY (Ch de Chamirey). See also PRIEUR.

Roederer, Louis Brut Premier NV, Rosé 75 83 85 and **71 73** 75 76 78 79 81 83 85 One of the best champagne-growers and merchants at Reims. V. reliable non-vintage wine with plenty of flavour. Luxury brand: Cristal Brut **79** 82 83 (in white glass bottles) needs time. 83 is v.young.

La Romanée B'y. r. **★★★ 76 78 80 82** 83 84 85 86 87 88
2-acre Grand Cru in VOSNE-ROMANÉE just uphill from ROMANÉE-CONTI, distributed by BOUCHARD.

Romanée-Conti B'y. r. **★★★★ 66 71 73 76 78 79 80 81 82** 83 **84** 85 86 87 88 89 4⅓-acre monopole Grand Cru in VOSNE-ROMANÉE. The most celebrated and expensive red wine in the world. Sometimes the best: '85 is astonishing.

Romanée-Conti, Domaine de la The grandest estate of Burgundy, owning the whole of ROMANÉE-CONTI and LA TACHE and major parts of RICHEBOURG, GRANDS ECHEZEAUX, ECHEZEAUX and ROMANÉE-ST-VIVANT. Also a very small part of LE MONTRACHET. Keep D.R.C. wines for decades.

Romanée-St-Vivant B'y. r. **★★★★ 71 76 78 79 80 82** 83 84 85 86 87 88 89 23-acre Grand Cru in VOSNE-ROMANÉE. Similar to ROMANÉE-CONTI but lighter and less sumptuous. Top grower: LEROY.

Ropiteau Burgundy wine-growers and merchants at MEURSAULT. Specialists in MEURSAULT and COTE DE BEAUNE wines.

Rosé d'Anjou Lo. p. **★** D.Y.A.
Pale, slightly sweet, rosé. Cabernet d'Anjou *should* be better.

Rosé de Loire Lo. p. dr. **★→★★** D.Y.A.
Appellation for dry Loire rosé (Anjou is sweet).

Roty, Joseph Small grower of classic GEVREY-CHAMBERTIN.

Rousseau, Domaine A. Major burgundy grower famous for CHAMBERTIN, etc. of highest quality.

Roussette de Savoie Savoie w. dr. ** D.Y.A.
  The tastiest of the fresh whites from s. of Geneva.

Roussillon See Côtes du Roussillon. "Grands Roussillons" are v.d.n.

Ruchottes-Chambertin B'y. r. *** 71 76 78 79 80 82 83 84 85 86 87 88
  89 7½-acre Grand Cru neighbour of CHAMBERTIN. Similar splendid
  long-lasting wine. Top growers: LEROY, Roumier, ROUSSEAU.

Ruinart Père & Fils NV, rosé 79 and Bl. de Blancs 71 73 75 76 78 79 81
  85 The oldest champagne house, owned by Moët-Hennessy. Luxury
  brand: Dom Ruinart, Blanc de Blancs 79 81. N.B. the v.g. Rosé.

Rully B'y. r. or w. dr. or (sp). ** 87 88 89
  Village of the CÔTE CHALONNAISE famous for sparkling burgundy. Still
  white and red are light but tasty and good value, esp. the whites.
  Growers incl. DELORME, FAIVELEY, Jacquesson, Dom de la Folie.

Sablet Rh. r. (p.) w. dr. ** 88 89
  Admirable CÔTE-DU-RHÔNE village, esp. Ch du Trignon, Dom. de
  Boissan, Dom. de Veropriére.

Saint-Amour B'y. r. ** 88 89
  Northernmost cru of BEAUJOLAIS: light, fruity, irresistible.

Saint-Aubin B'y. (r.) or w. dr. ** 83 85 86 87 88 89
  Little-known neighbour of CHASSAGNE-MONTRACHET, up a side-valley.
  Not top-rank, but typical and good value. Also sold as CÔTE-DE-BEAUNE-
  VILLAGES. Top growers: J. Lamy, JADOT, Bachelet, Roux, Clerget.

Saint Bris B'y. (r.) w. dr. * D.Y.A.
  Village w. of CHABLIS known for its fruity ALIGOTE, making good
  sparkling burgundy, but chiefly for SAUVIGNON-DE-ST-BRIS.

Saint Chinian Midi r. *→*** 88 89
  Hilly area of growing reputation in the COTEAUX DU LANGUEDOC.
  Appellation contrôlée since 1982. Tasty southern reds.

Sainte-Croix-du-Mont B'x. w. sw. ** 75 76 80 82 83 86 88 89
  Neighbour to SAUTERNES with similar golden wine. No superlatives but
  well worth trying, esp. Ch Loubens, Ch du Mont, Clos des Coulinats,
  Ch Lousteau Vieil. Often a bargain.

Saint-Emilion B'x. r. **→**** 70 71 75 76 78 79 81 82 83 85 86 88 89
  The biggest (13,000 acres) top-quality Bordeaux district; solid, rich,
  tasty wines from hundreds of ch'x, incl. CHEVAL-BLANC, AUSONE, CANON,
  MAGDELAINE, fiGEAC, etc. Also a v.g. coop.

Saint-Estèphe B'x. r. ** →**** 75 78 79 81 82 83 84 85 86 88 89
  Northern village of HAUT-MÉDOC. Solid, structured, occasionally superlative wines. Top ch'x: CALON-SEGUR, COS D'ESTOURNEL, MONTROSE, etc,
  and many notable CRUS BOURGEOIS.

St-Gall Brand-name used by Union-Champagne; the very good
  champagne-growers' cooperative at AVIZE.

Saint-Georges-Saint-Emilion B'x. r. ** 82 83 85 86 88 89
  Part of MONTAGNE-ST-EMILION with high standards. Best ch'x: ST-
  GEORGES, Belair-Montaiguillon, Marquis-St-G, Tour-du-Pas-St-G.

Saint-Joseph Rh. r. (p. or w. dr.) ** 78 83 85 86 88 89
  Northern Rhône appellation of second rank but reasonable price.
  Substantial wine often better than CROZES-HERMITAGE, esp. from
  JABOULET, Grippat, CHAPOUTIER, Chave.

Saint-Julien B'x. r. **→***** 70 75 76 78 79 81 82' 83' 84 85' 86 88'
  89 Mid-Médoc village with a dozen of Bordeaux's best ch'x, incl.
  three LEOVILLES, BEYCHEVELLE, DUCRU-BEAUCAILLOU, GRUAUD-LAROSE, etc.
  The epitome of harmonious red wine.

Saint-Laurent Village next to ST-JULIEN. Appellation HAUT-MÉDOC.

Saint-Nicolas-de-Bourgueil Lo. r. ** 82 83 84 85 86 88 89
  The next village to BOURGUEIL: the same lively and fruity CABERNET
  FRANC red. Top growers: Cognard, Jamet. Mabilleau, Taluan.

Saint-Péray Rh. w. dr. or sp. ** NV
  Rather heavy white from the n. Rhône, much of it made sparkling. A
  curiosity worth trying once.

Saint Pourçain Central France r. p. or w. dr ■ ★ D.Y.A.

The venerable local wine of Vichy. Made from GAMAY and/or PINOT NOIR, the (light) white from Tressalier and/or CHARD or SAUV BLANC.

Saint Romain B'y. r. w. dr. ★★ 85 86 87 88 89

Overlooked village just behind the COTE DE BEAUNE. Value, esp. for young whites. Top growers: LEROY, Thévenin, Gras, Fèvre.

Saint-Sauveur HAUT-MEDOC village just w. of PAUILLAC.

Saint-Seurin-de-Cadourne HAUT-MEDOC village just n. of ST-ESTÈPHE.

Saint-Véran B'y. w. dr. ★★ 88 89

Next-door appellation to POUILLY-FUISSE. Similar but better value: real character from the best slopes of MACON-VILLAGES. Try DUBOEUF'S.

Salon Le Mesnil 61 64 66 69 71 73 76 79

The original Blanc de Blancs champagne, from Le Mesnil. Fine very dry wine with extraordinary keeping qualities. Bought in 1988 by LAURENT-PERRIER.

Sancerre Lo. (r. p.) or w. dr. ★★★ 86 88 89

Very fragrant and fresh SAUVIGNON white almost indistinguishable from POUILLY-FUME, its neighbour over the Loire. Drink young. Also light P NOIR red (best drunk at 2-3 yrs) and rosé. Top growers incl. Cotat, Bonnard, Bourgeois, Bailly, Pinard, Crochet, CORDIER, Reverdy.

Santenay B'y. r. or (w. dr.) ★★★ 76 78 79 80 82 83 85 86 87 88 89

Very worthy, rarely rapturous, sturdy reds from the s. of the COTE DE BEAUNE. Best v'yds: Les Gravières, Clos de Tavannes, La Comme. Top growers: DOM DE LA POUSSE D'OR, Lequin-Roussot, Morey.

Saumur Lo. r. p. or w. dr. and sp. ★→ ★★

Versatile district in ANJOU. Fresh fruity whites, v.g. CREMANT, pale rosés and increasingly good CABERNET FRANC reds, the best from Saumur-Champigny, esp. Ch du Hureau, Dom. Fillatreau, Dubois, Duveau.

Sauternes B'x. w. sw. ★★ →★★★★ 67 71 75 76 78 79 80 81 82 83 84 85 86 88 89 District of five villages (incl. BARSAC) making France's best sweet wine: strong (14%+ alcohol) luscious and golden, demanding to be aged. Top ch's: D'YQUEM, SUDUIRAUT, COUTET, CLIMENS, GUIRAUD, etc. Also dry wines which cannot be sold as Sauternes.

Sauvignon Blanc See Grapes for white wine.

Sauvignon-de-St-Bris B'y. w. dr. ★★ D.Y.A.

A baby VDQS cousin of SANCERRE from near CHABLIS. To try.

Sauvion & Fils Ambitious and well-run MUSCADET house, based at the Ch de Cléray. Top wine: Cardinal Richard.

Sauzet, Etienne White burgundy estate at PULIGNY-MONTRACHET. Clearly-defined, well-bred wines at best superb.

Savennières Lo. w. dr./sw. ★★★ 75 76 78 82 83 84 85 86 88 89

Small ANJOU district of pungent, long-lived whites, incl. COULEE DE SERRANT, LA ROCHE AUX MOINES, Clos du Papillon.

Savigny-lès-Beaune B'y. r. or (w. dr.) ★★★ 78 83 85 86 87 88 89

Important village next to BEAUNE, with similar well-balanced middle-weight wines, often deliciously delicate and fruity. Best v'yds: Marconnets, Dominode, Serpentières, Vergelesses, les Guettes. Top growers incl: BIZE, Girard-Vollot, TOLLOT-BEAUT, CLAIR, LEROY, Ecard.

Savoie E. France r. or w. dr. or sp. ★★ D.Y.A.

Alpine area with light dry wines like some Swiss wine or minor Loires. CREPY, SEYSSEL and APREMONT are best known whites; ROUSSETTE is often more interesting. Also MONDEUSE red.

Schlumberger ALSACE grower-merchants of luscious wines at Guebwiller.

Schröder & Schyler Old Bordeaux merchants, owners of Ch KIRWAN.

Sciacarello Red grape of Corsica's best red, e.g. AJACCIO, Sartène.

Sec Literally means dry, though champagne so-called is medium-sweet (and better at breakfast and tea-time than Brut).

Selection de Grains Nobles Descriptions coined by HUGEL for Alsace equivalent to German BEERENAUSLESE. "Grains nobles" are individual grapes with "noble rot" (see p. 49).

Sèvre-et-Maine The département containing the best v'yds of MUSCADET.

Seyssel Savoie w. dr. or sp. ★★ NV
Delicate pale dry white making v. pleasant light sparkling wine.

Sichel & Co. Two famous merchant houses. In Bordeaux owners of Ch D'ANGLUDET and part-owners of Ch PALMER. In Germany, maker of BLUE NUN and respected trader.

Soussans Village just n. of MARGAUX, sharing its appellation.

Sylvaner See Grapes for white wine

Syrah See Grapes for red wine

La Tâche B'y. r. ★★★★ 69 70 71 73 76 78 79 80 81 82 83 84 85 86 87 88 89 15-acre Grand Cru of VOSNE-ROMANEE and one of the best v'yds on earth: dark, perfumed and luxurious wine, year after year. Owned by the DOMAINE DE LA ROMANEE-CONTI.

Taittinger NV, Collection Brut 78 and 71 73 75 76 78 79 80 82 83 Fashionable champagne growers and merchants of Reims with a light touch. Luxury brand: Comtes de Champagne 76 79 81 82 83 (also v.g. rosé 79 83).

Tastevin, Confrérie des Chevaliers du Burgundy's colourful and successful promotion society. Wine carrying their Tastevinage label has been approved by them and will usually be of a fair standard. A tastevin is the shallow silver wine-tasting cup of Burgundy. See panel on p. 34.

Tavel Rh. p. ★★★ D.Y.A.
France's most famous, though not her best, rosé, strong and dry. Best growers: Maby, Bernard, Ch de Trinoprevedal. Drink *very* young.

Tempier, Domaine Top grower of BANDOL, with noble reds (incl. single-v'yd wines) and rosé.

Téte de Cuvée Archaic term used of the best wines of a district.

Thénard, Domaine The major grower of GIVRY, but best known for his substantial portion (4½ acres) of LE MONTRACHET.

Thevenet, Jean A master maker of white Mâcon-Clessé (Domaine de la Bon Gran) at Quintaine-Clessé, near LUGNY.

Thorin, J. Grower and major merchant of BEAUJOLAIS, owner of the Château des Jacques, MOULIN A VENT. Owned by Racke of Germany.

Thouarsais, Vin de Lo. r. w. dr. ✴ D.Y.A.
Light GAMAY and SAUV BLANC VDQS area south of SAUMUR.

Tokay d'Alsace See Pinot Gris under Grapes for white wine

Tollot-Beaut Stylish burgundy grower with some 50 acres in the COTE DE BEAUNE, incl. CORTON, BEAUNE Grèves, SAVIGNY (Les Champs Chevrey) and at Chorey-lès-Beaune where he is based.

Tortochot, Domaine 25-acre estate at GEVREY-CHAMBERTIN. Classic wines.

Touraine Lo. r. p. w. dr./sw./sp. ✴→★★★
Big mid-Loire province with immense range of wines, incl. dry white SAUVIGNON, dry and sweet CHENIN BLANC (e.g. VOUVRAY), red CHINON and BOURGUEIL, light red CABERNETS, GAMAYS and rosés: often bargains. Amboise, Azay-le-Rideau and Mesland are sub-sections of the appellation.

Trimbach, F.E. Distinguished ALSACE grower and merchant at Ribeauvillé. Best wines incl. the austere Riesling Clos Ste Hune.

Tursan s.w. France r. p. w. dr. ★
Emerging VDQS in the Landes. Sound reds.

Vacqueyras Rh. r. ★★ 83 85 86 88 89
Prominent village of s. COTES-DU-RHONE, neighbour to GIGONDAS and often better value. Try JABOULET's version.

Valençay Lo. w. dr. ★ D.Y.A.
Neighbour of CHEVERNY: similar pleasant sharpish wine.

Val-Joannis, Ch de Prov. r. p. w. dr. ★★
Impressive new estate making v.g. COTES DU LUBERON wines.

Valréas Rh. r. (p. w. dr.) ★★
Côtes-du-Rhône-village with big coop and good red wines.

Varichon & Clerc Principal makers and shippers of SAVOIE sp. wines.

Varoilles, Domaine des Burgundy estate of 30 acres, principally in GEVREY-CHAMBERTIN. Tannic wines with great keeping qualities.

Vaudésir B'y. w. dr. ★★★★ **78 83 85 86 87** 88 89
  Arguably the best of 7 CHABLIS Grands Crus (but then so are the others).

VDQS Vin Délimité de Qualité Supérieure (see p. 23).

Vendange Harvest.

Vendange tardive Late vintage. In ALSACE equivalent to German AUSLESE, but stronger and usually less fine.

Veuve Clicquot NV ("Yellow label"), NV Demi-Sec (White Label) and (Gold Label) **73 75 76 78 79 80** 82 83 85 and rosé 83 Historic champagne house of the highest standing, now owned by Moët-Hennessy. Full-bodied wines. Cellars at Reims. Luxury brand: La Grande Dame **79** 83.

Vidal-Fleury, J. Long-established shippers and growers of top Rhône wines, esp. HERMITAGE and COTE-ROTIE. Bought in 85 by GUIGAL.

Vieilles Vignes "Old vines" – therefore the best wine. Used for such wine by BOLLINGER, DE VOGUE and others.

Viénot, Charles Grower-merchant of reputable burgundy owned by BOISSET at NUITS. 70 acres in Nuits, CORTON, RICHEBOURG, etc.

Vignoble Area of vineyards.

Vin de garde Wine that will improve with keeping. The serious stuff.

Vin de l'année This year's wine. See Beaujolais, Beaujolais-Villages.

Vin de paille Wine from grapes dried on straw mats, consequently very sweet, like Italian passito. Especially in the JURA.

Vin de Pays The junior rank of country wines. Well over 100 are now operational, mainly in the Midi. Don't turn up your nose; there are some gems, and many charming trinkets.

Vin de Table Standard everyday table wine, not subject to particular regulations about grapes and origin. Choose the previous entry.

Vin Doux Naturel ("VDN") Sweet wine fortified with wine alcohol, so the sweetness is "natural", not the strength. The speciality of ROUSSILLON. A vin doux liquoreux is several degrees stronger.

Vin Gris "Grey" wine is very pale pink, made of red grapes pressed before fermentation begins, unlike rosé, which ferments briefly before pressing. Oeil de Perdrix means much the same; so (though I blush to say it) does "blush".

Vin Jaune Jura w. dr. ★★★ (At least 7 years old.)
  Speciality of ARBOIS: odd yellow wine like fino sherry. Normally ready when bottled. The best is CHATEAU-CHALON.

Vin nouveau See Beaujolais Nouveau.

Vin vert A very light, acidic, refreshing white wine, a speciality of ROUSSILLON and v. necessary in summer in those torrid parts.

Vinsobres Rh. r. (p. or w. dr.) ★★ **85 86** 88 89
  Contradictory name of s. Rhône village. Potentially substantial reds, but much ordinary.

Viré B'y. w. dr. ★★ **88 89**
  One of the best white-wine villages of MACON. Good wines from coop, Ch de Viré, Clos du Chapitre, JADOT.

Visan Rh. r. p. or w. dr. ★★ **86 88** 89
  One of the better s. Rhône villages. Reds much better than white.

Viticulteur Wine-grower.

Vogüé, Comte Georges de First-class 30-acre burgundy domaine at CHAMBOLLE-MUSIGNY. At best the ultimate MUSIGNY and BONNES MARES.

Volnay B'y. r. ★★★ **78 79 80 82 83 85'** 86 87 88 89
  Village between POMMARD and MEURSAULT: often the best reds of the COTE DE BEAUNE, not strong or heavy but fragrant and silky. Best v'yds: Caillerets, Clos des Ducs, Champans, Clos des Chênes, etc. Best growers: POUSSE D'OR, d'ANGERVILLE, Lafarge, de Montille, HOSPICES DE BEAUNE.

Volnay-Santenots B'y. r. ★★★

Excellent red wine from MEURSAULT is sold under this name. Indistinguishable from VOLNAY.

Vosne-Romanée B'y. r. ★★★→★★★★ 76 78 79 80 82 83 84 85 86 87 88 89 The village containing Burgundy's grandest Crus (ROMANÉE-CONTI, LA TACHE, etc.). There are (or rather should be) no common wines in Vosne. Many good growers incl: Arnoux, JAYER, Gros, Mongeard-Mugneret, Grivot, ROMANÉE-CONTI, Castagnier, Engel.

Vougeot See Clos de Vougeot.

Vouvray Lo. w. dr./sw./sp. ★★→★★★★ 71 76 78 79 82 83 85 86 88 89

Small district of TOURAINE with very variable wines, at their best intensely sweet and almost immortal. Good dry sparkling. Best producers: Huet, Foreau, Allias, Bourillon-Dorléaus, Brisebarre, Fouguet, Ch Gaudrelle, Brédif, Poniatowski.

Willm, A Northerly ALSACE grower at Barr: with v.g. GEWÜRZ Clos Gaensbronnel.

"Y" (Pronounced ygrec) 78 79 80 84 85 86

Dry wine produced occasionally at Ch D'YQUEM.

Ziltener, André Swiss burgundy grower and merchant with cellars in GEVREY-CHAMBERTIN. Reds very sound.

Zind-Humbrecht 64-acre Alsace estate in Wintzenheim, Turckheim and Thann. First-rate individual v'yd wines (esp. Clos St Urbain Riesling).

MISE EN BOUTEILLES
AU DOMAINE

VOLNAY
LES CAILLERETS

APPELLATION CONTROLEE
DOMAINE DE LA POUSSE D'OR
A VOLNAY, COTE D'OR

Burgundy: a grower's own label

Domaine is the burgundy equivalent of château.
The Appellation Contrôlée is Volnay.
The individual v'yd in Volnay is called Les Caillerets.
The name and address of the grower/producer.
(The word propriétaire is often also used.)

GEVREY-CHAMBERTIN
CLOS ST JACQUES

APPELLATION CONTROLEE

REMOISSENET PERE ET FILS
NEGOCIANTS A BEAUNE

A merchant's label

The village.
The vineyard.
The wine qualifies for the Appellation Gevrey-Chambertin Premier Cru.
Remoissenet Père et Fils is a négociant, or merchant, who bought the wine from the grower to mature, bottle and sell.

Châteaux
of Bordeaux

Some 400 of the best-known Bordeaux châteaux are listed here. Information on the current state of each vintage of each château (whether it is ready for drinking or will benefit from keeping; whether it is a wine that its maker is specially proud of) is complete up to the 1988 vintage. The château wines of 1989 will not be bottled until spring 1991. It is too early to record specific judgements, but not too early to say that 1989 was another very good to excellent vintage, ripened and harvested in almost perfect conditions – and the earliest since 1893.

1989 was the sixth very good vintage of the decade; a particular success for the Merlot-rich wines of Pomerol and St Emilion, but remarkably even overall in producing deep-coloured, full and well-structured wines of classic proportions. It was a very good year for dry white wines and a wonderful one for Sauternes. 1987 caused no excitement; its honourable wines will be restaurant-fodder for the next few years. 1986 has proved even more exciting than expected in the Médoc and less so in St Emilion and Pomerol, where too much wine was made. Here it will mature quickly. 1985 is a magnificent vintage awaiting its hour. It should always be remembered that in Bordeaux the making of a vintage is only the prologue to its history . . .

MEDOC

R. Gironde

ST-SEURIN-DE-CADOURNE

ST-ESTEPHE **St Est**

PAUILLAC **Pau**

ST-SAUVEUR **St-Sau**
ST-LAURENT **St-Lau**
ST-JULIEN **St-Jul**

CUSSAC

LISTRAC-MEDOC
MOULIS

SOUSSANS-MARGAUX **Sou-Mar**
MARGAUX **Mar**

LABARDE-MARGAUX **Lab-Mar**

CANTENAC-MARGAUX **Cant-Mar**

ARSAC-MARGAUX **Ar-Mar**

HAUT MEDOC

FRONSAC
LALANDE
DE POMEROL

POMEROL

Bordeaux

Libourne

ST-GEORGES **St-Geo**

Castillion

ST-EMILION **St-Em**

R. Dordogne

GRAVES

R. Garonne

ENTRE-DEUX-MERS

BARSAC

SAUTERNES

Langon

d'Agassac Haut-Médoc r. ★★ 75′ 78 79 81 82′ 83 84 85 86 88

Sleeping Beauty 14th-century moated fort with 86 acres v. near Bordeaux suburbs. Same owners as Ch'x CALON-SEGUR and DU TERTRE. Very tasty wines.

Andron-Blanquet St-Est. r. ★★ 82 83 84 85′ 86 88

Sister-château to cos LABORY. Rather "open" and easy wine. 40 acres.

L'Angélus St-Em. r. ★★ 75′ 78 79′ 80 81′ 82 83 85′ 86 87 88

Well-situated classed-growth of 57 acres on the St-Emilion Côtes w. of the town. Looking very good recently.

d'Angludet Cant-Mar. r. ★★★ 70′ 75 76′ 78′ 79 80 81′ 82 83′ 84 85′ 86′ 87 88 75-acre Cru Exceptionnel of classed-growth quality owned by Peter A. Sichel. Lively fragrant Margaux of great style. Exceptional value.

d'Archambeau Graves r. and w. dr. (sw.) ★★ (r.) 85 86 87 88 (w.) 85 86 87 88 89 Up-to-date 54-acre property at Illats. V.g. fruity dry white; since '84 fragrant barrel-aged reds.

d'Arche Sauternes w. sw. ★★ 78 79 80 81 82 83′ 85 86 88

Substantial classed-growth of 88 acres rejuvenated since 1980. Rich juicy wines.

d'Arcins Central Médoc r. ★★

185-acre property of the Castel family (cf. Castelvin); sister-château to neighbouring Barreyres (160 acres).

l'Arrosée St-Em. r. ★★→★★★ 78 79 81 82 83 84 85′ 86′ 87 88

Substantial 24-acre Côtes property. Seriously fine wine with "stuffing", despite its name (which means watered). A top St-Emilion: opulence and structure.

Ausone St-Em. r. ★★★★ 76′ 78 79′ 80 81 82′ 83′ 84 85 86′ 87 88

Celebrated first-growth with 17 acres (about 2,500 cases) in the best position on the Côtes with famous rock-hewn cellars under the vineyard. The firmest, most elegant and subtle St-Emilion. See also Ch Belair.

Bahans-Haut-Brion Graves r. ★★★ NV and 82 83 87 88

The second-quality wine of Ch HAUT-BRION. Worthy of its noble origin.

Balestard-la-Tonnelle St-Em. r. ★★ 70′ 75′ 78 79 81 82 83 85 86′ 87 88

Historic 30-acre classed-growth on the plateau near the town. Big flavour; more finesse since '85.

de Barbe Côtes de Bourg r. (w.) ★★ 79′ 81 82′ 83 85 86 87 88

The biggest (148 acres) and best-known ch of the right bank of the Gironde. Good tasty, light but fruity, Merlot red.

Bastor-Lamontagne Sauternes w. sw. ★★ 76 79 80 82 83′ 84 85 86′ 87 88 89 Large "bourgeois" Preignac property at classed-growth standard. Excellent rich wines. 10,000 cases.

Batailley Pauillac r. ★★★ 70 75′ 78′ 79′ 81 82′ 83 84 85 86 87 88

The bigger of the famous pair of fifth-growths (with HAUT-BATAILLEY) on the borders of Pauillac and St-Julien. 110 acres. Fine, firm strong-flavoured wine. Home of the Castéja family of BORIE-MANOUX.

Beaumont Cussac, Haut-Médoc r. ★★ 78′ 79 81 82 83 84 85 86′ 87 88

200-acre+ Cru Bourgeois, well-known in France for rather light but increasingly serious wines. Second label: Ch Moulin d'Arvigny. 35,000 cases. In the same hands as Ch BEYCHEVELLE since '87.

Beauregard Pomerol r. ★★★ 75′ 79′ 81 82′ 83 85 86 87 88

32-acre v'yd with pretty 17th-century ch near LA CONSEILLANTE. Well-made but rather delicate wines to drink quite young.

Beau Séjour-Bécot St-Em. r. ★★★ 75′ 82′ 83 85 86′ 87 88

Half of the old Beau Séjour Premier Grand Cru estate on the w. slope of the Côtes. 45 acres. Controversially demoted in class in '85 but much revved-up since. The Bécots also owns Ch GRAND PONTET.

Beauséjour-Duffau-Lagarosse St-Em. r. ★★★ 75 78 81 82 83 85 86 88

The other half of the above, 17 acres in old family hands. Coasting in the '70s; more grip since '82.

Beau-Site St-Est. r. ✶✶ 75′ 78′ 79 81 82 83 84 85 86′ 87 88
55-acre Cru Bourgeois Exceptionnel in same hands as Ch'x BATAILLEY, etc. Quality and substance typical of St-Estèphe.

Belair St-Em. r. ✶✶✶ 70 71 75′ 76′ 78 79′ 80 82′ 83′ 85′ 86′ 88
Sister-ch and neighbour of AUSONE with 34.5 acres on the Côtes. Wine a shade heartier and less complex. V. high standard in recent vintages. Makes a NV, "Roc-Blanquant", in magnums only.

de Bel-Air Lalande de Pomerol r. ✶✶ 75′ 76 79 81 82′ 83 85 86
The best-known estate of this village just n. of Pomerol, with very similar wine. 25 acres.

Bel Air-Marquis d'Aligre Sou-Mar. r. ✶✶ 70′ 75′ 78 79 81 82′ 83 84 85 86 87 88   Cru Exceptionnel with 42 acres of old vines giving only 3,500 cases. The owner likes gutsy wine.

Belgrave St-Lau. r. ✶✶ 81 82 83 85 86′ 87 88
Obscure fifth-growth in St-Julien's back-country. 107 acres. Managed by DOURTHE since 1979. '86 shows real promise.

Bel-Orme-Tronquoy-de-Lalande St-Seurin-de-Cadourne (Haut-Médoc) r. ✶✶ 75′ 78 79′ 81 82′ 83 84 85 86 88   60-acre Cru Bourgeois n. of St-Estèphe. Old v'yd producing tannic wines.

Berliquet St-Em. r. ✶✶ 79 81 82 83 85 86 88
Tiny Grand Cru Classé recently v. well run (by the coop).

Beychevelle St-Jul. r. ✶✶✶ 61 66 70′ 75′ 78 79 81 82′ 83 84 85′ 86′ 87 88
170-acre fourth-growth with the Médoc's finest mansion. New owners (an insurance company). Wine of more elegance than power, patchy quality; since '85 a star again.

Bonnet Entre-Deux-Mers r. and w. dr. ✶✶ (w.) D.Y.A.
Big-scale producer (600 acres!) of some of the best Entre-Deux-Mers.

**CHATEAU
LANGOA-BARTON**

GRAND CRU CLASSE

APPELLATION ST-JULIEN
CONTROLEE

MIS EN BOUTEILLES AU
CHATEAU

A Bordeaux label

A château is an estate – not necessarily with a mansion or a big expanse of vineyard.

Reference to the local classification. It varies from one part of Bordeaux to another.

The Appellation Contrôlée: look up St-Julien in the France A-Z.

"Bottled at the château" – now the normal practice with classed-growth wines.

Bon-Pasteur, Le Pom. r. ✶✶✶ 70 75 76 78 79 81 82 83 84 85 86 87 88
Excellent small property (3,500 cases) on the St-Emilion boundary. Concentrated, sometimes even creamy, wines.

Boscq, Le St-Est. r. ✶✶ 82 83 84 85 86 87 88
Leading Cru Bourgeois giving excellent value in tasty St-Estéphe.

Le Bourdieu Haut-Médoc r. ✶✶ 75′ 78′ 79 81 82 83 85 86 88
Cru Bourgeois at Vertheuil with sister Ch Victoria (134 acres in all) known for well-made St-Estèphe-style wines.

Bourgneuf-Vayron Pomerol r. ✶✶-✶✶✶ 81 82 83 84 85′ 86 87 88
22-acre v'yd on chalky clay soil making fairly rich wines with typically plummy Pomerol perfume. 5,000 cases.

Bouscaut Graves r. w. dr. ✶✶ 70′ 75 78 79 81 82′ 83 85 86′ 88
Classed-growth bought in 1980 by Lucien Lurton, owner of Ch BRANE-CANTENAC, etc. 75 acres red (largely Merlot); 15 acres white. Never yet brilliant, but slowly getting there.

du Bousquet Côtes de Bourg r. ✶✶ 81 82 83 85 86 87 88
Reliable estate with 148 acres making attractive solid wine.

Boyd-Cantenac Margaux r. ✶✶✶ 75′ 78′ 79 81 82′ 83′ 84 85 86′ 87 88   44-acre third-growth often producing attractive wine, full of flavour, if not of third-growth class. See also Ch Pouget.

Branaire (Ducru) St-Jul. r. ★★★ 70′ 75′ 76 78 79′ 81 82′ 83 84 85 86 87
88 Fourth-growth of 125 acres producing notably spicy and flavoury wine in the '70s; still attractive and reliable, if not so striking. New owners in '87 and 2nd label: Dulac.

Brane-Cantenac Cant-Mar. r. ★★★ 75′ 78′ 79 81 82′ 83 84 85 86′ 87
88 Big (211 acres) well-run second-growth. Often gamey wines of strong character. Same owners as Ch'x DURFORT-VIVENS, VILLEGEORGE, CLIMENS, BOUSCAUT, etc. Second label: Ch Notton.

Brillette Moulis, Haut-Médoc r. ★★ 75 78 79 81′ 82 83 84 85′ 86 88
70-acre Cru Bourgeois. Reliable and attractive; fulfilling high promise.

La Cabanne Pomerol r. ★★ 75′ 78′ 79′ 81 82′ 83 85 86 88
Highly regarded 25-acre property near the great Ch TROTANOY. Recently modernized; expect to hear more.

Cadet Piola St-Em. r. ★★ 70′ 75′ 76 78 79 81 82 83′ 84 85′ 86
Distinguished little property just n. of the town of St-Emilion. 3,000 cases. Ch Faurie de Souchard has same owner; less robust wine.

Caillou Sauternes w. sw. ★★ 81 82 83 85 86 87 88′ 89′
Well-run second-rank 37-acre Barsac vineyard for firm, fruity wine. "Private Cuvée" (81 83 85 86 88) is a top selection.

Calon-Ségur St-Est. r. ★★★ 70 75 78′ 79′ 81 82′ 83 84 85′ 86 87 88′
Big (123-acre) third-growth of great reputation. A great classic for big hearty wines, but rather patchy in recent years. '86 and '88 look good.

Cambon-la-Pelouse Haut-Médoc r. ★★ 82 83 84 85 86 87 88
Big (145-acre) accessible Cru Bourgeois. A sure bet for fresh typical Médoc without wood ageing.

Camensac St-Lau. r. ★★ 75′ 78 79 81 82′ 83 84 85 86′ 87 88
149-acre fifth-growth, replanted in the '60s with new equipment and the same expert direction as LAROSE-TRINTAUDON. Good vigorous if not exactly classic wines.

Canon St-Em. r. ★★★ 75′ 78 79′ 81 82′ 83′ 85′ 86 87 88
Famous first-classed-growth with 44+ acres on the plateau w. of the town. Conservative methods; very impressive wine.

Canon Canon-Fronsac r. ★★ 81 82 83 85 86′ 88
Tiny property of Christian MOUEIX. Long-ageing wine.

Canon-la-Gaffelière St-Em. r. ★★ 82′ 83 85 86′ 87 88
47-acre classed-growth on the lower slopes of the Côtes with Austrian ownership. Total renovation in '85. Much more meat now.

Canon de Brem Canon-Fronsac r. ★★ 78 81 82′ 83 85 86 87 88 89′
One of the top Fronsac v'yds for vigorous wine. MOUEIX property.

Canon-Moueix Canon-Fronsac r. ★★ 83 85 86 87 88 89′
The latest MOUEIX investment in this rising appellation. V. stylish wine.

Cantemerle Macau r. ★★★ 61 70′ 75′ 78 79 81 82 83′ 84 85 86 87 88
Superb estate at the extreme s. of the Médoc, with a romantic ch in a wood and 150 acres of vines. Officially fifth-growth: potentially higher for its harmony of flavours. Problems hampered quality in late '70s. A new broom (CORDIER) since 1981 is fulfilling potential.

Cantenac-Brown Cant-Mar. r. ★★★ 70 75 78 79 81 82 83 84 85 86′ 87 88
Formerly old-fashioned 77-acre third-growth, with very promising recent vintages. Big wines. New owners since '87 investing heavily. 2nd label: Canuet.

Capbern-Gasqueton St-Est. r. ★★ 75 81 82 83 84 85 86 88
Good 85-acre Cru Bourgeois; same owner as CALON-SEGUR.

Cap de Mourlin St-Em. r. ★★ 70′ 75′ 78 79′ 81 82′ 83 84 85 86 87 88
Well-known 37-acre property of the Cap de Mourlin family, owners of Ch BALESTARD and Ch Roudier, Montagne-St-Em. Classic St-Emilion.

Carbonnieux Graves r. and w. dr. ★★★ (r.) 82 83 85 86′ 88
Historic estate at Léognan making rather light reds (since '85 much better). The whites of e.g. '83, '86, '88, '89 have the structure to age 10 yrs. Ch'x Le Pape and Le Sertre are also in the family.

Cardaillan Graves r. **
The trusty red wine of the distinguished (Sauternes) Ch de MALLE.

La Cardonne Blaignan (Médoc) r. ** 78 79 81' 82 83 84 85 86 87 88
Large (300+ acres) Cru Bourgeois in the n. Médoc bought in 1973 by
the Rothschilds of LAFITE. A safe bet for fairly early drinking.

Les Carmes-Haut-Brion Graves r. ** 75 78 79 81' 82' 83 85 86 87 88'
Small neighbour (9-acre) of HAUT-BRION with higher than bourgeois
standards. Old vintages show its potential. Alas only 1,800 cases.

Caronne-Ste-Gemme St-Lau. (Haut-Médoc) r. **→→** 75 78 79 81 82'
83 84 85 86 87 88 Cru Bourgeois of 100 acres. Steady quality repays
patience. At minor cru classé level.

du Castéra Médoc r. ** 75 81 82 83 84 85 86 87 88
Historic property at St-Germain in the n. Médoc. Recent investment;
to watch for tasty but not tannic wine.

Certan de May Pomerol r. *** 70 75 76 78 79 81 82' 83 84 85' 86
Neighbour of VIEUX-CHATEAU-CERTAN. Tiny property (1,800 cases) with
full-bodied rich and tannic wine consistently flying very high.

Certan-Giraud Pomerol r. *** 75 79 81 82 83' 85 86 88
Small (17-acre) property next to the great Ch PETRUS.

Chambert-Marbuzet St-Est. r. ** 78 79 81 82 83 84 85 86 88
Tiny (20-acre) sister-ch of HAUT-MARBUZET. Very good predominantly
cabernet wine aged in new oak relatively fast – but very tastily.

Chantegrive Graves r. w. dr. ** 81 82 84 85 88
215-acre estate half white, half red; modern Graves of high quality.
Cuvée Caroline is top white selection. Other labels incl. Mayne-
Levéque, Bon-Dieu-des-Vignes.

Chasse-Spleen Moulis r. *** 70' 75' 76 78' 79 81' 82' 83' 84 85 86 87
88 180-acre Cru Exceptionnel of classed-growth quality. Consistently good, usually outstanding, long-maturing wine. 2nd label:
Ermitage de C-S. One of the surest things in Bordeaux.

Chéret-Pitres Graves r. w. dr. *→**
Substantial estate in the up-and-coming village of Portets.

Cheval Blanc St-Em. r. **** 66 70 75' 76 78 79 80 81' 82' 83' 84 85' 86
87 88 This and AUSONE are the "first-growths" of St-Emilion. Cheval
Blanc is richer, more full-blooded, intensely vigorous and perfumed,
from 100 acres. Delicious young, and lasts almost forever.

Chicane Graves r. **
Satisfying and reliable product of the Langon merchant Pierre Coste.
Domaine de Gaillat is another. Drink at 2-6 years.

Cissac Cissac r. ** 70' 75' 76 78' 79 81 82' 83' 84 85 86 87 88
A pillar of the bourgeoisie. 80-acre Grand Bourgeois Exceptionnel
with a steady record for tasty long-lived wine.

Citran Avensan, Haut-Médoc r. ** 70' 75 78' 81 82 83 85 86 88
Grand Bourgeois Exceptionnel of 178 acres bought by Japanese in
'87. Major works. Expect stylish wine.

Clarke Listrac, Haut-Médoc r. (p.) ** 78 79 81 82 83 84 85' 86 87 88
Huge (350-acre) Cru Bourgeois Rothschild development, incl. visitor
facilities. 2nd labels: Ch'x Malmaison and Peyrelebade.

Clerc-Milon Pauillac r. *** 75' 78' 79 80 81 82' 83 84 85 86' 87 88
Once forgotten little fifth-growth bought by the late Baron Philippe de
Rothschild in 1970. Now 73 acres. Not normally thrilling in the '70s
(except 70), but a v.g. '85 and (esp.) '86, and now '88 and '89.

Climens Sauternes w. sw. *** 71' 75' 76' 78' 79 80' 81 82 83' 85' 86'
87 88 74-acre classed-growth at Barsac making some of the most
stylish (though not the very sweetest) wine in the world for a good
10 years' maturing. A superb '83. (Occasional) 2nd label: Les Cyprès.
Same owner as Ch BRANE-CANTENAC, etc.

Clinet Pomerol r. ** 79 81 83 85 86 87 88
17-acre property in central Pomerol making tannic wines from old
vines. Progress in recent vintages towards a juicier style.

Clos l'Eglise   Pomerol r.   ★★★ 75 78 79' 81 82' 83 85 86 88
14-acre v'yd in one of the best sites in Pomerol. Fine wine without great muscle or flesh. The same family owns Ch PLINCE.

Clos Floridéne   Graves w. dr.   ★★
Tour de force by one of the best white winemakers of B'x, Denis Dubourdieu. Drink young or keep 5 years.

Clos Fourtet   St-Em. r.   ★★★ 78 79 80 81 82' 83 85 86 88
Well-known 42-acre first-growth on the plateau with cellars almost in the town. Back on reasonable form after a middling patch. Same owners as CLIMENS, BRANE-CANTENAC, etc.

Clos Haut-Peyraguey   Sauternes w. sw.   ★★ 78 79 81 82 83 84 85 86' 87 88   Tiny production of good medium-rich wine. The v.g. Cru Bourgeois Ch Haut-Bommes is in the same hands.

Clos des Jacobins   St-Em. r.   ★★ 75' 78 79 81 82' 83' 85 86 87 88
Well-known and well-run little (18-acre) classed-growth owned by the shipper CORDIER. Wines of notable depth and style.

Clos du Marquis   St-Jul. r.   ★★ 75 78 79 81 82 83 84 85 86 87 88
The second wine of LEOVILLE-LAS CASES.

Clos René   Pomerol r.   ★★★ 75 81 82' 83 85 86 87 88
Leading ch on the w. of Pomerol. 38 acres making increasingly concentrated wine. Also sold as Ch Moulinet-Lasserre.

La Closerie-Grand-Poujeaux   Moulis (Haut-Médoc) r.   ★★
Small but respected traditional middle-Médoc. To keep 10 years.

La Clotte   St-Em. r.   ★★ 75' 81 82 83' 85 86 87 88
Tiny Côtes Grand Cru with fragrant supple wine. Drink at the owners' restaurant, La Cadine, in St-Em.

Colombier-Monpelou   Pauillac r.   ★★ 82 83 85 86' 88
Reliable small Cru Bourgeois made to a high standard.

La Conseillante   Pomerol r.   ★★★ 70' 75 79 81' 82' 83 84 85 86 87 88
29-acre historic property on the plateau between PETRUS and CHEVAL BLANC. At best some of the noblest and most fragrant Pomerol, worthy of its superb position.

Corbin (Giraud)   St-Em. r.   ★★ 75 79 81 82' 83' 85 86 88
28-acre classed-growth in n. St-Emilion where a cluster of Corbins occupy the edge of the plateau. Top vintages are very rich.

Corbin-Michotte   St-Em. r.   ★★ 75 81 82 83 85 86 88
Well-run 19-acre property; "generous" Pomerol-like wine.

Cos-d'Estournel   St-Est. r.   ★★★★ 61 66 70 73 75' 76' 78' 79 81' 82' 83' 84 85' 86' 87 88'   140-acre second-growth with eccentric chinoiserie building overlooking Ch LAFITE. Always full-flavoured, often magnificent, wine. Now regularly one of the best in the Médoc. 2nd label: Ch Marbuzet.

Cos Labory   St-Est. r.   ★★ 82' 83 84 85 86 88
Little-known fifth-growth neighbour of COS D'ESTOURNEL with 37 acres. Nowhere near classed-growth standard.

Coufran   St-Seurin-de-Cadourne (Haut-Médoc) r.   ★★ 78' 79 81 82' 83 85 86' 87 88   Coufran and Ch VERDIGNAN, on the northern-most hillock of the Haut-Médoc, are under the same ownership. Coufran has mainly Merlot vines; soft, supple wine. 148 acres.

Couhins-Lurton   Graves w. dr.   ★★ 85 86' 87' 88 89
Tiny quantity of very fine Sauvignon wine for maturing.

Coutet   Sauternes w. sw.   ★★★ 67' 70' 71' 73 75' 76 79 81 82 83' 84 85 86 87 88   Traditional rival to Ch CLIMENS; 91 acres in Barsac. Usually slightly less rich; at its best equally fine. "Cuvée Madame" is a v. rich selection of the best. A dry Graves sold under the same name is not so special.

Couvent des Jacobins   St-Em. r.   ★★ 75 78 79' 81 82' 83 85 86 87 88
Well-known vineyard of 22 acres adjacent to the town of St-Emilion on the east. Among the best of its kind.

Le Crock St-Est. r. ★★ 79 81 82 83 84 85 86 87 88
Well-situated Cru Bourgeois of 74 acres in the same family as Ch LEOVILLE-POYFERRE. Among the many good C.B's of the commune.

La Croix Pomerol r. ★★ 70′ 71′ 75′ 78 79′ 81 82′ 83 85 86
Well-reputed property of 32 acres. Appealing plummy Pomerol with a spine; matures well. Also La C.-St-Georges, La C.-Toulifaut, Castalot and Clos des Litanies.

La Croix de Gay Pomerol r. ★★★ 75′ 79 81 82′ 83′ 85 86 88
30 acres in the best part of the commune. Recently on fine form. Has underground cellars, rare in Pomerol. "La Fleur de Gay" is the best selection.

Croizet-Bages Pauillac r. ★★ 75′ 82′ 83 84 85 86
52-acre fifth-growth (lacking a château or a reputation) with the same owners as Ch RAUZAN-GASSIES. Wines with growing vigour (at last).

Croque-Michotte St-Em. r. ★★ 75 81 82′ 83 85 86 87 88
35-acre Pomerol-style classed-growth on the Pomerol border.

de Cruzeaux Graves r. w. dr. ★★
100-acre GRAVES-LEOGNAN v'yd recently developed by André Lurton of LA LOUVIERE etc. V. high standards; to try. Drink white at 1-3 years.

Curé-Bon-la-Madeleine St-Em. r. ★★★ 75 78 81 82′ 83 85 86 88
Small (12-acre) property among the best of the Côtes; between AUSONE and CANON. Managed by MOUEIX.

Why do the Châteaux of Bordeaux have such a large section of this book devoted to them? The reason is simple: collectively they form by far the largest supply of high-quality wine on earth.

A single typical Médoc château with 150 acres (some have far more) makes approximately 26,000 dozen bottles of identifiable wine a year – the production of two or three California "boutique" wineries. The tendency over the last two decades has been for the better-known châteaux to buy more land. Many classed-growths have expanded very considerably since they were classified in 1855. The majority have also raised their sights and invested the good profits of the past decade in better technology.

Dassault St-Em. r. ★★ 81 82 83 85 86 88
Consistent early-maturing middle-weight Grand Cru. 58 acres.

La Dauphine Fronsac ★★ 85 86 87 88 89
Famous old star of Fronsac rejuvenated by J-P MOUEIX.

Dauzac Lab-Mar. r. ★★→★★★ 75 79′ 81 82′ 83′ 84 85′ 86 87 88
Substantial fifth-growth near the river s. of Margaux. Doing well since '79; new owner in '89. 120 acres. 22,000 cases.

Desmirail Mar. r. ★★→★★★ 82 83′ 84 85 86 88
Third-growth, now 45 acres. A long-defunct name recently revived by the owner of BRANE-CANTENAC. So far wines for drinking young.

Doisy-Daëne Barsac w. sw. and dr. ★★★ 76′ 78 79 80 81 82 83′ 84 85 86 88 Forward-looking 34-acre estate making crisp dry white (incl. Riesling grapes) and red Ch Cantegril as well as notably fine (and long-lived) sweet Barsac.

Doisy-Dubroca Barsac w. sw. ★★ 75′ 76 78 79 80 81 83 84 85 86 87 88
Tiny (8½-acre) Barsac classed-growth allied to Ch CLIMENS.

Doisy-Védrines Sauternes w. sw. ★★★ 71 75′ 76′ 78 79 80 81 82′ 83′ 85 86 88′ 89′ 50-acre classed-growth at Barsac, near CLIMENS and COUTET, recently re-equipped. Deliciously sturdy rich wines designed for a long life.

Domaine de Chevalier Graves r. and w. dr. ★★★★ (r.) 66 70′ 75′ 76 78′ 79′ 80 81′ 82′ 83 84 85 86′ 87 Superb small estate of 36 acres at Léognan. The red is stern at first, richly subtle with age. The white is delicate but matures to rich flavours. (w. 78 79′ 81 82 83′ 84 85′ 87′ 88). Changed hands (but not management) in 1983. Up to 9,000 cases red, 1,000 cases white.

Domaine de l'Eglise Pomerol r. ★★ 79' 81 82' 83 85 86 88
Small property: solid wine distributed by BORIE-MANOUX.

Domaine la Grave Graves r. w. dr. ★★ 82 83 84 85 86 88
Innovative little estate with lively medal-winning reds made for a long life. Oak-aged delicious whites. Wines made at Ch de Landiras by Peter Vinding Diers.

La Dominique St-Em. r. ★★★ 70 71' 75 76 78 79 81 82' 83 86' 87 88 Fine 45-acre classed-growth next door to Ch CHEVAL BLANC, making wine almost as arresting.

Ducru-Beaucaillou St-Jul. r. ★★★★ 61 66 70' 75' 76 78'79 81 82' 83' 84 85' 86' 87 88 Outstanding second-growth; 120 acres overlooking the river. 2nd label: La Croix-Beaucaillou. The owner, M. Borie, makes classic claret for v. long ageing. See also Grand-Puy-Lacoste, etc.

Duhart-Milon-Rothschild Pauillac r. ★★★ 75' 78 79 81 82' 83 85 86 87 88 Fourth-growth neighbour of LAFITE under the same management. Maturing vines; increasingly fine quality. 110 acres.

Duplessis-Fabre Moulis r. ★★ 82 83 84 85 86 87 88' Former sister-château of FOURCAS-DUPRE, since '89 owned by DOURTHE of Ch. MAUCAILLOU. To watch.

Durfort-Vivens Margaux r. ★★★ 78' 79' 81 82' 83 85' 86 87 88' Relatively small (49-acre) second-growth owned by M. Lurton of BRANE-CANTENAC. Recent wines (except '84) have real class.

Dutruch-Grand-Poujeaux Moulis r. ★★ 78 79 81 82' 83 84 85 86 87 88 One of the leaders of MOULIS; full-bodied, and tannic wines.

L'Eglise-Clinet Pomerol r. ★★★ 70 71 75 76 78 79 81 82' 83' 84 85' 86 11 acres. Ranked very near the top; full, fleshy wine. Changed hands in '82; '85 is noble. 1,700 cases. 2nd label: La Petite Eglise.

L'Enclos Pomerol r. ★★ 70 75 76 78 79 81 82' 83 85 86 87 88 Respected 26-acre property on the w. side of Pomerol, near CLOS-RENE. Big, well-made, long-flavoured wine.

L'Evangile Pomerol r. ★★★ 75' 78 79 82' 83' 84 85' 86 88 33 acres between PETRUS and CHEVAL BLANC. Impressive wines. In the same area and class as LA CONSEILLANTE.

Fargues Sauternes w. sw. ★★★ 70' 71' 75' 76' 78 79 80 81 83 85' 86 87 25-acre v'yd in same ownership as Ch YQUEM. Fruity and extremely elegant wines, maturing earlier than YQUEM.

Faurie de Souchard St Em. r. ★★ 85 86 88
Small Grand Cru Classé on the Côtes.

Ferrande Graves r. (w. dr.) ★★ 82 83 84 85 86 87 88 Major estate of Castres with 100+ acres. Easy enjoyable red and v.g. white at 1-4 yrs. Early drinking is fun; the proprietor prefers to wait.

Ferrière Margaux r. ★★ 75 78 79 81 82 83 85 86 87 88 Phantom third-growth of only 10+ acres. Now in the same capable hands as CHASSE-SPLEEN.

Feytit-Clinet Pomerol r. ★★ 75' 79 81 82' 83 85' 86 87 88' Little property next to LATOUR-POMEROL. Has made some fine big ripe wines. Managed by J-P MOUEIX.

Fieuzal Graves r. and (w. dr.) ★★★ 75' 78' 79 80 81' 82' 83 84 85' 86' 87 88 75-acre classed-growth at Léognan. Finely made memorable wines of both colours esp. since '84. Whites since '85 are keepers.

Figeac St-Em. r. ★★★ 70' 75' 76' 78 79 81 82' 83 84 85' 86 87 88 Famous first-growth neighbour of CHEVAL BLANC. 98-acre gravelly v'yd gives one of Bordeaux's most stylish, rich but elegant wines, maturing relatively quickly, but lasting almost indefinitely.

Filhot Sauternes w. sw. and dr. ★★★ 75 76' 79' 80 82' 83' 85 86' 87 88 Second-rank classed-growth with splendid ch, 148-acre v'yd. Lightish (Sauvignon) sw. wines for fairly early drinking, a little dry, and red.

La Fleur St-Em. r. ★★ 75 78 79 81 82′ 83 85 86 88

16-acre Côtes estate producing consistently fruity wines.

Lafleur See under L.

La Fleur-Gazin Pomerol r. ★★ 78 79 80 81 82 83 85′ 86 88

Tiny MOUEIX-run property. Appealing, not over-aweing wines.

La Fleur-Pétrus Pomerol r. ★★★ 70 75′ 78 79 81′ 82 83′ 84 85 86 87 88′ 89′ 18-acre v'yd flanking PETRUS and under the same management. Exceedingly fine plummy wines; Pomerol at its most stylish.

Fombrauge St-Em. r. ★★ 79 81 82′ 83 85 86 87 88

Major property of St-Christophe-des-Bardes, e. of St-Emilion, with 120 acres. Reliable early-drinking St-Emilion making great efforts.

Fonbadet Pauillac r. ★★ 70 75 78 79 81′ 82′ 83 84 85 86 87 88

Cru Bourgeois of high repute with 38 acres next door to PONTET-CANET. Old vines and no oak give solid wine needing long bottle-age. Value.

Fonplégade St-Em. r. ★★ 75 78 79 81 82′ 83 85 86 88

48-acre Grand Cru Classé on the Côtes w. of St-Emilion in another branch of the MOUEIX family. Fragrant and appealing.

Fonréaud Listrac r. ★★ 78′ 79 81 82′ 83 84 85′ 86′ 87 88

One of the bigger (96 acres) and better Crus Bourgeois of its area. New broom (and barrels) since '83. See also Ch Lestage.

Fonroque St-Em. r. ★★★ 70 75′ 78 79 81 82 83′ 84 85′ 86 87 88 89′

48 acres on the plateau n. of St-Emilion, MOUEIX property. Big deep dark wine that nonetheless opens up quite young.

Les Forts de Latour Pauillac r. ★★★ 70′ 75 76 78′ 79 80 81 82′ 83

The second wine of Ch LATOUR; well worthy of its big brother. Unique in being bottle-aged at least three years before release. Spectacular '82.

Fourcas-Dupré Listrac r. ★★ 70′ 75 78′ 79 81 82′ 83′ 84 85′ 86′ 87 88 A top-class 100-acre Cru Bourgeois Exceptionnel making consistent and elegant wine. To follow. 2nd label: Ch. Bellevue-Laffont.

Fourcas-Hosten Listrac r. ★★→★★★ 70 75 78′ 79 81 82′ 83′ 84 85 86′ 87 88 96-acre Cru Bourgeois currently considered the best of its commune. Firm wine with a long life.

La Gaffelière St-Em. r. ★★★ 70 79 81 82′ 83′ 85 86′ 87 88′

61-acre first-growth at the foot of the Côtes below Ch BEL-AIR. "Elegant", not rich wines, but justifying its reputation since '82 after a bad patch.

La Garde Graves r. (w. dr.) ★★ 75′ 78 79 81 82′ 83′ 84 85 86 88

Substantial ESCHENAUER property making reliably sound red.

Le Gay Pomerol r. ★★★ 70 75′ 76′ 78 79 82′ 83′ 85 86 88

Well-known 14-acre v'yd on the northern edge of Pomerol. Same owner as Ch LAFLEUR, different management since '85. Splendid wine.

Gazin Pomerol r. ★★★ 81 82 83 85 86 87 88

Large property (for Pomerol) with 58 acres. Not quite as splendid as its position next to PETRUS. 2nd label: Ch l'Hospitalet.

Gilette Sauternes w. sw. ★★★ 37 49 53 55 59 61 62

Extraordinary small Preignac château which stores its sumptuous wines in cask to a great age. Only about 5,000 bottles of each. Ch Les Justices is the sister-château.

Giscours Lab-Mar. r. ★★★ 70 71′ 75′ 76 78′ 79′ 81′ 82′ 83 84 85 86 87 88

Splendid 182-acre third-growth s. of CANTENAC. Dynamically run and making excellent vigorous wine in '70s. Recently distinctly lighter and patchy.

du Glana St-Jul. r. ★★ 81 82′ 83 85 86 88

Big Cru Bourgeois in centre of St-Julien. Undemanding; undramatic.

Gloria St-Jul. r. ★★★ 70′ 75′ 76 78′ 79 81 82′ 83 84 85 86 87 88

Outstanding Cru Bourgeois making wine of vigour and finesse, among classed-growths in quality. 110 acres. The owner, Henri Martin, bought Ch ST-PIERRE in 1982. Recent return to long-maturing style.

Grand-Barrail-Lamarzelle-Figeac St-Em. r. ★★ 75 78 79 81 82' 83 85 86 87 88   48-acre property near FIGEAC, incl. Ch La Marzelle. Well-reputed and popular, if scarcely exciting.

Grand-Corbin-Despagne St-Em. r. ★★ 70 75 78 79 81 82' 83 85 86 88   One of the biggest and best of the Grands Crus on the CORBIN plateau.

Grand Mayne St Em. ★★ 82 83 84 85 86 87 88   40-acre Grand Cru Classé on western Côtes. To watch.

Grand-Pontet St-Em. r. ★★ 82' 83 85 86' 87 88   Widely distributed 35-acre sister-château of Ch BEAU SEJOUR-BECOT; like it revitalized since '85. To watch.

Grand-Puy-Ducasse Pauillac r. ★★★ 75 78 79 81 82' 83 84 85 86 87 88   Well-known little fifth-growth bought in '71, renovated and enlarged to 90 acres under expert management. A best buy. 2nd label: Ch Artigues Arnaud.

Grand-Puy-Lacoste Pauillac r. ★★★ 75 78' 79' 81' 82' 83 84 85 86' 87 88   Leading fifth-growth famous for excellent full-bodied vigorous Pauillac. 110 acres among the "Bages" ch'x s. of the town, owned by the Borie family of DUCRU-BEAUCAILLOU. 2nd label: Lacoste-Borie.

Gravas Sauternes w. sw. ★★ 83' 85 86 88   Small Barsac property; impressive firm wine.

La Grave Trigant de Boisset Pom. r. ★★★ 75' 76' 78 79 81' 82' 83 84 85 86' 87 88   Verdant ch with small but first-class v'yd owned by Christian MOUEIX. Firm, beautifully structured Pomerol.

Gressier Grand Poujeaux Moulis. r. ★★★ 70 75' 78 79' 81 82 83' 84 85 86 87 88   Good Cru Bourgeois, neighbour of CHASSE-SPLEEN. Fine firm wine with a good track record.

Greysac Médoc r. ★★ 79' 81' 82 83 85 86 88   Elegant 140-acre property. Easy, early-maturing wines.

Gruaud-Larose St-Jul. r. ★★★ 70' 75' 76 78' 79 81 82' 83 84 85 86 87 88   One of the biggest and best-loved second-growths. 189 acres making smooth rich stylish claret. Owned by CORDIER. The excellent second wine is called Sarget de Gruaud-Larose.

Guadet-St-Julien St-Em. r. ★★ 82 83 85 86 88   Extremely well-made wines from v. small Grand Cru Classé.

Guiraud Sauternes (r.) w. sw. (dr.) ★★★ 70' 76 78' 79' 81 82 83' 84 85 86' 87 88   Newly restored classed-growth of top quality. 250+ acres. At best excellent sweet wine of great finesse and a small amount of red and dry white. The '86, '88 and '89 will be superb in time.

La Gurgue Margaux r. ★★ 79 81 82 83' 84 85 ' 86 87 88   Small (30-acre) well-placed property making Margaux of the fruitiest sort, recently bought by owners of Ch CHASSE-SPLEEN. To watch.

Hanteillan Cissac r. ★★ 81 82' 83 84 85' 86 87 88   Large (200+ acres) v'yd renovated and enlarged since 1973. Very fair bourgeois wine. Ch Larrivaux-Hanteillan is second quality. 50,000 cases.

Haut-Bages-Averous Pauillac r. ★★ 81 82 83 84 85 86 87   The second wine of Ch LYNCH BAGES. Delicious easy drinking.

Haut-Bages-Libéral Pauillac r. ★★ 75 78 81 82'83 84 85 86' 87 88   Lesser-known fifth-growth of 64 acres in same stable as CHASSE-SPLEEN since '83. The results are excellent, full of Pauillac vitality.

Haut-Bages-Monpelou Pauillac r. ★★ 75' 78 79 80 81 82' 83 84 85 86   25-acre Cru Bourgeois stable-mate of Ch BATAILLEY on former DUHART-MILON land. Good minor Pauillac.

Haut-Bailly Graves r. ★★★ 70' 78 79' 81' 82 83 84 85 86' 87 88   70+ acre estate at Léognan famous for ripe, round, intelligently made, sometimes "feminine" wine since '79. 2nd label: La Parde de H-B.

Haut-Batailley Pauillac r. ★★★ 70' 75' 78' 79 81 82' 83 84 85 86' 87 88   The smaller section of the fifth-growth Batailley estate: 49 acres. Often in a gentler vein than its sister ch, GRAND-PUY-LACOSTE. 2nd label La Tour-l'Aspic.

Haut-Brignon Premières Côtes r. and w. dr. ★
Big producer of standard wines at Cénac, owned by a major Champagne coop. Do not confuse with the next!

Haut-Brion Pessac, Graves r. (w.) ★★★★ 61 64 66 70′ 71′ 75′ 78′ 79′ 81 82′ 83 84 85′ 86′ 87 88 The oldest great ch of Bordeaux and the only non-Médoc first-growth of 1855. 108 acres. Reds of singular balance, particularly good since 1975. A little full dry white in 78 79 81 83 84 85 86 87 88. See Bahans-Haut-Brion, La Mission H-B.

Haut-Marbuzet St-Estèphe r. ★★ 75′ 78′ 79 80 81 82′ 83 84 85 86 87 88
One of the best of many good St-Estèphe Crus Bourgeois. 100 acres, mainly MERLOT. 2nd label Ch Tour de Marbuzet. CHAMBERT-MARBUZET, MacCarthy-Moula are in same hands. New oak gives them all classic style.

Haut-Pontet St-Em. r. ★★ 70 75 78 79 81 82′ 83 85 86 88
12-acre v'yd of the Côtes well deserving its Grand Cru status.

Haut-Quercus St-Em. r. ★★
Oak-aged cooperative wine to a very high standard.

Haut-Sarpe St-Em. r. ★★ 79 81 82 83′ 85 86 87 88
Grand Cru Classé (6,000 cases) with a very elegant château and park. Same owner as Ch LA CROIX, Pomerol.

Arguments for and against Decanting

Fierce arguments take place between wine-lovers over whether it is a good or a bad thing to decant wine from its bottle into a carafe. The argument in favour is that it allows the wine to "breathe" and its bouquet to expand: against, that its precious breath is dissipated – or at the least that it makes no difference.

Two additional practical reasons in favour concern old wine which has deposited dregs, which can be left in the bottle by careful decanting, and young wine being consumed before it is fully developed: thorough aeration helps to create the illusion of maturity. An aesthetic one is that decanters are handsome on the table.

Decanting is done by pouring the wine into another container very steadily until any sediment reaches the shoulder of the bottle. To see the sediment clearly hold the bottle's neck over a light bulb or a candle.

Hortevie St-Jul. r. ★★ 81 82 83 84 85′ 86 87 88
One of the few St Julien Crus Bourgeois. This tiny v'yd and its bigger sister TERREY-GROS-CAILLOU are shining examples. Needs bottle-age.

Houissant St-Estèphe r. ★★ 78 79 80 81 82 83 84 85 86 87 88
Typical, robust, well-balanced St-Estèphe Cru Bourgeois Exceptionnel, also called Ch Leyssac; well known in Denmark.

d'Issan Cant-Mar. r. ★★★ 70 75′ 78 79′ 81 82′ 83′ 84 85 86 87 88
Beautifully restored moated ch with 75-acre third-growth v'yd well known for fragrant, virile but delicate wine.

Kirwan Cant-Mar. r. ★★★ 78 79′ 81 82′ 83′ 84 85 86 87 88
Well-run 86-acre third-growth owned by SCHRÖDER & SCHYLER. New planting of '60s now mature and recent results tasting v. good.

Labégorce Margaux r. ★★ 75′ 78 79 81′ 82′ 83′ 84 85 86 87 88
Substantial 69-acre property north of Margaux with long-lived wines of true Margaux quality.

Labégorce-Zédé Margaux r. ★★ 75′ 78 79 81′ 82′ 83′ 84 85 86 87 88
Outstanding Cru Bourgeois on the road n. from Margaux. 62 acres. Typical delicate, fragrant Margaux, truly classic since '81. The same family as VIEUX-CHATEAU-CERTAN. 2nd label: Domaine Zédé.

Lacoste-Borie The second wine of Ch GRAND-PUY-LACOSTE.

Lafaurie-Peyraguey Sauternes w. sw. ★★★ 75′ 76′ 78′ 80 81′ 82 83′ 85 86 Fine classed-growth of only 49 acres at Bommes, belonging to CORDIER. After a lean patch, good, rich and racy wines.

Lafite-Rothschild Pauillac r. ★★★★ 70′ 75′ 76 78 79 81′ 82′ 83 84 85 86′ 87 88 First-growth of fabulous style and perfume in its great vintages, which keep for decades. Off-form for several years but resplendent since '76. Amazing circular cellars opened '87; joint ventures in Chile ('88) and California ('89). 2nd wine: MOULIN DES CARRUADES. 225 acres. Also owns Ch'x DUHART-MILON, RIEUSSEC.

Lafleur Pomerol r. ★★★ 70' 75' 78 81 82' 83' 85 **86 87** 88 89'
Property of 12 acres just n. of PETRUS. Resounding wine of the tannic, less "fleshy" kind. Same owner as LE GAY. MOUEIX oenology.

Lafleur-Gazin Pomerol r. ★★ 70 75' 78 **79 81** 82' **83** 85' **86 87** 88'
Distinguished small MOUEIX estate on the n.e. border of Pomerol.

Lafon-Rochet St-Est. r. ★★ 70' 75 79 **81** 82 83' 85 86' 87 88
Fourth-growth neighbour of Ch COS D'ESTOURNEL, restored in the '60s and again recently. 110 acres. Rather hard, dark, full-bodied St-Estèphe. Same owner as Ch PONTET-CANET. 2nd label: Numero 2.

Lagrange Pomerol r. ★★★ 70' 75' **78 81** 82' **83** 85' **86** 87 88
20-acre v'yd in the centre of Pomerol run by the ubiquitous house of MOUEIX. Maturing vines are giving deeper flavour.

Lagrange St-Jul. r. ★★★ 70' 75' 79 **81 82 83**/ **84 85**' **86 87** 88' 89
Formerly run-down third-growth inland from St-Julien, bought by Suntory in 1982. 123+ acres, restored to tip-top condition. To watch. Second label: Les Fiefs de Lagrange **83**' 85 **86 87** 88

La Lagune Ludon r. ★★★ 70' 75' 76' 78' 79 81 82' **83 84** 85 86' 87 88'
Well-run ultra-modern 160-acre third-growth in the extreme s. of the Médoc. Attractively rich and fleshy wines; usually brilliant quality.

Lalande-Borie St-Jul. r. ★★ **78 79 81 82 83 84 85** 86 87 88
A baby brother of the great DUCRU-BEAUCAILLOU created from part of the former v'yd of Ch LAGRANGE.

Lamarque Lamarque (Haut-Médoc) r. ★★ 75' **81**' **82 83**' **84** 85 86 87 88
Splendid medieval fortress of the central Médoc with 113 acres giving admirable and improving wine of high "Bourgeois" standard.

Lanessan Cussac (Haut-Médoc) r. ★★ 75' 78' **79 81** 82' 83 **84** 85 86' 87 88 Distinguished 108-acre Cru Bourgeois Exceptionnel just s. of St-Julien. Lots of flavour.

Langoa-Barton St-Jul. r. ★★★ 70' 75' 76 78' **79 81** 82' 83 **84** 85 86 87 88 49-acre third-growth sister-ch to LEOVILLE-BARTON. V. old and beautiful family property with impeccable standards, and value.

Larcis-Ducasse St-Em. r. ★★ 75' **81 82**' **83 84** 85' **86 87** 88
The top property of St-Laurent, eastern neighbour of St-Emilion, on the Côtes next to Ch PAVIE. 30 acres. Coasting.

Larmande St-Em. r. ★★ 75' 78 **79 81** 82 83 **84** 85 86 87 88
Substantial 54-acre property related to CAP-DE-MOURLIN. Replanted and now making rich, strikingly scented wine.

Laroque St-Em. r. ★★ 75' 78 **79 81** 82' **83 84** 85 86 88
Important 108-acre v'yd with an impressive mansion on the St-Emilion côtes in St Christophe.

Larose-Trintaudon St-Lau. (Haut-Médoc) r. ★★ 75' **81 82 83** 85 86' 87 88 The biggest v'yd in the Médoc: 388 acres. Modern methods make reliable fruity and charming Cru Bourgeois wine.

Laroze St-Em. r. ★★ 75' 79 **81 82 83** 85 **86 87** 88'
Big v'yd (74 acres) on the w. Côtes. Relatively light wines from sandy soil; soon enjoyable. Sometimes excellent.

Larrivet-Haut-Brion Graves r. (w.) ★★ 75' 76 79' **81 82**' 83 **84** 85 86 87 88 Little property at Léognan with perfectionist standards. Also 500 cases of white to age up to 5 years.

Lascombes Margaux r. (p.) ★★★ 70' 75' 78 **79 81** 82 83 **84** 85 86 87 88
240-acre second-growth owned by the British brewers Bass-Charrington and lavishly restored. After a poor patch, some new vigour since '82, but still not tasting like a 2nd growth. Second wine: Ch Segonnes.

Latour Pauillac r. ★★★★ 61 62 64 66 67 70' 71 73 75' 76' 78' 79 **80** 81' 82' 83 **84** 85 86' 87 88' First-growth. The most consistent great wine in Bordeaux, and probably the world: rich, intense and almost immortal in great years, almost always classical and pleasing even in bad ones. British-owned (though different company since '89). 150 acres sloping to the R. Gironde. Second wine LES FORTS DE LATOUR.

Latour à Pomerol Pomerol r. ******** 70′ 76′ 79′ 81′ 82 83 **84** 85′ **86** 87 88 89 Top growth of 19 acres under MOUEIX management. Pomerol of great power and perfume, yet also ravishing finesse.

des Laurets St-Em. r. ****** 75′ 78 **79 81 82 83 85 86** 88 Major property of Puisseguin and Montagne-St-Emilion (to the e.) with 160 acres (40,000 cases) on the Côtes. Sterling wine distributed by J.P. MOUEIX.

Laville-Haut-Brion Graves w. dr. ******** 75 76 78 **79 81 82 83**′ **84** 85 86 87 88 A tiny production of one of the very best white Graves for long maturing, made at Ch LA MISSION-HAUT-BRION.

Léoville-Barton St-Jul. r. ******* 61 66 70′ 75′ 76 78′ **79 80 81** 82′ 83 **84** 85 86 87 88 90-acre portion of the great second-growth Léoville v'yd in the Anglo-Irish hands of the Barton family for over 150 years. Powerful and classic claret; traditional methods. Major recent investment is raising already v. high standards.

Léoville-Las Cases St-Jul. r. ******** 61 66 70′ 75′ 76 78′ **79** 81 82′ 83 **84** 85′ 86′ 87′ 88 The largest portion of the old Léoville estate, 210 acres, with one of the highest reputations in Bordeaux. Elegant, complex, powerful but never heavy wines, built for immortality. Second label: Clos du Marquis.

Léoville-Poyferré St-Jul. r. ******* 75′ **79 81** 82′ 83 **84** 85 86′ 87 88 For years the least outstanding of the Léovilles; since 1980 again living up to the great name. '82 is a triumph and '86 even better. 156 acres. Second label: Ch Moulin-Riche.

Lestage Listrac r. ****** 81 82′ 83 **84 85** 86′ 87 88 130-acre Cru Bourgeois in same hands as Ch FONREAUD. Light, quite stylish wine, aged in oak since '85.

Liot Barsac w. sw. ****** 70′ 71 75′ 76 78 79′ **80 81** 83 **85 86** 88 Consistent fairly light golden wines from 94 acres.

Liversan St-Sau. (Haut-Médoc) r. ****** 75′ 78 **81** 82′ 83 **84** 85 86′ 87 88 116-acre Grand Cru Bourgeois inland from Pauillac. Change of regime in 1984 has greatly improved standards. Ch Fonpiqueyre is a second wine in certain markets.

Livran Médoc r. ****** 78′ **79** 81 82′ 83 85 88 Big Cru Bourgeois at St-Germain in the n. Médoc. Consistent round wines (half Merlot).

Loudenne St-Yzans (Médoc) r. ******* (r.) 78′ **81** 82′ 83 85 86′ 87 88 Beautiful riverside ch owned by Gilbeys since 1875. Well-made Cru Bourgeois red and a very agreeable dry white from 120 acres. The white is best at 2-3 years ('89 v.g.).

Loupiac-Gaudiet Loupiac w. sw. ****** **85 86 87** 88 89 Reliable source of good-value almost-Sauternes, just across the river Garonne. 7,500 cases.

La Louvière Graves r. and w. dr. ****** (r.) 78 **81** 82′ 83 **84** 85 86 87 (w.) 88 Noble 135-acre estate at Léognan. Excellent white for drinking or maturing, and red recently of classed-growth standard.

de Lussac St-Em. r. ****** 75′ 78′ **81 82 83** 85 **86** 88 One of the best estates in Lussac-St-Emilion (to the n.e.).

Lynch-Bages Pauillac r. ******* 61 66 70 75′ 78′ **79** 81 82′ 83′ **84** 85′ 86′ 87 88 Always popular, but now one of Pauillac's regular stars. 200 acres making rich robust wine: deliciously brambly; occasionally great. Recent vintages esp. notable. 2nd wine: HAUT-BAGES-AVEROUX.

Lynch-Moussas Pauillac r. ****** 75′ 78 79 81 82′ 83 **84** 85 86 88 Fifth-growth restored by the director of Ch BATAILLEY since 1969. Now 60+ acres and new equipment are making serious wine, gaining depth as the vines age, but only at high cru bourgeois level.

du Lyonnat Lussac-St-Em. r. **★★ 82 83 85 86'** 88
120-acre estate with well-distributed reliable wine.

Magdelaine St-Em. r. **★★★ 70' 71' 73 75 76 78 79 81** 82 83' 85' 86 87 88
89 Leading first-growth of the Côtes, 28 acres next to AUSONE owned by J-P MOUEIX. Beautifully balanced wine. On top form.

Magence Graves r. w. dr. **★★** (r.) w. dr.
Go-ahead 45-acre property at St Pierre de Mons, in the s. of the Graves. Distinctly SAUVIGNON-flavoured dry white, and fruity red. Both age well 2-6 years.

Malartic-Lagravière Graves r. and (w. dr.) **★★★** (r.) **70' 75' 76' 78 79 81** 82' 83 **84** 85 86' **87** 88 (w.) **79 81' 82 83 85 86** 87 88 89
Well-known Léognan classed-growth of 34 acres making well-structured, rather hard red and a very little excellent fruity SAUVIGNON white, hard to resist young, but well worth cellaring.

Malescasse Lamarque (Haut-Médoc) r. **★★ 78 79' 81 82 83** 85 86 87 88
Renovated Cru Bourgeois with 100 acres in a good situation, owned by M. Tesseron of Ch LAFON-ROCHET. 2nd label: Le Tana de M.

Malescot-St-Exupéry Margaux r. **★★★ 70' 75' 78' 79 81** 82' 83' **84** 85 86 **87** 88 Third-growth of 84 acres. Often tough when young, but eventually fragrant and stylish Margaux, if not of 3rd-growth class.

de Malle Sauternes r. w. sw./dr. **★★★** (w. sw.) **75 76 78 79 80 81' 82 83** 85 86' 88 Famous and beautiful ch with Italian gdns. at Preignac. 124 acres. Good sweet and dry w. and r. (Graves) Ch de CARDAILLAN.

de Malleret Haut-Médoc r. **★★ 82 83 84 85** 86 88
Big well-run Cru Bourgeois with beautiful château and park at Le Pian near Bordeaux. Reliable quality.

Maquin-St-Georges St-Em. r. **★★ 81 82 83 85** 86 88
Steady producer of delicious "satellite" St-Em. at St-Georges.

de Marbuzet St-Est. r. **★★ 75 78 79 81 82 83 84** 85 86 87 88
Effectively the second label of Ch COS D'ESTOURNEL, and correspondingly well made.

Margaux Margaux r. (w. dr.) **★★★★ 61 70 78' 79 80 81'** 82' 83' **84** 85 86' 87 88 First-growth (with 209 acres of vines), the most penetrating and fabulously perfumed of all in its (very frequent) best vintages. "Pavillon Rouge" **(81 82' 83' 84 85** 86 87 88) is the second wine. "Pavillon Blanc" is the best white (SAUVIGNON) wine of the Médoc, for up to 10 years' ageing (82, 83, 86).

Marquis-d'Alesme Margaux r. **★★ 75' 78 79 81 82 83 84** 85 86 88
Tiny (17-acre) third-growth, formerly made with Ch MALESCOT; independent since '79. Better than its reputation.

Marquis-de-Terme Margaux r. **★★★ 75' 79 81' 82 83** 85 86' 87 88
Renovated fourth-growth of 84 acres. Fragrant, fairly lean style has been replaced in '85, '86 by splendid big wines.

Martinens Margaux r. **★★ 75 78' 79' 81 82 83 84** 85 86 87 88
Worthy 75-acre Cru Bourgeois at Cantenac, re-equipped in '89.

Maucaillou Moulis r. **★★ 75' 78 79 81 82 83' 84** 85' 86' 87 88
130-acre Cru Bourgeois with cru classé standards, property of DOURTHE family. Full, richly fruity, "Cap de Haut-M." is second wine.

Meyney St-Est. r. **★★★→★★★★ 75' 78' 79 81** 82' 83 **84** 85 86 87 88
Big (125-acre) riverside property next door to Ch MONTROSE, one of the best of many steady Crus Bourgeois in St-Estèphe. Owned by CORDIER. Second label: Prieur de Meyney.

Millet Graves r. w. dr. **★★ 81 82 83 85** 86 88
160-acre estate at Portets; useful Graves.

La Mission-Haut-Brion Graves r. **★★★★ 61 64 66 71' 74 75' 76 78'** 79 81 82' 83 **84** 85' 86 87 88 Neighbour and long-time rival to Ch HAUT-BRION, since 1984 in the same hands. New equipment in '87. Serious and grand old-style claret for long maturing, usually "bigger" than Haut-Brion. 30 acres. Ch Latour-H-B is its second-quality wine.

Monbousquet St-Em. r. ★★ 75 78' 79' **81 82 83 84 85** 86 88
Fine 75-acre estate in the Dordogne valley below St-Emilion. Attractive early-maturing wine from deep gravel soil lasts well.

Monbrison Ar-Mar. r. ★★ **81** 82 **83 84** 85 86 **87** 88
A new name to watch in Margaux. Top bourgeois standards. 4,000 cases plus 2,000 of 2nd label, Ch. Cordet.

Montrose St-Est. r. ★★★ **61 66 70'** 75' 76 78 79 81 82' 83 **84** 85 86' 87 88 158-acre family-run second-growth well known for deeply coloured, forceful, old-style claret. But vintages between 78-86 (except '82) were far lighter. 2nd wine: La Dame de Montrose.

Moulin-à-Vent Moulis r. ★★ **70' 75' 78' 79 81** 82' **83 84** 85 86
60-acre property in the forefront of this booming appellation. Lively, forceful wine. La Tour Blanche (Médoc) has same owners.

Moulin des Carruades The second-quality wine of Ch LAFITE.

Moulin du Cadet St-Em. ★★ **75' 81 82' 83 85 86 87** 88 89
First-class little v'yd on the Côtes managed by MOUEIX.

Moulinet Pomerol r. ★★ 75 78 79 81 82 83 85 86 88
One of Pomerol's bigger ch'x, 43 acres on lightish soil; wine ditto.

Mouton-Baronne-Philippe Pauillac r. ★★★ **70' 75' 78' 79 81** 82' 83 **84** 85 86' 87 88 Substantial fifth-growth nurtured by the late Baron Philippe de Rothschild, 125 acres making gentler, less rich and tannic wine than MOUTON, but still outstanding in its class..

Mouton-Rothschild Pauillac r. ★★★★ **61 66 70' 71** 75' **76 78'** 79 81 82' 83 84 85 86' 87 88 Officially a first-growth since 1973, though for 40 years worthy of the title. 175 acres (87% CABERNET SAUVIGNON) make wine of majestic richness ('82 and '86 are imperial). Also the world's greatest museum of works of art relating to wine. Baron Philippe, the greatest champion of the Médoc, died in 1988, to be succeeded by his daughter Philippine.

Nairac Sauternes w. sw. ★★ **73** 75 76' 78 79 80 **81 82** 83' 85 86' 88
Barsac classed-growth with perfectionist owner. Fascinating wines to lay down.

Nenin Pomerol r. ★★★ **70'** 75' **78 83** 85' **86** 87 88
Well-known 66-acre estate; on an upsurge since '85.

Olivier Graves r. and w. dr. ★★ (r.) 79' **81 82 83 84** 85 86 88
90-acre classed-growth, surrounding a moated castle at Léognan. 9,000 cases r., 12,000 w., both in need of a promised upgrade. Recent wines are intended for longer maturing.

Les Ormes-de-Pez St-Est. r. ★★ **75' 78'79 81'** 82' 83' **84** 85 86' 87 88
Outstanding 72-acre Cru Bourgeois managed by Ch LYNCH BAGES. Increasingly notable full-flavoured St-Estèphe.

Les Ormes Sorbet Médoc r. ★★ **81 82 83** 85 86 87 88
Emerging smaller producer of good solid red aged in new oak at Couquèques. 2nd label: Ch de Conques.

Palmer Cant-Mar. r. ★★★★ **61' 66' 70 71'** 75'76 78' 79' 81 82 83' **84** 85 86' 87 88 The star ch of CANTENAC; a third-growth often on a level just below the first-growths. Wine of power, flesh and delicacy. 110 acres with Dutch, British and French owners. 2nd wine: Réserve du Général (value).

Pape-Clément Graves r. and (w. dr.) ★★★ 75' 78' 82' **83 84 85'** 86 87 88
Ancient v'yd at Pessac, with record of seductive, scented not ponderous reds, but recent vintages less even. New resolve since '85 (and more white).

Patache d'Aux Bégadan (Médoc) r. ★★ 79' **81 82' 83'** 85 86' **87** 88
90-acre Cru Bourgeois of the n. Médoc. Fragrant, largely Cabernet, wine.

Paveil-de Luze Margaux r. ★★ **75' 78 79 81 82' 83 84** 85 86' **87** 88
Old family estate at Soussans. Small but highly regarded.

Pavie St-Em. r. ★★★ **75' 78 79' 81** 82' 83' **84** 85' 86 87 88
Splendidly sited first-growth of 92 acres on the slope of the Côtes.

Typically rich and tasty St-Em., particularly since '82. The family owns the smaller Ch'x PAVIE-DECESSE and La Clusière.

Pavie-Decesse St-Em. r. ★★ 24 acres

Pavie-Macquin St-Em. r. ★★ 75 78 79 82 83 85' 86 87 88
Reliable 25-acre Côtes v'yd e. of St-Em. New energy since '86.

Pedesclaux Pauillac r. ★★ 75' 78 81 82' 83 **84** 85 86 88
50-acre fifth-growth on the level of a good Cru Bourgeois. Solid strong wines loved by Belgians. Grand-Duroc-Milon and Bellerose are second labels.

Petit-Village Pomerol r. ★★★ 75' 78 79 81 82' **83 84** 85 86 88
One of the best-known little properties: 26 acres next to VIEUX-CH-CERTAN, same owner as Ch COS D'ESTOURNEL. Powerful plummy wine.

Petrus Pomerol r. ★★★★ 61 64 66 67 70' 71' 73 75' 76' 78 79' 80 81 82' 83 **84** 85' 86 87 88' 89' The great name of Pomerol. 28 acres of gravelly clay giving massively rich and concentrated wine. 95% Merlot vines. Each vintage adds lustre (84 and 87 were in tiny quantities). The price, too, is legendary.

Peyrabon St-Sauveur r. ★★ 75 78 81 82 83 **84** 85 **86 87** 88
Serious 82-acre Cru Bourgeois popular in the Low Countries.

Peyreau St-Em. r. ★★
Sister-ch of CLOS L'ORATOIRE.

de Pez St-Est. r. ★★★ 66 70' 75' 76 78' 79 81 82' 83 **84** 85 86 87 88 Outstanding Cru Bourgeois of 60 acres. As reliable as any of the classed growths of the village, and nearly as fine. Needs v. long storage. (e.g. '66 was ideal in '88.)

Phélan-Ségur St-Est. r. ★★ 75' 81 82' 85 86
Big and important Cru Bourgeois (125 acres) with some fine old vintages. New owners in 1985 have put their foot down hard.

Pichon-Longueville, Baron de Pichon-Longueville Pauillac r. ★★★ 79' 81 82' 83 **84** 85 86' 87 88 77-acre second-growth whose wines have varied widely. Under new and highly ambitious management since '87. Revitalised wine-making matched by spectacular building programme.

Pichon-Longueville, Comtesse de Lalande Pauillac r. ★★★★ 61 66 70' 75' 76 78' 79' 80 81' 82' 83' **84** 85 86 87 Second-growth neighbour to Ch LATOUR. 148 acres. Consistently among the very top performers; classic long-lived wine of fabulous breed, even in lesser years. 2nd wine: Réserve de la Comtesse. Rivalry from across the road (last entry) wil be fun to watch.

Pique-Caillou Graves r. ★★ 85 86 87 88
Near Bordeaux airport. Recently refurbished and worth watching. Also next-door Ch. Chênevert.

Pindefleurs St-Em. r. ★★ 79 81 82' 83 85 **86** 88
Steady 25-acre v'yd on the St-Emilion plateau.

Piron Graves (r.) w. dr. ★★
Producer of seductively fruity modern white Graves at St Morillon.

de Pitray Castillon r. ★★ 81 82 83 85 86 87 88
Substantial (62 acre) v'yd on the Côtes de Castillon e. of St-Emilion. Good flavoursome, chewy wines.

Plagnac Médoc r. ★★ 79 81 82 83 85 86 88
Cru Bourgeois at Bégadan restored by CORDIER. To follow.

Plince Pomerol r. ★★ 75 79 80 81 82 83 85 **86** 88
Reputable 20-acre property near Libourne. Attractive, perhaps rather simple wine from sandy soil.

La Pointe Pomerol r. ★★→★★★ 81 82 83' 85 **86** 87 88
Prominent 63-acre estate, well made, but relatively spare of flesh until '86, when a new consultant started work. Ch LA SERRE is in the same hands.

Pontac-Monplaisir Graves r. (w. dr.) ★★ 85 86 87 88 89
Another Graves property suddenly offering delicious white wine.

Pontet-Canet Pauillac r. ✱✱✱ 70 75′ 78′ 79′ 80 81′ 82′ 83′ 85 86 87 88
One of the biggest classed-growths. 182 acres, neighbour to MOUTON. Dragged its feet for many years. Current owners (same as LAFON-ROCHET) have re-equipped and shown new resolve since '85. Expect potent long-lived wines. 2nd label: Les Hauts de Pontet.

Potensac Potensac (Médoc) r. ✱✱ 78′ 79 81′ 82′ 83 84 85′ 86 87 88
The best-known Cru Bourgeois of the n. Médoc. The neighbouring Ch'x Lassalle and Gallais-Bellevue belong to the same family, the Delons, owners of LÉOVILLE-LASCASES. Class shows.

Pouget Margaux ✱✱ 70′ 75 78 79 81 82′ 83 85 86 87 88
19-acre v'yd attached to Ch BOYD-CANTENAC. In 1983 separate chais were built. Similar, rather lighter, wines.

Poujeaux (Theil) Moulis r. ✱✱ 70′ 75′ 76 78 79′ 81 82′ 83′ 84 85 86 87
88 Family-run Cru Exceptionnel of 120 acres. 20,000-odd cases of characterful, tannic and concentrated wine for a long life. 2nd label: La Salle de Poujeaux. Also Ch Arnauld (83′).

Prieuré-Lichine Cant-Mar. r. ✱✱✱ 70 75 76 78 79′80 81 82′ 83′ 84 85
86′ 87 88 143-acre fourth-growth brought to the fore by the late Alexis Lichine since 1952. Excellent full-bodied and fragrant Margaux.

Puy-Blanquet St-Em. r. ✱✱ 75′ 81 82′ 83 85 86 88
The major property of St-Etienne-de-Lisse, e. of St-Emilion, with over 50 acres. Early-maturing St-Em., if behind the leaders.

Puy-Razac St-Em. r. ✱✱ 78 79 81′ 82′ 83 85 86 88
Tiny brother to MONBOUSQUET at the foot of the Côtes near Ch PAVIE.

Puygueraud Côte de Francs r. ✱✱ 82 83 85 86 87 88
Leading ch of this rising district. Wood-aged wines of surprising class.

Rabaud-Promis Sauternes w. sw. ✱✱ 75 76 78 79 81 83 85 86 88 89
74-acre classed-growth at Bommes. Little seen outside France.

Rahoul Graves r. and w. dr. ✱✱ (r.) 78′ 81 82 83 85 86 87 88 (w.) 85 86′
87 88 37-acre v'yd at Portets making particularly good wine in the '80s from maturing vines; 80% red. White is aged in oak, too.

Ramage-la-Batisse Haut-Médoc r. ✱✱ 75′ 78 79 81 82 83′ 86 87 88
Potentially outstanding Cru Bourgeois of 130 acres at St-Sauveur, west of Pauillac. Increasingly attractive since '85. Ch. Tourteran is 2nd wine.

Rausan-Ségla Margaux r. ✱✱✱ 70′ 81 82 83′ 84 85 86′ 87 88
106-acre second-growth; famous for its fragrance; a great Médoc name trying hard to regain its rank. New British owners in '89.

Rauzan-Gassies Margaux r. ✱✱ 61 75′ 78′ 79′ 82 83 85 86 87 88
75-acre second-growth neighbour of the last with little excitement to report for two decades, now seemingly perking up – but still far to go.

Raymond-Lafon Sauternes w. sw. ✱✱✱ 75 76 78′ 79 80′ 81′ 82 83′ 85
86′ 87 88 Serious Sauternes estate run by the ex-manager of Ch D'YQUEM. Splendid wines for long ageing. Among the top Sauternes today.

de Rayne-Vigneau Sauternes w. sw. ✱✱✱ 67 71′ 76′ 78 81 83 85 86 88
164-acre classed-growth at Bommes. Standard sweet wine and a little dry, "Raynesec". New equipment in 1980: looking better.

Respide-Médeville Graves (r.) w. dr. ✱✱ (w.) 83 84 85 86 87 88
One of the better unclassified white-wine ch'x. Full-flavoured wines for ageing. (N.B. '85 Cuvée Kauffman).

Reynon Premières Côtes de Bordeaux r. and w. dr. ✱✱
100 acres producing extraordinary dry white from very old Sauvignon vines ("Vieilles Vignes": 85 86 87 88 89). Also "CLOS FLORIDÈNE" barrel-fermented white (86 87′ 88 89) and red since '85, D.Y.A. white and serious red (82 83 85 86).

Reysson Vertheuil Haut-Médoc r. ✱✱ 81 82′ 83 84 85 86 87 88
Recently replanted, up-and-coming 120-acre Cru Bourgeois with the same owners as Ch CHASSE-SPLEEN.

Ricaud Loupiac w. sw. (or dr.) or r. ★★ **81 82 83' 85 86'** 88 89
> Substantial grower of Sauternes-like dessert wine, just across the river. New owners are working hard.

Rieussec Sauternes w. sw. ★★★ **70 71' 75' 76' 80** 81' **82** 83' 85 86 87 88 89 Worthy neighbour of Ch D'YQUEM with 136 acres in Fargues, bought in 1984 by the (Lafite) Rothschilds. Not the sweetest; can be exquisitely fine. Also dry "R" and super-wine "Crême de Tête".

Ripeau St-Em. r. ★★ **75 78 79 81 82 83** 85 86 **87** 88
> Increasingly high-performance Grand Cru in the centre of the plateau. 49 acres.

La Rivière Fronsac r. ★★ **85 86** 87 88
> The biggest and most impressive Fronsac property. Tannic but juicy wines win prizes in youth and stay youthful for a decade.

de Rochemorin Graves r. (w. dr.) ★★ **81 82 83 84** 85 86 87 88
> An important restoration at Martillac by the owner of CH LA LOUVIÈRE. 165 acres of new vines promise great things.

Romer du Hayot Sauternes w. sw. ★★ **79 80 81 82 83** 85 **86'** 88 89
> A minor classed-growth with a growing reputation.

Roquetaillade-la-Grange Graves r. w. dr. ★★
> Substantial estate establishing a name for fine red (s.) Graves.

Roudier Montagne-St-Em. r. ★★
> 75-acre "satellite" St-Em. with the flavour of the real thing.

Rouget Pomerol r. ★★ **75' 76'** 78 **79 81** 82' 83 85' **86** 88
> Attractive old estate with rising standards on the n. edge of Pomerol.

Royal St-Emilion Brand name of the important and dynamic growers' cooperative. See also Haut Quercus, Berliquet.

Ruat-Petit-Poujeaux Moulis r. ★★ **79 81 82 83 84 85** 86 87 88
> 45-acre v'yd gaining in reputation for vigorous wine.

St-André Corbin St-Em. r. ★★ **75' 78 79 81** 82' 83' **84** 85 86 87 88
> Considerable 54-acre property in Montagne-St-Emilion with a long record of above-average wines.

St-Bonnet Médoc r. ★★
> Big n. Médoc estate at St-Christoly. V. flavoury wine.

St-Estèphe, Marquis de St-Est. r. ★ **81 82 83 84 85** 86
> The growers' cooperative; over 200 members. Good value.

St-Georges St-Geo., St-Em. r. ★★ **75 79 81 82 83 85 86** 87 88
> Noble 18th-century ch overlooking the St-Emilion plateau from the hill to the n. 125 acres; v. good wine sold direct to the public.

St-Georges-Côte-Pavie St-Em. r. ★★ **79 81 82 83'** 85' **86** 88
> Perfectly placed little v'yd on the Côtes. Run with dedication.

Saint-Pierre St-Jul. r. ★★★ **70 75' 78 79 81'** 82' 83' **84** 85 86 87 88
> Small (50-acre) fourth-growth many years in Belgian ownership; bought in 1982 by Henri Martin of Ch GLORIA. A name to follow.

St-Pierre Graves (r.) w. dr. ★★ **81 84 85 86 87** 88 89
> Mainstream white Graves of notable character and flavour.

de Sales Pomerol r. ★★★ **75' 81 82' 83 85 86 87** 88
> The biggest v'yd of Pomerol (116 acres), attached to the grandest château. Not poetry but excellent prose. Second labels: Ch Chantalouette and Ch du Delias.

Sénéjac Haut-Médoc r. (w. dr.) ★★ **75 76' 78 79 81 82' 83' 84** 85 **86'** 87 88
> 60-acre Cru Bourgeois in s. Médoc run by a New Zealander with zeal and new equipment. 2nd label Dom. de l'Artigue. All-Sémillon white to age.

La Serre St-Em. r. ★★ **81 82 83 85** 86 87 88
> Small Gr. Cru, same owner as LA POINTE. Fresh approach since '86.

Sigalas-Rabaud Sauternes w. sw. ★★★ **76' 78 79 81 82** 83' **85** 86 88 89
> The lesser part of the former Rabaud estate: 34 acres in Bommes, usually making first-class sweet wine in a fresh, grapey style.

Siran Lab-Mar. r. ★★★ **61 66 70 75' 78'79 81'** 82' **83 84** 85 86 87 88
> 74-acre property of Cru Classé quality. Elegant, long-lived wines.

Smith-Haut-Lafitte Graves r. and (w. dr.) ★★→★★★ (r.) **82' 83 84 85 86**
88 89 (w: age 2-3 years.) Classed-growth at Martillac restored in the
'70s. New British owners (same as RAUSAN-SÉGLA) in '89. 122 acres
(14 of white). The white wine is light and fruity; the red light. Recent
efforts have improved matters.

Sociando-Mallet Haut-Médoc r. ★★ **70 75 78 79 81** 82 83 **84** 85 86 88
Splendid Cru Grand Bourgeois at St-Seurin in the n. 65 acres.
Conservative big-boned wines to lay down.

Soutard St-Em. r. ★★ 70' **71 75' 76 78' 79 80 81 82' 83** 85' 86 87 88
Excellent reliable 48-acre classed-growth. A long-term keeper.

Suduiraut Sauternes w. sw. ★★★ **67 70 75 76' 78 79' 81 82' 83 84 85** 86
88' 89 One of the best Sauternes – though rarely super-rich. Over
173 acres of the top class. Selection: Cuvée Madame **(82, 85)**.

Taillefer Pomerol r. ★★ **70 75 78 79 81 82' 83** 85 86 88
24-acre property on the edge of Pomerol owned by another branch
of the MOUEIX family. Give it time.

Talbot St-Jul. r. (w.) ★★★ **70' 75' 78'79 81** 82' 83 **84 85** 86' **87** 88'
Important 240-acre fourth-growth, sister-ch to GRUAUD-LAROSE, wine
similarly attractive: rich, satisfying, reliable and good value. (V.g)
second label: Connétable Talbot. White is called "Caillou Blanc".

Tayac Sou-Mar. r. ★★ **81 82 83** 85 86 88
Margaux's biggest Cru Bourgeois. Reliable if not noteworthy.

Terrefort-Quancard Bordeaux r. w. dr. ★★ **82 83 84 85** 86
Huge producer of good value wines at St-André-de-Cubzac. Rocky
sub-soil contributes to surprising quality. 33,000 cases.

du Tertre Ar-Mar. r. ★★★ **70' 75 78 79' 81** 82' 83' **84** 85 86 **87** 88'
Fifth-growth, isolated s. of Margaux; restored to excellence by the
owner of CALON-SÉGUR. Fragrant and long-lived.

Le Tetre-Rôteboeuf St Em. ★★★ **85 86** 87 88
A new star making concentrated, even dramatic wine since '83.

Tertre-Daugay St-Em. r. ★★★ **78 79 81** 82' 83' 85 **86**
Small, spectacularly sited, Grand Cru. Restored to its proper place
since purchase in '78 by the owner of LA GAFFELIÈRE.

Thieuley Entre-Deux-Mers r. p. w. dr. ★★
Substantial supplier, esp. of "clairet" (rosé) and grapey SAUVIGNON.

Timberlay Bordeaux r. (w. dr.) ★ **82 83 85 86 87** 88
The biggest property of Cubzac; 185 acres. Pleasant light wines.

Toumilon Graves r. w. dr ★★
Notable ch in St-Pierre-de-Mons. Fresh and charming r. and w.

La Tour-Blanche Sauternes w. sw. (r.) ★★★ **75' 76 79 81' 83' 85** 86 87 88
Not among the leaders for a long time. But since '83 v.g.

La Tour-Carnet St-Lau. r. ★★ **79 80 81 82' 83 84** 85 86' 87 88   Fourth-
growth reborn from total neglect. Lightish, pretty wine. ('86 is bolder).

La Tour de By Bégadan (Médoc) r. ★★ **78' 79' 81** 82' **83 84** 85 86 87
88' Very well-run 144-acre Cru Bourgeois in the n. Médoc steadily
increasing its reputation for sturdy, impressive yet appealing wine.

La Tour-de-Mons Sou-Mar r. ★★ **70' 75' 78 81** 82' **83** 85 86' 87 88'
Distinguished Cru Bourgeois of 75 acres, three centuries in the same
family. After a dull patch, five good vintages in a row.

La Tour-du-Pin-Figeac St-Em. r. ★★
26-acre Grand Cru worthy of restoration.

La Tour-du-Pin-Figeac-Moueix St-Em. r. ★★ **81 82 83** 85 **86** 88
Another 26-acre section of the same old property, owned by a branch
of the famous MOUEIX family. Looking good, not inspired.

La Tour-Figeac St-Em. r. ★★ **75 81 82'** 83 85 **86** 88
34-acre Grand Cru between Ch FIGEAC and Pomerol, not quite showing
the form that such a site suggests.

La Tour-Haut-Brion Graves r. ★★★ **70 75 78 79 81** 82' **83** 85 86 87 88
Formerly 2nd label of LA MISSION-HAUT-BRION. Up to '83 a plainer, very
tannic wine for long life. Now a separate v'yd, and easier wines.

La Tour-Martillac Graves r. and w. dr. ★★ (r.) 75'78 79 81 82' 83 **84** 85 86 **87** 88 Small but serious property at Martillac. 10 acres of white grapes; 37 of black. The white can age admirably. The owner, Jean Kressmann, is resurrecting the neighbouring Ch Lespault.

La Tour St-Bonnet Médoc r. ★★ 78' 79 81 82' 83 85 86 87 87 88 Consistently well-made n. Médoc from St-Christoly. 100 acres.

La Tour du Haut Moulin Cussac (Haut-Médoc) r. ★★ 78 79 80 81 82 83 **84** 85 86 88 Little-known property; concentrated wines to age.

Tournefeuille Lalande de Pomerol r. ★★ 75' 78 81' 82' 83' 85' 86 88 Best-known chateau of Néac. 43 acres making very sound wine.

des Tours Montagne-St-Em. r. ★★ 82 83 85 86 87 88 Spectacular ch with modern 170-acre v'yd. Sound, easy wine.

Toutigeac, Domaine de Entre-Deux-Mers r. (w. dr) ★ Enormous producer of useful Bordeaux at Targon.

Tronquoy-Lalande St-Est. r. ★★ 70 75 78 79 81 82' 83 85 86 88 40-acre Cru Bourgeois making typical high-coloured St-Estèphe needing long ageing. Distributed by DOURTHE.

Troplong-Mondot St-Em. r. ★★ 82' 83 85 86 88 70-acre Grand Cru well sited on the Côtes above Ch PAVIE. To watch.

Trotanoy Pomerol r. ★★★★ 61' 70' 71' 73 75' 76' 78 79 81 82' 83 84 85 86' 87 88' 89' Perhaps the second Pomerol after PETRUS, from the same stable. Only 27 acres but a glorious fleshy perfumed wine.

Trottevieille St-Em. r. ★★★ 79' 82' 83 85 86 88 Grand Cru of 27 acres on the Côtes. Dragged its feet for years. '83 '85 '86 look better. Same owners as BATAILLEY. To watch.

Le Tuquet Graves r. and w. dr. ★★ 81 82 83 85 86 87 88 Big estate at Beautiran. Light fruity wines; the white better.

Verdignan Médoc r. ★★ 79 81 82 83 85 86 87 88 Substantial Grand Bourgeois sister property to Ch COUFRAN. More Cabernet than Coufran; Jack Sprat and his wife.

Vieux-Château-Certan Pomerol r. ★★★ 75 78 79 80 81 82' 83 84 85 86' 87 88 Traditionally rated close to PETRUS in quality, but totally different in style; almost Médoc build. 34 acres. Same (Belgian) family owns LABEGORCE-ZEDE and another tiny Pomerol, Le Pin.

Vieux-Château-Landon Médoc r. ★★ 82 83 85 86 88 Up-to-date grower of vigorous wine worth keeping 3-4 years.

Vieux-Château-St-André St-Em. r. ★★ 75' 78 79' 81 82' 83 85' 86 87 88 Small v'yd in Montagne-St-Emilion owned by the leading winemaker of Libourne. To follow. 2,500 cases.

Villegeorge Avensan r. ★★ 81 82 83' 85 86 87' 88 24-acre Cru Exceptionnel to the n. of Margaux with the same owner as Ch BRANE-CANTENAC. Enjoyable rather tannic wine.

Villemaurine St-Em. r. ★★ 81 82' 83 84 85' 86 88 Small Grand Cru with splendid cellars well sited on the Côtes by the town. Firm wine with a high proportion of Cabernet.

Vraye-Croix-de-Gay Pomerol ★★★ 75' 81 82' 83 85 86 88 Very small ideally situated v'yd in the best part of Pomerol.

Yon-Figeac St-Em. r. ★★ 81 82 83 85 86 88 59-acre Grand Cru to follow for savoury and scented wine.

d'Yquem Sauternes w. sw. (dr.) ★★★★ 67' 71' 73 75' 76' 77 78 79 80 81 82 83' 84 86 The world's most famous sweet-wine estate. 250 acres making only 500 bottles per acre of very strong, intense, luscious wine kept 4 years in barrel. Most vintages improve for at least 15 yrs. Also dry "Ygrec" in 78 79 80 84 85 86 (v. little) 87 88.

More Bordeaux châteaux are listed under Canon-Fronsac, Côtes de Bourg, Cubzac, Fronsac, Côtes-de-Castillon, Côtes de Francs, Lalande de Pomerol, Loupiac, Ste-Croix-du-Mont, Premières Côtes de Blaye, Premières Côtes de Bordeaux in the A-Z of France, pages 26-55.

Switzerland has no truly great wines, but almost all (especially whites) are enjoyable and satisfying – and very expensive. Switzerland has some of the world's most efficient and productive vineyards. Costs are high and nothing less is viable. All the most important are in French-speaking Switzerland, along the south-facing slopes of the upper Rhône valley and Lake Geneva, respectively the Valais and the Vaud. Wines from German-and Italian-speaking zones (see map) are mostly drunk locally. Wines are known by place-names, grape-names, and legally controlled type-names. All three, with those of leading growers and merchants, appear in the following list. D.Y.A.

Aigle Vaud w. dr. ★★→★★★★
    Principal town of CHABLAIS, between L. Geneva and the VALAIS. Dry CHASSELAS whites: at best strong and well balanced.
Amigne Traditional white grape of the VALAIS. Heavy but tasty wine, usually made dry.
Arvine Another old VALAIS white grape, similar to the last; perhaps better. Makes good dessert wine. Petite Arvine is similar.
Auvernier Neuchâtel r. p. w. dr. (sp.) ★★
    Village s. of NEUCHÂTEL known for light PINOT NOIR, CHASSELAS and OEIL DE PERDRIX.
Blauburgunder PINOT NOIR: grown in German-speaking Switzerland.
Bonvin Old-established growers and merchants at SION.
Chablais Vaud (r.) w. dr. ★★→★★★
    The district between Montreux on L. Geneva and Martigny where the Rhône leaves the VALAIS. Good DORIN whites. Best villages: AIGLE, YVORNE, Bex, Ollon, VILLENEUVE.
Chasselas The principal white grape of French-speaking areas, neutral in flavour but taking remarkable local character. Known as FENDANT in VALAIS, DORIN in VAUD and PERLAN round Geneva.
Clevner (or Klevner) Another name for BLAUBURGUNDER.
Completer Rare Grisons (see map) grape giving liquorous wine.
Cortaillod Neuchâtel r. (p. w.) ★★
    Village near NEUCHÂTEL specializing in light PINOT NOIR reds.
Côte, La N. shore of L. Geneva from Geneva to Lausanne. V. good DORIN, OEIL DE PERDRIX, SALVAGNIN. Best villages incl. Féchy, Rolle, Mont-sur-Rolle, Luins, Aubonne, Coppet, Morges, Prangins, Perroy, Vufflens.

Dézaley Vaud w. dr. ★★★

  Best-known village of LAVAUX, between Lausanne and Montreux.
  Steep s. slopes to the lake make fine, strong, fruity DORIN. Dôle
  Blanche is a kind of rosé, akin to Baden's Weissherbst.

Dôle Valais r. ★★

  Term for red VALAIS wine of PINOT NOIR or GAMAY or both grapes,
  reaching a statutory level of strength and quality.

Dorin Vaud w. dr. ★★

  Obsolescent name for CHASSELAS wine in the VAUD, the equivalent of
  FENDANT from the VALAIS. Most wines are known by village names.

Epesses Vaud w. dr. and r. ★★

  Well-known lakeside village of LAVAUX. Good dry DORIN.

Ermitage VALAIS name for white wine from MARSANNE grapes. Rich,
  concentrated and heavy; usually dry.

Fendant Valais w. dr. ★→★★★

  The name for CHASSELAS wine in the VALAIS, where it reaches its ripest,
  strongest and smoothest. SION is the centre. All too easy to swallow.

Flétri Withered, late-picked grapes for making sweet wine, often
  MALVOISIE.

Gamay The Beaujolais grape; makes pretty thin wine.

Glacier, Vin du Almost legendary long-matured white stored at high
  altitudes. Virtually extinct today.

Goron Red VALAIS wine that fails to reach the DOLE standard.

Grand Cru Vaudois term for estate wines from top areas.

Hallau Main wine village of Schaffhausen in N. Switz.

Hammel Major merchant and grower of LA COTE at Rolle with wide range
  of good value wines. One of the few exporters.

Herrschaft Grisons r. (w. sw.) ★→★★★

  District near the border of Austria and Liechtenstein. Small amount
  of light PINOT NOIR reds and a few sweet whites.

Humagne Old VALAIS grape. Some red Humagne is sold: decent country
  wine. The strong white is a rare speciality.

Johannisberg The Valais name for SYLVANER, which can make excellent
  stiff, dense and high-flavoured dry wine here, comparable to
  Frankenwein (see Germany).

Lausanne, Ville de Producer of fine wines in surrounding villages for
  centuries (e.g Clos des Moines, la Côte and Clos des Abbayes, Lavaux),
  now incl. late-harvest CHARDONNAY.

Lavaux Vaud r. w. dr. ★→★★★

  The n. shore of L. Geneva between Lausanne and Montreux. The e.
  half of the VAUD. Best villages for CHASSELAS, lively and generous, incl.
  DEZALEY, RIEX, CORSEAUX, EPESSES, Villette, Lutry, ST-SAPHORIN.

Légèrement doux Most Swiss wines are dry. Any with measurable sugar
  must be labelled thus or as "avec sucre résiduel".

Malvoisie VALAIS name for PINOT GRIS. Makes some wonderful late-picked
  sweet wines.

Mandement Geneva r. (p.) w. dr. ★

  Wine district just w. of Geneva, (see Vin-Union-Genève). Very light
  reds, chiefly GAMAY, and whites (PERLAN and increasingly Chardonnay).

Marsanne The white grape of Hermitage on the French Rhône, used in
  the VALAIS to make ERMITAGE.

Merlot Bordeaux red grape (see Grapes for red wine) used to make the
  better wine of Italian Switzerland (TICINO). See also Viti.

Mont d'Or, Domaine du Valais w. dr. sw. ★★★★

  Often considered the best wine estate of Switzerland: 60 acres of
  steep hillside near SION. Good FENDANT, JOHANNISBERG, AMIGNE, etc., and
  real Riesling. Very rich concentrated wines.

Montreux The town's v'yds make some of the best CHASSELAS of the Vaud,
  juicy, ripe and resonant.

Neuchâtel Neuchâtel r. p. w. dr. sp. ★→★★★
    City and the wine from the n. shore of its lake. Pleasant light PINOT
    NOIR and attractive sometimes sparkling CHASSELAS.

Nostrano Word meaning "ours" applied to the lesser red wine of the
    TICINO, made from a mixture of native and Italian grapes, in contrast
    to MERLOT from Bordeaux.

Oeil de Perdrix Pale rosé of PINOT NOIR.

Orsat Long-established wine firm at Martigny, VALAIS, recently changed
    hands. See next entry.

Orsat, J. A. and P. L. Members of the original Orsat family have started
    this firm to maintain high standards and good value in FENDANT, etc.

Perlan Geneva w. dr. ★
    The MANDEMENT name for the ubiquitous CHASSELAS, here at its palest,
    driest and least impressive.

Provins The excellent central cooperative of the VALAIS.

Rèze The grape, now very rare, used for VIN DU GLACIER.

Riesling-Sylvaner Swiss name for MÜLLER-THURGAU, common in e. Swit-
    zerland (Thurgau), where it was bred by Dr. Müller. "A prophet is not
    without honour . . ."

Rivaz Vaud r. w. dr. ★★
    One of the better known villages of LAVAUX.

St-Saphorin Vaud w. dr. ★★
    One of the principal villages of LAVAUX: wines drier and more austere
    than DEZALEY or EPESSES.

Salvagnin Vaud r. ★→★★
    Red VAUD wine of tested quality: the equivalent of DOLE.

Savagnin Swiss name for the TRAMINER, called Païen in the VALAIS.

Schafiser Bern (r.) w. dr. ★→★
    The n. shore of L. Bienne (Bielersee) is well known for very dry and
    light CHASSELAS sold as either Schafiser or Twanner.

Schenk, S.A. The biggest Swiss wine firm, based at Rolle in the VAUD, with
    570 acres as well as other world-wide interests.

Sion Valais w. dr. ★→★★
    Centre of the VALAIS wine region, famous for its FENDANT.

Sierre Important centre for some of the best VALAIS wines.

Spätburgunder PINOT NOIR: by far the commonest grape of German-
    speaking Switzerland, making very light wines.

Testuz, V. & P. Well-known growers and merchants at Dézaley, LAVAUX.

Thurgau E. Switz. canton beside Bodensee. BLAUBURGUNDER and RIESLING
    SYLVANER, best v'yds: Weinfelden, Ottoberg, Arenenberg

Ticino Italian-speaking s. Switzerland. Recent trials with Cabernet, Sauv
    Bl, Semillon. See Merlot, Viti, Nostrano.

Twanner See Schafiser.

Valais The Rhône valley between Brig and Martigny. Its n. side is an
    admirable dry sunny and sheltered v'yd, planted mainly to the
    CHASSELAS grape, which here makes its most potent wine.

Vaud The region of L. Geneva. Its n. shore is Switzerland's biggest v'yd
    and in places as good as any. DORIN and SALVAGNIN are the main wines.

Vétroz Valais (r.) w. dr. ★★
    Village near SION in the best part of the VALAIS.

Villeneuve Top-rate village for CHASSELAS between Montreux and the
    CHABLAIS slopes of YVORNE.

Vevey Town near Montreux with a famous wine festival once every 30-
    odd years. The last was in 1977.

Vin-Union-Genève Big growers' cooperative at Satigny in the MANDEMENT.
    Light Gamay reds and white PERLAN are Geneva's local wine.

Viti Ticino r. ★★
    Legal designation of better-quality TICINO red, made of MERLOT and
    with at least 12% alcohol.

Yvorne Village near AIGLE with some of the best CHABLAIS v'yds.

Italy

Sangevesi grape go
castello de Ama Chianti
classica

VALLE D'AOSTA

PIEMONTE
LIGUR

Switzerland

Turin

Mila

Genoa

Italian wine at the start of the 1990s is in a revolutionary state. The 30-year-old DOC system, the basis of the country's wine laws, is more or less discredited. Its original purpose, of defining Italy's myriad winemaking traditions, is increasingly seen more as hindrance than help when most of the best winemakers are experimenting with untraditional ideas, grape varieties and techniques.

A Denominazione di Origine Controllata (DOC) is granted by the government in Rome to any grower or growers who can plead convincingly for a distinctive regional style and claim that it is "traditional". Once in place, a DOC stultifies progress – and has very little bearing on quality. Most regions can make more attractive (and saleable) wine by adopting the international top-selling grape varieties than by persisting with Italy's indigenous but often degenerate types. Sangiovese and the rest can be very good; but it takes time and trouble to select and propagate the best vines. So to plant Cabernet is a short-cut.

Ironically the only appellation available to non-DOC wines, however good, is the most basic of all: vino da tavola, or plain table wine. The confidence of good growers in their new products is such that they wear this apparent stigma as a talisman. As always it is the maker's name that matters most.

Meanwhile the DOC system remains, for all its faults, the only general key to the Italian wine maze. It is the approximate equivalent of France's Appellations Contrôlées. Most of Italy's traditional wines have defined areas and standards under the system. A few, like Chianti Classico, it must be said, had them long before. An increasing number, however, have not – and DOCs have been granted to many areas of only local interest: so the mere existence of a DOC proves little. The entries in this book ignore a number of unimportant DOCs and include considerably more non-DOCs. They also include a larger number of grape-name entries.

Italian wines are named in a variety of ways: some geographical, some historical, some merely whimsical, and many of the best from their grapes. These include old "native" grapes such as Barbera and Sangiovese and more and more the international favourites. Many of the DOCs, particularly in the north-east, are area names applying to widely different wines from more than a dozen different varieties. No overall comment on the quality of such a diversity is really possible, except to say that general standards are rising steadily and a growing number of producers have proved themselves outstanding.

The best advice to buyers of Italian wine in 1990 and 1991 is to be bold. Do not cling limply to familiar names like Valpolicella. Look for distinctive labels on designer bottles – and be prepared to pay more for quality.

The map is the key to the province names used for locating each entry. The following abbreviations are used in the text.

Abr. Abruzzi	**Camp.** Campania	**Lat.** Latium
		Lig. Liguria
Apu. Apulia	**Em-Ro.** Emilia Romagna	**Lom.** Lombardy
		Mar. Marches
Bas. Basilicata		**M.** Molise
	Fr-VG. Fruili-Venezia-	**Piem.** Piemonte
Cal. Calabria	Giulia	**Sard.** Sardinia
		Sic. Sicily
		Tr-Aad. Trentino-Alto-Adige
		Tusc. Tuscany
		Umbr. Umbria
		V d'A. Valle d'Aosta
		Ven. Veneto

Abbazia di Rosazzo Leading estate of COLLI ORIENTALI. White Ronco delle Acacie and Ronco di Corte and red Ronco dei Roseti are v.g. single v'yd wines.

Abboccato Semi-sweet.

Adanti Umbrian maker of v.g. Sagrantino di MONTEFALCO; also V.D.T. Rosso d'Arquata, outstanding BARBERA/Canaiolo/MERLOT blend.

Aglianico del Vulture Bas. DOC r. (s/sw. sp.) ★★★ 82 85 86 87 88 Among the best wines of s. Italy. Ages well to rich aromas. Called Vecchio after 3 yrs, Riserva after 5. Top grower: Fratelli D'Angelo, also makes v.g. pure Aglianieno V.D.T., "Canneto".

Alba Major wine-centre of PIEMONTE.

Albana di Romagna Em-Ro. DOCG w. dr. s/sw. (sp.) ★★★ D.Y.A. Absurdly Italy's first DOCG for white wine. Produced for several centuries in Romagna from Albana grapes. Cold fermentation now robs it of what little character it had. Fattoria PARADISO makes some of the best. AMABILE is often better than dry. Fattoria ZERBINA's botrytis-affected PASSITO is outstanding.

Alcamo Sic. DOC w. dr. ▨ Soft neutral whites from w. Sicily. Rapitalà is the best brand.

Aleatico Red, slightly muscat-flavoured grape, chiefly of the south.

Aleatico di Gradoli Lat. DOC r. sw. or f. ★★ Aromatic, fruity; alcohol: 17.5%. Made near Viterbo.

Aleatico di Puglia Apu. DOC r. sw. or f. ★★ Aleatico grapes make good dessert wine in limited quantities. Two distinct types have 15% or 18.5% alcohol.

Alezio Apu. DOC (r.) p. dr. ★★ 85 86 87 88 89 Recent DOC at Salento, esp. for delicate rosé.

Allegrini Top-quality producer of Veronese wines, incl. VALPOLICELLA from prime new v'yds.

Altesino Highly regarded estate producing BRUNELLO DI MONTALCINO and V.D.T. Palazzo Altese.

Alto Adige Tr-Aad. DOC r. p. w. dr. sw. sp. ★★→★★★ A DOC covering some 19 different wines, usually named after their grape varieties, in 33 villages round Bolzano.

Ama, Castello di Modern CHIANTI CLASSICO estate nr. Gaiole. San Lorenzo and Bellavista are excellent top wines. V.g. CHARDONNAY, SAUVIGNON, MERLOT (Vigna L'Apparita) and pure PINOT NERO.

Amabile Semi-sweet, but usually sweeter than ABBOCCATO.

Amaro Bitter. When prominent on a label the content is a "bitters".

Amarone See Recioto.

Anghelu Ruju Port-like version of CANNONAU from Sella & Mosca in Sardinia.

Anselmi, Roberto A leader in SOAVE with his single v'yd Capitel Foscarino and exceptional sweet dessert RECIOTO dei Capitelli.

Antinori Immensely influential, long-established Tuscan house of the highest repute producing first-rate CHIANTI (esp. PEPPOLI, Tenute Marchese Antinori and BADIA A PASSIGNANO), and ORVIETO. Distinguished for pioneering new V.D.T. styles: e.g. TIGNANELLO, SOLAIA, Cervaro DELLA Sala. See also Sassacaia.

Argusto Oak-aged DOLCETTO from VILLA BANFI.

Arneis Piem. w. dr. ★★ D.Y.A. Revival of this ancient wine is much in vogue. Now DOC under Roero, a zone n. of Alba. Good producers incl. Bruno GIACOSA, Castello di Neive, Blangé (Ceretto).

Artimino Ancient hill-town w. of Florence, known for its DOC CARMIGNANO.

Assisi Umbr. r. (w. dr.) ★★ D.Y.A. Rosso and Bianco di Assisi are very attractive V.D.Ts. Drink cool.

Asti Major wine-centre of PIEMONTE.

Asti Spumante Piem. DOC w. sp. ★★★ NV Sweet and very fruity muscat sparkling wine. Low in alcohol.

Avignonesi MONTEPULCIANO house with range of excellent wines incl. VINO NOBILE, blended red Grifi, first-rate CHARD, SAUV BL., MERLOT and superlative VIN SANTO.

Azienda agricola (or agraria) A farm producing crops, often incl. wine.

Azienda vinicola or casa vinicola Wine firm using bought-in grapes.

Azienda vitivinicola A (specialized) wine estate.

Badia a Coltibuono 71 75 82 83 85 86 88
Fine Chianti-maker at Gaiole with a restaurant and remarkable collection of old vintages. Also V.D.T. "Sangioveto" 80 81 82 83 85 86 88

Banfi See Villa Banfi.

Barbacarlo Lomb. r. dr. or sw. sp. ★★ 85 86 88 Delicate wines with slightly bitter after-taste, from Oltrepò Pavese.

Barbaresco Piem. DOCG r. dr. ★★★→★★★★ 78 79 82 85 86 87 88 89
Neighbour of BAROLO from the same grapes but lighter, ageing sooner. At best deep, palate-cleansing, subtle and fine. At 4 yrs becomes Riserva. Best producers incl. GAJA, Bruno GIACOSA, Marchesi di Gresy, Produttori del B, Castello di Neive, CERETTO.

Barbera Dark acidic red grape, the second most planted in Italy after SANGIOVESE; a speciality of Piemonte also used in Lombardy, Emilia-Romagna and other northern provinces. Its best wines are:

Barbera d'Alba Piem. DOC r. dr. ★★→★★★★ 82 83 84 85 86 87 88 89
Tasty, tannic, fragrant red. Superiore can age 7 years. Round ALBA, NEBBIOLO is sometimes added to make a VINO DA TAVOLA. Top growers incl. GAJA, Prunotto, A. CONTERNO.

Barbera d'Asti Piem. DOC r. dr. ★★→★★★★ 82 83 84 85 86 87 88 89
To many the best of the Barberas; all Barbera grapes; tangy and appetizing, drunk young or aged up to 7 years. Top growers incl. Bertelli, Chiarla-Duca d'Asti, Carnevale.

Barbera del Monferrato Piem. DOC r. dr. ★ 85 86 87 88 89
From a large area in the province of Alessandria and ASTI. Pleasant, slightly fizzy, sometimes sweetish.

Barberani Leading ORVIETO producer; Calcaia is sweet, botrytis-affected.

Bardolino Ven. DOC r. dr. (p.) ★★ D.Y.A.
Pale, light, slightly bitter red from e. shore of La Garda. Bardolino Chiaretto is even paler and lighter. Top maker: Riccardi.

Berlucchi, Guido Italy's biggest producer of sparkling METODO CLASSICO, at FRANCIACORTA. Steady quality.

Barolo Piem. DOCG r. dr. ★★★→★★★★★ 78 79 82 83 85′ 86 87 88 89
Small area s. of Turin with one of the highest-rated Italian red wines, dark, rich, alcoholic (minimum 13°), dry but deep in flavour. From NEBBIOLO grapes. Ages for up to 15 yrs, Riserva after 5. Best producers incl. VIETTI, GIACOSA, CONTERNO, Pio Cesare, Marcarini, MASCARELLO, CERETTO, PRUNOTTO, CORDERO, RATTI, Rinaldi, ROCCHE DEI MANZONI, FONTANA FREDDA, Sandrone, Voerzio, Altare, Clerico. The coop "Terre del Barolo" is also good.

Bellavista Franciacorta estate rivalling CA'DEL BOSCO for sparkling wines (notable Crémant), with good V.D.T. reds from CABERNET and Pinot Noir.

Beradenga-Felsina Top CHIANTI CLASSICO estate, plus fine V.D.T. Fontalloria.

Bertani Well-known producers of quality Veronese wines (VALPOLICELLA, VALPANTENA, SOAVE, etc.), including aged AMARONE.

Bianco White.

Bianco d'Arquata Umbr. w. dr. ★★ 87 88 89
A limpid and inspiring light and fruity white from near Perugia.

Bianco di Custoza Ven. DOC w. dr. (sp.) ★★ D.Y.A.
Twin of SOAVE from w. of Verona often rivals or surpasses it in quality.

Bianco di Pitigliano Tusc. DOC w. dr. ★ D.Y.A.
A soft, fruity, lively wine made near Grosseto.

Bianco Vergine della Valdichiana Tusc. DOC w. dr. ★ D.Y.A.

Pale dry light wine from Arezzo. But what music in the name.

Bigi, Luigi & Figlio Famous producers of ORVIETO and other wines of Umbria and Tuscany. Their Torricella v'yd produces v.g. dry Orvieto.

Biondi-Santi The original producer of BRUNELLO with cellars in MONTALCINO (Siena). His Il Greppo v'yd is only 45 acres. Prices are v. high but ancient vintages unique.

Boca Piem. DOC r. dr. ★★ 82 85 86 88 89

From same grape as BAROLO in n. of PIEMONTE. See VALLANA.

Bolla Famous Veronese firm producing VALPOLICELLA, SOAVE, etc. Top wines: Jago, Castellaro (one of the v. best Soaves).

Bonarda Minor red grape widely grown in PIEMONTE and Lombardy.

Bonarda (Oltrepò Pavese) Lomb. DOC r. dr. ★★ 86 87 88

Soft, fresh, pleasant red from south of Pavia.

Bosca PIEMONTE producers of ASTI SPUMANTE and Vermouths.

Boscarelli, Poderi Small estate with v.g. VINO NOBILE DI MONTEPULCIANO.

Botticino Lomb. DOC r. dr. ★★ 85 86 87 88 89

Rare, strong, full-bodied rather sweet red from Brescia.

Brachetto d'Acqui Piem. DOC r. sw. (sp.) ★★ D.Y.A.

Sweet sparkling red with enticing muscat aroma. Only 7% alcohol.

Bramaterra Piem. DOC. r. dr. ★★ 82 85 86 88 89

A stylish addition to Piemonte's reds. NEBBIOLO grapes predominate.

Breganze Ven. DOC ★→★★★ 82 83 85 86 88

A catch-all for many varieties around Vicenza. CABERNET and PINOT BIANCO are best. Top producer: MACULAN.

Bricco dell'Uccellone Piem. r. dr. ★★★ 82 83 85 86 87 88 89

Barrique-aged BARBERA from firm of Giacomo Bologna. Bricco della Bigotta is another.

Bricco Manzoni Piem. r. ★★★ 82 85 86 88 89

Excellent blend of NEBBIOLO and BARBERA from Monforte d'Alba.

Brolio One of the oldest (c. 1200) and most famous CHIANTI CLASSICO estates, now owned by a British group. Good whites as well as red.

Brunello di Montalcino Tusc. DOCG r. dr. ★★★★ 71 75 79 80 81 82 83 85 86 88 With BAROLO, Italy's most celebrated red wine. Strong, full-bodied, high-flavoured and long-lived. After 5 yrs is called Riserva. Produced for over a century 25 miles s. of Siena. Top producers incl. BIONDI-SANTI, CAPARZO, Case Basse, Altesino, Costanti, Il Poggione, VILLA BANfi. Fattoria dei Barbi, Col d'Orcia, LISINI. N.B. ROSSO DI MONTALCINO is a less expensive alternative.

Brusco dei Barbi Piem. r. dr. ★★ 85 86 87 88

Lively variant on BRUNELLO, using old Chianti *governo* method.

Ca'del Bosco FRANCIACORTA estate making some of Italy's v. best sparkling wine, CHARDONNAY, and excellent reds (Pinot Noir, MAURIZIO ZANELLA and FRANCIACORTA).

Cabernet Much used in n.e. Italy and increasingly in Tuscany and the S.

Cacchiano, Castello di First-rate CHIANTI CLASSICO estate at Gaiole.

Cafaggio, Villa A solid CHIANTI CLASSICO estate with a good red V.D.T. called Solatio Basilica.

Caldaro or Lago di Caldaro Tr-Aad. DOC r. dr. ★→★★ D.Y.A.

Alias KALTERERSEE. Light, soft, slightly bitter-almond red. Classico from a smaller area is better. From south of Bolzano.

Caluso Passito Piem. DOC w. sw. (f.) ★★★

Made from Erbaluce grapes left to partly dry; delicate scent, velvety taste. Tiny production from a large area. Best from Vittorio Borrato.

Cannonau di Sardegna Sard. DOC r. (p.) dr. or s/sw. ★★ 85 86 87 88

Cannonau is Sardinia's basic red grape; its wine often formidably strong (min. 13.5% alc.). Less potent Cannonaus without the DOC can be easier to like.

Cantina 1. Cellar or winery. 2. Cantina Sociale = growers' coop.

Capannelle Good producer of Tuscan V.D.T. (formerly CHIANTI CLASSICO), though overrated and overpriced.

Caparzo, Tenuta MONTALCINO estate with excellent BRUNELLO La Casa; also CHARDONNAY and red blend Ca'del Pazzo.

Capezzana, Tenuta di (or Villa) The Tuscan estate of the ancient Contini Bonacossi family, producers of excellent CHIANTI MONTALBANO and CARMIGNANO. Also a Bordeaux-style red, GHIAIE DELLA FURBA.

Carpenè Malvolti Leading producer of classic PROSECCO and other sp. wines at Conegliano, Veneto.

Capri Camp. DOC r. w. p. ★
Widely abused name of the famous island. Better to drink e.g. RAVELLO.

Carema Piem. DOC r. dr. ★★ **82 85** 86 88 89
Old speciality of N. PIEMONTE, NEBBIOLO grapes traditionally fermented Beaujolais-style before crushing. (See France: macération carbonique.) More conventional today. Best from Luigi Ferrando (or the coop).

Carmignano Tusc. DOC r. dr. (p. br.) ★★★ **82 83 85 86** 87 88
Section of CHIANTI using 10% of CABERNET to make increasingly good, and some very fine, wine. See Capezzana. DOCG imminent.

Carso r-VG. DOC r. w. dr. D.Y.A.
DOC near Trieste includes good MALVASIA. Terrano del C. is a soft REFOSCO-like red.

Casa fondata nel . . . Firm founded in .

Castel del Monte Apu. DOC r. p. w. dr. ★★ **83 84 85 86** 87 88
Dry, fresh, well-balanced southern wines. The red becomes Riserva after 3 yrs. Rosé most widely known. Il Falcone stands out.

Castel San Michele Tr-Aad. r. dr. ★★ **85 86 87** 88
A good red made of CABERNET and MERLOT grapes by the Trentino Agricultural College near Trento.

Castellare Small but admired CHIANTI CLASSICO producer with first-rate Sangiovese V.D.T. I Sodi di San Niccoló and sprightly Governo del Castellare, a modern version of old-style Chianti.

Castell'in Villa v.g. Chianti Classico estate.

Castello della Sala ANTINORI'S estate at ORVIETO. Borro is regular white. Top wine is Cervaro della Sala: CHARDONNAY and GRECHETTO aged in oak (**86 87** 88)

CAVIT CAntina VITicultori, a group of good-quality coops near Trento.

Cellatica Lomb. DOC r. dr. ★★ **88 89**
Light red with slightly bitter after-taste of Schiava grapes.

Cerasuolo Abr. DOC p. dr. ★★
The rosato version of MONTEPULCIANO D'ABRUZZO.

Ceretto High-quality grower of v. expensive BARBARESCO, BAROLO, etc. Barb is called Bricco Asili, Barolo Bricco Rocche.

Cervaro see Castello della Sala.

Cerveteri Lat. DOC w. dr. s/sw. ★ **87 88**
Sound wines produced n.w. of Rome between Bracciano and the sea.

Chardonnay Has recently joined permitted varieties for several n. Italian DOCs. Some of the best (e.g. GAJA) are still only VINI DA TAVOLA.

Chianti Tusc. DOC r. dr. ★→★★ **85 86 87 88**
The lively local wine of Florence. Fresh but warmly fruity when young, still locally sold in straw-covered flasks. Variously age-worthy. Montalbano, RUFINA and Colli Fiorentini, Senesi, Aretini, Colline Pisane are sub-districts. RUFINA is recommended.

Chianti Classico Tusc. DOCG r. dr. ★→★★★ **82 83 85 86 87** 88 Senior Chianti from the central area. Many estates make powerful slightly astringent wine. Riservas (after 3 yrs) often have the bouquet of age in oak. Members of the Consorzio use the badge of a black rooster, but several top firms do not belong.

Chianti Putto Tusc. DOCG r. dr. ★→★★★★
  Often high-quality Chianti from a league of producers outside the
  Classico zone. Neck-label is a pink and white cherub.

Chiaretto Rosé (the word means "claret") produced esp. around Lake
  Garda. See Bardolino, Riviera del Garda.

Cinqueterre Lig. DOC w. dr. or sw. or pa. ★★
  Fragrant fruity white made for centuries near La Spezia. The PASSITO
  is known as Sciacchetrà.

Cinzano Major Vermouth company also known for its ASTI SPUMANTE from
  PIEMONTE and Floria MARSALA. Owns MONTALCINO estate of Col d'Orcia.

Cirò Cal. DOC r. (p.w.) dr. ★★ 83 85 86 87 88 89
  Very strong red, fruity white (to drink young).

Classico Term for wines from a restricted area within the limits of a DOC.
  By implication, and often in practice, the best of the region.

Collavini, Cantina Quality producers of COLLIO, COLLI ORIENTALI and GRAVE
  DEL FRIULI wines: PINOT GRIGIO, RIESLING, MERLOT, PINOT NERO and sp.

Colle Picchioni Estate s. of Rome making the best MARINO white; also red
  (CAB/MERLOT) V.D.T., Vigna del Vassallo, perhaps Latium's best.

Colli Means "hills" in many wine-names.

Colli Albani Lat. DOC w. dr. or s/sw. (sp.) ★→★★ D.Y.A.
  Soft fruity wine of the Roman hills.

Colli Berici Ven. DOC r. w. p. dr. ★★ 85 86 88
  CABERNET is the best wine of these hills south of Vicenza.

Colli Bolognesi Em-Ro. DOC r. p. w. dr. ★★ D.Y.A. (w.) 85 86 87 88
  From the hills s.w. of Bologna. Six possible grape varieties. Terre
  Rosse is top estate.

Colli del Trasimeno Umb. DOC r. w. dr. ★★ 85 86 87 88
  Lively wines from the province of Perugia.

Colli di Catone Reliable producer of FRASCATI.

Colli Euganei Ven. DOC r. w. dr. or s/sw. (sp.) ★ 87 88
  A DOC applicable to 7 wines produced s.w. of Padua. Red is adequate;
  white and sparkling sweet and pleasant.

Colli Orientali del Friuli r-VG. DOC r. w. dr. or sw. ★★→★★★★ 85 86
  88 89 18 different wines are produced under this DOC on the hills
  east of Udine and named after their grapes, esp v.g. whites.

Colli Piacentini Tusc. DOC r. p. w. dr. ★→★★★
  DOC incl. traditional GUTTURNIO and Monterosso Val d'Arda among 11
  types grown round Piacenza. Good fizzy MALVASIA.

Collio (Goriziano) Fr-VG. DOC r. w. dr. ★★→★★★★ 85 86 88 89
  12 different wines named after their grapes from a small area
  between Udine and Gorizia nr. the Yugoslav border. V.g. whites.

Coltassala Tusc. r. dr. ★★★ 82 83 85 86 87 88
  Notable V.D.T. red of SANGIOVESE from the ancient CHIANTI CLASSICO
  estate of CASTELLO DI VOLPAIA at Radda. "Balifico " includes Cabernet.

Coltiva – Gruppo Italiano Vini Complex of coops and wineries, now
  apparently world's third largest producer. Sells 10% of all Italian
  wine.

Conterno, Aldo and Giacomo Highly regarded growers of BAROLO, etc,
  with separate estates at Monforte d'Alba.

Contratto Piemonte firm known for ASTI SPUMANTE, BAROLO, etc.

Copertino Apu. DOC r. dr (p.) ★★ 82 85 86 87 88
  Savoury and age-worthy dark red of NEGROAMARO from the heel of
  Italy.

Cordero di Montezemolo-Monfallettu Tiny producer of top-class BAROLO.

Cori Lat. DOC w. r. dr./sw. ★ D.Y.A.
  Soft and well-balanced wines made 30 miles south of Rome.

Cortese di Gavi See Gavi.

Cortese (Oltrepò Pavese) Lomb. DOC w. dr. ★→★★ D.Y.A.
  Delicate fresh white from western Lombardy.

Corvo-Duca di Salaparuta Sic. r. w. dr. ★★ 85 86 87 88 89
> Popular Sicilian wines. Sound dry red, pleasant soft whites. Excellent new "barrique" red called Duca Enrico from Nero d'Avola grapes.

Costanti, Emilio Tiny estate producing top-quality BRUNELLO DI MONTALCINO.

d'Albola, Castello Famous CHIANTI CLASSICO estate owned by ZONIN.

D'Ambra Well-known producer of ISCHIA and other wines of that island.

Darmagi Piem. r. dr. ★★★★ 82 83 85 86 87 88 89
> CABERNET SAUVIGNON grown in a choice plot in BARBARESCO by GAJA has become Piemonte's most discussed and admired "foreign" (V.D.T.) red.

Decugnano dei Barbi Top ORVIETO estate with an ABBOCCATO version known as "Pourriture Noble" and a good red V.D.T.

Di Majo Norante Molise's lone star with v.g. Biferno DOC MONTEPULCIANO and white Falanghina under the Ramitello label. Also lighter, more aromatic Molí. Fine value.

Dolce Sweet.

Dolceacqua See Rossese di Dolceacqua.

Dolcetto Popular low-acid red grape of PIEMONTE, the everyday wine of BAROLO and BARBARESCO-producing areas, giving its name to:

Dolcetto d'Acqui Piem. DOC r. dr. ★ 88 89
> Pale, quick-maturing table wine from s. of ASTI.

Dolcetto d'Alba Piem. DOC r. dr. ★★ 88 89
> Among the best Dolcetti, with a trace of bitter-almond.

Dolcetto di Diano d'Alba Piem. DOC ★★ 88 89
> A rival to Dolcetto d'Alba; often more potent.

Dolcetto di Dogliani Piem. DOC r. ★★ 88 89
> Often regarded as the top Dolcetto sub-region.

Dolcetto di Ovada Piem. DOC r. dr. ★★ 85 86 87 88 89
> Reputedly the sturdiest and longest-lived of Dolcetti.

Donnafugata Sic. r. w. ★★ 87 88 89
> Sound red and zesty white from the Belici hills near Agrigento.

Donnaz Vd'A. DOC dr. ★★ 82 85 86 88 89
> A mountain NEBBIOLO, fragrant, pale and faintly bitter. Aged for a statutory 3 yrs. Now part of the VALLE D'AOSTA regional DOC.

Elba Tusc. r. w. dr. (sp.) ★ 85 86 87 88 89
> The island's white is drinkable with fish. Decent dry red.

Enfer d'Arvier Vd'A. DOC r. dr. ★★ 85 86 88 89
> Alpine speciality (cf. DONNAZ); pale, pleasantly bitter, light red.

Enoteca "Wine library". There are many; the impressive original being the Enoteca Italiana of Siena. Also used for wine shops.

Erbaluce di Caluso See Caluso Passito.

Est! Est!! Est!!! Lat. DOC w. dr. or s/sw. ★ D.Y.A.
> Soft fruity white from Montefiascone, n. of Rome that has traded for centuries on its odd-ball name.

Etna Sic. DOC r. p. w. dr. ★→★★ 87 88 89
> Wine from the volcanic slopes. The red is warm, full, balanced and can age well; the white is distinctly grapey. See Villagrande.

Falerio dei Colli Ascolani Mar. DOC w. dr. ★ D.Y.A.
> Made near Ascoli Piceno. Pleasant, fresh, fruity; a summer wine.

Falerno del Massico Camp. DOC r. w. dr. ★★ 88 89
> As Falernum, one of the best-known wines of ancient times. Strong red from Aglianico, fruity white from Falanghina, improving in quality.

Fara Piem. DOC r. dr. ★★ 82 85 86 88 89
> Good NEBBIOLO wine from Novara, n. PIEMONTE. Fragrant; worth ageing. Small production.

Faro Sic. DOC r. dr. ★★ 86 87 88 89
> Rare strong Sicilian red, made in sight of the Straits of Messina.

Fazi-Battaglia Well-known producer of VERDICCHIO, etc.

Felluga Brothers Livio and Marco (Russiz Superiore) have separate companies in the COLLIO and COLLI ORIENTALI. Both highly esteemed.

Ferrari Firm making some of Italy's best dry sparkling wines by the champagne method near Trento, Trentino-Alto Adige.

Fiano di Avellino Cam. w. dr. ★★→★★★ **87 88 89**
Considered the best white of Campania, smooth, pale, dry but not otherwise remarkable. Only from MASTROBERADINO.

Fiorano Lat. r. w. dr. s/sw. ★★ **81 82 83 85 86** 87 88
Interesting Roman reds of CABERNET and MERLOT.

Flaccianello della Pieve See Fontodi.

Florio The major producer of Marsala, controlled by CINZANO.

Foianeghe Tr-Aad. r. ★★
Trentino CABERNET/MERLOT red to age 7-10 years.

Folonari Large run-of-the-mill merchant at Brescia, Lombardy.

Fontana Candida One of the biggest producers of FRASCATI. Single v'yd Santa Teresa stands out.

Fontanafredda One of the biggest producers of Piemontese wines, incl. BAROLO from single v'yds and a range of ALBA DOCs. Also v.g. sp. wines.

Fonterutoli High-quality CHIANTI CLASSICO estate at Castellina with noted V.D.T. Concerto.

Fontodi Rising CHIANTI CLASSICO estate producing one of Italy's most highly regarded V.D.T. in Flaccianello della Pieve.

Franciacorta Pinot Lomb. DOC w. (p.) dr. (sp.) ★★→★★★
Pleasant soft white and some v.g. sparkling wines made of PINOT BIANCO, NERO OR GRIGIO and CHARD. CA'DEL BOSCO is outstanding. Bellavista, Monte Rossa and Cavalleri also v.g.

Franciacorta Rosso Lomb. DOC r. dr. ★★ **85 86 87 88**
Lightish red of mixed CABERNET and BARBERA from Brescia.

Frascati Lat. DOC w. dr. s/sw. sw. (sp.) ★→★★★ D.Y.A.
Best-known wine of the Roman hills: should be soft, ripe, golden, tasting of whole grapes. Most is disappointingly neutral today: look for dated wines from small producers (e.g. Conte Zandotti, Villa Simone, Colli Catone or single v'yd Santa Teresa from Fontana Candida). The sweet version is known as Cannellino.

Freisa Piem. r. dr. s/sw. or sw. (sp.) ★★ D.Y.A.
Sometimes sweet, often FRIZZANTE red, said to taste of raspberries and roses. With enough acidity it can be highly appetizing.

Frescobaldi Ancient noble family, leading pioneers of CHIANTI PUTTO at NIPOZZANO, e. of Florence. Also white POMINO and PREDICATO SAUV BLANC (Vergena) and CABERNET (Mormoreto). See also Montesodi.

Friuli-Venezia Giulia The n.e. province on the Yugoslav border. Many wines; the DOCs COLLIO and COLLI ORIENTALI include most of the best.

Frizzante Semi-sparkling; used to describe wines such as LAMBRUSCO.

Gaja Old family firm at BARBARESCO with inspired direction. Top-quality (and price) Piemonte wines, esp. BARBARESCO (single v'yds Sori Tildin, Sorì San Lorenzo, Costa Russi). Now setting trends with excellent CHARDONNAY (Gaia & Rey **84 85 86** 87 88), CABERNET (DARMAGI) and SAUV BLANC. Vignarey is excellent BARBERA.

Galestro Tusc. w. dr. ★
Name for v. light grapey white from shaley soil in Chianti country.

Gambellara Ven. DOC w. dr. or s/sw. (sp.) ★ D.Y.A.
Neighbour of SOAVE. Dry wine similar. Sweet (known as RECIOTO DI GAMBELLARA) agreeably fruity. Also VIN SANTO.

Gancia Famous ASTI SPUMANTE house from Piemonte, also produces vermouth and dry sparkling wines. New Torrebianco estate in Apulia is making good V.D.T. whites; CHARDONNAY, SAUVIGNON, PINOT BIANCO.

Garganega The principal white grape of SOAVE.

Garofoli Notable style in VERDICCHIO Macrina and Serra Fiorese; also champenoise. ROSSO CONERO Piancarda and Grosso Agontano are outstanding.

Gattinara Piem. DOC r. dr. ★★→★★★ 78 79 82 85 86 88 89
  Very tasty big-scale BAROLO-type red from northern PIEMONTE. Made
  from NEBBIOLO, locally known as Spanna. Best are Monsecco and
  single v'yd wines from Antoniolo.

Gavi (or Cortese di Gavi) Piem. w. dr. ★★→★★★ 87 88 89 (usually
  D.Y.A.) At best substantial yet subtle dry white of Cortese grapes.
  La Scolca is best known, Castello di Tassarolo top quality, La
  Giustiniana and Tenuta San Pietro admirable. But high prices rarely
  justified.

Ghemme Piem. DOC r. dr. ★★→★★★ 82 85 86 88 89
  Neighbour of GATTINARA, capable of Bordeaux-style finesse. Best is
  Antichi Vigneti di Cantalupo.

Ghiaie della Furba Tusc. r. dr. ★★★ 82 83 85 86 88
  Bordeaux-style CABERNET blend from the admirable Tenuta di
  CAPEZZANA, CARMIGNANO.

Giacobazzi Well-known producers of LAMBRUSCO near Modena.

Giacosa, Bruno Inspired loner making excellent BARBARESCO, BAROLO and
  other Piemonte wines at Neive (Cuneo). Also excellent P Nero sp.

Girò di Cagliari Sard. DOC r. dr. or sw. ★
  A formidably alcoholic red, most sympathetic when some of its sugar
  content is left unfermented.

Goldmuskateller Aromatic grape made into irresistible dry white, esp. by
  TIEFENBRUNNER.

Gradi Degrees (of alcohol), i.e. percent by volume.

Grai, Giorgio Merchant and consultant to top ALTO-ADIGE and other
  estates.

Grave del Friuli Fr-VG. DOC r. w. dr. ★★ 85 86 87 88
  A DOC covering 15 different wines named after their grapes, from
  near the Yugoslav border. Good MERLOT and CABERNET.

Gravner COLLIO estate with range of superb whites, led by CHARD and SAUV.

**SOAVE
CLASSICO**

VINO A DENOMINAZIONE DI
ORIGINE CONTROLLATA

IMBOTTIGLIATO DAL
PRODUTTORE ALL 'ORIGINE

CANTINA SOCIALE DI SOAVE

Most Italian wines have a single name, in
contrast to the combination village and vineyard
names of France and Germany.

Soave is the name of this wine. It is qualified
only by the word Classico, a legal term for the
central (normally the best) part of many long-
established wine regions.
"Denominazione di Origine Controllata" is the
official guarantee of authenticity.
Imbottigliato . . . all'origine means bottled by
the producer. Cantina Sociale di Soave means
the growers' cooperative of Soave.

Grechetto A traditional white grape with far more flavour than the
  ubiquitous Trebbiano, increasingly used in Umbria. Greco ("Greek")
  is less specific.

Greco di Bianco (or Greco di Gerace) Cal. DOC w. sw. ★★ 85 86 87 88
  An original smooth and fragrant dessert wine from Italy's toe. See
  also Mantonico.

Greco di Tufo Camp. DOC w. dr. (sp.) ★★★ 87 88 89
  One of the best whites of the south, fruity and slightly "wild" in
  flavour. A character.

Grignolino d'Asti Piem. DOC r. dr. ★ D.Y.A.
  Pleasant lively standard wine of PIEMONTE.

Grumello Lomb. DOC r. dr. ★★ 79 82 83 85 86 88
  NEBBIOLO wine from VALTELLINA, can be delicate (or meagre).

Guerrieri-Rizzardi Top producer of BARDOLINO and other Veronese wines
  from various family estates (esp. Villa Rizzardi, 86').

Gutturnio dei Colli Piacentini   Em-Ro. DOC r. dr. (s/sw.) ★★ 85 86 87 88
Full-bodied BARBERA/BONARDA blend from the hills of Piacenza. Ages admirably. (DOC is Colli Piacentini.)

Inferno   Lomb. DOC r. dr. ★★ 82 83 85 86 88
Similar to GRUMELLO and like it classified as VALTELLINA Superiore.

Ischia   Camp. DOC (r.) w. dr. ★ D.Y.A.
The wine of the island off Naples. Slightly sharp Superiore is best.

Isole e Olena   Up and coming CHIANTI CLASSICO estate with fine red V.D.T. called Cepparello. V.g. VIN SANTO.

Isonzo   Fr-VG. DOC r. w. dr. ★★ 85 86 87 88
DOC covering 10 varietal wines in the extreme north-east. Best whites and CABERNET (esp. from Stelio Gallo) compare with top COLLIO wines.

Jermann   Estate in Collio producing top-ranked V.D.T., including the singular VINTAGE TUNINA white blend.

Kalterersee   German name for Lago di CALDARO.

Lacryma Christi del Vesuvio   Camp. r. p. w. (f.) dr. (sw.) ★—→★★ 87 88 89
Famous but usually ordinary wines in great variety from Vesuvius. (DOC is Vesuvio.) MASTROBERARDINO makes the only good example.

Lageder, Alois   The senior producer of the Bolzano DOCs: STA MADDALENA, etc. Exciting wines, incl. barrel-aged CHARD and CAB. Löwengang. Single v'yd SAUV BL. is called Lehenhof, PINOT BIANCO Haberlehof, PINOT GRIGIO Benefizium Porer. Also Portico dei Leoni CHARD.

Lago di Caldaro   See Caldaro.

Lagrein   Tr-Aad. DOC r. p. dr. ★★ 83 85 86 88
A Tyrolean grape with a bitter twist. Good fruity wine – at best v. satisfying. The rosé is called Kretzer, the dark Dunkel.

Lamberti   Producers of SOAVE, VALPOLICELLA and BARDOLINO at Lazise on the east shore of Lake Garda.

Lambrusco   DOC (or not) r. p. (w.) s/sw. ❋ D.Y.A.
Bizarre, highly popular fizzy red, generally drunk secco (dry) in Italy but best-known in its sweet version in the USA.

Lambrusco di Sorbara   Em-Ro. DOC r. (w.) dr. or s/sw. sp. ★★ D.Y.A.
The best of the Lambruscos. From near Modena.

Lambrusco Grasparossa di Castelvetro   Em-Ro. DOC r. dr. or s/sw. sp. ★★ D.Y.A. Often rivals above. Highly scented, pleasantly acidic; good with rich food.

Lambrusco Salamino di Santa Croce   Em-Ro. DOC r. dr. or s/sw. sp. ★ D.Y.A Similar to above. Fruity smell, high acidity and a thick "head".

Langhe   The hills of central PIEMONTE, home of BAROLO, BARBARESCO, etc. Candidate for its own DOC. The name is seen on many V.D.Ts.

Latisana   Fr-VG. DOC r. w. dr. ★★ 87 88 89
DOC for 7 varietal wines from some 50 miles n.e. of Venice. Particularly good TOCAI FRIULANO.

Leone de Castris   Leading producer of Apulian wines with an estate at SALICE SALENTINO, near Lecce.

Lessona   Piem. DOC r. d. ★★ 82 83 85 86 87 88
Soft, dry, claret-like wine produced in the province of Vercelli from NEBBIOLO, Vespolina and BONARDA grapes.

Liquoroso   Strong and usually sweet (whether fortified with alcohol or not), e.g. Tuscan VIN SANTO.

Lisini   Small estate producing some of the finest recent vintages of BRUNELLO DI MONTALCINO.

Locorotondo   Apu. DOC w. dr. (sp.) ★ D.Y.A.
A pleasantly fresh southern white.

Lugana   Lomb. DOC w. dr. (sp.) ★★★ D.Y.A.
One of the best white wines of s. Lake Garda: fragrant, smooth, full of body and flavour. Visconti is the best producer.

Lungarotti   The leading producer of TORGIANO wine (which see), with cellars and a wine museum near Perugia. Recently also fine CHARDONNAY and PINOT GRIGIO.

Maculan The top producer of DOC BREGANZE. Also Torcolato, dessert VINO DA TAVOLA (★★★) and Prato di Cangio (CHARD, P.BIANCO and P.GRIGIO).

Malfatti Estate with modern methods, near Lecce, Apulia, producing Bianco, Rosso and SALICE SALENTINO of medium quality.

Malvasia Important white or red grape for luscious wines, incl. Madeira's Malmsey. Used all over Italy for dry and sweet, still and sp. wines. An outstanding mature example is TORRICELLA.

Malvasia di Bosa Sard. DOC w. dr. sw. ★★ 85 86 87 88 89
A wine of character. Strong, aromatic finish.

Malvasia di Cagliari Sard. DOC w. dr. s/sw. or sw. ★★ 85 86 87 88 89 Interesting strong Sardinian wine, fragrant and slightly bitter.

Malvasia di Casorzo d'Asti Piem. DOC r. sw. sp. ★★ D.Y.A.
Fragrant grapey sweet red, sometimes sparkling.

Malvasia di Castelnuovo Don Bosco Piem. DOC r. sw. (sp.) ★★
Peculiar method of interrupted fermentation gives very sweet aromatic red.

Malvasia delle Lipari Sic. DOC w. sw. (pa. f.) ★★★ 85 86 87 88 89
Among the very best Malvasias, aromatic and rich, from the Lipari or Aeolian Islands n. of Sicily. Top producer: Carlo Hauner.

Malvoisie de Nus Vd'A. DOC w. dr. s/sw. ★★★
Rare Alpine white, with a deep bouquet of honey. Small production and high reputation. Can age remarkably well.

Mandrolisai Sard. DOC r. p. dr. ★ 87 88
CANNONAU at a lower strength and more approachable style.

Manduria (Primitivo di) Apu. DOC r. s/sw. (f. dr. or sw.) ★★ 86 87 88 89
Heady red, naturally strong but often fortified. From nr. Taranto. Primitivo is a southern grape related to ZINFANDEL.

Mantonico Cal. w. dr. or sw. f. ★★ 85 86 87 88
Fruity deep amber dessert wine from Reggio Calabria. Can age remarkably well. See also Greco di Bianco.

Marino Lat. DOC w. dr. or s/sw. (sp.) ★★ D.Y.A.
A neighbour of FRASCATI with similar wine, often a better buy. Look for COLLE PICCHIONI brand.

Marrano Umb. w. dr. ★★★
Pungent white from GRECHETTO grapes grown by BIGI near ORVIETO.

Marsala Sic. DOC br. dr. s/sw. or sw. f. ★★★ NV
Dark sherry-type wine invented by the Woodhouse Brothers from Liverpool in 1773; excellent apéritif or for dessert. The dry ("virgin"), sometimes made by the solera system, must be 5 years old. Top producers: VECCHIO SAMPERI, Pellegrino, Diego RALLO, FLORIO.

Martina Franca Apu. DOC w. dr. (sp.) ★ D.Y.A.
Rather neutral southern white, cousin to LOCOROTONDO.

Martini & Rossi Well-known vermouth and sparkling wine house, also famous for its splendid wine museum in Pessione, near Turin.

Marzemino (del Trentino) Tr-Aad. DOC r. dr. ★ 87 88 89
Pleasant local red of Trento. Fruity fragrance; slightly bitter taste.

Mascarello The name of two top producers of BAROLO, etc.: Bartolo M. and Giuseppe M. & Figli.

Masi, Agricola Well-known specialist producers of VALPOLICELLA, RECIOTO, SOAVE, etc., including fine red Campo Fiorin and v.g. single v'yd AMARONE.

Mastroberardino The leading wine-producer of Campania, incl. TAURASI, LACRYMA CHRISTI DEL VESUVIO, GRECO DI TUFO and FIANO DI AVELLINO.

Melini Long-established important producers of CHIANTI CLASSICO at Pontassieve. Inventors of the straw-covered *fiasco*, or flask.

Melissa Cal. DOC r. w. dr. ★★ 83 85 86 87 88 89
Mostly made from Gaglioppo grapes in the province of Catanzaro. Delicate, balanced, ages rather well. CIRO is identical.

Meranese di Collina Tr-Aad. DOC r. dr. ★ D.Y.A.
Light red of Merano, known in German as Meraner Hügel.

Merlot Adaptable red Bordeaux grape widely grown in n.e. Italy and elsewhere. For example:

Merlot di Aprilia Lat. DOC r. dr. ★ **87 88 89**
Harsh at first, softer after 2-3 yrs.

Merlot Colli Berici Ven. DOC r. dr. ★ **86 87 88** 89
Pleasantly light and soft. Campo del Lago V.D.T. from Villa dal Ferro is one of Italy's best MERLOTS.

Merlot Colli Orientali del Friuli Fr-VG. DOC r. dr. ★★ **83 85 86 88**
Pleasant herby character, best at 2-3 yrs (Riserva). Some ages well; notably Vigne dal Leon.

Merlot Collio Goriziano Fr-VG. DOC r. dr. ★★ **86 88**
Grassy scent, slightly bitter taste. Best at 2-3 yrs.

Merlot Grave del Friuli Fr-VG. DOC r. dr. ★★ **85 86 88**
Pleasant light wine, usually best at 1-2 yrs, but potentially a keeper.

Merlot Isonzo Fr-VG. DOC r. dr. ★★ **85 86 88**
A DOC in Gorizia. Dry, herby, agreeable wine.

Merlot Lison-Pramaggiore Ven. DOC r. dr. ★★ **85 86 88**
A cut above most other MERLOTS. Riserva after 2 yrs.

Merlot del Piave Ven. DOC r. dr. ★★ **85 86 88**
Sound tasty red, best at 2-4 yrs.

Merlot (del Trentino) Tr-Aad. DOC r. dr. ★ **85 86 88**
Full flavour, slightly grassy scent, Riserva after 2 yrs. (ALTO ADIGE has better; esp. from Margreid and Siebeneich v'yds.)

Metodo classico or tradizionale Terms increasingly in use to identify champagne method sparkling wines.

Monica di Cagliari Sard. DOC r. dr. or sw. (f. dr. or sw.) ★★ **87 88** 89
Strong spicy red, often fortified and comparable with Spanish Malaga. Monica is a Sardinian grape.

Monica di Sardegna Sard. DOC r. dr. ★ **86 87** 88 89
Dry version of above, not fortified.

Monsanto Esteemed CHIANTI CLASSICO estate, esp. for IL POGGIO v'yd.

Montalcino Village in the province of Siena, Tuscany, famous for its deep red BRUNELLO and lighter ROSSO DI MONTALCINO.

Monte Vertine Top estate at Radda in Chianti. ★★★ V.D.T. Le Pergole Torte and Sodaccio.

Montecarlo Tusc. DOC w. dr. r. ★★ D.Y.A.
One of Tuscany's best whites, smooth and delicate. Now applies to a CHIANTI-style red too.

Montecompatri Colonna Lat. DOC w. dr. or s/sw. ★ D.Y.A.
A neighbour of FRASCATI. Similar wine.

Montefalco Umb. DOC r. dr. or sw. ★★ **85 86 87** 88 89
M. Rosso is standard red, Sagrantino (named for the grape) has sweetness and bite. Top producer ADANTI. Adanti's Rosso d'Arquata V.D.T. stands out.

Montepulciano, Vino Nobile di See Vino Nobile di Montepulciano.

Montepulciano d'Abruzzo (or Molise) Abr & M. DOC r. p. dr. ★★★ **82 83 85 86 87** 88 89 At its best one of Italy's best reds, full of flavour and warmth, from the Adriatic coast round Pescara. See also Cerasuolo, Valentini.

Monterosso (Val d'Arda) Em-Ro. DOC w. dr. or sw. (sp.) ★ D.Y.A.
Agreeable minor white from Piacenza. (DOC Colli Piacentini.)

Montesodi Tusc. r. ★★★ **82 83 85** 86 88
Tip-top CHIANTI Rufina Riserva from FRESCOBALDI.

Moscato ruitily fragrant grape grown all over Italy.

Moscato d'Asti Piem. DOC w. sw. sp. ★★ NV
Low-strength sweet fruity sparkler, delicious from Rivetti, Saracco, Dogliotti, Bera, Vignaioli di Santo Stefano, Carbonere, Gatti. ASTI SPUMANTE is the (theoretically) superior version.

Moscato dei Colli Euganei Ven. DOC w. sw. (sp.) ★★ D.Y.A.
Golden wine, fruity and smooth, from near Padua.

Moscato (Oltrepò Pavese) Lomb. DOC w. sw. (sp.) ★ D.Y.A.
The Lombardy equivalent of MOSCATO D'ASTI. Rarely as good.

Moscato di Pantelleria Sic. DOC w. sw. (sp.) (f. pa.) ★★★★
Italy's best muscat, from the island of Pantelleria off the Tunisian
coast; rich, fruity and aromatic. Ages well. Top wine: Bukkuram from
De Bartoli.

Moscato di Sorso Sennori Sard. DOC w. sw. (f.) ✷ D.Y.A.
Strong golden dessert wine from Sassari, n. Sardinia.

Moscato di Trani Apu. DOC w. sw. or f. ★
Another strong golden dessert wine, sometimes fortified, with a
"bouquet of faded roses".

Müller-Thurgau Makes wine to be reckoned with in TRENTINO-ALTO ADIGE
and FRIULI, esp. TIEFENBRUNNER'S "Feldmarschall".

Nasco di Cagliari Sard. DOC w. dr. or sw. (f. dr. or sw.) ★
Sardinian speciality, light bitter taste, high alcoholic content.

Nebbiolo The best red grape of PIEMONTE and Lombardy.

Nebbiolo d'Alba Piem. DOC r. dr. s/sw. (sp.) ★★ 85 86 87 88 89
Like lightweight BAROLO; sometimes easier to appreciate than the
more powerful classic wine. Roero is a new DOC from n. of ALBA.

Negroamaro Literally "black bitter"; Apulian red grape with potential for
quality. See Copertino.

Neive, Castello di A leading producer of BARBARESCO, in the castle where
Louis Oudart pioneered cask-ageing of NEBBIOLO in 1850s.

Nipozzano, Castello di The FRESCOBALDI estate nr. Florence producing
Montesodi CHIANTI. The most important outside the CLASSICO zone.

Nozzole amous estate in the heart of CHIANTI CLASSICO n. of Greve.

Nuragus di Cagliari Sard. DOC w. dr. ✷ D.Y.A.
Lively Sardinian white, not too strong.

Oliena Sard. r. dr. ★★
Interesting strong fragrant CANNONAU red; a touch bitter.

Oltrepò Pavese Lomb. DOC. r. w. dr. sw. sp. ★→★★
DOC applicable to 15 wines produced in the province of Pavia, mostly
named after their grapes. Top growers incl: Tenuta Mazzolino, Doria,
Monsupello, Anteo, Fontanachiara.

Ornellaia New estate of Lodovico Antinori nr. Bolgheri on Tuscan coast.
To watch for CAB/MERLOT and SAUV BLANC called Poggio delle Gazze.

Orvieto Umb. DOC w. dr. or s/sw. ★★→★★★ D.Y.A.
The classical Umbrian golden-white, smooth and substantial, formerly rather dull but recently more interesting, esp. in sweet
versions. O. Classico is superior. Only the finest examples e.g. BIGI,
DECUGANO DEI BARBI, BARBERANI, age well. But see Castello della Sala.

Pagadebit di Romagna Em-Ro. DOC w. dr./s.sw. D.Y.A.
Pleasant traditional "payer of debts" from round Bertinoro.

Paradiso, Fattoria Century-old family estate near Bertinoro (EM-RO).
Good ALBANA and PAGADEBIT and unique red BARBAROSSA. V.g. SANGIOVESE.

Parrina Tusc. r. or w. dr. ★★ 86 87 88
Light red and fresh appetizing white from s. Tuscany.

Pasolini Dall'Onda Noble family with estates in CHIANTI Colli Forentini
and ROMAGNA producing fine traditional-style wines.

Passito Strong sweet wine from grapes dried on the vine or indoors.

Peppoli Estate owned by ANTINORI producing excellent CHIANTI CLASSICO in
a full, round, youthful style – first vintage **85**.

Per'e Palummo Camp. r. dr. ★★ 87 88 89
Appetizing light tannic red from the island of Ischia.

Petit Rouge Vd'A. ✷✷ 85 86 88 89
Good dark lively REFOSCO-like red. Part of VALLE D'AOSTA DOC.

Piave Ven. DOC r. or w. dr. ✷✷ 85 86 88 (w. D.Y.A.)
Flourishing DOC covering 8 wines, 4 red and 4 white, named after
their grapes. CAB, MERLOT and RABOSO reds all need ageing.

Picolit (Colli Orientali del Friuli) Fr–VG. DOC w. s/sw. or sw. ★★★ **85 86 88** Delicate, well-balanced, very sweet dessert wine. Ages up to 6 years, but wildly overpriced.

Piemonte The most important Italian region for quality wine. Turin is the capital, Asti and ALBA the wine-centres. See Barolo, Barbera, Dolcetto, Barbaresco, Grignolino, Moscato, etc.

Pieropan Outstanding producers of SOAVE that deserves its fame.

Pigato New DOC under Riviera Ligure di Ponente. Often outclasses VERMENTINO as Liguria's finest white, with rich texture and structure.

Pighin, Fratelli Solid producers of COLLIO and GRAVE DEL FRIULI.

Pinot Bianco Popular grape in n.e., esp. good for sparkling wine.

Pinot Bianco (Alto Adige) Tr–Aad. DOC. w. dr. ★★ **86 88 89** Italy's best and longest-lived wine of this variety.

Pinot Bianco (dei Colli Berici) Ven. DOC w. dr. ★★ D.Y.A. Straight, satisfying dry white.

Pinot Bianco (Colli Orientali del Friuli) r–VG. DOC w. dr. ★★ **88 89** Good white; smooth rather than showy.

Pinot Bianco (Collio Goriziano) Fr–VG. DOC w. dr. ★★ **88 89** Similar to the above.

Pinot Bianco (Grave del Friuli) Fr–VG. DOC w. dr. ★★ D.Y.A. Not normally up to the standard of the last two.

Pinot Grigio Tasty, low-acid white grape increasingly popular in n.e. Italy. Best from A. ADIGE, COLLIO. Also in e.g. Tuscany (see Villa Banfi).

Pinot Grigio (Collio Goriziano) Fr–VG. DOC w. dr. ★★ D.Y.A. Fruity, soft, agreeable dry white. The best age well.

Pinot Grigio (Grave del Friuli) Fr–VG. DOC w. dr. ★★ D.Y.A. Second choice to Collio or Colli Orientali.

Pinot Grigio (Oltrepò Pavese) Lomb. DOC w. dr. (sp.) ★★ D.Y.A. Lombardy's P.G. is usually at least adequate.

Pinot Nero Tr–Aad. DOC r. dr. ★★ **85 86 88** Pinot Nero (Noir) gives lively burgundy-scented light wine in much of n.e. Italy, incl. Trentino. Riserva after 2 yrs. Also fine sparkling.

Pio Cesare A producer of top-quality red wines of PIEMONTE, incl. BAROLO.

Podere Il Palazzino Small estate with admirable CHIANTI CLASSICO and V.D.T. Grosso Senese.

Poggio al Sole CHIANTI CLASSICO estate. Less distinguised than formerly.

Poggione, Tenuta Il Perhaps the most consistent top estate for BRUNELLO and ROSSO DI MONTALCINO.

Pojer & Sandri Top producers of TRENTINO V.D.T. MÜLLER-THURGAU, CHARD.

Pomino Tusc. DOC (r.) w. dr. (br.) ★★★ **85 88** Fine white, partly CHARDONNAY ("Il Benefizio" is 100%) and a SANGIOVESE/CABERNET blend. Also Vin Santo. From FRESCOBALDI.

Polyphemo Monster monocular Sicilian overfond of Greek red.

Predicato Name for four kinds of VINI DA TAVOLA from central Tuscany. They illustrate the headlong rush from tradition. P. del Muschio is CHARD, P BIANCO, P. del Selvante is SAUV BLANC., P. di Biturica is CAB SAUV with SANGIOVESE, P. di Cardisco is SANGIOVESE straight. RUFFINO's Cabreo brand are examples.

Primitivo di Apulia See Manduria.

Prosecco di Conegliano Ven. DOC w. dr. or s/sw. (sp.) ★★★ D.Y.A. Popular sparkling wine of the n.e. Slight fruity bouquet, the dry pleasantly bitter, the sweet fruity; the best are known as Superiore di Cartizze. Carpené-Malvolti is famous old maker, now surpassed in quality by Pino Zardetto, Nino Franco, Canevel, Cardinal.

Prunotto, Alfredo Very serious ALBA company with v.g. BAROLO, BARBAR-ESCO, NEBBIOLO, etc. Now controlled by ANTINORI.

Quintarelli, Giuseppe True artisan producer of VALPOLICELLA, RECIOTO and AMARONE, at the top in both quality and price.

Raboso del Piave (now DOC) Ven. r. dr. ★★ 82 83 85 86 88
Powerful, sharp, interesting country red; needs age.

Rallo, Nuova A leader in MARSALA with 1st class Vergine and other wines.

Ramandolo See Verduzzo Colli Orientali del Friuli.

Ramitello See Di Majo Norante.

Rampolla, Castello dei Top CHIANTI CLASSICO estate at Panzano; also excellent Cabernet-based V.D.T. Sammarco.

Rapitalà See Alcamo.

Ratti, Renato Maker of v.g. BAROLO and other ALBA wines. Signor Ratti (d. 1988) was a highly respected leader of the Piemonte industry.

Ravello Camp. r. p. w. dr. ★★ 87 88 89
Among the best wines of Campania: full dry red, fresh clean white. Caruso is the best-known brand.

Recioto Wine made partly of half-dried grapes. Speciality of Veneto since the great days of the Venetian empire.

Recioto di Gambellara Ven. DOC w. s/sw. sp. ★ D.Y.A.
Sweetish golden wine, often half-sparkling.

Recioto di Soave Ven. DOC w. s/sw. (sp.) ★★ 86 87 88 89
Soave made from selected half-dried grapes; sweet, fruity, fresh, slightly almondy: high alcohol. Top makers: ANSELMI, PIEROPAN.

Recioto della Valpolicella Ven. DOC r. s/sw. sp. ★★ 80 81 83 85 86 88
Strong late-harvested red, sometimes sparkling. "Amabile" is sweet.

Recioto Amarone della Valpolicella Ven. DOC r. dr. ★★★★ 80 81 83 85 86 88
Dry version of the above; strong concentrated flavour, rather bitter. Impressive and expensive.

Refosco (Colli Orientali del Friuli) r-VG. DOC r. dr. ★★ 82 83 85 86 88
Full-bodied dry red; Riserva after 2 yrs. Refosco is said to be the same grape as the MONDEUSE of Savoie (France).

Refosco (Grave del Friuli) r-VG. DOC r. dr. ★★ 83 85 86 87 88
Similar to above but slightly lighter.

Regaleali Sic. w. r. p. ★★ 83 84 85 86 87 88 89
Perhaps the best Sicilian table wines, produced between Palermo and Caltanissetta to the s.e.

Ribolla (Colli Orientali del Friuli) r-VG. DOC w. dr. ★ D.Y.A.
Clean and fruity north-eastern white.

Ricasoli amous Tuscan family, "inventors" of CHIANTI, whose Chianti Classico is named after their BROLIO estate and castle.

Riecine Tusc. ★★★
First-class CHIANTI CLASSICO estate at Gaiole started 20 years ago by an Englishman, John Dunkley.

Riesling Formerly referred to as Italian Riesling (R. Italico or "Welschriesling"). German Riesling, now ascendant, is R. Renano.

Riesling Alto Adige DOC w. dr. ★★ 87 88 89
Can often be Italy's best Riesling.

Riesling (Oltrepò Pavese) Lomb. DOC w. dr. (sp.) ★★
The Lombardy version, quite light and fresh. Occasionally sparkling. Keeps well. Made of both types of Riesling.

Riesling (Trentino) Tr-Aad. DOC w. dr. ★★ D.Y.A.
Delicate, slightly acid, very fruity.

Riserva Wine aged for a statutory period, usually in barrels.

Riunite One of the world's largest coop cellars near Reggio Emilia producing huge quantities of LAMBRUSCO and other wines.

Rivera Reliable winemakers at Andria, near Bari, with good red Il Falcone and CASTEL DEL MONTE rosé. Also Vigna al Monte label.

Riviera del Garda Chiaretto Ven. and Lom. DOC p. dr. ★★ D.Y.A.
Charming cherry-pink, fresh and slightly bitter, from s.w. Garda.

Riviera del Garda Rosso Ven. DOC r. dr. ★★ 86 87 88
Red version of the above; ages surprisingly well.

Rocche dei Manzoni, Podere Go-ahead estate at MONFORTE D'ALBA. Excellent BAROLO, BRICCO MANZONI, ALBA wines and Valentino Brut sp.

Roero See Nebbiolo d'Alba.

Ronco del Gnemiz Tiny property with outstanding COLLIO ORIENTALI DOCs and V.D.T. CHARDONNAY made in "barriques."

Rosa del Golfo Apu. p. dr. ★★ D.Y.A.
  An outstanding V.D.T. rosato of ALEZIO.

Rosato Rosé.

Rosato del Salento Apu. p. dr. ★→★★ D.Y.A.
  Strong but refreshing southern rosé from round Brindisi.

Rossese di Dolceacqua Lig. DOC r. dr. ★★ 87 88
  Well-known fragrant light red of the Riviera, as clean as claret.

Rosso Red.

Rosso Cònero Mar. DOC r. dr. ★★★ 82 85 86 87 88 89
  Some of the best MONTEPULCIANO (varietal) reds of Italy, e.g. Umani Ronchi's Cumaro and San Lorenzo, Garofoli's Piancarda.

Rosso d'Arquata See Adanti.

Rosso delle Colline Lucchesi Tusc. DOC r. dr. ★★ 86 88
  Produced round Lucca but not greatly different from CHIANTI.

Rosso di Montalcino Tusc. DOC r. dr. ★★→★★★ 86 87 88 89
  Recent DOC for younger wines from BRUNELLO grapes. Still variable but potentially a winner (e.g. Centine from Villa Banfi).

Rosso di Montepulciano Tusc. DOC r.dr. ★★
  Equivalent of the last for junior VINO NOBILE, just introduced.

Rosso Piceno Mar. DOC r. dr. ★→ ★★ 83 85 86 88 89
  Adriatic red with a touch of style. Can be Superiore from classic zone near Asedi.

Rubesco The excellent popular red of TORGIANO.

Rubino di Cantavenna Piem. DOC r. dr. ★★ D.Y.A.
  Lively red, principally BARBERA, from a well-known coop s.e. of Turin.

Rufina Important sub-region of CHIANTI in the hills east of Florence.

Ruffino The biggest and best known of all CHIANTI merchants. Riserva Ducale is the top wine. N.B. New PREDICATO wines.

Sagrantino See Montefalco.

Salice Salentino Apu. DOC r. ★★ 79 80 81 83 85 86 87 88 89
  Strong red from NEGROAMARO grapes. Riserva after 2 yrs, smooth when mature. Top makers: Taurino, De Castris.

San Felice Rising star in CHIANTI with fine Classico Poggio Rosso. Also prize-winning red V.D.T. Vigorello and PREDICATO di Biturica.

Sangiovese or Sangioveto Principal red grape of Italy, esp. Tuscany. Many forms incl. the noble BRUNELLO and Prugnolo Gentile (of MONTEPULCIANO), also:

Sangiovese d'Aprilia Lat. DOC r. or p. dr. ★ D.Y.A.
  Strong dry rosé from south of Rome.

Sangiovese di Romagna Em-Ro. DOC r. dr. ★★ 85 86 87 88 89.
  Pleasant standard red; gains character with a little age.

San Giusto a Rentennano One of the best CHIANTI CLASSICO producers; stunning '85 at a reasonable price. Excellent V.D.T. red Percarlo.

San Polo in Rosso, Castello di CHIANTI CLASSICO estate with first-rate red V.D.T. Cetinaia, (aged in standard casks, not "barriques").

San Severo Apu. DOC r. p. w. dr. ★
  Sound neutral southern wine; not particularly strong.

Santa Maddalena Tr-Aad. DOC r. dr. ★★ 88 89
  Perhaps the best Tyrolean red. Round and warming, slightly almondy.

Santa Margherita The Veneto winery that popularized PINOT GRIGIO, now on a broad base with many good wines.

Sassella (Valtellina) Lomb. DOC r. dr. ★★★ 82 83 85 86 88
  Considerable NEBBIOLO wine, tough when young. Known since Roman times, mentioned by Leonardo da Vinci.

Sassicaia Tusc. r. dr. ★★★★ 75 76 77 78 79 80 81 82 83 85 86' 87 88 Outstanding pioneer CABERNET from the Tenuta San Guido of the Incisa family, at Bolgheri near Livorno. Limited production.

Sauvignon Sauvignon Blanc: used in n.e., perhaps best at TERLANO, ALTO ADIGE. Very good in COLLIO and COLLI ORIENTALI.

Sauvignon (Colli Berici) Ven. DOC w. dr. ★ D.Y.A.
Fresh white from near Vicenza.

Sauvignon (Colli Orientali del Friuli) Fr-VG. DOC w. dr. ★★ 88 89
Full, smooth, freshly aromatic n.e. white.

Sauvignon (Collio Goriziano) Fr-VG. DOC w. dr. ★★ 88 89
Very similar to the last; slightly higher alcohol.

Savuto Cal. DOC r. p. dr. ★★ 86 88 89
Fragrant juicy wine produced in the provinces of Cosenza and Catanzaro.

Schiava Good red grape of TRENTINO-ALTO ADIGE with characteristic bitter after-taste, used for SANTA MADDALENA, etc.

Sciacchetrà See Cinqueterre.

Sebaste Young Barolo-maker to watch in joint venture with GANCIA.

Secco Dry.

Secentenario Tusc. r. ★★★★
ANTINORI's red V.D.T., bottled (in magnums) for the firm's 600th anniversary in 1985.

Sella & Mosca Major Sardinian growers and merchants at Alghero. Their port-like Anghelu Ruju is good. Also pleasant white TORBATO.

Selvapiana RUFINA estate owned by Giuntini family. One of the finest Chiantis of all, rivalled by few Classicos.

Settesoli Sicilian growers' coop with range of sometimes v.g. table wines.

Sforzato (Valtellina) Lomb. DOC r. dr. ★★★ 78 79 80 82 83 85 86 88
Valtellina equivalent of RECIOTO AMARONE made with partly dried grapes. Velvety, strong, ages remarkably well. Also called Sfursat.

Sfursat See Sforzato.

Sizzano Piem. DOC r. dr. ★★ 82 83 85 86 87 88
Attractive full-bodied red produced at Sizzano in the province of Novara, mostly from NEBBIOLO. Ages up to 10 years.

Soave Ven. DOC w. dr. ★★★ D.Y.A.
Famous, if not very characterful, Veronese white. Fresh with v. attractive texture. Standards are rising (at last). S. Classico is more restricted and better. Top growers incl. PIEROPAN, ANSELMI, BOSCAINI. See also Bolla.

Solaia Tusc. r. ★★★★ 83 85 86 88
Very fine Bordeaux-style wine of CAB. SAUV and now 25% SANGIOVESE from ANTINORI, first made in 1979.

A top category, DOCG, Denominazione Controllata e Garantita, is gradually being added to the Italian wine classification. It is awarded only to certain wines from top-quality zones which have been bottled and sealed with a government seal by the producer. The first five areas to be "guaranteed" were Barolo, Barbaresco, Brunello di Montalcino, Chianti and Vino Nobile di Montepulciano. The sixth (and first white) was Albana di Romagna, for no discernable reason. But it should be remembered that many of Italy's best wines are not covered by the DOC system and are officially only vino da tavola – V.D.T. in this book. Examples are Sassicaia, Tignanello, Venegazzù, Bricco Manzoni, etc, etc.

Solopaca Camp. DOC r. w. dr. ★★ 86 87 88 89
Up-and-coming from near Benevento; rather sharp when young, the white soft and fruity.

Sorni Tr-Aad. r. w. dr. ★★ D.Y.A.
Made in the Province of Trento. Light, fresh and soft. Drink young.

Spanna See Gattinara.

Spumante Sparkling, as in sweet Asti or many good dry wines, incl. both METODO CLASSICO and tank-made cheapos.

Squinzano Apu. DOC r. p. dr. ★ 83 85 86 87 88 89
Strong southern red from Lecce. Riserva after 2 yrs.

Stravecchio Very old.

Taurasi Camp. DOC r. dr. ★★★ **79 80 82 83 85 86** 87 88 89
The best Campanian red, from MASTROBERARDINO of Avellino, has a cult following in the USA. Harsh when young. Riserva after 4 yrs.

Tedeschi, Fratelli Leading small producer of VALPOLICELLA, RECIOTO and AMARONE. V.g. Capitel San Rocco red and white V.D.T.

Terlano Tr-Aad. DOC w. dr. ★★ **88 89**
A DOC for 7 white wines from the province of Bolzano, named by their grapes, esp. outstanding SAUVIGNON. Terlaner in German.

Teroldego Rotaliano Tr-Aad. DOC r. p. dr. ★★→★★★ **83 85 86 88 89**
The attractive local red of Trento. Blackberry-scented, slight bitter after-taste, can age v. well. Top maker: Foradori.

Terre Rosse Distinguished small estate near Bologna. CABERNET, CHARD., SAUV BL, PINOT GRIGIO, etc., are the best of the region.

Tiefenbrunner Distinguished grower of some of the very best ALTO ADIGE white and red wines at Schloss Turmhof, Kurtatsch (Cortaccio).

Tignanello Tusc. r. dr. ★★★ **78 79 80 81 82 83** 85 86 88
The leader of the new style of Bordeaux-inspired Tuscan reds, made by ANTINORI.

Tocai Friulano (Collio). ★★ **88 89**
North-east Italian white grape; no relation of Hungarian or Alsace Tokay. Light dry wine. The Tocais of the COLLI ORIENTALI DEL FRIULI and COLLIO GORIZIANO are best.

Tocai di Lison Ven. DOC w. dr. ★★ D.Y.A.
From e. Veneto, delicate scent, fruity taste. Classico is better.

Tocai (Colli Berici) Ven. DOC w. dr. ★ D.Y.A.
A more modest wine altogether.

Tocai (Grave del Friuli) r-VG. DOC w. dr. ★★ D.Y.A.
Similar to TOCAI DI LISON, generally rather milder.

Tocai di S. Martino della Battaglia Lomb. DOC w. dr. ★★ D.Y.A.
Small production s. of Lake Garda. Light, slightly bitter.

Torbato di Alghero Sard. w. dr. (pa.) ★★ D.Y.A.
Good n. Sardinian table wine. Top maker: SELLA & MOSCA.

Torgiano (Rubesco di) Umb. DOC r. w. dr. ★★★ **75 78 82 83 85 86 87** 88 89 The creation of the LUNGAROTTI family. Excellent red from near Perugia comparable with top CHIANTI CLASSICO. RUBESCO is the standard quality. Riserva Monticchio is superb. Keep 10 years. V.D.T. San Giorgio involves CABERNET to splendid effect. White Torre di Giano, of TREBBIANO and GRECHETTO, also ages well. See also under Lungarotti.

Torricella Tusc. w. dr. ★★★ **81 82 83 85 86** 87 88
Remarkable aged, soft, buttery MALVASIA dry white from BROLIO.

Toscana The region of Tuscany.

Traminer Aromatico Tr-Aad. DOC w. dr. ★★ D.Y.A.
Delicate, aromatic, rather soft Gewürztraminer.

Trebbiano The principal white grape of Tuscany, found all over Italy. Ugni Blanc in French. Rarely remarkable unless blended.

Trebbiano d'Abruzzo Abr. & M. DOC w. dr. ★→★★ D.Y.A.
Gentle, rather neutral, slightly tannic. From round Pescara. Valentini is much the best producer (also of MONTEPULCIANO D'ABRUZZO).

Trebbiano d'Aprilia Lat. DOC w. dr. ★ D.Y.A.
Heady, mild-flavoured, rather yellow. From south of Rome.

Trebbiano di Romagna Em-Ro. DOC w. dr. or s/sw. (sp.) ★ D.Y.A.
Clean, pleasant white from near Bologna.

Trentino Tr-Aad. DOC r. w. dr. or sw. ★→★★★
DOC for as many as 20 different wines, mostly named after their grapes. Best are CHARD, P BIANCO, MARZEMINO and esp. VIN SANTO.

Umani Ronchi A leading producer of quality wines of the Marches; notably VERDICCHIO, Casal di Serra and Villa Bianchi and ROSSO CONERO, Cumaro and San Lorenzo.

Uzzano, Castello di Fine old CHIANTI CLASSICO estate at Greve.

Valcalepio Lomb. DOC r. w. dr. ★ **88** 89
From nr. Bergamo. Pleasant red; lightly scented, fresh white.

Valdadige Tr-Aad. DOC r. w. dr. or s/sw. ★
Name for the table wines of the Adige valley – in German Etschtal.

Val d'Arbia Tusc. DOC w. dr. ★→★★ D.Y.A.
Another DOC for a pleasant white and VIN SANTO from CHIANTI country.

Valentini, Edoardo Outstanding traditionalist maker of TREBBIANO and MONTEPULCIANO D'ABRUZZO.

Valgella (Valtellina) Lomb. DOC r. w. dr. ★★ **82 83 85** 86 88
One of the VALTELLINA NEBBIOLOS: good dry red. Riserva at 4 yrs.

Vallana, Antonio & Figlio The protagonist of the "SPANNA" (Nebbiolo) near Novara, Piem. Uses the DOC name BOCA. Rich-flavoured reds.

Valle d'Aosta/Vallée d'Aosta Vd'A. DOC
Regional DOC for 15 Alpine wines including DONNAZ, etc. A mixed bag.

Valle Isarco Tr-Aad. DOC w. dr. ★→★★ **88 89**
A DOC applicable to 5 varietal wines made n.e. of Bolzano. Outstanding MÜLLER-THURGAU, SYLVANER.

Valpantena Valley in the VALPOLICELLA zone. Rival to CLASSICO. See Bertani.

Valpolicella Ven. DOC r. dr. ★→ ★★★ **88** 89
Attractive light red from nr. Verona; most attractive when young. Delicate nutty scent, slightly bitter taste. (None of this is true of Valpolicella sold in litre and bigger bottles.) Classico more restricted; Superiore has 12% alcohol and 1 yr of age. Best wines from ALLEGRINI, MASI, Quintarelli.

Valtellina Lomb. DOC r. dr. ★★→★★★ **85 86 88** 89
A DOC for tannic wines made principally from Chiavennasca (NEBBIOLO) grapes in the province of Sondrio, n. Lombardy. V. Superiore is GRUMELLO, INFERNO, SASSELLA or VALGELLA.

Vecchio Samperi Sic. des. ★★★
The outstanding wine of MARSALA today, although not DOC. A dry apéritif not unlike Amontillado sherry.

Velletri Lat. DOC r. w. dr. or s/sw. ★★ (r.) **86 87** 88
Agreeable Roman dry red and smooth white. Drink young.

Vendemmia Harvest or vintage.

Venegazzù Ven. r. w. dr. sp. ★★★ **82 83 85** 86 88
Remarkable rustic Bordeaux-style red produced from CABERNET grapes nr. Treviso. Rich bouquet, soft, warm taste, "della Casa" is best quality. Also sparkling white.

Verdicchio dei Castelli di Jesi Mar. DOC w. dr. (sp.) ★→★★★ D.Y.A.
Ancient, famous and very pleasant fresh pale white from nr. Ancona. Goes back to the Etruscans. Classico is more restricted. Traditionally comes in amphora-shaped bottles: today also standard bottles of notable class from Umani Ronchi, Garofoli, Brundri, Bucci, Monte Schiaro; also Fazi-Battaglia.

Verdicchio di Matelica Mar. DOC w. dr. (sp.) ★★ D.Y.A.
Similar to the last, though less well known. Bigger wines than Jesi.

Verdiso Rare native white grape of n.e. Italy, used with PROSECCO.

Verduzzo (Colli Orientali del Friuli) r-VG. DOC w. dr. s/sw. or sw. ★★ **88 89** Full-bodied white from a native grape. The best sweet is called Ramandolo. Top maker: Giovanni Dri.

Verduzzo (Del Piave) Ven. DOC w. dr. ★ D.Y.A. A dull little white.

Vermentino Lig. w. dr. DOC ★★ D.Y.A.
The best seafood white of the Riviera: from Pietra Ligure and San Remo. DOC is Rivera Ligure del Ponente. See Pigato.

Vermentino di Gallura Sard. DOC w. dr. ★★ D.Y.A.
Soft, dry, rather strong white from northern Sardinia.

Vernaccia di Oristano Sard. DOC w. dr. (sw.) (f.) ★★★ **82 83 84 85** 86 88 89 Sardinian speciality, like light sherry, a touch bitter, full-bodied and interesting. Superiore with 15.5% alcohol and 3 yrs of age. Top producer Contini.

Vernaccia di San Gimignano Tusc. DOC w. dr. (f.) ★★ **86 87 88 89**
Should be a distinctive strong high-flavoured wine from near Siena. Michelangelo's favourite. Much today is light and bland but signs of improvement. Try Teruzzi & Puthod, Falchini or (old-style) Pietrafitta. Riserva after 1 yr.

Vernaccia di Serrapetrona Mar. DOC r. s/sw. sp. ★★ D.Y.A.
From Macerata; aromatic, with pleasantly bitter after-taste.

Vernatsch German for SCHIAVA.

Vicchiomaggio Important CHIANTI CLASSICO estate near Greve.

Vietti Excellent small producer of some of Piedmont's most characterful wines, incl. BAROLO. At Castiglione Falletto, Prov. Cuneo.

VIDE Grouping of better-class producers for marketing estate wines.

Vignamaggio Historic and beautiful CHIANTI CLASSICO estate near Greve.

Villa Banfi The production department of the biggest US importer of Italian wine. Huge new plantings at MONTALCINO, incl. SHIRAZ, P, NERO, CABERNET, CHARDONNAY, are part of a drive for quality plus quantity. BRUNELLO is proving excellent. Centine is ROSSO DI MONTALCINO. In PIEMONTE Banfi produces v.g. sp. Banfi Brut, Principessa GAVI, BRACCHETO D'ACQUI, Pinot Grigio.

Villagrande Imposing old estate on the slopes of Mt Etna, Sicily, DOC ETNA.

Vino da arrosto "Wine for roast meat", i.e. good robust dry red.

Vino da pasto "Mealtime" wine, i.e. nothing special.

Vino da tavola "Table wine": intended to be the humblest class of Italian wine, with one specific geographical or other claim to fame, but increasingly the category to watch (with reasonable circumspection) for top-class wines not conforming to DOC regulations. They are referred to in the A-Z as V.D.T. It is the maker's name that counts.

Vino Nobile di Montepulciano Tusc. DOCG r. dr. ★★★ **82 83 85 86 88** Impressive Chianti-like red with bouquet and style, rapidly making its name and fortune. Aged for 3 yrs Riserva; for 4 yrs Riserva Speciale. Best estates incl. BOSCARELLI, AVIGNONESI, Fognano, Poliziano, Bindella, Tennta Trerose.

Vino novello Italy's equivalent of France's "primeurs", (as in BEAUJOLAIS).

Vinsanto or **Vin Santo** Term for certain strong sweet wines esp. in Tuscany: usually PASSITI. Can be v. fine, esp. in Tuscany and Trentino.

Vin Santo di Gambellara Ven. DOC w. sw. ★★
Powerful velvety, golden: made near Vicenza and Verona.

Vin Santo Toscano Tusc. w. s/sw. ★★→★★★
Aromatic bouquet, rich and smooth. Aged in very small barrels known as Caratelli. Can be astonishing.

Vintage Tunina r-VG. w. dr. ★★★ **86 88** 89
A notable blended COLLIO white from the JERMANN estate.

Voerzio, Roberto Young pace-maker in Barolo with refreshing wines.

Volpaia, Castello di First-class CHIANTI CLASSICO estate at Radda. See Coltassala.

VQPRD Often found on the labels of DOC wines to signify "Vini di Qualita Prodotti in Regioni Delimitate", or quality wines from restricted areas in accordance with EEC regulations.

Zagarolo Lat. DOC w. dr. or s/sw. ★★ D.Y.A.
Neighbour of FRASCATI, similar wine.

Zanella, Maurizio Owner of CA'DEL BOSCO. His name is on top CAB/MERLOT blend, one of Italy's best (**82 83 84 85** 86 87 88).

Zerbina, Fattoria New leader in Romagna with best Albana DOCG to date (a rich passita), good SANGIOVESE and a SANGIOVESE-CABERNET V.D.T. in "barrique" called Marzeno di Marzeno.

Zonin One of Italy's biggest privately owned estates and wineries, based at GAMBELLARA, with DOC VALPOLICELLA, etc. Other large estates are at ASTI and in CHIANTI, San Gimignano and FRIULI. Also at Barboursville, Virginia, USA.

Germany

Of all the world's fine wines those of Germany are currently the most underrated (and therefore often the best value for money). Yet to the regret of those who admire the many fine examples of her unique style that truly represent her traditions, her climate and soil, her wine industry is in disarray; better known abroad for its banal products than for its masterpieces.

The fault lies with the government, whose wine laws, passed in 1971 and marginally modified in 1989, suffer from a fatal flaw. They try to democratize quality. The definition of "quality" wine mocks the word – and so do the official definitions of the grades of superior qualities – Kabinett, Spätlese and Auslese – that used to be proud talismans. Unlike the the French and Italian wine laws, until 1989 those of Germany put no limit on the amount produced from a given vineyard. Inflation of quantity and dilution of quality together have nearly been Germany's undoing. The regulations introduced in 1989 are so perfunctory as to make serious growers snort in derision.

If the tide is turning at last, it is because Germany's best growers have resolved to ignore government decrees and make the best wine they can, in a style that has not been seen for half a century. They have turned their backs on flowery, sugar-watery wine. Most of their wines are now dry, with sweetness reserved as the exception, for Spätleses and Ausleses – and not always even for these. They have been helped by two excellent vintages, after a decade with only one that was memorable. On the home market, especially in restaurants, these fine dry wines are all the rage, but abroad they have yet to be fully understood.

German wine law is based on the ripeness of the grapes at harvest time. Vintages vary, but most German wine, like most French wine, needs sugar added before fermentation to increase its strength, and make up for missing sunshine.

Unlike in France wine from grapes ripe enough not to need sugar is kept apart as Qualitätswein mit Prädikat or QmP. Within this top category its natural sugar content is expressed by traditional terms – in ascending order of ripeness: Kabinett, Spätlese, Auslese, Beerenauslese, Trockenbeerenauslese.

The second category, "Qualitätswein bestimmte Anbaugebiete" (QbA), is for wines that needed additional sugar before fermentation.

The third level, tafelwein, has no pretensions to quality.

Though there is very much more detail in the laws this is the gist of the quality grading. Where it differs completely from the French system is in ignoring geographical difference. There are no Grands Crus, no VDQS. In theory all any German vineyard has to do to make the best wine is to grow the ripest grapes.

The law distinguishes only between degrees of geographical exactness. In labelling quality wine the grower or merchant is given a choice. He can (and almost always will) label the relatively small quantities of his best wine with the name of the precise vineyard or Einzellage where it was grown. Germany

The following
abbreviations of
regional names
are used in the text.

Bad. Baden
Frank. Franken
M-M Mittel-Mosel
M-S-R Moselle Saar Ruwer
Na. Nahe
Rhg. Rheingau
Rhh. Rheinhessen
Rhpf. Rheinpfalz
Wurtt. Württemberg

has about 2,600 Einzellage names. Obviously only particularly good ones are famous enough to help sell the wine. Therefore the 1971 law created a second class of vineyard name: the Grosslage. A Grosslage is a group of neighbouring Einzellages of supposedly similar character. Because there are fewer Grosslage names, and far more wine from each, they have the advantage of familiarity. The law was thus responsible for confusing the public, and the industry is now suffering as a result.

Thirdly the grower or merchant (more likely the latter) may choose to sell his wine under a regional name: the word is Bereich. To cope with the vast demand for "Bernkasteler" or "Niersteiner" or "Johannisberger" these world-famous names have been made legal for considerable districts. "Bereich Johannisberg" is the whole of the Rheingau. By this logic the whole of the Médoc could be Margaux. Beware the Bereich.

A fourth alternative, now gaining ground, is to use the community (or village) name only, not mentioning the vineyard. Do not confuse these with Bereich wines. One golden rule: the name of the producer is the key.

Recent vintages

Mosel-Saar-Ruwer

Mosels (including Saar and Ruwer wines) are so attractive young that their keeping qualities are not often enough explored, and wines older than seven years or so are unusual. But well-made wines of Kabinett class gain from three or more in bottle, Spätleses by longer, and Ausleses and Beerenausleses by anything from 10 to 20 years.

As a rule, in poor years the Saar and Ruwer make sharp, thin wines, but in the best years they can surpass the whole of Germany for elegance and "breed".

1989 Large and outstandingly good, with noble rot giving great Ausleses, etc.
1988 Excellent vintage. Much ripe QmP, esp. in Mittelmosel. For long keeping.
1987 Rainy summer but warm Sept/Oct. 90% QbA wines, crisp and lively, keeping well.
1986 Fair Riesling year despite autumn rain: 13% QmP wines, mostly Kabinett. Mostly ready.
1985 A modest summer but beautiful autumn. 40% of the harvest was QmP. Very good Riesling vintage from best v'yds, incl. Eiswein. Drinking well.
1984 A late and rainy year. Two-thirds QbA, one-third Tafel or Landwein. Almost no QmP. But good acidity means some wines (esp. Ruwers) have kept well.
1983 The best between 1976 and '88, much good QbA, a little Kabinett, 31% Spätlese, Ausleses few but some fine. No hurry to drink.
1982 A huge ripe vintage marred by rain which considerably diluted the wines. Most is plain QbA but good sites made Kabinett, Spätlese and Auslese. Drink up.
1981 A wet vintage but some good middle Mosels up to Spätlese. Also Eiswein. Drink up.
1980 A terrible summer. Some pleasant wines but little more. Avoid.
1979 A patchy vintage after bad winter damage. But several excellent Kabinetts and better. Light but well-balanced wines should be drunk up.
1978 A similar vintage to '77, though very late and rather small. Very few sweet wines but many with good balance. Drink up.
1977 Big vintage of serviceable quality, mostly QbA. Drink up.
1976 Very good small vintage, with some superlative sweet wines and almost no dry. Most wines now ready; the best will keep a little longer.
1975 Very good; many Spätleses and Ausleses. Almost all now ready.
1971 Superb, with perfect balance. At its peak.
Older fine vintages: '69, '67, '64, '59, '53, '49, '45.

Rheinhessen, Nahe, Rheinpfalz, Rheingau

Even the best wines can be drunk with pleasure after two or three years, but Kabinett, Spätlese and Auslese wines gain enormously in character by keeping for longer. Rheingau wines tend to be longest-lived, improving for 10 years or more, but wines from the Nahe and Palatinate can last nearly as long. Rheinhessen wines usually mature sooner, and dry Franconian wines are best at 3-6 years.

1989 Serious summer storms reduced quantity in Rheingau. V.g. quality; in most areas up to Auslese level.
1988 Not quite so outstanding as the Mosel, but comparable with 1983.
1987 Good average quality: lively, round and fresh. 80% QbA (keep 2-4 years), 15% QmP (keep 3-6 years).
1986 Well-balanced Rieslings, mostly QbA but some Kabinett and Spätlese, esp. in Rheinhessen and Nahe. No hurry to drink.
1985 Frost, hail and drought led to sadly small crops, but good quality, esp. Riesling. Average 65% QmP. Comparable quality to 1983. Keeping well.
1984 Poor flowering and ripening. Three-quarters QbA, with QmP only in Rheinhessen, Rheinpfalz, Baden and Nahe. But flavour can be good. Drink soon.
1983 Very good Rieslings, esp. in the Rheingau and central Nahe. Generally about half QbA, but plenty of Spätleses. No hurry to drink.
1982 A colossal vintage gathered in torrential rain. All '82s should be drunk up.
1981 Poor conditions in the Rheingau but better in Nahe and Rheinhessen and good in Palatinate. Generally ready.
1980 Bad weather from spring to autumn. Only passable wines. Avoid.
1979 Few great wines but many typical and good, esp. in Palatinate. Drink up.
1978 Satisfactory vintage saved by late autumn. 25% QmP, but very few Spätleses. Some excellent wines in the south. Drink up.
1977 Big and useful; few Kabinett wines or better. Drink up.
1976 The richest vintage since 1921 in places. Very few dry wines. Balance less consistent than 1975. Generally mature.
1975 A splendid Riesling year, a high percentage of Kabinetts and Spätleses. Drink soon.
1971 A superlative vintage, now at its peak.
Older fine vintages: '69, '67, '66, '64, '59, '57, '53, '49, '45.

N.B. On the German vintage notation

Vintage notes after entries in the German section are given in a different form from those elsewhere, to show the style of the vintage as well as its quality. Three styles are indicated: The classic, super-ripe vintage with a high proportion of natural (QmP) wines, including Spätleses and Ausleses. Example: **88**

The "normal" successful vintage with plenty of good wine but no great preponderance of sweeter wines. Example: 86

The cool vintage with generally poor ripeness but a fair proportion of reasonably successful wines, tending to be over-acid. Few or no QmP wines, but correspondingly more selection in the QbA category. Such wines sometimes mature better than expected. Example: *84*

Where no mention is made the vintage is generally not recommended, or most of its wines have passed maturity.

Achkarren Bad. (r.) w. ******
> Well-known wine village of the KAISERSTUHL, esp. for SILVANER, RULÄNDER. Best site: Schlossberg. Good wines from coop.

Adelmann, Graf Famous grower with 37 acres at Kleinbottwar, WÜRTTEMBERG. Uses the name "Brussele". Light reds; good RIESLINGS.

Ahr Ahr r. ***→** 76 83** 85 86 87 88 **89**
> Germany's best-known red-wine area, s. of Bonn. Very light pale SPÄTBURGUNDERS, esp. from STATE DOMAIN Kloster Marienthal.

Amtliche Prüfungsnummer See Prüfungsnummer.

Anheuser Name of two distinguished growers of the NAHE; August (***) and Paul (**).

Annaberg Rhpf. w. ***** 75 76** 79 **83** *84* 85 86 87 **88 89**
> 18-acre v'yd at Dürkheim famous for stylish and pungent wines, esp. SCHEUREBES, with prodigious keeping qualities.

A.P.Nr. Abbreviation of AMTLICHE PRÜFUNGSNUMMER.

Assmannshausen Rhg. r. ***→*** 71 75 76 83** 85 86 87 88 **89**
> RHEINGAU village known for its pale, sometimes sweet, reds. Top v'yd: Höllenberg. Grosslagen: Steil and Burgweg. Growers incl. the State Domain at ELTVILLE, August Kessler, VON MUMM, Allendorf.

Auslese Specially selected wine with high natural sugar content; the best affected by "noble rot" and correspondingly unctuous in flavour.

Avelsbach M-S-R (Ruwer) w. ***** 71 75 76** 79 **83** 84 85 86 87 **88 89**
> Village near TRIER. Supremely delicate wines. Growers: Staatliche Weinbaudomäne (see Staatsweingut), BISCHÖFLICHE WEINGÜTER. Grosslage: Römerlay.

Ayl M-S-R (Saar) w. ***** 71 75 76** 79 **83** *84* 85 86 87 **88** 89
> One of the best villages of the SAAR. Top v'yds: Kupp, Herrenberger. Grosslage: Scharzberg. Growers incl. BISCHÖFLICHE WEINGÜTER.

Bacchus Modern highly perfumed grape variety, best for sweet wines.

Bacharach Romantic old town, a tourist centre of the MITTELRHEIN.

Bacharach (Bereich) ***→****
> District name for the s. Mittelrhein v'yds downstream from the RHEINGAU. Steely, racy wines, some v. pleasant. Growers incl. Toni Jost.

Baden Huge south-western area of scattered wine-growing. The style is substantial, relatively low in acid, well adapted for mealtimes. Best areas are KAISERSTUHL and ORTENAU.

Badische Bergstrasse/Kraichgau (Bereich) Widespread district of n. BADEN. RIESLING and RULÄNDER are best.

Bad Dürkheim See Dürkheim, Bad.

Badischer Winzerkeller New name for the former ZBW, Germany's (and Europe's) biggest ultra-modern cooperative, at Breisach, BADEN, with 25,000 grower-members with 12,000 acres, producing 80% of Baden's wine at all quality levels.

Badisches Frankenland (Bereich) Minor district name of n. BADEN; Franconian-style wines.

Bad Kreuznach Nahe w. ★★→★★★ **75 76** 79 **83** *84* 85 86 87
Main town of the NAHE with some of its best wines. Many fine v'yds, incl. Brückes, Kahlenberg, Steinweg, Krötenpfuhl. Grosslage: Kronenberg. Growers incl. ANHEUSERS, Finkenauer, PLETTENBERG.

Balbach Erben, Bürgermeister One of the best-known NIERSTEIN growers. 44 acres, 80% Riesling. Best v'yds: Pettenthal, Ölberg.

Barriques A few German growers are experimenting with fashionable new-oak small-barrel ageing. Higher prices are only positive result.

Basserman-Jordan 117-acre MITTELHAARDT family estate with many of the best v'yds in DEIDESHEIM, FORST, RUPPERTSBERG, etc. 100% Riesling.

Becker, J.B. Excellent family estate and brokerage house at WALLUF, Rheingau. 30 acres in WALLUF, ELTVILLE, MARTINSTHAL.

Beerenauslese Extremely sweet and luscious wine from exceptionally ripe selected individual bunches, their sugar and flavour concentrated by "noble rot". Very rare and expensive.

Bereich District within an Anbaugebiet (region). See introduction and under Bereich names, e.g. Bernkastel (Bereich). The word on a label should be treated as a warning.

Bergweiler-Prüm Erben (Dr. Pauly-Bergweiler), Zach., Weingut Fine 27-acre estate based at BERNKASTEL. V'yds there and in WEHLEN, etc. Also Nicolay wines from ÜRZIG and ERDEN.

Bergzabern, Bad Rhpf. (r.) w. ★→★★ **76** 79 83 *84* 85 86 87 88 **89**
Town of SÜDLICHE-WEINSTRASSE. Pleasant light wines. Grosslage: Liebfrauenberg.

Bernkastel M-M w. ★★→★★★★ **71** **75 76** 79 **83** *84* 85 86 87 **88 89**
Top wine-town of the Mosel; the epitome of RIESLING. Best v'yds: Doctor (8 acres), Graben, Bratenhöfchen, etc. Grosslagen: Badstube (★★★) and Kurfürstlay (★★). Top growers incl. FRIEDRICH WILHELM GYMNASIUM, VEREINIGTE HOSPITIEN, THANISCH, PRÜM, WEGELER-DEINHARD, LAUERBURG, LOOSEN, STUDERT-PRÜM, BERGWEILER, etc.

Bernkastel (Bereich) Wide area of deplorably mixed quality but hopefully flowery character. Includes all the Mittelmosel.

Bingen Rhh. w. ★★→★★★ **71** **75 76** 79 **83** *84* 85 86 87 88 **89**
Town on Rhine and Nahe with fine v'yds, incl. Scharlachberg. Grosslage: Sankt Rochuskapelle. Top grower: VILLA SACHSEN.

Bingen (Bereich) District name for w. Rheinhessen.

Bischöfliche, Weinguter Verwaltung der Famous M-S-R estate at TRIER, a union of the Cathedral properties with two other famous charities, the Bischöfliches Priesterseminar and the Bischöfliches Konvikt. 260 acres of top v'yds in AVELSBACH, WILTINGEN, SCHARZHOFBERG, AYL, KASEL, EITELSBACH, PIESPORT, TRITTENHEIM, ÜRZIG, etc. Regrettably inconsistent.

Blankenhornsberg Well-known KAISERSTUHL estate; 62 acres at IHRINGEN.

Blue Nun The best-selling brand of LIEBFRAUMILCH, from SICHEL.

Bodenheim Rhh. w. ★★
Village nr. NIERSTEIN with delicate wines, esp. from Silberberg. Top grower: Liebrecht.

Bodensee (Bereich) Minor district of s. BADEN, on Lake Constance.

Bocksbeutel lask-shaped bottle used for FRANKEN wines.

Brauneberg M-M w. ★★★ **71** **75 76** 79 **83** *84* 85 86 87 88 **89**
Village near BERNKASTEL with 750 acres. Excellent full-flavoured Rieslings. Best v'yd: Juffer. Grosslage: Kurfürstlay. Growers incl, BERGWEILER, Paulinshof, RICHTER, HAAG, VON KESSELSTATT, Karp-Schreiber.

Breisach Baden
Frontier town on Rhine nr. KAISERSTUHL. Seat of the largest German cooperative, the BADISCHER WINZERKELLER.

Breisgau (Bereich) Minor district of BADEN, just n. of KAISERSTUHL. Best known for very pale pink WEISSHERBST.

Brentano, von 25-acre old family estate in WINKEL, Rhg. Uneven quality.

Breuer, G. Weingut Family estate of 36 acres in RÜDESHEIM, with 6 acres of Berg Schlossberg setting the pace for the district. Brilliant quality and new ideas. See also Scholl & Hillebrand.

Buhl, von, Reichsrat Historic RHEINPFALZ family estate. 250+ acres in DEIDESHEIM, FORST, RUPPERTSBERG, etc. New Japanese owners.

Bullay M-S-R ★→ ★★ 76 **83** 85 86 87 **88 89**
Lower Mosel village. Good light wines. Growers incl. Drathen.

Bundesweinprämierung The German State Wine Award, organized by the DLG (see below): gives gold, silver or bronze medallion labels.

Bürgerspital zum Heiligen Geist Ancient charitable estate at WÜRZBURG. 333 acres in WÜRZBURG, RANDERSACKER, etc., make rich dry wines.

Bürklin-Wolf, Dr Great RHEINPFALZ family estate. 247 acres in WACHENHEIM, FORST, DEIDESHEIM and RUPPERTSBERG. Many wines more worthy than inspirational recently.

Castell'sches, Fürstlich Domänenamt Historic 142-acre princely estate in STEIGERWALD. Noble FRANKEN wines: SILVANER, RIESLANER. Also SEKT.

Chardonnay A small acreage of Chardonnay has been experimentally, and sometimes illegally, planted – e.g. on an island in the Rhine. It is the wrong grape for Germany.

Charta Organization of top RHEINGAU estates making HALBTROCKEN RIESLINGS. The wines are made to considerably higher standards than the dismally permissive laws require.

Crown of Crowns Popular brand of LIEBFRAUMILCH from LANGENBACH & CO.

Crusius 30-acre family estate at TRAISEN, Nahe. Excellently made, vivid RIESLINGS from Bastei and Rotenfels v'yds age v. well. Also SEKT of high quality and freshly fruity SPÄTBURGUNDER dry rosé.

Dahlem Erben, Dr Long-established 67-acre estate in OPPENHEIM. Some fine RIESLING and SYLVANER.

Deidesheim Rhpf. w. (r.) ★★→★★★★ **71** 75 76 79 **83** 84 85 86 87 **88 89**
Biggest top-quality wine-village of RHEINPFALZ with 1,000 acres. Rich, high-flavoured, lively wines. V'yds incl. Grainhübel, Herrgottsacker, Leinhöhle, Hohenmorgen, Kieselberg, Paradiesgarten, etc. Grosslagen: Hofstück (★★), Mariengarten (★★★). Top growers: BASSERMANN-JORDAN, DEINHARD, Bilfar, BÜRKLIN-WOLF, Fitz-Ritter, VON BUHL.

Deinhard Famous old Koblenz merchants and growers of top-quality wines in RHEINGAU, MITTELMOSEL, RUWER and RHEINPFALZ (see Wegeler-Deinhard), also makers of v.g. SEKT (brand name: Lila). Launched in '88 the Heritage range of single-village TROCKEN wines. Leaders in both quality and new ideas.

Deinhard, Dr 62-acre family estate in DEIDESHEIM with many of best v'yds.

Deutscher Tafelwein TAFELWEIN from Germany (only). See also Tafelwein.

Deutsches Weinsiegel A quality "seal" (i.e. neck label) for wines which have passed a statutory tasting test. Seals are yellow = dry, green = medium dry, red = sweet.

Deutsche Weinstrasse Popular tourist road of the southern Palatinate, Bockenheim to Schweigen.

DLG (Deutsche Landwirtschaft Gesellschaft) The German Agricultural Society at Frankfurt. Awards national medals for quality.

Dhron See Neumagen-Dhron.

Diabetiker Wein Wine with minimal residual sugar (less than 4gms/litre); thus suitable for diabetics – or those who like *very* dry wine.

Diel auf Burg Layen, Schlossgut Fashionable 30 acre NAHE estate; known for ageing RIESLING (also RULANDER) in French barriques.

Dienheim Rhh. w. ★★ 76 **83** 85 86 87 88 **89**
Southern neighbour of OPPENHEIM. Mainly run-of-the-mill wines. Best v'yds: Kreuz, Herrenberg, Schloss. Grosslagen: Güldenmorgen, Krötenbrunnen. Growers incl. Braun, DAHLEM, Wolf-Metternich.

Dom German for Cathedral. Wines from the famous TRIER Cathedral properties have "Dom" before the v'yd name.

Domäne German for "domain" or "estate". Sometimes used alone to mean the "State domain" (Staatliche Weinbaudomäne).

Durbach Baden w. (r.) ★★→ **★★★** 76 **83** *84* 85 86 87 88 **89**
775 acres of the best v'yds of BADEN. Top growers: Schloss Staufenberg, Wolf-Metternich, von Neveu, H. Männle. Choose their KLINGELBERGERS (Rieslings) and KLEVNERS (Traminers). Grosslage: Fürsteneck.

Dürkheim, Bad Rhpf. w. or (r.) ★★→★★★ 76 79 83 *84* **85** 86 87 88 **89**
Main town of the MITTELHAARDT with the world's biggest barrel (converted into a tavern). Top v'yds: Hochbenn, Michelsberg. Grosslagen: Feuerberg, Schenkenböhl, Hochmess. Top growers: BÜRKLIN-WOLF, Fitz-Ritter, Karst, Koehler-Ruprecht.

Edel Means "noble". Edelfäule means "noble rot": the condition which gives the greatest sweet wines (see p. 49).

Egon Müller zu Scharzhof Top Saar estate of 32 acres at WILTINGEN. Its delicate, racy SCHARZHOFBERGER Rieslings are among the world's greatest wines, esp. in vintages that produce AUSLESES.

Eiswein Wine made from frozen grapes with the ice (e.g. water content) rejected, thus very concentrated in flavour and sugar, of Beerenauslese ripeness or more. Rare and very expensive. Sometimes produced as late as the January or February following the vintage. Alcohol content can be as low as 5.5%. High acidity gives them long life.

Eitelsbach Ruwer w. ★★→★★★ **71** 75 76 **83** *84* 85 86 87 **88 89**
RUWER village now part of TRIER, incl. superb KARTHÄUSERHOFBERG estate. Grosslage: Römerlay.

Elbling Traditional but generally inferior grape widely grown on upper Mosel but capable of great freshness and vitality in the best conditions (e.g. at MENNIG or in the Mittelmosel).

Eltville Rhg. w. **★★→★★★** **71** 75 76 79 **83** *84* **85** 86 87 88 **89**
Major wine-town with cellars of the Rheingau State domain, FISCHER and VON SIMMERN estates. Excellent wines. Top v'yds: Sonnenberg, Taubenberg. Grosslage: Steinmächer.

Enkirch M-M w. ★★→ **★★★** **71** 76 **83** *84* 85 86 87 **88 89**
Minor MITTELMOSEL village, often overlooked but with lovely light tasty wine. Grosslage: Schwarzlay. Best v'yds: Steffensberg, Herrenberg.

Erbach Rhg. w. ★★★→★★★★ **71** 76 79 **83** *84* 85 86 87 88 **89**
One of the best parts of the Rheingau with powerful, perfumed wines, incl. the great MARCOBRUNN; other top v'yds: Schlossberg, Siegelsberg, Honigberg, Michelmark. Grosslage: Deutelsberg. Major estates: SCHLOSS REINHARTSHAUSEN, VON SCHÖNBORN. Also WEIL, BECKER, RESS, Knyphausen, etc.

Erben Word meaning "airs", often used on old-established estate labels.

Erden M-M w. ★★→★★★ **71** 75 76 **83** *84* 85 86 87 **88 89**
Village between Ürzig and Kröv with full-flavoured vigorous wine. Top v'yds: Prälat, Treppchen. Growers incl: BISCHÖFLICHE WEINGÜTER, BERGWEILER-PRÜM, LOOSEN, Christoffel, MÖNCHHOF, Nicolay. Grosslage: Schwarzlay.

Erzeugerabfüllung Estate-bottled; bottled by the producer.

Escherndorf rank. w. ★★→★★★ 76 **83** 86 87 88
Important wine-town near WÜRZBURG. Similar tasty dry wine. Top v'yds: Lump, Berg. Grosslage: Kirchberg. Growers incl: JULIUSSPITAL.

Remember that vintage information about German wines is given in a different form from the ready/not ready distinction applying to other countries. Read the explanation on page 104.

Fischer, Dr. Weingut 60-acre estate of top quality at OCKFEN, incl. whole of 25-acre WAWERNER Herrenberg.

Fischer Erben, Weingut 18-acre RHEINGAU estate at ELTVILLE with highest traditional standards. Immensely long-lived classic wines.

Fitz-Ritter High-profile Bad Dürkheim estate. 54 acres, fine Rieslings.

Forschungsanstalt See Hessische Forschungsanstalt für Wein-Obst-&
  Gartenbau . . .

Forst Rhpf. w. ★★→★★★★ **71** 75 76 79 **83** *84* **85** 86 87 88 **89**
  MITTELHAARDT village with 500 acres of Germany's best v'yds. Ripe,
  richly fragrant, full-bodied but subtle wines. Top v'yds: Kirchenstück,
  Jesuitengarten, Ungeheuer. Grosslagen: Mariengarten, Schnepfenflug. Many excellent growers.

Franken Franconia: region of excellent distinctive dry wines, esp.
  SILVANER, always bottled in round-bellied flasks. The centre is
  WÜRZBURG. BEREICH names: MAINDREIECK, STEIGERWALD.

Freiburg Baden w. (r.) ★→★★ D.Y.A.
  Wine centre in n. of MARKGRÄFLERLAND. Good GUTEDEL.

Freinsheim Rhpf. w. r. ★★
  Well-known village of Lower Haardt with high proportion of Riesling.
  Earthy, spicy wines. Top grower: LINGENFELDER.

Friedrich Wilhelm Gymnasium Superb 111-acre charitable estate based
  in TRIER with v'yds in BERNKASTEL, ZELTINGEN, GRAACH, TRITTENHEIM,
  OCKFEN, etc., all M-S-R.

Fuhrmann See Pfeffingen.

Geheimrat 'J' Brand-name of v.g. dry Riesling Spätlese from WEGELER-
  DEINHARD, Oestrich since '85. Epitomizes new thinking in German
  wine.

Geisenheim Rhg. w. ★★→★★★ **71** 76 **83** *84* 85 86 87 88 **89**
  Village famous for Germany's leading wine-school and fine aromatic
  wines. Best v'yds incl. Rothenberg, Kläuserweg. Grosslagen: Burgweg
  and Erntebringer. Many top Rhg. growers have v'yds here.

Gemeinde A commune or parish.

Gewürztraminer Spicy grape, speciality of Alsace, used a little in
  Germany, esp. RHEINPFALZ, Rheinhessen and BADEN. Also called
  Traminer.

Gimmeldingen Rhpf. w. ★→★★★ 76 **83** *84* 85 86 87 88 **89**
  Village just s. of MITTELHAARDT. At their best, similar wines. Grosslage:
  Meerspinne. Top growers: Müller-Catoir, Stolleis, Mugler.

Goldener Oktober Brand of Rhine and Mosel blends from ST URSULA.

Graach M-M w. ★★→ ▐▐▐▐ **71** 75 76 **83** *84* 85 86 87 **88 89**
  Small village between BERNKASTEL and WEHLEN. Top v'yds: Himmel-
  reich, Domprobst, Abstberg, Josephshöfer. Grosslage: Münzlay. Many
  top growers incl: J.J. PRÜM, DEINHARD, THANISCH, etc.

Green Label Best-selling MOSEL (BEREICH BERNKASTEL). Brand-name of
  DEINHARD.

Grosslage See Introduction, p.103.

Gunderloch-Usinger Currently top-rate 30-acre NACKENHEIM estate. 70%
  Riesling.

Guntersblum Rhh. w. ★→★★ 76 **83** *84* 85 86 87 88 **89**
  Big wine-town s. of OPPENHEIM. Grosslagen: Krötenbrunnen, Vogels-
  gärten. Top-growers: Rappenhof, DAHLEM.

Guntrum, Louis Fine 164-acre family estate in NIERSTEIN. OPPENHEIM, etc.,
  and merchant house with high and reliable standards. Fine SILVANERS
  and GEWÜRZ as well as RIESLINGS.

Gutedel German for the Chasselas grape, used in S. BADEN.

Gutsverwaltung Estate administration.

Haag, Fritz Top-quality little (12 acres) estate at BRAUNEBERG.

Halbtrocken Medium-dry. Containing less than 18 but more than 9
  grams per litre unfermented sugar. An increasingly popular category
  of wine intended for meal-times, often better-balanced than TROCKEN.
  All CHARTA wines are halbtrocken.

Hallgarten Rhg. w. ★★→★★★ **71** 76 **83** *84* 85 86 87 88 **89**
  Important little wine-town behind HATTENHEIM. Robust, full-bodied
  wines. Top v'yds incl. Schönhell, Jungfer. Grosslage: Mehrhölzchen.
  Top growers incl: LÖWENSTEIN, DEINHARD, WEIL, Eser.

Hallgarten, House of Well-known London-based wine-merchant.

Hanns Christof Estimable Rhine-wine brand from DEINHARD.

Hattenheim Rhg. w. ★★→★★★★ **71 75 76 83** 84 85 86 87 88 **89**

Superlative 500-acre wine-town. V'yds incl. STEINBERG, NUSSBRUNNEN, MANNBERG, HASSEL etc. Grosslage: Deutelsberg. MARCOBRUNN lies on the ERBACH boundary. Many fine estates incl: SCHLOSS SCHÖNBORN, STATE DOMAIN, KNYPHAUSEN, RESS, etc.

Heilbronn Württ. w. r. ★→★★★ **76 83** 85 86 87 88 **89**

Wine-town with many small growers and a big coop. Seat of DLG competition. Top growers: Heinrich, Drautz-Able, Amalienhof.

Hessische Bergstrasse w. ★★→★★★ **76** 83 84 85 86 87 88 **89**

Germany's smallest wine-region (1,000 acres) n. of Heidelberg. Pleasant Riesling from State domain v'yds in Heppenheim and Bensheim, Stadt Bensheim and Bergstrasser coop.

Hessische Forschungsanstalt für Wein-Obst-& Gartenbau . . .

Germany's top wine-school and research establishment, at GEISENHEIM, Rheingau. Label (good wines incl. reds) is "Forschungsanstalt".

Heyl zu Herrnsheim 72-acre estate, perhaps the best in NIERSTEIN, 60% Riesling.

Hochgewächs Term for a superior level of QbA, esp. in MOSEL-SAAR-RUWER.

Hochheim Rhg. w. ★★→★★★ **71 75 76** 79 **83** 84 85 86 87 **88 89**

600-acre wine-town 15 miles e. of the main part of the RHEINGAU. Similar fine wines with a softness and fragrance of their own. Top v'yds.: Domdechaney, Kirchenstück, Hölle, Königin Viktoria Berg. Grosslage: Daubhaus. Growers incl.: Aschrott, RESS, SCHÖNBORN, WERNER.

Hock English term for Rhine-wine, derived from HOCHHEIM.

Huesgen, Adolph Important merchant house at TRABEN-TRARBACH.

Huxelrebe Modern very aromatic grape variety; mainly for sweet wines.

Ihringen Bad. r. w. ★→★★★ 81 **83** 84 85 86 87 88 **89**

One of the best villages of the KAISERSTUHL, BADEN. Proud of its SPÄTBURGUNDER red, WEISSHERBST and v.g. SILVANER. Top growers: Heger, Stigler, Blankenhornberg.

Ilbesheim Rhpf. w. ▰★→★★★ **83** 85 86 87 88 **89**

Base of important growers' cooperative of SÜDLICHE WEINSTRASSE. See also Schweigen.

Ingelheim Rhh. r. or w. ★ 85 86 87 88 89

Town opposite the RHEINGAU historically known for SPÄTBURGUNDER.

Iphofen Frank. w. ★★→★★★ 75 76 **83** 85 87 88 89

Village e. of WÜRZBURG. Superb top v'yd: Julius-Echter-Berg. Grosslage: Burgweg. Growers: STAATLICHER HOFKELLER, JULIUSSPITAL, Wirsching, Ruck.

Jahrgang Year – as in "vintage".

Jesuitengarten 15-acre vineyard in FORST. One of Germany's best.

Johannisberg Rhg. w. ★★→★★★★ **71 75 76** 79 **83** 84 85 86 87 88 **89**

260-acre village with superlative subtle RIESLINGS. Top v'yds incl. SCHLOSS JOHANNISBERG, Hölle, Klaus, etc. Grosslage: Erntebringer. Many good growers. But beware "Bereich Johannisberg" wines (see next entry).

Johannisberg (Bereich) District name of the entire RHEINGAU.

Josephshöfer Fine v'yd at GRAACH, the property of von KESSELSTATT.

Juliusspital Ancient religious charity at WÜRZBURG with 374 acres of top FRANKEN v'yds. Look for SILVANERS.

Kabinett The term for the lightest category of natural unsugared (QmP) wines. Low in alcohol (average 7-9%) but capable of sublime finesse.

Kaiserstuhl-Tuniberg (Bereich) One of the top districts of BADEN. Villages incl. ACHKARREN, IHRINGEN.

Kallstadt Rhpf. w. (r.) ★★→★★★ **75 76** 83 *84* 85 86 87 88 **89**
Village of n. MITTELHAARDT. Fine rich wines. Top v'yd: ANNABERG.
Grosslagen: Feuerberg, Kobnert. Growers incl. Koehler-Ruprecht,
Henninger, Stumpf-Fitz.

Kammerpreismünze See Landespreismünze.

Kanzem M-S-R (Saar) w. ★★★ **71 75 76** 83 *84* 85 86 87 **88 89**
Small but excellent neighbour of WILTINGEN. Top v'yds: Sonnenberg,
Altenberg. Grosslage: Scharzberg. Growers incl. Le Gallais, Othegra-
ven, Reverchon, BISCHÖFLICHEN WEINGUTER, etc.

Kasel M-S-R (Ruwer) w. ★★→★★★ **71 75 76** 83 *84* 85 86 87 **88 89**
Village with wonderfully attractive light wines. Best v'yd: Nies'chen.
Grosslage: Römerlay. Growers incl. DEINHARD, BISCHÖLFLICHEN WEIN-
GUTER, VON KESSELSTATT, von Beulwitz, von Nele.

Keller Wine-cellar.

Kellerei Winery.

Kerner Modern grape variety, earlier-ripening than Riesling, of fair
quality but without the inbuilt harmony of Riesling.

Kesselstatt, von The biggest private Mosel estate, 600 years old. Over
200 acres in GRAACH (Josephshöfer), PIESPORT, KASEL, MENNIG, WILTINGEN,
etc., plus substantial rented or managed estates, making light and
fruity typical Mosels. Now belongs to Gunther Reh of Leiwen.

Kesten M-M w. ★→★★★ **71 75 76** 79 83 *84* 85 86 87 **88 89**
Neighbour of BRAUNEBERG. Best wines (from Paulinshofberg v'yd)
similar. Grosslage: Kurfürstlay. Top grower: DEINHARD.

Kiedrich Rhg. w. ★★→★★★★ **71 76** 79 83 *84* 85 86 87 88 **89**
Neighbour of RAUENTHAL; almost as splendid and high-flavoured. Top
v'yds: Gräfenberg, Wasseros, Sandgrub. Grosslage: Heiligenstock.
Top growers: Schloss Groensteyn, WEIL, STATE DOMAIN, FISCHER,
Knyphausen, etc.

Klevner (or Clevner) Red Klevner (synonym, Blauer Frühburgunder),
grown in WÜRTTEMBERG, is supposedly either a mutation of Pinot Noir
or Italian Chiavenna, an early-ripening black Pinot. Also an ORTENAU
(BADEN) synonym for TRAMINER.

Klingelberger BADEN term for the RIESLING, esp. at DURBACH.

Kloster Eberbach Glorious 12th-century Abbey at HATTENHEIM, Rheingau,
now State domain property and H.Q. of the German Wine Academy.

Klüsserath M-M w. ★★→ ★★★ 76 83 *84* 85 86 88 **89**
Minor Mosel village worth trying in good vintages. Best v'yds:
Bruderschaft, Königsberg. Grosslage: St Michael. Top growers:
FRIEDRICH WILHELM GYMNASIUM, Kirsten.

Koehler-Ruprecht Top-rated little (22-acre) estate at KALLSTADT, Pfalz.

Kraichgau Small BADEN region s. of Heidelberg. Best-known wines are
from villages of Neckarzimmern and Wiesloch.

Kreuznach (Bereich) District name for the entire northern NAHE. See also
Bad Kreuznach.

Kröv M-M w. ★→★★★ 76 83 85 86 87 **88 89**
Popular tourist resort famous for its Grosslage name: Nacktarsch,
meaning "bare bottom".

Landespreismünze Prizes for quality at state, rather than national, level.
Considered by some more discriminating than DLG medals.

Landgräflich Hessisches Weingut Wide-ranging 75-acre estate in JOHAN-
NISBERG, WINKEL, KIEDRICH and ELTVILLE. "Prinz von Hessen" is an
excellent KABINETT blend.

Landwein A category of better quality TAFELWEIN (the grapes must be
slightly riper) from 15 designated regions. It must be TROCKEN or
HALBTROCKEN. Similar in intention to France's Vins de Pays.

Lauerburg One of the four owners of the famous Doctor v'yd, with 10
acres, all in BERNKASTEL. Excellent racy wines.

Liebfrauenstift 26-acre v'yd in the city of Worms, said to be the origin of
the name LIEBFRAUMILCH.

Liebfraumilch A much-abused name, accounting for 50% of all German wine exports – much to the detriment of Germany's better products. Legally defined as a QbA "of pleasant character" from RHEINHESSEN, RHEINPFALZ, NAHE or RHEINGAU, of a blend with at least 51% of RIESLING, SILVANER, KERNER or MÜLLER-THURGAU. Most is mild semi-sweet wine from RHEINHESSEN and RHEINPFALZ. The rules now say it must have more than 18 gms. per litre unfermented sugar. Sometimes very cheap and of inferior quality, depending on brand/shipper. Its definition makes a mockery of the term "Quality wine".

Lieser M-M w. ★→ ██ ★★ 71 76 83 *84* 85 86 87 **88 89**
Little-known neighbour of BERNKASTEL. Best v'yd: Schlossberg. Grosslage: Kurfürstlay. Growers incl. DEINHARD, THANISCH.

Lingerfelder Weingut Small innovative estate at Grosskarlbach (Rhpf.) making Germany's best Burgundy-style SPÄTBURGUNDERS and full-bodied RIESLING etc.

Loosen, Dr, Weingut 20-acre St Johannishof estate in BERKASTEL, GRAACH, WEHLEN, URZIG. Lovely quality in '88.

Lorch Rhg. w. (r.) ★→★★ 71 76 83 85 86 87 88 **89**
At extreme w. end of Rheingau. Some fine light RIESLINGS more like MITTELRHEIN wines. Best growers: von Kanitz, Altenkirch.

Löwenstein, Fürst 66-acre FRANKEN estate: classic dry powerful wines. 45-acre HALLGARTEN property rented by MATUSCHKA-GREIFFENCLAU.

Maikammer Rhpf. w. (r.) ★→ ██ ★★ **83** 85 86 87 88 **89**
Village of n. SÜDLICHE WEINSTRASSE. Very pleasant wines incl. those from coop at Rietburg. Grosslage: Mandelhöhe.

Maindreieck (Bereich) The central part of FRANKEN, incl. WÜRZBURG.

Marcobrunn Historic RHEINGAU v'yd; one of Germany's best. See Erbach.

Markgräflerland (Bereich) District s. of Freiburg (BADEN). GUTEDEL wine is delicious refreshment when drunk very young.

Martinsthal Rhg. w. ★★→ ██ ★★★ 71 75 76 **83** *84* 85 86 87 88 89
Little-known neighbour of RAUENTHAL. Top v'yds: Langenberg, Wild-sau. Grosslage: Steinmächer. Growers incl. BECKER, Diefenhardt.

Matuschka-Greiffenclau, Graf Erwein Owner of the ancient SCHLOSS VOLLRADS estate and tenant of the Fürst LÖWENSTEIN Weingut at Hallgarten, now in a joint venture with Suntory at the DR. WEIL estate. President of the VDP association.

Maximin Grünhaus M-S-R (Ruwer) w. ★★★★ 71 75 76 79 **83** *84* 85 86 87 **88 89** Supreme RUWER estate of 80 acres at Mertesdorf. Wines of firm elegance to mature 20 years +.

Maximinhof Top-quality 12-acre estate in WEHLEN, GRAACH, BERNKASTEL. Owner: Stephan Studert-Prüm.

Mertesdorf See Maximin Grünhaus.

Mittelheim Rhg. w. ★★→ ██ ★★★ 71 75 76 79 **83** *84* 85 86 87 88 89
Relatively minor village between WINKEL and OESTRICH. Top grower: WEGELER-DEINHARD. Grosslage: Honigberg.

Mittelhaardt The north-central and best part of RHEINPFALZ, incl. FORST, DEIDESHEIM, RUPPERTSBERG, WACHENHEIM, largely planted with RIESLING.

Mittelhaardt-Deutsche Weinstrasse (Bereich) District name for the northern and central part of RHEINPFALZ.

Mittelmosel The central and best part of the Mosel, incl. BERNKASTEL, WEHLEN, PIESPORT, etc. Its best sites are (or should be) entirely RIESLING.

Mittelrhein Northern Rhine area of domestic importance, incl. BACHARACH. Some attractive steely RIESLINGS, esp. in 1983, 1985, 1986, 1988.

Mönchhof, Weingut Top-quality 12-acre estate in URZIG, Erden, ZELTINGEN and WEHLEN.

Morio-Muskat Stridently aromatic grape variety now on the decline.

Mosel The TAFELWEIN name of the area. All quality wines from the area must be labelled MOSEL-SAAR-RUWER. (Moselle is the French – and English – spelling for this beautiful river.)

Moselland, Winzergenossenschaft The biggest coop of the M-S-R, based at Bernkastel, incl. Saar-Winzerverein at WILTINGEN. Its 5,200 members produce 25% of the M-S-R wines. Formerly Zentralkellerei M-S-R.

Moseltaler New registered name for MOSEL-SAAR-RUWER QbA, intended to simplify selection (cf. LIEBFRAUMILCH) but maintain a higher standard than the latter.

Mosel-Saar-Ruwer 31,000-acre QUALITÄTSWEIN region between TRIER and KOBLENZ. Includes MITTELMOSEL, SAAR, RUWER and lesser areas. Grows more RIESLING than any region on earth.

Müller-Catoir Leading estate of Neustadt, Pfalz, with 40 acres and many varieties.

Müller, Felix Fine small SAAR estate with delicate SCHARZHOFBERGER, now run by VON KESSELSTATT.

Müller zu Scharzhof, Egon See Egon Müller.

Müller-Thurgau Fruity, early-ripening, usually low-acid grape variety; the commonest in RHEINPFALZ and RHEINHESSEN, the NAHE, BADEN and FRANKEN, and increasingly planted in all areas, including the Mosel; generally to the detriment of quality.

Germany's Quality Levels

The official range of qualities in ascending order is

1) *Deutscher Tafelwein: sweetish light wine of no special character.*
2) *Landwein: dryish Tafelwein with some regional style.*
3) *Qualitätswein: dry or sweetish wine with sugar added before fermentation to increase the strength, but tested for quality and with distinct local and grape character.*
4) *Kabinettwein: dry or dryish natural (unsugared) wine of distinct personality and distinguishing lightness. Can be very fine.*
5) *Spätlese: stronger, often sweeter than Kabinett. Full bodied. The trend today is towards drier or even completely dry Spätleses.*
6) *Auslese: sweeter, sometimes stronger than Spätlese, often with honey-like flavours, intense and long.*
7) *Beerenauslese: very sweet and usually strong, intense, can be superb.*
8) *Eiswein: (Beeren-or Trockenbeerenauslese) concentrated, sharpish and very sweet. Extraordinary and everlasting.*
9) *Trockenbeerenauslese: intensely sweet and aromatic; alcohol slight.*

Mumm, von
Excellent 173-acre estate in JOHANNISBERG, RUDESHEIM, etc. Under the same control as SCHLOSS JOHANNISBERG.

Munster Nahe w. ★→★★★★ **71 75 76 83** *84* 85 86 87 88 **89**
Best village of northern NAHE, with fine delicate wines. Top grower: State Domain. Grosslage: Schlosskapelle.

Nackenheim Rhh. w. ★→ ★★★ **75 76** 79 **83** 85 86 87
Neighbour of NIERSTEIN; best wines (Engelsberg, Rothenberg) similar. Grosslagen: Spiegelberg (★★★), Gutes Domtal (★). Top growers: GUNTRUM, Gunderloch-Usinger.

Nahe Tributary of the Rhine and high quality wine region. Balanced, fresh and clean but full-flavoured wines; the best are RIESLING. Two Bereiche: KREUZNACH and SCHLOSS BÖCKELHEIM.

Nahesteiner Brand name of new NAHE HALBTROCKEN blend of RIESLING, SILVANER and MÜLLER THURGAU. Distinctive bottle and modern label.

Neef M-S-R w. ★→ ★★ **71 76 83** 85 86 87 88 **89**
Village of lower Mosel with one fine v'yd: Frauenberg.

Neipperg, Graf von 71-acre top WÜRTTEMBERG estate at Schwaigern, esp. known for red wines and TRAMINER.

Nell, von (Weingut Thiergarten) 40-acre family estate at TRIER and AYL.

Neumagen-Dhron M-M w. ★★→★★★ **71 75 76 83** *84* 85 86 87 88 **89**
Neighbours of PIESPORT. Top v'yd: Hofberger. Grosslage: Michelsberg. Growers: VON KESSELSTATT, Milz, FRIEDRICH WILHELM GYMNASIUM.

Neustadt Central town of RHEINPFALZ, with a famous wine school.

Niederhausen Nahe w. ★★→★★★★ **71 75 76** 79 **83** *84* 85 86 87 88 **89**
 Neighbour of SCHLOSS BÖCKELHEIM and H.Q. of the Nahe State Domain.
 Wines of grace and power. Top v'yds incl. Hermannshöhle, Hermann-
 sberg, Steinberg. Grosslage: Burgweg. Top growers: STATE DOMAIN,
 Schneider, Sitzius, CRUSIUS.

Niederwalluf See Walluf.

Nierstein (Bereich) Large e. RHEINHESSEN district of very mixed quality.

Nierstein Rhh. w. ★→★★★ **71 75 76 83** *84* 85 86 87 **88 89**
 Famous but treacherous name. 1,300 acres incl. superb v'yds:
 Hipping, Ölberg, Pettenthal, etc., and their Grosslagen Rehbach,
 Spiegelberg, Auflangen: ripe aromatic wines with great "elegance".
 But beware Grosslage Gutes Domtal: no guarantee of anything.
 Growers to choose: HERNSHEIM, GUNTRUM, BALBACH, Braun, F. K.
 Schmitt, G. A. Schmitt, Schuh, Senfter, Wolf-Metternich.

Nobling New white grape variety giving light fresh wine in BADEN, esp.
 Markgräflerland.

Norheim Nahe w. ★→★★★ **71 76** 79 **83** *84* 85 86 87 **88 89**
 Neighbour of NIEDERHAUSEN. Top v'yds: Klosterberg, Kafels, Kirsch-
 heck. Grosslage: Burgweg. Growers: CRUSIUS, P. ANHEUSER.

Novum Completely new style of wine from SICHEL, softened by malolactic
 fermentation. Aromatic, gentle, full and versatile.

Oberemmel M-S-R (Saar) w. ★★→★★★ **71 75 76 83** 85 86 87 **88 89**
 Next village to WILTINGEN. Very fine wines from Rosenberg, Hütte, etc.
 Grosslage: Scharzberg. Growers incl. von Hövel, Reverchon, von
 Volxem.

Obermosel (Bereich) District name for the upper Mosel above TRIER.
 Generally uninspiring wines from the Elbling grape unless v. young.

Ockfen M-S-R (Saar) w. ★★→★★★ **71 75 76 83** *84* 85 86 87 **88 89**
 200-acre village with superb fragrant austere wines. Top v'yds:
 Bockstein, Herrenberg. Grosslage: Scharzberg. Growers incl. Dr.
 Fischer, FRIEDRICH WILHELM GYMNASIUM, Zilliken, Reverchon.

Oechsle Scale for sugar-content of grape-juice (see page 19).

Oestrich Rhg. w. ★★→★★★ **71 75 76 83** *84* 85 86 87 88 89
 Big village: variable but capable of splendid Riesling Ausleses. V'yds
 incl. Doosberg, Lenchen, Klosterberg. Grosslage: Gottes-thal. Major
 grower: WEGELER-DEINHARD.

Oppenheim Rhh. w. ★→★★★ **71 75 76** 79 **83** *84* 85 86 87 **88 89**
 Town s. of NIERSTEIN with a famous 13th-century church. Best wines
 (Kreuz, Sackträger) similar. Grosslagen: Guldenmorgen (★★★),
 Krötenbrunnen (★). Growers incl. GUNTRUM, Dahlem, Baumann,
 Schuh.

Ortenau (Bereich) District just s. of Baden-Baden. Good KLINGELBERGER
 (Riesling) and RÜLANDER. SPÄTBURGUNDER (not so good) is a speciality.
 Best village DURBACH.

Palatinate English for RHEINPFALZ.

Perlwein Semi-sparkling wine.

Pfalz See Rheinpfalz.

Pfeffingen, Weingut Messrs Fuhrmann and Eymael make outstanding
 Riesling and Scheurebe on 26 acres of UNGSTEIN.

Piesport M-M w. ★★→★★★★ **71 75 76 83** *84* 85 86 87 **88 89**
 Tiny village with famous amphitheatre of vines giving (at best)
 glorious, gentle, fruity RIESLINGS. Top v'yds: Goldtröpfchen, Falken-
 berg. Treppchen is on flatter land and inferior. Grosslage: Michelsberg (much planted with MÜLLER-THURGAU). Top growers: BISCHOF-
 LICHEN WEINGUTER, VON KESSELSTATT, VEREINIGTE HOSPITIEN, Grans-
 Fassian.

Plettenberg, von ine 100-acre Nahe estate at BAD KREUZNACH. Wines
 recently very "commercial".

Pokalwein Wine by the glass. A pokal is a big glass.

Portugieser Second-rate red-wine grape now often used for WEISSHERBST.

Prädikat Special attributes or qualities. See QmP.

Prüfungsnummer The official identifying test-number of a quality wine.

Prüm, J. J. Superlative and legendary 34-acre Mosel estate in WEHLEN, GRAACH, BERNKASTEL. Delicate, long-lived wines, esp. in Wehlener Sonnenuhr.

Prüm, S. A., Erben Small separate part of the Prüm family estate making fine Wehleners, etc.

Qualitätswein bestimmter Anbaugebiete (QbA) The middle quality of German wine, with sugar added before fermentation (as in French "chaptalization"), but controlled as to areas, grapes, etc.

Qualitätswein mit Prädikat (QmP) Top category, incl. all wines ripe enough to be unsugared, from KABINETT to TROCKENBEERENAUSLESE.

Rappenhof, Weingut 90-acre Rheinhessen estate at Alsheim with wide range of varieties and techniques, incl. barrique-ageing, Chardonnay and deep-coloured SPÄTBURGUNDER.

Randersacker rank. w. ★★→★★★ **76** 79 *83* 86 87 88 89
Leading village for distinctive dry wine. Top v'yds incl. Teufelskeller. Grosslage: Ewig Leben. Growers incl: BURGERSPITAL, STAATLICHER HOFKELLER, JULIUSSPITAL, Schmitt.

Rauenthal Rhg. w. ★★★ →★★★★ **71 75 76** 79 **83** *84* 85 86 87 88 **89**
Supreme village for spicy complex wine. Top v'yds incl. Baiken, Gehrn, Wulfen. Grosslage: Steinmächer. The State Domain is an important grower. Also VON SIMMERN, SCHLOSS SCHÖNBORN, SCHLOSS REINHARTSHAUSEN.

Rautenstrauch Erben Owners of the Karthäuserhof, EITELSBACH.

Reh, Franz & Sohn Thriving wine-merchant at Leiwen (Mosel) with two small estates.

Ress, Balthasar RHEINGAU grower with 50 acres of good land, cellars in HATTENHEIM. Also runs SCHLOSS REICHARTSHAUSEN. Fine fresh wines; highly original artists' labels.

Restsüsse Unfermented sugar remaining in wine to give it sweetness. New-style TROCKEN wines have very little, if any.

Reverchon, Eddie Substantial SAAR estate in Filzen, WILTINGEN, etc.

Rheinart Erben 26-acre SAAR estate known for its OCKFENER BOCKSTEIN.

Rheinburgengau (Bereich) District name for v'yds of the MITTELRHEIN round the Rhine gorge. Wines with "steely" acidity needing time to mature.

Rheingau The best v'yd region of the Rhine, near Wiesbaden. 7,000 acres. Classic, substantial but subtle RIESLING. Bereich name, for the whole region, JOHANNISBERG.

Rheinhess New name for blended HALBTROCKEN Rheinhessen wines.

Rheinhessen Vast region (61,000 acres of v'yds) between Mainz and Worms, bordered by the river NAHE, most second-rate, but incl. top wines from NIERSTEIN, OPPENHEIM, etc.

Rheinhessen Silvaner (RS) New uniform label for dry wines from Silvaner designed to give a modern quality image to the region.

Rheinpfalz 56,000-acre v'yd region s. of Rheinhessen. (See Mittelhaardt and Südliche Weinstrasse.) This and RHEINHESSEN are the chief sources of LIEBFRAUMILCH. Grapes ripen to relatively high degrees. The classics are rich wines, but TROCKEN and HALBTROCKEN increasingly fashionable.

Rhodt Village of SÜDLICHE WEINSTRASSE with well-known cooperative. Agreeable fruity wines. Grosslage: Ordensgut.

Richter, Max Ferd, Weingut 37-acre MITTELMOSEL family estate based at Mülheim. Fine barrel-aged RIESLINGS from WEHLEN, GRAACH, BRAUNEBERG (Juffer), Mülheim (Helenenkloster).

Rieslaner Cross between SILVANER and RIESLING; has made fine Auslesen in FRANKEN, where most is grown.

Riesling The best German grape: fine, fragrant, fruity, long-lived. Only Chardonnay can compete as the world's best white grape.

Roseewein Rosé wine made of red grapes fermented without their skins.

Rotwein Red wine.

Rüdesheim Rhg. w. ★★→★★★★ **71 75 76** 79 *81* 82 **83** *84* 85 86 87 88 **89** Rhine resort with 650 acres of excellent v'yds; the three best called Rüdesheimer Berg . . . Full-bodied wines, fine-flavoured, often remarkable in "off" vintages. Grosslage: Burgweg. Most top Rheingau estates own some Rüdesheim v'yds.

Rüdesheimer Rosengarten Rüdesheim is also the name of a NAHE village near BAD KREUZNACH. Do not be misled by the ubiquitous blend going by this name. It has nothing to do with Rheingau RÜDESHEIM.

Ruländer The PINOT GRIS: grape giving soft, full-bodied wine, alias Grauburgunder. Best in BADEN.

Ruppertsberg Rhpf. w. ★★→★★★ **75 76** 79 **83** *84* 85 86 87 88 89 Southern village of MITTELHAARDT. Top v'yds incl. Hoheburg. Reiterpfad, Linsenbusch. Grosslage: Hofstück. Growers incl. BASSERMANN-JORDAN, DEINHARD, BÜRKLIN-WOLF, VON BUHL.

Ruwer Tributary of Mosel near TRIER. Very fine, delicate but well-structured wines. Villages incl. EITELSBACH, MERTESDORF, KASEL.

Saar Tributary of Mosel s. of RUWER. Brilliant, austere, "steely" RIESLINGS. Villages incl. WILTINGEN (SCHARZHOFBERG), AYL, OCKFEN, SERRIG. Grosslage: Scharzberg. Many fine estates.

Saar-Ruwer (Bereich) District incl. the two above.

Salem, Schloss 188-acre estate of Margrave of Baden near L. Constance in s. Germany. MÜLLER-THURGAU and WEISSHERBST.

St Ursula Well-known merchants at BINGEN; owners of VILLA SACHSEN.

Scharzberg Grosslage name of WILTINGEN and neighbours.

Scharzhofberg Saar w. ★★★★ **71 75 76** 79 **83** *84* 85 86 87 88 **89** Superlative 67-acre SAAR v'yd: austerely beautiful wines, the perfection of RIESLING. Do not confuse with above. Top estate: EGON MÜLLER.

Schaumwein Sparkling wine.

Scheurebe Fruity grape of good quality used in RHEINHESSEN and RHEINPFALZ.

Schillerwein Light red or rosé QbA, speciality of WÜRTTEMBERG (only).

Scholl & Hillebrand RÜDESHEIM merchants with fine BREUER estate wines and highly successful "Riesling Dry".

Schlossböckelheim Nahe w. ★★→★★★★ **71 75 76** 79 **83** *84* 85 86 87 88 **89** Village with the best NAHE v'yds, incl. Kupfergrube, Felsen-berg. Firm yet delicate wine. Grosslage: Burgweg. Top growers: STATE DOMAIN, A. ANHEUSER, CRUSIUS.

Schloss Böckelheim (Bereich) District name for the whole southern NAHE.

Schloss Groenesteyn Top-grade Rheingau estate (80 acres) in KIEDRICH and RÜDESHEIM, owned by Baron von Ritter zu Groenesteyn.

Schloss Johannisberg Rhg. w. ★★★★ **76** 79 **83** *84* 85 86 87 **88 89** Famous RHEINGAU estate of 86 acres owned by Prince Metternich and the Oetker family. The "first growth" of the Rhine, back on superb form since '88 after a less brilliant spell. Wines incl. fine SPÄTLESE and KABINETT TROCKEN.

Schloss Reichartshausen 10-acre HATTENHEIM v'yd run by RESS.

Schloss Reinhartshausen ine 165-acre estate in ERBACH, HATTENHEIM, etc. Changed hands in 1987. The mansion is now a Japanese-owned luxury hotel.

Schloss Vollrads Rhg. w. ★★★→★★★★ **71 76 83** 85 86 87 88 89 Great estate at WINKEL, since 1300. 116 acres producing classical RHEINGAU RIESLING, esp. since 1977. TROCKEN and HALBTROCKEN wines a speciality. The owner, Graf MATUSCHKA GREIFFENCLAU, leads the "German wine with food" campaign, rents the LÖWENSTEIN estate and runs DR. WEIL.

Schmitt, Gustav Adolf Merchant house with fine old 250-acre family estate at NIERSTEIN.

Schmitt, Franz Karl Even older 74-acre ditto.

Schönborn, Schloss One of the biggest and best Rheingau estates, based at HATTENHEIM. Full-flavoured wines, at best excellent. Also v.g. SEKT.

Schoppenwein Café wine: i.e. wine by the glass.

Schorlemer, Freiherr von Historically important MOSEL estate of 116 acres in 5 parts. Current financial and other problems have clouded its reputation.

Schubert, von Owner of MAXIMIN GRÜNHAUS.

Schweigen Rhpf. w. *→ ★★ 83 *84* 85 86 87 88 **89**
Southernmost Rheinpfalz village with important cooperative, Deutsches WEINTOR. Grosslage: Guttenberg.

Sekt German (QbA) sparkling wine, best when RIESLING is on the label. SEKT B.A. is the same thing, but from a specified area.

Senfter, Reinhold NIERSTEIN grower with 32 acres. Best v'yds: Niersteiner Hipping and Oppenheimer Sackträger.

Serrig M-S-R (Saar) w. ★★→★★★ 71 75 76 79 83 *84* 85 86 87 **88 89**
Village known for "steely" wine, excellent in hot years. Top growers: VEREINIGTE HOSPITIEN and State Domain. Grosslage: Scharzberg. Growers incl. Schloss Saarstein, STATE DOMAIN, VEREINIGTE HOSPITIEN, Bert Simon.

Sichel H., Söhne Famous wine-merchants of London and Mainz with new KELLEREI in Alzey, Rhh. Owners of "Blue Nun" LIEBFRAUMILCH and creators of revolutionary NOVUM.

Silvaner The third most-planted German white grape, best in FRANKEN and the KAISERSTUHL. But look for good Silvaners from RHEINHESSEN, too.

Simmern, Langwerth von Top 120-acre family estate at ELTVILLE. Famous v'yds: Mannberg, MARCOBRUNN, Baiken etc. Some of the very best, most typical RHEINGAU RIESLINGS.

Sonnenuhr "Sun-dial." Name of several v'yds, esp. the famous one at WEHLEN.

Spätburgunder PINOT NOIR: the best red-wine grape in Germany esp. in BADEN and WÜRTEMBERG – though its wines are not widely appreciated outside Germany.

Spätlese "Late gathered." One better (stronger/sweeter) than KABINETT. Wines to age *at least* three years. Dry Spätleses can be v. fine.

Spindler, Wilhelm ine 33-acre family estate at FORST, Rheinpfalz.

Staatlicher Hofkeller The Bavarian State Domain. 287 acres of finest FRANKEN v'yds with spectacular cellars under the great baroque Residenz at WÜRZBURG.

Staatsweingut (or Staatliche Weinbaudomäne) The State wine estate or domain. There are several: ELTVILLE, TRIER, SCHLOSSBOCKELHEIM are the principal.

Staufenberg, Schloss 69-acre DURBACH estate of the Margrave of Baden. Fine "Klingelberger" (RIESLING).

Steigerwald (Bereich) District name for eastern part of FRANKEN.

Steinberg Rhg. w. ★★★ →★★★★ 71 75 76 79 **83** *84* 85 86 87 88 89
Famous 79-acre v'yd at HATTENHEIM walled by Cistercians 700 yrs. ago. Now property of the State Domain, ELTVILLE.

Steinwein Wine from WÜRZBURG's best v'yd, Stein. In the past the term was loosely used for all Franconian wine.

Stuttgart Chief city of WÜRTTEMBERG, producer of some pleasant wines (esp. Riesling), recently beginning to be exported.

Südliche Weinstrasse (Bereich) District name for the S. RHEINPFALZ. Quality has improved tremendously in the last 25 years.

Tafelwein "Table wine." The vin ordinaire of Germany. Mostly blended with other EEC wines. But DEUTSCHER TAFELWEIN must come from Germany alone. (See also Landwein.)

Thanisch, Weingut Wwe. Dr. H 16-acre BERNKASTEL family estate of top quality, incl. part of Doctor v'yd. 16 acres changed hands in 1987; the new name is Erben Müller-Burggraef.

Traben-Trarbach M-M w. ★★ 76 83 85 86 87 88 89
Secondary wine-town, some good light wines. Top v'yds incl. Würzgarten, Schlossberg. Grosslage: Schwarzlay.

Traisen Nahe w. ★★★ **71** 75 76 79 **83** *84* 85 86 87 88 89
Small village incl. superlative Bastei and Rotenfels v'yds, making RIESLINGS of great concentration and class. Top grower: CRUSIUS.

Traminer See Gewürztraminer.

Trier M-S-R w. ★★→★★★
Important wine city of Roman origin, on the Mosel, adjacent to RUWER, now incl. AVELSBACH and EITELSBACH. Grosslage: Römerlay. The big Mosel charitable estates have their cellars here.

Trittenheim M-M w. ★★ **71** 75 76 **83** *84* 85 86 87 88 89
Attractive light wines from the s. end of the Mittelmosel. Top v'yds Apotheke, Altärchen. Grosslage: Michelsberg. Top grower: Milz.

Trocken Dry. On labels Trocken *alone* means with a statutory maxiumum of unfermented sugar (9 grams per litre). But see next entry. See also Halbtrocken.

Trockenbeerenauslese The sweetest and most expensive category of wine, extremely rare and with concentrated honey flavour, made from selected withered grapes (esp. Riesling). See also Edel.

Trollinger Common red grape of WÜRTTEMBERG: locally very popular.

Ungstein Rhpf. w. ★★→ ★★★ **71** 75 76 **83** *84* 85 86 87 88 89
MITTELHAARDT village with fine harmonious wines. Top v'yd Herrenberg. Top growers: WEINGUT PFEFFINGEN, FITZ-RITTER, BASSERMANN-JORDAN. Grosslages: Honigsäckel, Kobnert.

Ürzig M-M w. ★★★ **71** 75 76 79 **83** *84* 85 86 87 **88** 89
Village famous for lively spicy wine. Top v'yd: Würzgarten.
Grosslage: Schwarzlay. Growers incl. MÖNCHHOF.

Valckenburg, P.J. Major merchants at Worms, with Madonna LIEBFRAUMILCH and a small estate with good Rieslings. Also Riesling Dry.

VdP Verband Deutscher Prädikats und Qualitätsweinguter, an association of premium growers.

Vereinigte Hospitien "United Hospitals." Ancient charity at Trier with large holdings in SERRIG, WILTINGEN, TRIER, PIESPORT, etc.

Verwaltung Administration (of property/estate etc.).

Villa Sachsen 67-acre BINGEN estate belonging to ST URSULA Weingut.

Wachenheim Rhpf. w. ★★★ →★★★★ **71** 75 76 79 **83** *84* 85 86 87 88 **89** 840 acres, incl. exceptionally fine Rieslings. V'yds incl. Gerümpel, Böhlig, Rechbächel. Top grower: BÜRKLIN-WOLF. Grosslagen: Schenkenböhl, Schnepfenflug, Mariengarten.

Waldrach M-S-R (Ruwer) w. ★★ 75 76 79 **83** *84* 85 87 88 **89**
Some charming light wines. Grosslage: Römerlay.

Wallhausen, Schloss The 25-acre estate of the Prince Zu Salm at Dalberg, NAHE, one of Germany's oldest. 65% Riesling. V.g. TROCKEN.

Walluf Rhg. w. ★★ 75 76 79 **83** *84* 85 87 88 89
Neighbour of ELTVILLE; formerly Nieder-and Ober-Walluf. Underrated wines. Grosslage: Steinmächer. Growers incl. BECKER.

Walporzheim Ahrtal (Bereich) District name for the whole AHR valley.

Walthari-Hof Much-discussed estate at Edenkoben, Rheinpfalz, making wine without recourse to sulphur dioxide.

Wawern M-S-R (Saar) w. ★★→★★★ **71** 75 76 **83** *84* 85 86 87 88 **89**
Small village with fine RIESLINGS. Grosslage: Scharzberg.

Wegeler-Deinhard 136-acre RHEINGAU estate. V'yds in OESTRICH, MITTELHEIM, WINKEL, GEISENHEIM, RÜDESHEIM, etc. Consistent quality; dry SPÄTLESES, classic AUSLESES, finest EISWEIN. Also 67 acres in MITTELMOSEL, incl. major part of BERNKASTELER DOCTOR (WEHLENER, SONNENUHR etc.) and 46 acres in MITTELHAARDT (FORST, DEIDESHEIM, RUPPERTSBERG).

Wehlen M-M w. ★★★ →★★★★ **71** 75 76 79 **83** *84* 85 86 87 **88** 89
Neighbour of BERNKASTEL with equally fine, somewhat richer, wine. Best v'yd: Sonnenuhr. Top growers: PRÜM family branches, led by J.J.P, and DEINHARD. Grosslage: Münzlay.

Weil, Dr. Fine 84-acre estate at KIEDRICH, now owned by Suntory of Japan and MATUSCHKA-GREIFFENCLAU.

Weinbaugebiet Viticultural region for TAFELWEIN (e.g. Mosel, Rhein).

Weingut Wine estate. Can only be used on the label by estates that grow all their own grapes, make their wines from these grapes and bottle these same wines.

Weinkellerei Wine cellars or winery. See Keller.

Weinstrasse "Wine road." Scenic route through v'yds. Germany has several, the most famous the Deutsche Weinstrasse in RHEINPFALZ.

Weintor, Deutsches See Schweigen.

Weissherbst Very pale pink or "blush" wine of QbA standard or above, even occasionally BEERENAUSLESE, the speciality of BADEN, WÜRTTEMBERG, and RHEINPFALZ. Currently v. popular in Germany.

Werner, Domdechant Fine 25-acre family estate on the best slopes of HOCHHEIM. 95% Riesling.

Werner Klein (Mosbacher Hof) 25-acre estate, 90% Riesling, in FORST and DEÏDESHEIM. Good TROCKEN wines.

Remember that vintage information about German wines is given in a different form from the ready/not ready distinction applying to other countries. Read the explanation on page 104.

Wiltingen Saar w. ★★→★★★★ 71 75 76 79 83 85 86 87 **88** 89
The centre of the Saar. 790 acres. Beautiful subtle austere wine. Top v'yds incl. SCHARZHOFBERG, Braune Kupp, Braunfels, Klosterberg. Grosslage: Scharzberg. Top growers: EGON MÜLLER, BISCHÖFLICHEN WEINGUTER, VON KESSELSTATT, le Gallais, Reverchon, etc.

Winkel Rhg. w. ★★★→★★★★ 71 75 76 79 83 *84* 85 86 87 88 89
Village famous for fragrant wine, incl. SCHLOSS VOLLRADS. V'yds incl. Hasensprung, Jesuitengarten. Grosslagen: Honigberg, Erntebringer. Growers incl. DEINHARD, SCHLOSS SCHONBORN, LANDGRAFLICH HESSISCHES, VON MUMM, RESS, etc.

Winningen M-S-R. w. ★★ Village of lower Mosel near Koblenz with some fine delicate RIESLING. Best v'yds: Uhlen, Röttgen. Growers, Heymann-Löwenstein, Richter.

Wintrich M-M w. ★★→★★★ 71 75 76 83 *84* 85 86 87 **88** 89
Neighbour of PIESPORT; similar wines. Top v'yds: Grosser Herrgott, Ohligsberg, Sonnenseite. Grosslage: Kurfürstlay.

Winzergenossenschaft Wine-growers' cooperative, usually making good and reasonably priced wine. Referred to in this text as "coop".

Winzerverein The same as the last.

Wirsching, Hans Well-known estate in IPHOFEN, FRANKEN. Robust, full-bodied wines. 100 acres in top v'yds: Julius-Echter-Berg, Kalb, etc.

Wonnegau (Bereich) District name for S. RHEINHESSEN.

Württemberg Vast S. area little known for wine outside Germany. Some good RIESLINGS, esp. from Neckar valley. Also TROLLINGER.

Würzburg Frank. ★★→★★★★ 71 76 81 *83* 85 86 87 88 89
Great baroque city on the Main, centre of Franconian (FRANKEN) wine: fine, full-bodied and dry. Top v'yds: Stein, Leiste, Schlossberg. No Grosslage. See also Maindreieck. Top growers: STAATLICHER HOFKELLER, JULIUSSPITAL, BURGERSPITAL.

Zell M-S-R w. ★→★★ 76 83 85 86 87 **88** 89
The best-known lower Mosel village, esp. for its Grosslage name Schwarze Katz ("Black Cat"). RIESLING on steep slate gives aromatic light wines.

Zell (Bereich) District name for the whole lower Mosel.

Zeltingen-Rachtig M-M w. ★★ →★★★★ 71 75 76 79 83 *84* 85 86 87 **88** 89 Important Mosel village next to WEHLEN. Typically lively crisp RIESLING. Top v'yds: Sonnenuhr, Schlossberg. Grosslage: Münzlay. Many estates hold v'yds here.

Zilliken, Forstmeister Geltz Former estate of the Prussian royal forester at Saarburg, Saar. Old-style Riesling wines for maturing.

Zwierlein, Freiherr von 55-acre family estate in Geisenheim. 100% Riesling. Best v'yds: Rothenberg, Kläuserweg.

Spain & Portugal

The following abbreviations of regional names are used in the text.

Alen. Alton Alentejo	**Est'a** Estremadura	**N.Cas.** New Castile
Alg. Algarve	**Ext.** Extremadura	**O.Cas.** Old Castile
And. Ándalucia	**Gal.** Galicia	**R'a.A.** Rioja Alta
Ara. Aragon	**g.** see Vino generoso	**R'a.Al.** Rioja Alavesa
B'a.al. Beira Alta	**Gui.** Guipuzcoa	**R'a.B.** Rioja Baja
Bei. Lit.	**Lev.** Levante	**Res.** Reserva
Beira Littoral	**M'o.** Minho	**Trás-os-m.**
Cat. Catalonia	**Nav.** Navarra	Trás-os-Montes

Since 1986, when Spain and Portugal joined the European Common Market, their wine industries have boomed in both quality and variety. Modern ideas have arrived to enrich (and often replace) their traditions. The continuing state of ferment is highly productive, and some splendid new wines have appeared both in their few traditional quality areas, and in former bulk-wine regions.

Currently in Spain (apart from sherry country), Catalonia, Rioja, Navarra, Rueda and Ribera del Duero still hold most interest; in Portugal (apart from port and madeira) Bairrada, the Douro, the Ribatejo, Alentejo and Estremadura, and the Minho. In Portugal especially, new delimited ("VQPRD") areas are tending to overshadow such old-fashioned appellations as e.g. Dão.

The listing here includes the best and most interesting types and regions of each country, whether legally delimited or not. Geographical references (see map) are to the traditional division of Spain into kingdoms and Portugal into provinces.

Sherry, port and madeira are listed separately on pp 133-138.

Spain

A.G.E., Bodegas Unidas R'a.A. r. (p.) w. dr. or sw. res. ★→★★ **73 74 75 78 80 81** 82 83 84 85 Large bodega making a wide range of wines. Best are red Marqués de Romeral and Siglo Gran Reserva.

Alavesas, Bodegas R'a.Al. r. (w. dr.) res ★★→★★★ **73 74 75 76 78 80 81 83** 85 86 87 Pale orange-red SOLAR DE SAMANIEGO was always one of the most delicate of the soft, fast-maturing Alavesa wines. But quality since 1983 has been seriously variable; some wines excessively light.

Albariño del Palacio Gal. w. dr. ★★ D.Y.A.
Flowery and pétillant wine from FEFINANES near Cambados, made with the Albariño grape, the best of the region.

Alella Cat. r. (p.) w. dr. or sw. ★★
Small demarcated region just n. of Barcelona. Pleasantly fresh and fruity wines. (See Marfil and Marqués de Alella.)

Alicante Lev. r. (w.) ★
Demarcated region: wines still tend to be "earthy" and overstrong.

Aloque N. Cas. r. ★ D.Y.A.
A light (though not in alcohol) variety of VALDEPEÑAS, made by fermenting together red and white grapes.

Almendralejo Ext. r. w. ★
Commercial wine centre of the Extremadura. Much of its wine is distilled to make the spirit for fortifying sherry.

Alvear, S.A. And. g. ★★★
The largest producer of excellent sherry-like apéritif and dessert wines in MONTILLA-MORILES.

Ampurdan, Cavas del Cat. w. dr. p. r. res. sp. ★→★★
Producers of big-selling white Pescador, red Cazador table wines and CUVE CLOSE sparklers.

Año 4° Año (or Años) means 4 years old when bottled.

Bach, Masia Cat. r. p. w. dr. or sw. res. ★★ →★★★ **70 74 78 80 81 82 83** 85 Spectacular villa-winery nr. SAN SADURNI DE NOYA, now owned by CODORNIU. Formerly best known for luscious oaky white Extrisimo Bach. Now making waves with a dry white Extrisimo and good red reservas.

Banda Azul R'a.A. r. ★★ **75 76 80 81** 84 85
Big-selling wine, very variable in quality, from BODEGAS PATERNINA.

Barril, Masia Cat. r. res. br. ★★→★★★ **81 81 83** 86 87
Tiny family estate in DO PRIORATO making powerful fruity reds – the 1983 was 18°! – and providing superb RANCIO to better-known firms.

Berberana, Bodegas R'a.A. r. (w. dr.) res. ★→★★★ **64** 66 **70 73 74 75 76 78 80 81 82 83** 84 85 The fruity, full-bodied reds are best: the 3° año Carta de Plata, the 5° año Carta de Oro and the velvety reservas.

Beronia, Bodegas R'a.A. r. w. dr. res. ★★→★★★ **73 75 77 78 80** 81 82 83 84 A small modern bodega making excellent reds in the traditional oaky style. Owned by GONZALEZ BYASS.

Bilbainas, Bodegas R'a.A. r. (p.) w. dr. sw. or sp. res. ★★ →★★★ **66 69 70 72 73 75 76 78 81** 82 83 Large bodega in HARO. Wide and reliable range includes dark Viña Pomal, lighter Viña Zaco, Vendimia Especial Reservas and "Royal Carlton" CAVA.

Blanco White.

Bodega Spanish for 1. a wineshop; 2. a concern occupied in the making, blending and/or shipping of wine and 3. a cellar.

Campanas, Las See Vinicola Navarra.

Campo Nuevo Nav. r. p. w. dr. ★
Everyday red and white Navarra from the Murchantina Coop.

Campo Viejo, Bodegas R'a.A. r. (w. dr.) res. ★ →★★★ **70 71 73 75 76 78 80 81** 82 83 84 Branch of Savin S.A., one of Spain's largest wine companies. Makes the popular and tasty 2° año San Asensio and some big, fruity red reservas, esp. Marqués de Villamagna.

Can Rafols de Caus Cat. r. w. dr. **∗∗ 84 85** 86
> Young small PENEDES bodega, growing its own fruity estate CAB SAUV and pleasant white blend of CHARDONNAY, Xarel-lo and Chenin Blanc.

Cañamero Ext. w. ∗
> Remote village near Guadalupe whose wines grow FLOR and acquire a sherry-like taste.

Caralt, Cavas Conde de Cat. sp. r. w. res. **∗∗ 73 78 80 81 82 83** 84 85
> "CAVA" wines from SAN SADURNI DE NOYA; also pleasant still wines.

Carbonell And. br. **∗∗**
> Producer of good Montilla ("Sombra"). Also olive oil, at Cordoba.

Cariñena Ara. r. (p. w.) ∗
> Demarcated region and large-scale supplier of strong everyday wine, dominated by cooperatives. Now being invigorated (and its wines lightened) by modern technology.

Casar de Valdaiga O.Cas. r. w. dr. **∗∗**
> Producer in El Bierzo, n. of LEON, with a light, very dry CLARETE of fair quality.

Castellblanch Cat. sp. **∗∗**
> PENEDES CAVA firm, owned by FREIXENET. Currently much praised for Brut Zero and slightly sweeter Cristal Seco.

Castillo Ygay See Marqués de Murrieta.

Cava The official term for any Spanish sparkling wine made by the champagne method. Also the bodega making it.

Cenalsa Nav. r. w. dr. **∗∗**
> A marketing organization shipping a range of Navarra wines, incl. a flowery new-style white and a fruity red "Agramont".

Cenicero Wine township in the RIOJA ALTA with ancient Roman origins.

Cepa Wine or grape variety.

Chacolí Gui. (r.) w. ∗ D.Y.A.
> Alarmingly sharp, often fizzy, wine from the Basque coast. It contains only 9% to 11% alcohol.

Chaves, Bodegas Gal. w. dr. **∗∗→∗∗∗ 81 82 84** (D.Y.A.)
> Small family firm making a good and fragrant, though slightly acidic, ALBARINO; arguably the best Galician wine exported.

Chivite, Bodegas Julin Nav. r. (p.) w. dr. or sw. res. **∗∗ 81 82** 83 84 86 Biggest bodega in NAVARRA, producing full-bodied, fruity red wines and a flowery, well-balanced white.

Clarete Traditional term for light red wine (occasionally dark rosé).

Codorníu, S.A. Cat. sp **∗∗→∗∗∗**
> One of the two largest and best known of the firms in SAN SADURNI DE NOYA making good CAVA by the champagne method. Non Plus Ultra is matured. Many prefer the fresher Ana de Codorníu.

Compañía Vinícola del Norte de España (CVNE) R'a.A. r. (p.) w. dr. or sw. res. **∗∗→∗∗∗ 66 70 73 74 75 76 78 80** 81 82 83 84 85
> Top Rioja bodega. The 3° año is among the best young red Riojas and Monopole one of the best slightly oaky whites. Excellent red Imperial and Viña Real reservas. CVNE is pronounced "Coonay."

Conca de Barber Cat. (r. p.) w. dr.
> Demarcated region growing Parellada grapes for making CAVA. Its best wine is the TORRES Milmanda Chardonnay.

Consejo Regulador Official organization for the defence, control and promotion of a DENOMINACION DE ORIGEN.

Contino R'a.Al. r. res. **∗∗ 74 75 76 78 80 81 82** 84
> Superior single-vineyard red made by a subsidiary of COMPAÑIA VINICOLA DEL NORTE DE ESPAÑA.

Corral S.A., Bodegas R'a.A. r. (p. w. dr.) res. **∗∗→∗∗∗ 73 75 78 80 81** 85 Long-established bodega now in improved new premises at Navarrete. Best-known for red Don Jacobo.

Cosecha Crop or vintage.

Cosecheros Alaveses R'a. Al. r. ★★ 87 88

Up-and-coming cooperative. Its young unoaked red has won golden opinions in Spain.

Criado y embotellado por . . . Grown and bottled by . . .

Crianza Literally, "nursing"; the ageing of wine. New or unaged wine is "sin crianza". Wines labelled crianza must be at least 2 years old, of which one year is in barrel.

Cumbrero See Montecillo, Bodegas.

De Muller Cat. (r. w. dr.) br. ★★→★★★

Old TARRAGONA firm specializing in altar wines, making a good PRIORATO and superb v. old solera-aged dessert wines, perhaps Spain's most sumptuous, incl. PRIORATO DULCE and PAXARETE. Also fragrant Moscatel Seco.

Denominación de origen Officially regulated wine region. (See p. 119).

Diaz e Hijos, Jesus N. Cas. w. dr. p. r. res. ★★→★★★ 86

The red wines from this small bodega near Madrid have won many prizes and been compared with those of the Rioja and Catalonia.

Domecq, S.A. R'a.Al. r. (w. dr.) res. ★★→★★★ 73 74 76 78 80 82 83 84 85 Rioja outpost of Sherry firm. Best wines are the fruity red Domecq Domain, exceptional in '76, and Marqués de Arienzo RESERVAS.

Dulce Sweet.

Elaborado y añejado por . . . Made and aged by . . .

El Coto, Bodegas R'a.Al. r. (w. dr.) res. ★★→★★★ 76 78 80 81 82 84 85 Bodega best-known for light, soft red El Coto and Coto de Imaz.

Espumoso Sparkling (but see Cava).

Fariña, Bodegas O.Cas. r. res. w. dr. ★★→★★★ 82 85 86

Rising star of the new DO TORO, making good spicy reds. Its Gran Colegiata is aged in cask; Colegiata is not.

Faustino Martinez, S.A. R'a.Al. r. w. dr. (p.) res. ★★ →★★★ 64 70 72 73 74 75 76 78 80 81 82 83 85 Good red wines and light, fruity white Faustino V. Gran Reserva is Faustino I. Do not be put off by the repellent fake-antique bottles.

Felix Solis Valdepeñas r. ★★

Bodega setting a new pace with oak-aged reds, Viña Albaldi, Reservas (78) and fresh white.

Ferrer, José L. Majorca r. res. ★★ 78 80 84 85

The best-known bodega of Majorca, at Binisalem. 2nd best-known is Vinos Oliver, at Felanix.

Flor A floating yeast peculiar to FINO sherry and certain other wines that oxidize slowly and tastily under its influence.

Franco-Españolas, Bodegas R'a.A. r. w. dr. or sw. res. ★→★★ 70 73 74 75 76 78 79 82 83 85 Reliable wines from LOGROÑO. Bordón is a fruity red. The semi-sweet white Diamante is a favourite in Spain.

Freixenet, S.A., Cavas Cat. sp. ★★→★★★

CAVA, rivalling CODORNIU in size through many acquisitions, making a range of good sparkling wines; notably its Cordon Negro in black bottles. Also owns GLORIA FERRER in California and the Champagne house of Henri Abelé in Reims. Paul Cheneau is a low-price brand.

Gonzalez y Dubosc, S.A., Cavas Cat. sp. ★★

A branch of the sherry giant GONZALES BYASS. Pleasant sparkling wines exported as "Jean Perico".

Gran Vas Pressurized tanks (*cuves closes*) for making inexpensive sparkling wines; also used to describe this type of wine.

Gurpegui, Bodegas R'a.B. r. (p. w. dr.) res. ★→★★ 75 78 80 81 82 83 84 Large family firm making some of the best wines from the RIOJA BAJA, labelled as Berceo. They incl. a fresh rosé.

Haro The wine centre of the RIOJA ALTA, a small but stylish old town.

Huelva And. r. w. br. ★→★★

Demarcated region w. of Cadiz. White table wines and sherry-like *generosos*, formerly an important resource of JEREZ for blending.

Irache, S.L. Nav. r. p. (w. dr) res. ✶✶ **64 70 73 78 81 82**
Well-known bodega with substantial exports.

Jean Perico See Gonzalez y Dubosc.

Jerez de la Frontera The capital city of sherry. (See p. 135).

Jumilla Lev. r. ✶ (w. dr. p.) ✶→✶✶
Demarcated region in the mountains n. of MURCIA. Its overstrong (up to 18%) wines are being lightened by earlier picking and better winemaking, esp. by French-owned Bodegas Vitivino, e.g. their Altos de Pío.

Juvé y Camps Cat. sp. ✶✶→✶✶✶
Family firm aiming for and achieving top quality CAVA, made with free-run juice, esp. Reserva de la Familia.

Labastida, Cooperativa Vinícola de R'a.Al. r. res. ✶✶ **70 75 78 82**
Makers of very drinkable Manuel Quintano, fruity, well-balanced Montebuena, Gastrijo and Castillo Labastida reservas and gran reservas, and a tasty fresh dry white.

La Granja Remélluri R'a.Al. r. res. ✶✶ **74 76 79 80 81** 83 84
Small firm (since 1970), making good traditional red Riojas.

Laguardia Picturesque walled town at the centre of LA RIOJA ALAVESA.

Lagunilla, Bodegas R'a.A. r. ✶✶ **70 73 75 78 81** 83 84
Modern firm owned by the British Grand Met. Co. Easy oaky light reds incl. Viña Herminia and Gran Reserva.

Lan, Bodegas R'a.A. r. (p. w.) res. ✶✶→✶✶✶ **70 73 75 78 80 82** 85
Huge modern bodega, lavishly equipped and making aromatic red Riojas, incl. the good Lancorta and fresh white Lan Blanco.

La Rioja Alta, Bodegas R'a.A. r. (p.) w. dr. (or sw.) res. ✶✶→✶✶✶ **64 68 70 73 76 78 80 81 83** 84 Excellent wines, esp. the red 3° año Viña Alberdi, the velvety 5° año Ardanza, the lighter 6° año Araña, the splendid Reserva 904 and marvellous Reserva 890. This bodega is now making only reservas and gran reservas.

León O.Cas. r. p. w. ✶→✶✶ **78 81** 82 83 84
Northern region on the move. Its wines, esp. those from the unfortunately named V.I.L.E. (e.g. the young Coyanza and full-blooded Don Suero reserva), can be fruity, dry and refreshing.

León, S.A., Jean Cat. r. w. dr. res ✶✶✶ **74 75 77 78 79 80 81 82** 83
Small firm owned by a Los Angeles restauranteur. Good oaky CHARDONNAY and deep, full-bodied CABERNET that repays long bottle-ageing, though less so since 1980.

Rioja Vintages

Thanks to the more consistent climate and the blending of wine from better vintages with poor years, Riojas do not vary to the same extent as e.g. Bordeaux. The best vintages of the last 40 years have been: 52 55 58 64 66 68 70 73 76 78 80 81 82 83 85 86 and 87. (Those in bold type were outstanding.)

Riojas are put on the market when they are ready to drink. The best reservas of the best vintages, however, have very long lives and improve with more bottle age. The best '64s are still at their peak.

Logroño Principal town of the RIOJA region. HARO has more charm and more bodegas.

López de Heredia, S.A. R'a.A. r. (p.) w. dr. or sw. res. ✶✶→ ✶✶✶ **64 68 70 73 76 78 80 81 82 83** 84 85 Superb old established bodega in HARO with exceptionally long-lasting, very traditional wines. Viña Tondonia reds and whites are delicate and fine; Viña Bosconia fine and beefy.

López Hermanos Malaga ✶✶
Large bodega for commercial Malaga wines, incl. popular Malaga Virgen and Moscatel Flor de Malaga.

Los Llanos N.Cas. r. (p. w. dr.) res. ✶✶ **75 78 81**
One of the few VALDEPENAS bodegas to age wine in oak. Señorio de Los

Llanos Gran Reserva is remarkably scented and silky; a winner. Also a clean and fruity white "Armonioso".

Magaña, Bodegas Nav. r. res. **80 81** 82 ★★

Tiny, young bodega making vigorous red with MERLOT (vines bought from Petrus) and CABERNET SAUVIGNON.

Majorca José FERRER, Vinos Oliver and Vino d'Or make the only wines of any interest.

Málaga And. br. sw. ★★→★★★

Demarcated region around the city of Málaga. At their best, its dessert wines yield little to tawny port. See SCHOLTZ.

Mancha, La N.Cas. r. w. ★

Large demarcated region n. and n.e. of VALDEPEÑAS. Mainly white wines, lacking the lively freshness of the best Valdepeñas, but showing distinct signs of improvement. To watch.

Marfil Cat. r. (p.) w. ★★

Brand name of Alella Vinicola (Bodegas Cooperativas), best known of the producers in ALELLA. Means "ivory".

Marqués de Alella Cat. w. dr. (sp.) ★★→★★★ 86 87 88 (D.Y.A.)

Small bodega making light and fragrant white ALELLA wines, some from CHARDONNAY, by modern methods. Also a little CAVA.

Marqués de Cáceres, Bodegas R'a.A. r. p. w. dr. res. ★★→★★★ 70 73 75 76 78 80 81 82 83 84 85 86 87 Good red Riojas of various ages made by modern French methods from CENICERO (R'a.A.) grapes and also a surprisingly light and fragrant white (D.Y.A.).

Marqués de Griñon O.Cas. (r.) w. dr. ★★★ (r.) 82 83 84 85

Enterprising nobleman making very fine CABERNET nr. Toledo, south of Madrid, not a recognized wine region. Also refreshing white from Verdejo grapes in RUEDA.

Marqués de Monistrol, Bodegas Cat. w. r. (dr. or sw.) sp. res. ★★ 75 77 78 80 82 Old bodega now owned by Martini & Rossi. Refreshing whites, esp. the Vin Nature, a good red reserva and an odd sweet red wine.

Marqués de Murrieta, S.A. R'a.A. r. p. w. dr. res. ★★★→ ★★★★ 34 42 60 62 64 68 70 73 74 75 76 78 79 80 81 82 83 84 85 Historic, much-respected bodega near LOGROÑO making some of the best of all Riojas. Makes 4° año Etiqueta Blanca, superb red Castillo Ygay, an "old-style" oaky white, dry, fruity, and worth bottle-ageing, and a wonderful old-style ROSADO.

Marqués de Riscal, S.A. R'a.Al. r. (p. and w. dr.) res. ★★→★★★★ 64 65 68 71 73 75 76 78 80 81 82 83 84 The best-known bodega of the RIOJA ALAVESA. Its red wines are relatively light and dry. Old vintages are very fine; some recent ones have disappointed; current ones are back on form. Its white wines from RUEDA, incl. a v.g. SAUV BLANC, are some of the best from this region.

Marqués de Romeral R'a.A. r. w. dr. ★★ 76 78 80

Everyday Romeral and Gran Reserva are both v.g. value.

Marqués del Puerto R'a.A. r. (p. w. dr.) res. ★★→★★★ 73 76 78 80 81 83 84 Small concern, founded as Bodegas Lopez Agos, making a red reserva Señorío de Agos highly praised in Spain.

Martinez-Bujanda R'a.Al. r. w. dr. res ★★★ 73 75 80 81 82 83 85

Refounded (1985) family-run RIOJA bodega, remarkably equipped. Excellent wines, incl. fruity SIN CRIANZA and irresistible rosado as well as noble Valdemar reservas, incl. sumptuous Centenario.

Martinez Lacuesta, S.A. R'a, A. r. res. ★→★★★ 73 76 84 87

For long a main supplier to Iberia airlines, Lacuesta has bounced back with first rate Campeador **80** & **81** and Martinez Lacuesta **84** & 87.

Mascaró, Cavas Cat. sp. (w. dr. r.) ★★→ ★★★

Maker of some of the best Spanish brandy, good sparkling wine and a refreshing dry white Viña Franca.

Mauro, Bodegas O.Cas. r. ★★★ **81 83** 84

Young bodega in Tudela del Duero nr. Valladolid with v.g. round, fruity Tinta Fina red.

Méntrida N.Cas. r. w. ★

Demarcated region w. of Madrid, source of everyday red wine.

Milmanda See Conca de Barberá, Torres.

Monopole See Compañía Vinícola del Norte de España (CVNE).

Montánchez Ext. r. g. ★

Village near Mérida, interesting because its red wines grow FLOR yeast like FINO sherry.

Montecillo, Bodegas R'a.A. r. (p.) res. ★★★ **75 76 78 80 81** 82 84 85

"State of the art" Rioja bodega owned by Osborne (see Sherry). Red and fresh dry white Cumbrero are currently among the best 3° año wines. Viña Monty is the worthy Reserva. "Gran Reserva Especial" is rare but first rate.

Montecristo, Bodegas ★★

Well-known brand of MONTILLA-MORILES wines.

Monterrey Gal. r. ★

Region near the n. border of Portugal; strong wines like those of VERIN.

Montilla-Moriles And. g. ★★→★★★

Demarcated region near Cordoba. Its crisp, sherry-like FINO and AMONTILLADO contain 14% to 17.5% natural alcohol and remain unfortified and singularly toothsome.

Muga, Bodegas R'a.A. r. (w.) res. (sp.) ★★★ **70 73 75 76 78 80 81 82** 84 Small family firm in HARO, making some of Rioja's best reds by strictly traditional methods. Wines are light but intensely aromatic, with long complex finish. The best is Prado Enea. Whites and CAVA not of the same standard.

Navarra Nav. r. p. (w.) ★→ ★★

Demarcated region; mainly fruity rosés and sturdy reds, but some reservas up to Rioja standards. See Cenalsa, Chivite, Magaña, etc.

Nuestro Padre Jésus del Perdón, Coop de N.Cas. r. w. dr. ★ D.Y.A.

Look for bargain Yuntero, Casa la Teja and fresh white Lazarillo.

Ochoa, S.A. Nav. w. p. r. res. ★★ **82** 84

Small family bodega now producing an excellent white, but better known for its well-made red and rosé wines.

Olarra, Bodegas R'a.A. r. (w. p.) res. ★★→★★★ **70 73 75 76 78 80 81 82** 84 85 87 Vast modern bodega near LOGROÑO, one of the show-pieces of RIOJA, making good red and white wines and excellent Cerro Añon reservas. Since '81, Añares is the top reserva.

Palacio de Arganza O.Cas. r. p. w. dr. res. ★★→★★★ **58 65 70 74 76 79 80** Best-known bodega in El Bierzo, between LEON and GALICIA. White Vega Burbia and red Almena del Bierzo are characters worth meeting.

Palacio de Fefiñanes Gal. w. res. ★★★

Illustrious for untypical ALBARIÑO wine: no bubbles and oak-aged 3-5 years.

Rioja's Characteristic Style

To the Spanish palate the taste of luxury in wine is essentially the taste of oak. Oak contains vanillin, the taste of vanilla. Hence the characteristic vanilla flavour of all mature Spanish table wines of high quality – exemplified by the reservas of Rioja (red and white). Fashion has swung (perhaps too far) against the oaky flavour of old Rioja whites. But the marriage of ripe fruit and oak in red Rioja is still highly appreciated.

Paternina, S.A., Bodegas R'a.A. r. (p.) w. dr. or sw. res. ★→★★★ **28 59 67 68 71 73 75 76 78 82** 83 A household name, esp. for Banda Azul red and Banda Dorada white. The Conde de los Andes label was fine but recent vintages have been disappointing. Most consistent red is Viña Vial.

Paxarete Traditional, intensely sweet dark brown almost chocolaty speciality of Tarragona. Not to be missed. See De Muller.

Pazo Gal. r. p. w. dr. ★ D.Y.A.
Brand name of the cooperative at RIBEIRO, making wines akin to Portuguese VINHOS VERDES. The rasping red is the local favourite. Pleasant slightly fizzy Pazo and Xeiro whites are safer, and the Viña Costeira has real quality.

Peñafiel O.Cas. r. and w. dr. res. ★★ 64 74 76 79 80 82 83 85 86 87
Village on the R. Duero near Valladolid. Best wines are fruity reds from the Coop de RIBERO DEL DUERO, incl. the v-tasty 5° año PROTOS.

Penedès Cat. r. w. dr. sp. ★→★★★
Demarcated region including Vilafranca del Penedès, SAN SADURNI DE NOYA and SITGES. See also Torres.

Perelada Cat. (r. p.) w. sp. ★★
In the demarcated region of Ampurdán on the Costa Brava. Best known for sparkling wines made both by the CAVA and tank or CUVE CLOSE systems.

Pérez Pascua Hnos. O.Cas. r. (p.) res. ★★★ 81 83 85 86 87
Immaculate tiny family bodega in RIBERO DEL DUERO. In Spain its fruity and complex red Viña Pedrosa is rated one of the country's best.

Pesquera O.Cas. r. ★★★ 80 82 84 85 86
RIBERA DEL DUERO red made in small quantity by Alejandro Fernandez. Robert Parker has rated it a match for Bordeaux GRANDS CRUS. Janus is an (even more expensive) special bottling.

Piqueras, Bodegas N.Cas. r. ★ 82 83
Makers of inexpensive and drinkable red Marius with more style than most Castilian wine.

Priorato Cat. br. dr. r. ★★
Demarcated region, an enclave in that of TARRAGONA, known for its alcoholic "rancio" wines and also for almost black splendidly full-bodied reds, often used for blending. Lighter blended Priorato is a good carafe wine in Barcelona. See De Muller, Scala Dei.

Protos See Peñafiel.

Raimat Cat. r. w. p. sp. ★→★★★ (Cab) 76 81 82 83 84 85
Thrillingly clean, structured and highly promising wines from old v'yds near Lérida, replanted by CODORNIU with CABERNET, CHARDONNAY and other foreign vines. Also a good 100% CHARD CAVA.

René Barbier Cat. r. w. dr. res. ★★ 83 85
Part of the FREIXENET group known for fresh white Kraliner and red R.B. Reservas.

Reserva Good-quality wine matured for long periods. Red reservas must spend at least 1 year in cask and 2 in bottle; Gran Reservas 2 in cask and 3 in bottle. Thereafter many continue to mature for decades.

Ribeiro Gal. r. (p.) w. dr. ★→★★
Demarcated region on the n. border of Portugal making wines similar to Portuguese VINHO VERDE – and others.

Ribera del Duero Historic demarcated region e. of Valladolid, now revealed as excellent for Tinto Fino (TEMPRANILLO) reds. See Vega Sicilia, Peñafiel, Mauro, Torremilanos, Pesquera, Pérez Pascua.

Rioja O.Cas. r. p. w. dr. sp. esp. 64 66 68 70 73 75 76 78 80 81 82 83 85 86 87
This upland region along the R. Ebro in the n. of Spain produces most of the country's best table wines in some 50 BODEGAS DE EXPORTACION. It is sub-divided into:

Rioja Alavesa North of the R. Ebro, the R'a.Al. produces fine red wines, mostly light in body and colour.

Rioja Alta South of the R. Ebro and w. of LOGRONO, the R'a.A. grows most of the finest red and white wines; also some rosé.

Rioja Baja Stretching e. from LOGRONO, the Rioja Baja makes coarser red wines, high in alcohol and often used for blending.

Riojanas, Bodegas R'a.A. r. (w. p.) res. ★★→★★★ **34 42 56 64 66 68 70 73 74 75 76 78 80** 81 **82** 83 85 Old bodega making a good traditional Viña Albina. Monte Real reservas are big and mellow.

Rioja Santiago, S.A. R'a.A. r. (w. dr. or sw. p.) res. ★→★★★ **78** 82
Bodega at HARO with well-known brands. Appropriately, as until recently it belonged to Pepsi-Cola, it makes the biggest-selling bottled SANGRIA. Top reds, Condal and Gran Enologica are respectable.

Rosado Rosé.

Rovellats S.A. Cat. sp. ★★→★★★
Small family firm making only exclusive and expensive CAVA, stocked in some of Spain's leading restaurants.

Rovira S.A., Pedro Cat. r. p. w. dr. or sw. br. res. ★→★★
Large firm with bodegas in the DOs TARRAGONA, TERRA ALTA and PENEDES, making beverage, apéritif and dessert wines.

Rueda O.Cas. br. w. dr. ★→★★
Small historic demarcated area w. of Valladolid. Traditional producer of flor-growing sherry-like wines up to 17° alcohol, now making fresh whites incl. those of the MARQUES DE RISCAL and MARQUES DE GRINON.

Ruiz, Santiago Gal. w. dr. ★★★ D.Y.A.
Small but prestigious bodega in the new Galacia DO Rias Baixas, whose Albariño is of the very best.

Salceda, S.A., Bodegas Viña R'a.Al. r. res. ★★→★★★ **73 75 78 80 81 82** 83 84 **85** Makes fruity, light but well-balanced red wines.

Sangre de Toro Brand name for a rich-flavoured red from TORRES.

Sangría Cold red wine cup traditionally made with citrus fruit, fizzy lemonade, ice and brandy. Also repulsive cheap commercial fizz.

Sanlúcar de Barrameda Centre of the Manzanilla district. (See Sherry.)

San Sadurní de Noya Cat. sp. ★★→★★★
Town s. of Barcelona, hollow with cellars where dozens of firms produce CAVA by the champagne method. Standards can be very high, though the flavour is distinct from champagne.

San Valero, Bodega Cooperative Ara. r. p. (w.) res. ★→★★
Large CARINENA coop with some modern wines. Good red CRIANZA Monte Ducay; fresh Perçebal rosado with slight spritz; and good value young, unoaked Don Mendo red.

Sarría, Señorio de Nav. r. (p. w. dr.) res. ★★→★★★ **64 73 74 75 76 78 81 82** 84 The vineyards and model winery near Pamplona produce wines up to (high) RIOJA standards.

Scala Dei, Cellers de Cat. r. res. ★★ **76 78 82** 87
One of the few bodegas in the tiny DO PRIORATO. Wines are full-bodied reds replete with fruit, body and alcohol – less so recently.

Scholtz, Hermanos, S.A. And. br. ★★→ ★★★
Makers of the best MALAGA, including a good, dry 10-year-old amontillado, excellent Moscatel and traditional Dulce y Negro. Best of all is the dessert Solera Scholtz 1885.

Seco Dry.

Segura Viudas, Cavas Cat. Sp. ★★→★★★
CAVA of PENEDES. Buy the Brut Vintage ('83) or Reserva Heredad (despite its wildly kitsch bottle).

Serra, Jaume Cat. w. dr. r. res. ★★→★★★ **84**
With establishments in both ALELLA and the PENEDES, the firm makes fresh white wines and fruity, well-balanced reds.

Sin Crianza See Crianza.

Sitges Cat. w. sw. ★★
Coastal resort s. of Barcelona formerly noted for its sweet dessert wine made from Moscatel and MALVASIA grapes.

Tarragona Cat. r. w. dr. or sw. br. ★→★★★
1. Table wines from the demarcated region; of little note. 2. Dessert wines from the firm of DE MULLER.

Tinto Red.

Toro O.Cas. r. ★→★★

Newly demarcated region 150 miles n.w. of Madrid, traditionally making over powerful (up to 16°) red wines, but now producing some tasty, balanced reds. See Bodega Fariña.

Torremilanos O.Cas. r. res. **★★ 76 79 81 82 83** 85 86 87

Label of Bodegas López Peñalba, a fast-expanding family firm near Aranda de Duero. Their red Tinto Fino (TEMPRANILLO) are lighter and more Rioja-like than most. Also labelled "Peñalba".

Torres, Bodegas Cat. r. w. dr. or semi-sw. p. res. **★★→★★★★ 64 70 71 73 74 75 76 77 78 79 80 81 82 83 84** 85 86 87 Distinguished family firm making the best wines of PENEDES, and indeed Spain; esp. flowery white Viña Sol and Gran Viña Sol, MILMANDA oak-fermented CHARD, semi-dry aromatic Esmeralda, Waltraud RIESLING, red Tres Torres and Gran Sangredetoro, superlative Gran Coronas (Cabernet) reservas, fresh and soft Los Torres Merlot and Santa Digna Pinot Noir. The family now also has vineyards in Chile and California.

Utiel-Requeña Lev. r. (w.) p.

Demarcated region w. of Valencia. Sturdy reds and chewy vino de doble pasta for blending; also really light and fragrant rosé.

Valbuena O.Cas. r. **★★★ 75 76 77 78 79 80 82** 83

Made with the same grapes as VEGA SICILIA but sold as 3° año or 5° año. Best at about 10 years. Some prefer it to its elder brother.

Valdeorras Gal. r. w. dr. **★→★★★**

Demarcated region e. of Orense. Dry and refreshing wines.

Valdepeñas N.Cas. r. (w.) ★→ **★★**

Demarcated region near the border of Andalucia. Its mainly red wines, though high in alcohol, can be surprisingly light in flavour. Some superior wine (e.g. LOS LLANOS and FELIX SOLIS) is oak-matured.

Valencia Lev. r. w. ★

Demarcated region producing high-strength blending wine.

Vega de la Reina, s.a. O. Cas. w. dr. r. res. ★★★ 80

Rueda bodega making old-style oaky reds with something of the quality of the famous VEGA SICILIA.

Vega Sicilia O.Cas. r. res. ★★★★ **41 48 53 59 60 61 62 64 66 67 69 72 73 76** One of the very best Spanish wines, full-bodied, fruity, piquant and fascinating. Contains up to 16% alcohol. VALBUENA is the same wine with less time in oak (**78 79 80 82** 83 84).

Vendimia Vintage.

Verín Gal. r. ★

Town near n. border of Portugal. Its wines are the strongest from Galicia, without a bubble, and up to 14% alcohol.

Viña Literally, a vineyard. But wines such as Tondonia (LOPEZ DE HEREDIA) or Zaco (BILBAINAS) are not necessarily made with grapes exclusively from the vineyard named.

Vinícola de Castilla N.Cas. r. p. w. dr. **★**

Large firm in LA MANCHA. Red Castillo de Alhambra is palatable.

VINIVAL Lev. r. w. ★

Huge Valencian consortium marketing the most widely drunk wine in the region, Torres de Serrano.

Vino Blanco White wine.

Vino comun/corriente Ordinary wine. **clarete** Light red wine.

dulce Sweet wine. **espumoso** Sparkling wine.

generoso Apéritif or dessert wine rich in alcohol.

rancio Maderized (brown) white wine. **rosado** Rosé wine.

seco Dry wine. **tinto** Red wine.

verde Wine akin to Portuguese VINHO VERDE.

Yecla Lev. r. w. ★

Demarcated region n. of Murcia. Its cooperative, "La Purisima", is said to be Spain's biggest. Best to avoid its wine.

Ygay See Marqués de Murrieta.

Portugal

For port and madeira see pages 133-138.

Adega   A cellar or winery.

Alentejo   Alen. r. (w.) ✶→✶✶✶
   Vast tract of southern Portugal with only sparse vineyards near the
   Spanish border. The great bulk of its wine is cooperative-made.
   Estate wines from ROSADO FERNANDES, Quinta de Mouchão and Esporao
   show remarkable potential. Best coops are at Redondo, BORBA and
   REGUENGOS DE MONSARRAZ. Growing excitement here.

Algarve   Alg. r. w. ✶
   Demarcated region in the holiday area. Its wines are nothing to write
   home about.

Aliança, Caves   r. w. dr. sp. res.   ✶✶→✶✶✶✶
   Large BAIRRADA-based firm making champagne-method sparkling.
   Reds and whites incl. good BAIRRADA wines and mature DAOS. Aliança
   Tinta Velha is the best-selling red in Portugal.

Almodovar, Casa Agricola   Alen. w. dr. r. res. ✶✶ 84 86 87
   The whites of this Vidigueira-based company are better-known, but
   its reds are worth trying.

Amarante   Sub-region in the VINHOS VERDES area. Rather heavier and
   stronger wines than those from farther north.

Arruda, Adega Cooperative de   B'a.al. r. res.   ✶
   Vinho Tinto Arruda is a best buy. Avoid the Reserva.

Aveleda   Douro w. dr. ✶✶ D.Y.A.
   A first-class VINHO VERDE made on the Aveleda estate of the Guedes
   family. Sold dry in Portugal but sweetened for export.

Bacalhôa, Quinta da   Est'a. r. res.   ✶✶✶ 81 82 83 84 85
   American-owned estate near Setúbal, whose harmonious, fruity, mid-
   weight CABERNET SAUVIGNON wine is vinified by João PIRES.

Bairrada   Bei. Lit. r. w. dr. and sp. ✶→   ✶✶ 66 70 75 76 77 78 79 82 85
   Recently demarcated region supplying much of Oporto's carafe wine
   and some excellent red GARRAFEIRAS. Also good-quality sparkling
   wines by the champagne method. A potential star.

Barca Velha   ("Ferreirinha") Trs-os-m. r. res. ✶✶✶✶ 57 64 65 66 78
   Perhaps Portugal's best red, made in very limited quantity by the port
   firm of FERREIRA. Powerful, resonant wine with deep bouquet.

Barrocão Cavas do   Bei. Lit. r. w. dr. res. ✶→   ✶✶✶
   Based in the BAIRRADA, the firm blends good red DAOS and makes first-
   rate old BAIRRADA garrafeiras, such as 60 and 64.

Basto   A sub-region of the VINHOS VERDES area on the R. Tamego,
   producing more astringent red wine than white.

Borba   Alen. r. ✶
   Small VQPRD area nr Evora, making some of best wine from ALENTEJO.

Borba, Adega Cooperative de   Alen. r. res. (w. dr.) ✶✶ 82 87
   A producer of big, fruity, mouth-filling wines, often at best when young.

Borges & Irmão   Merchants of port and table wines at Vila Nova de Gaia.
   Brands incl. Gatâo and (better) Gamba VINHOS VERDES. Also Fita Azul
   sparkling.

Braga   Sub-region of the VINHOS VERDES area, good red and white.

Buçaco   B'a.al. r. (p.) w. res.   ✶✶✶✶ r. 51 53 57 58 60 63 67 70 72 75
   77; w. 56 65 66 70 72 75   The legendary speciality of the luxury Palace
   hotel at Buçaco nr. Coimbra, not seen elsewhere. Variable, at best
   incredible quality.

Bucelas   Est'a. w. dr. ✶✶✶ 79 84
   Tiny demarcated region just n. of Lisbon. CAVES VELHAS make delicate,
   perfumed wines with 11% to 12% alcohol.

Camarate, Quinta de   Est'a. r.   ✶✶ 74 78 80 82 83 84 85
   Notable CLARETE from FONSECA at Azeit s. of Lisbon, incl. detectable
   CABERNET SAUVIGNON.

Carcavelos Est'a. br. sw. ★★★

Minute demarcated region w. of Lisbon. Its excellent but very rare sweet apéritif or dessert wines average 19% alcohol and resemble honeyed MADEIRA.

Cartaxo Ribatejo r. w. ★

A district in the RIBATEJO n. of Lisbon, now a VQPRD area making everyday wines popular in the capital.

Carvalho, Ribeiro & Ferreira B'a. al. r. w. des. ★★→★★★

Large merchants bottling and blending SERRADAYRES and excellent RIBATEJO GARRAFEIRAS.

Casa Ferreirinha Tras-os-m. r. res. ★★★ SO

The second wine to BARCA VELHA, made in less than ideal vintages.

Casa de Sezim M'o. w. dr. ★★→★★★ D.Y.A.

One of the best estate-bottled VINHO VERDES from a member of the new association of private producers, APEVV.

Casal García Douro w. dr. ★★ D.Y.A.

One of the biggest-selling VINHOS VERDES in Portugal, made by SOGRAPE.

Casal Mendes M'o. w. dr. ★★ D.Y.A.

The VINHOS VERDES from CAVES ALIANCA.

Casaleiro Trademark of Caves Dom Teodosio-João T. Barbosa, who make a variety of reliable wines: DAO, VINHOS VERDES, etc.

Caves Velhas Bei. Lit. r. w. dr. res ★★→★★★

Only maker of BUCELAS; also good DAO and "Romeira" GARRAFEIRAS.

Cepa Velha M'o. (r.) w. dr. ★★★

Brand name of Vinhos de Monção Lda. Their Alvarinho, from the grape of that name, is one of the best VINHOS VERDES.

Clarete Relatively light red wine.

Colares Est'a. r. ★★★ D.O.A.

Small demarcated region on the sandy coast w. of Lisbon. Its antique-style dark red wines, rich in tannin, are from vines which have never suffered from phylloxera. Drink the oldest available: it needs ten years (see PAULO DA SILVA).

Conde de Santar B'a.al. r. (w. dr.) res. ★★→★★★ **70 73 78** 85

The only estate-grown DAO, later matured and sold by the port firm of CALEM. Reservas are fruity, full-bodied and exceptionally smooth.

Dão B'a.al. r. w. res. ★★ **69 70 71 74 75 80 83** 85

Demarcated region found Viseu on the R. Mondego. Produces some of Portugal's best-known, but often disappointing table wines: solid reds of some subtlety with age: substantial dry whites. All are sold under brand names.

Douro The northern river whose valley produces port and some of Portugal's most exciting new table wines. See BARCA VELHA, QUINTA DO COTTO and others. Watch this space.

Esporão Heredade do Alen. r. ★★ 87

The owners, Finagra S.A., have planted CAB SAUV and Touriga Nacional on a large scale and built one of the largest, most modern ADEGAS, just coming on stream.

Esteva Tras-os-m. m. r. ★→★★ D.Y.A.

Very drinkable young "Nouveau" Douro red from Ferreira.

Evelita Trás-os-m. r. ★→★★ 75 79

Reliable middle-weight red made near VILA REAL by Real Companhia Vinícola do Norte de Portugal. Ages well.

Fonseca, J.M. da Est'a. r. w. dr. br. res. ★→★★★

Large, old-established family firm in Azeitão nr. Lisbon, making a wide range of good wines, incl. the red PERIQUITA, PASMADOS and QUINTA DE CAMARATE (formerly known as Palmela) and Terras Altas DAO, as well as the famous MOSCATEL DE SETUBAL.

Fonseca Internacional J.M. da Est'a p. ★

Formerly part of the last, now owned by Grand Met. Co. Produces LANCERS rosé and sparkling LANCERS Brut.

Gaeiras Est'a. r. ★★

Dry, full-bodied and well-balanced red made near Obidos.

Garrafeira The "private reserve" wine of a merchant aged for a minimum of 2 years in cask and 1 in bottle, but often much longer. Usually his best, though often of indeterminate origin.

Gatão M'o. w. dr. ★★ D.Y.A.

Reliable VINHO VERDE from the firm of Borges & Irmão fragrant but a little sweetened.

Gazala M'o. w. dr. ★★ D.Y.A.

A new VINHO VERDE made at Barcelos by SOGRAPE since the AVELEDA estate went to a different branch of the Guedes family.

Grão Vasco B'a.al. r. w. res. ★★ 70 73 75 78 80 81 83

One of the best brands of DAO, blended and matured at Viseu by SOGRAPE. Fine red reservas; fresh young white (D.Y.A.)

Lagosta M'o. w. dr. ★★ D.Y.A.

Well-known VINHO VERDE from the Real Companhia Vinícola do Norte de Portugal.

Lancers Est'a. p. w. sp. ★

Sweet carbonated rosé and sparkling white extensively shipped to the USA by FONSECA INTERNACIONAL.

Lima Sub-region in the n. of the VINHOS VERDES area making mainly astringent red wines.

Madeira Island br. dr./sw. ★★→★★★★

Source of famous apéritif and dessert wines. See pp. 133-138.

Mateus Rosé Trs-os-m. p. (w.) ★

World's biggest-selling medium-sweet carbonated rosé, made by SOGRAPE at VILA REAL and Anadia in the BAIRRADA.

Monção **Sub-region of the** VINHOS VERDES area on R. Minho, producing the best of them from the ALVARINHO grape.

Palacio de Brejoeira M'o. (r.) w. dr. ★★★

Outstanding estate-made VINHOS VERDE from MONCAO, with astonishing fragrance and full, fruity flavour.

Paulo da Silva, Antonio Bernardino Est'a (w. dr.) r. res. ★★→★★★ 68 70 74 His COLARES Chita is one of the best of those classics still made.

Penafiel Sub-region in the s. of the VINHOS VERDES area.

Periquita Est'a. r. ★★ 71 74 77 78 80 84 85 86 87

One of Portugal's most enjoyable robust reds, made by FONSECA at Azeitão s. of Lisbon from a grape much used in the ALENTEJO.

Pinhel B'a.al. (r.) w. sp. ★

VQPRD region e. of the DAO, making similar white wine, mostly processed into sparkling.

Planalto Douro w. dr. ★★

Good white wine from SOGRAPE.

Pires, João Est'a r. w. dr./sw. res. ★★→★★★

Producers of red TINTO DE ANFORA, a young red Quinta de Santo Amoro made by maceration carbonique, white dry Moscato, Catarina CHARDONNAY and CAB SAUV. (See Bacalhoa, Quinta da.)

Ponte de Lima, cooperativa de M'o. r. ★★

Maker of one of the best bone dry *red* VINHOS VERDES and also of a first-rate dry and fruity white.

Porta dos Cavalheiros B'a. al. ★★→★★★ 75 80 83

One of the best red DAOS, matured by CAVES SAO JOAO in BAIRRADA.

Quinta da Insua Ba.al. r. w. ★★

One of the very few single estate DAOS, made with a proportion of CAB SAUVIGNON in an old cellar recently re-equipped and modernized.

Quinta da Pacheca Trs-os-m. r. w. ★★ 82

Superior Douro table wines, estate-grown, made and bottled.

Quinta de Ribeirinho Bei. Lit. r. sp. ★★→★★★ 80

Luis Pato makes some of the best estate-grown BAIRRADA wines: fruity red and fresh méthode champenoise sparkling.

Quinta de S. Claudio M'o. w. dr. ★★★ D.Y.A.

Estate at Esposende perhaps the best VINHO VERDE outside MONCAO.

Quinta do Côtto Trás-os-m. r. w. dr. res. ★★→★★★ 82 85

Red Grande Escolha and Q. do Côtto are dense, fruity, tannic wines that will repay long keeping. Also port.

Quinta do Corval Trás-os-m. r. ★★

Estate near Pinhão making good light CLARETES.

Raposeira B'a.al. sp. ★★

One of the best-known Portuguese sparkling wines, made by the champagne method at Lamego. Ask for the Bruto.

Redondo See Alentejo.

Reguengos de Monsarraz, Cooperativa de Alen. r. res. (w. dr.) ★★ 82 83 86 87 Important cooperative making steadily better wines, the best of them red, since modernization.

Ribalonga, Vinícola B'a.al. r. res. ██ ★★ ██ 71 74 76 78 80 82 83

Makers of a sound and very reasonably priced red DAO.

Ribatejo Region on the R. Tagus n. of Lisbon. Source of several good GARRAFEIRAS, etc.

Rosado Fernandes, José de Sousa Alen. r. res. ★★★ 71 75 79 83 86

Small private firm, recently acquired by J.M da FONSECA, producing the most sophisticated of the full-bodied wines from the Alentejo, fermenting them in pottery *tinajas* and ageing them in oak.

São João, Caves Bei. Lit. r. w. dr. sp. res. ★★→ ██ ★★★ ██ 75 76 78 80 82 One of the best firms in the BAIRRADA, known for its fruity and full-bodied reds and PORTO DOS CAVALEIROS DAOS. Also fizz.

Serradayres Est'a. r. (w.) res. ★

Blended RIBATEJO table wines from CARVALHO, RIBEIRO & FERREIRA. Usually sound and very drinkable, but recently very tart.

Setúbal Est'a. br. ★★★

Small demarcated region s. of the R. Tagus, where J.M. da FONSECA make an aromatic dessert muscat, 6 and 20 yrs old.

Sogrape Sociedad Comercial dos Vinhos de Mesa de Portugal. Largest wine concern in the country, making VINHOS VERDES, DAO, MATEUS ROSE, VILA REAL red, etc., and now owners of FERREIRA port.

Terras Altas B'a. al. r. w. res. ★★ 75 76 78 79 80 82 83 84 85

Good DAO wines made by J.M. da FONSECA.

Tinto de Anfora Est'a r. ██ ★★ ██ 78 80 81 82 84 85 86

Deservedly popular juicy and fruity red from JOAO PIRES.

Torres Vedras Est'a r. w. dr. ★

Area n. of Lisbon famous for Wellington's "lines". Major supplier of bulk wine with one of the biggest coops in Portugal.

Vila Real Trás-os-m. r. ★→ ██ ██████

Town in the demarcated DOURO region, now making some good reds.

Vinho branco White wine.

    consumo Ordinary wine.

    doce Sweet wine.

    espumante Sparkling wine.

    garrafeira A reserve with min. 2 years in cask and 1 in bottle.

    generoso Apéritif or dessert wine rich in alcohol.

    maduro A mature table wine – as opposed to a VINHO VERDE.

    rosado Rosé wine.

    seco Dry wine.

    tinto Red wine.

    verde See under Vinhos Verdes.

Vinhos Verdes M'o. and Douro. r. ★ w. dr. ★→★★★

Demarcated region between R. Douro and n. frontier with Spain, producing "green wines": wine made from barely ripe grapes and undergoing a special secondary fermentation which leaves it with a slight sparkle. Ready for drinking in the spring after the harvest. It may be white or red. "Green wine" is not an official term.

Sherry, Port & Madeira

The original authentic sherries of Spain, ports of Portugal and madeiras of Madeira are listed below. References to their many imitators in South Africa, California, Australia, Cyprus, Argentina will be found under their respective countries. (N.B. "British Sherry" is an outrageous theft of the name to describe a drink made of dehydrated must and water – not legally wine at all.)

The map on page 119 locates the port and sherry districts. Madeira is an island 400 miles out in the Atlantic from the coast of Morocco, a port of call for west-bound ships: hence its historical market in North America.

In this section most of the entries are shippers' names followed by a brief account of their wines. The names of wine-types are included in the alphabetical listing.

Almacenista Individual old unblended sherry; high-quality, usually dark dry wines for connoisseurs. Often superb quality and value. See Lustau.

Amontillado In general use means medium sherry; technically means a FINO which has been aged in the bodega beyond its normal span to become more powerful and pungent.

Amoroso Type of sweet sherry, not much different from a sweet OLOROSO.

Barbadillo, Antonio The largest SANLUCAR firm, with a range of 50-odd MANZANILLAS and sherries, incl. Sanlúcar Fino, Solear Manzanilla Pasada, Fino de Balbaina, etc. Also fresh young Castillo de San Diego table wines.

Barbeito Shippers of good-quality madeira, the last independent family firm in the business. Wines include one of the driest and best apéritif madeiras "Island Dry". Also Crown range and vintage wines, e.g. Malmsey 1901.

Barros Almeida Large family-owned port house with several brands (incl. Kopke, Feuerheerd), making an excellent 20-y-o TAWNY.

Bertola Sherry shippers, best known for their Bertola Cream Sherry.

Blandy Historic family firm of Madeira shippers. Duke of Clarence Malmsey is their most famous wine. 10-year-old Reserve Malmsey is v. popular.

Blazquez Sherry bodega at JEREZ (owned by DOMECQ) with outstanding FINO, "Carta Blanca", and "Carta Oro" amontillado "al natural" (unsweetened).

Brown sherry British term for a style of dark sweet sherry.

Bual One of the best grapes of Madeira, making a soft smoky sweet wine, not usually as sweet as Malmsey.

Burmester Old small port house with fine soft sweet 20-y-o TAWNY. Vintages **48 50 55 58 60 63 75** 77 83 85

Caballero Sherry shippers at Puerto de Santa Maria best known for Pavon Fino, Oloroso Mayoral Cream, excellent "Burdon" sherries and Ponche orange liqueur.

Cálem Old family-run Portuguese house with a good reputation, esp. for vintage wines. Owning the excellent Quinta da Foz (82 84 87). Vintages: **50** 58 **60 63** 70 **75** 77 80 83 85 87. Adequate light tawny.

Churchill The only recently-founded port shipper, already respected for excellent vintages '82 and '85. Also a good crusted. Quinta da Agua Alta is Churchill's single-quinta port: 87.

Cockburn British-owned port shippers with a range of good wines incl. 20-year-old "Directors' Reserve". Fine vintage port from very high v'yds can look deceptively light when young, but has great lasting power. Vintages: **55 60 63 67** 70 75 77 83 85.

Cossart Gordon Leading firm of Madeira shippers founded 1745, best known for their "Good Company" range of wines but also producing old vintages (latest, 1952) and soleras (esp. superb Sercial Duo Centenary).

Cream Sherry A style of amber sweet sherry made by sweetening a blend of well-aged OLOROSOS.

Croft One of the oldest firms shipping vintage port: 300 years old in 1978. Bought early this century by Gilbey's. Well-balanced vintage wines last as long as any. Vintages: **55 60 63 66** 70 **75** 77 82 85, and lighter vintage wines under the name of their Quinta da Roeda in several other years (**78** 80 83 87). Also now in the sherry business with Croft Original (PALE CREAM), Croft Particular (medium), Delicado (FINO), and good PALO CORTADO.

Crusted Term for a vintage-style port, but usually blended from several vintages not one, bottled young and aged in bottle, so forming a "crust" in the bottle. Needs decanting.

Delaforce Port shippers owned by I.D.V., particularly well known in Germany. "His Eminence's Choice" is an excellent tawny. "Vintage Character" is also good. Vintage wines are very fine, among the lighter kind: **55 58 60 63 66 70 75** 77 82 85. "Quinta da Côrte" in **78** 80 84 87.

Delgado Zuleta Old-established Sanlùcar firm best-known for its marvellous La Goya Manzanilla Pasada.

Diez-Merito S.A. Fast-growing JEREZ firm owned by BODEGAS INTERNACIONALES specializing in "own-brand" sherries. Latest acquisition is Zoilo Ruiz-Mateos, formerly part of the ill-fated Rumasa empire. Its own Fino Imperial and Oloroso Victoria Regina are excellent. DON ZOILO wines are superb.

Domecq Giant family-owned sherry bodegas at JEREZ. Double Century Original Oloroso is their biggest brand, La Ina their excellent FINO. Other famous wines incl. Celebration Cream, Botaina (old amontillado) and the magnificent Rio Viejo (dry oloroso) and Sibarita (PALO CORTADO). Recently introduced a range of old solera sherries. Now also in Rioja.

Don Zoilo Luxury sherries, incl. velvety FINO, sold by DIEZ-MERITO.

Dow's Old name used on the British market by the port shippers Silva & Cosens, well known for their relatively dry but nonetheless splendid vintage wines, said to have a faint "cedarwood" character. Also v.g. "Vintage Character" and Boardroom Tawny, a 15-year-old Tawny. Quinta do Bomfim is their single-quinta port. Vintages: **55 60 63 66** 70 72 **75** 77 80 83 85. Dow, WARRE, GRAHAM, GOULD CAMPBELL, QUARLES HARRIS and SMITH WOODHOUSE all belong to the Symington family.

Dry Fly A household name in the UK, this crisp, nutty AMONTILLADO is made in Jerez for its British proprietors, Findlater, Mackie, Todd & Co.

Dry Sack See Williams & Humbert.

Duff Gordon Sherry shippers best known for their El Cid AMONTILLADO. Also good Nina dry OLOROSO. Owned by Bodegas OSBORNE.

Duke of Wellington Luxury range of sherries from BODEGAS INTERNACIONALES.

Eira Velha, Quinta da Small port estate with old-style vintage wines shipped by HARVEY of Bristol. Vintages: **72** 78 80 82 85 87.

Ferreira The biggest Portuguese-owned port growers and shippers (since 1751) recently bought by Sogrape, well-known for old tawnies and good, relatively light, vintages: **60** 63 **66 70 75** 77 78 80 82 83 85 87. Also Dona Antónia Personal Reserve and v.g. tawny Duque de Braganza.

Fino Term for the lightest and finest of sherries, completely dry, very pale and with great delicacy. Fino should always be drunk cool and fresh: it deteriorates rapidly once opened. TIO PEPE is the classic example.

Flor The characteristic natural yeast which gives FINO sherry its unique flavour.

Fonseca Guimaraens British-owned port shipper of stellar reputation, connected with TAYLOR. Robust, deeply coloured vintage wine, sometimes said to have a slight "burnt" flavour. Vintage Fonseca: **70 75 77 80** 83 85; Fonseca Guimaraens 76, 78. Quinta do Panascal 78 is a new single-quinta wine. Also popular Vintage Character "Bin 27".

Forrester Port shippers and owners of the famous Quinta da Boa Vista. Their vintage wines tend to be round, "fat" and sweet, good for relatively early drinking. Baron Forrester is v.g. TAWNY. Vintages: **60 62 63 66 67 70 72 75** 77 80 82 83 85 87.

Garvey's Famous old sherry shippers at JEREZ. Their finest wines are Fino San Patricio, Tio Guillermo Dry Amontillado and Ochavico Dry Oloroso. San Angelo Medium Amontillado is the most popular. Also Bicentenary Pale Cream.

Gonzalez Byass Enormous concern shipping the world's most famous and one of the best FINO sherries: Tio Pepe. Other brands incl. La Concha Medium Amontillado, Elegante Dry Fino, San Domingo Pale Cream, Nectar Cream and Alfonso Dry Oloroso. Matusalem and Apostoles are respectively sweet and dry old olorosos of rare quality.

Gould Campbell See Smith Woodhouse.

Graham Port shippers famous for one of the richest and sweetest of vintage ports, largely from their own Quinta Malvedos, also excellent brands, incl. "Six Grapes" Ruby, Late Bottled, and 10-and 20-year-old tawnies. Vintages: **55 58 60 63 66** 70 **75** 77 80 83 85.

Harvey's Probably the largest sherry firm, having recently bought PALOMINO and DE TERRY. World-famous Bristol shippers of Bristol Cream and Bristol Milk sweet sherries, Club Amontillado and Bristol Dry, which are medium. Luncheon Dry and Bristol Fino, which are dry, and excellent PALO CORTADO. Also a very good range of quality sherries: "1796". Harvey's also control COCKBURN.

Sherry, Port & Madeira & Food

By a quirk of fashion the wines of sherry, Madeira and to some extent port are currently being left on the sidelines by a world increasingly hypnotized by a limited range of "varietal" wines. Yet all three include wines with every quality of "greatness", and far more gastronomic possibilities than the world seems to realize. It is notorious that for the price of e.g. a bottle of top-class white burgundy you can buy three of the very finest fino sherry, which with many dishes (see Wine & Food) will make an equally exciting accompaniment. Mature madeiras give the most lingering farewell of any wine to a splendid dinner. Tawny port is a wine of many uses. Perhaps it is because the New World cannot rival these Old World classics that they are left out of the headlines.

Henriques & Henriques Well-known independent Madeira shippers of Funchal. Their wide range includes a good dry apéritif wine: Ribeiro Seco and (sometimes) fine old reservas.

Internacionales, Bodegas Once the pride of the now-defunct Rumasa concern and incorporating such famous houses as BERTOLA, Varela and DIEZ-MERITO, Internacionales is now the cornerstone of a new empire embracing PATERNINA and FRANCO-ESPANOLAS in Rioja. Its own best-known sherries are the Duke of Wellington range.

Jerez de la Frontera Centre of the sherry industry, between Cadiz and Seville in s. Spain. The word sherry is a corruption of the name, pronounced in Spanish "Hereth". In French, Xérès.

Late-bottled vintage Port of a single vintage kept in wood for twice as long as vintage port (about 5 years). Therefore lighter when bottled and ageing quicker. A real "L.B.V." will "throw a crust" like vintage port. Few (incl. WARRE, SMITH WOODHOUSE) qualify.

Leacock One of the oldest Madeira shippers. 10-year-old Special Reserve Malmsey and 13-year-old Bual are excellent.

Lustau One of the largest independent family-owned sherry bodegas in JEREZ, making many wines for other shippers, but with a very good "Dry Lustau" range (particularly the OLOROSO) and "Jerez Lustau" PALO CORTADO. Also shippers of excellent ALMACENISTA and "landed age" wines.

Macharnudo One of the best parts of the sherry v'yds. n. of Jerez, famous for wines of the highest quality, both FINO and OLOROSO.

Malmsey The sweetest form of madeira; dark amber, rich and honeyed yet with madeira's unique sharp tang.

Manzanilla Sherry, normally FINO, which has acquired a peculiar bracing salty character from being kept in bodegas at Sanlucar de Barrameda, on the Guadalquivir estuary near JEREZ.

Manzanilla Pasada A mature MANZANILLA half-way to an amontillado-style wine.

Martinez Gassiot Port firm, subsidiary of Harveys of Bristol, known esp. for excellent Directors 20-y-o TAWNY.

Morgan A subsidiary of CROFT port, best known in France.

Offley Forrester See Forrester.

Oloroso Style of sherry, heavier and less brilliant than FINO when young, but maturing to greater richness and pungency. Naturally dry, but generally sweetened for sale, as CREAM.

Osborne Big Spanish firm with well-known brandy but also good sherries include Fino Quinta, Coquinero, dry AMONTILLADO, 10 R.F. Oloroso.

Pale Cream Increasingly popular style of sherry made by sweetening FINO, pioneered by CROFT's "Original".

Palo Cortado A style of sherry close to OLOROSO but with some of the character of an AMONTILLADO. Dry but rich and soft. Not often seen.

Palomino & Vergara Sherry shippers of JEREZ bought in 1986 by HARVEY's, best known for Palomino Cream, Medium and Dry. Best FINO: Tio Mateo.

Ponche An aromatic digestif made with old sherry and brandy, flavoured with herbs and orange, and presented in eye-catching silvered bottles. See Caballero and De Soto.

Puerto de Santa María Second city of the sherry area, with important bodegas.

P.X. Short for Pedro Ximénez, the grape part-dried in the sun used in JEREZ for sweetening blends.

Quarles Harris One of the oldest port houses, since 1680, now owned by the Symingtons (see Dow). Small quantities of L.B.V. mellow and well-balanced. Vintages: **60 63** 66 70 **75** 77 80 83 85.

Quinta Portuguese for "estate". Used to denote vintage ports which are usually, but not invariably, from the estate's vineyards. Made in good but not exceptional vintages.

Quinta do Côtto Single vineyard port from Miguel Champalimaud, best-known of the new association of grower-bottlers. V.g. vintage '82.

Quinta do Noval Great Portuguese port house making intensely fruity, structured and elegant vintage port; a few pre-phylloxera vines still at the Quinta make a small quantity of "Nacional" – very dark, full and slow-maturing wine. Also v.g. 20-year-old Tawny. Vintages: **55 58 60 63 66 67 70 75** 78 80 82 85.

Rainwater A fairly light, not very sweet blend of madeira – in fact of VERDELHO wine – traditionally popular in N. America.

Real Tesoro, Marqués de One of the smaller family firms of JEREZ, with excellent MANZANILLA La Bailadora and a range of good sherries, esp. their AMONTILLADO.

Rebello Valente Name used for the vintage port of ROBERTSON. Their vintage wines are light but elegant and well-balanced, maturing rather early. Vintages: **55 60 63 66 67** 70 72 **75** 77 80 83 85.

La Riva Distinguished firm of sherry shippers making one of the best finos, Tres Palmas, among many good wines.

Rivero, J.M. The famous "C.Z." brand of the oldest sherry house now belongs to Antonio Núñez who makes and markets Rivero sherries as well as his own.

Passing the Port

Vintage port is almost as much a ritual as a drink. It always needs to be decanted with great care (since the method of making it leaves a heavy deposit in the bottle). The simplest and surest way of doing this is by filtering it through clean muslin or a coffee filter-paper into either a decanter or a well-rinsed bottle. All except very old ports can safely be decanted the day before drinking. At table the decanter is traditionally passed from guest to guest clockwise. Vintage port can be immensely long-lived. Particularly good vintages older than those mentioned in the text include 1950, '48, '45, '35, '34, '27, '20, '11, '08, '04.

Robertson Subsidiary of SANDEMAN, shipping REBELLO VALENTE vintage and L.B.V. and Robertson's Privateer Reserve, 10-year-old Pyramid and 20-year-old Imperial.

Rozes Port shippers controlled by Moët-Hennessy. Tawny very popular in France; also Ruby. Vintages: **63 67** 77 78 81 83 85 87.

Ruby The youngest (and cheapest) style of port: simple, sweet and red. The best are vigorous and full of flavour. Others can be merely strong and rather thin.

Rutherford & Miles Madeira shippers with one of the best known of all Bual wines: Old Trinity House. Also Old Custom House Sercial and Old Artillery House Malmsey.

Sanchez Romate amily firm in JEREZ since 1781. Best known in Spanish-speaking world esp. for their brandy, Cardinal Mendoza. Makes good sherry – Fino Cristal, Oloroso Don Antonio, Amontillado N.P.U. ("Non Plus Ultra").

Sandeman Giant of the port trade and a major figure in the sherry one, owned by Seagrams. Founder's Reserve is their well-known vintage character; their vintage wines are robust – some of the old vintages were superlative (**55 60 63 66 67** 70 **75** 77 80 82 85). Of the sherries, Medium Dry Amontillado is best-seller, Don Fino is v.g. and a new range of wonderful luxury dry old sherries incl. Royal Ambrosante, Imperial Corregidor, Character Oloroso, etc. Not to be missed.

Sanlúcar Seaside sherry-town (see Manzanilla).

Sercial Grape grown in Madeira to make the driest of the island's wines – a good apéritif.

Smith Woodhouse Port firm founded in 1784, now owned by the Symington family (see Dow). GOULD CAMPBELL is a subsidiary. Wines incl. His Majesty's Choice 20-year-old, Old Lodge Tawny **60** 70 **75** 77 80 83 85.

Solera System used in making both sherry and (in modified form) madeira, also some port. It consists of topping up progressively more mature barrels with slightly younger wine of the same sort: the object to attain continuity in the final wine. Most commercial sherries are blends of several solera wines.

Soto, José de Best-known for inventing PONCHE, this family firm also makes a range of excellent sherries.

Tarquinio Lomelino Madeira shippers famous for their collection of antique wines. Standard range is Dom Henriques; top range, "Lomelino".

Tawny A style of port aged for many years in wood (in contrast to vintage port, which is aged in bottle) until tawny in colour. Many of the best are 20-year-old. Low-price tawnies are blends of red and white ports. Taste the difference.

Taylor Perhaps the best port shippers, particularly for their full, rich, long-lived vintage wine and tawnies of stated age (40-year-old, 20-year-old, etc.). Their Quinta de Vargellas is said to give Taylor's its distinctive scent of violets. Vintages: **55 60 63 66** 70 **75** 77 80 83 85. Vargellas is shipped unblended in certain (lesser) vintages (**67 72 74** 76 78). Their L.B.V. is also better than most.

Terry, Fernando A. de Bodega at PUERTO DE SANTA MARÍA with a good range of sherries (and famous brandies), bought in 1986 by HARVEY'S.

Tio Pepe The most famous of fino sherries (see Gonzalez Byass).

Valdespino Famous family-owned bodega at JEREZ, owner of the Inocente v'yd, making the excellent aged FINO of the same name. Tio Diego is their splendid dry AMONTILLADO, Solera 1842 a ditto oloroso, Matador the name of their popular range.

Varela Sherry shippers best known for their Medium and Cream.

Verdelho Madeira grape making fairly dry wine without the distinction of SERCIAL. A pleasant apéritif. Some fine old vintage wines.

Vintage Port The best port of exceptional vintages is bottled after only 2 years in wood and matures very slowly, for up to 20 years or even more, in its bottle. It always leaves a heavy deposit and therefore needs decanting.

Vintage Character Somewhat misleading term used for a good-quality full and meaty port like a first-class RUBY made by a version of the solera system. Lacks the splendid "nose" of vintage port.

Warre Probably the oldest of all British port shippers (since 1670), now owned by the Symington family (see Dow). Fine long-maturing vintage wines, a good TAWNY, Nimrod and Vintage Character Warrior. Their single-v'yd Quinta da Cavadinha is a new departure. Vintages: **55 58 60** 63 **66** 70 **75** 77 80 83 85

White Port Port made of white grapes, golden in colour. Formerly made sweet, now more often dry: a good apéritif but a heavy one.

Williams & Humbert amous and first-class sherry bodega, recently bought by Antonio Barbadillo. Dry Sack (medium AMONTILLADO) is their best-selling wine. Pando is an excellent FINO. Canasta Cream and Walnut Brown are good in their class. Dos Cortados is their famous old oloroso.

Wisdom & Warter Not a magic formula for free wine, but an old bodega with good sherries, incl. fine Wisdom MANZANILLA.

Masters of Wine

The Institute of Masters of Wine was founded in London in 1953 to provide an exacting standard of qualification for the British wine trade. A small minority pass its very stiff examinations, even after rigorous training, both theoretical and practical. (They must be able to identify wines "blind", know how they are made, and also know the relevant EC and Customs regulations.) In all, only 141 people have qualified to become Masters of Wine. Fourteen "Masters" are women.

In 1988 the Institute, aided by a grant from the Madame Bollinger Foundation, opened its examinations for the first time to non-British candidates. "Masters of Wine" (or M.W.) should eventually become the equivalent of a Bachelor of Arts degree in the worldwide wine trade.

England

The English wine industry started again in earnest in the late 1960s after a pause of some 400 years. Well over a million bottles a year are now being made from nearly 2,500 acres; almost all white and generally Germanic or Alsace in style, many from new German and French grape varieties designed to ripen well in cool weather. Natural acidity is high, which means that good examples have a built-in ability (and need) to age. Four years is a good age for many, and up to ten for some. Mature wines can be really excellent. The annual Gore-Browne Trophy and medals are awarded for the best English wine. The English Vineyards Association (EVA) seal is worn by wines which pass quality tests. N.B. Beware "British Wine", which is neither British nor wine, and has nothing to do with the following.

Adgestone nr. Sandown, Isle of Wight.
: Prize-winning 8½-acre v'yd on chalky hill site. Vines are MÜLLER-THURGAU, Reichensteiner, SEYVAL BLANC. First vintage 1970. Light, fragrant, dryish wines age exceedingly well.

Astley Stourport-on-Severn, Worcestershire.
: 4½ acres producing good KERNER. Won prizes for its '85s.

Barkham Manor Vineyard Uckfield, Sussex.
: 34 acres of MÜLLER-THURGAU, KERNER etc, planted 1985-87.

Barton Manor East Cowes, Isle of Wight.
: 10-acre v'yd producing an aromatic medium-dry blend, regular prize-winner. Consistently good. Now an acre of GEWURZ under plastic tunnels.

Beaulieu nr. Lymington, Hampshire.
: 4.6-acre v'yd, principally of MÜLLER-THURGAU established in 1960 by the Gore-Browne family on an old monastic site.

Biddenden nr. Tenterden, Kent.
: 20-acre mixed v'yd planted in 1970, making crisp medium-dry white of MÜLLER-THURGAU and Ortega; also a rosé with PINOT NOIR. Also makes wine for other growers. Gore-Browne Trophy winner in 1986. Also good cider.

Breaky Bottom nr. Lewes, Sussex.
: Good dry wines, esp. SEYVAL BLANC from 5.5-acre vineyard.

Bruisyard nr. Saxmundham, Suffolk.
: 10 acres of MÜLLER-THURGAU making medium-dry wines since 1976.

Carr Taylor Vineyards nr. Hastings, Sussex.
: 21 acres, planted 1974. Gutenborner, Huxelrebe, KERNER and Reichensteiner. Also a KERNER/Reichenstiener méthode champenoise (Gold Medal in Gore-Browne, 1988) and a PINOT NOIR méthode champenoise rosé. Exports to France.

Chiddingstone Edenbridge, Kent.
: 28-acre vineyard with stress on dry, "French-style" wines. Barrique-ageing is used.

Chilford Hundred Linton, nr. Cambridge.
: 21 acres of MÜLLER-THURGAU, Schönburger, Huxelrebe, Siegerrebe and Ortega making fairly dry wines since 1974.

Chilsdown nr. Chichester, Sussex.
: 10 acres of MÜLLER-THURGAU, Reichensteiner and SEYVAL BLANC making full dry French-style white since 1974.

Chiltern Valley Wines Hambleden, Oxfordshire.
: Small, modern winery drawing on 3 acres of own v'yds, high up on the chalk, and neighbouring growers; producing four white wines. Gold medal winner in 1988. Impressive quality.

Cranmore   Cranmore, Isle of Wight.

   5-acre vineyard planted with MÜLLER-THURGAU and Gutenborner.
   Recent change of ownership.

Denbies Lane Estate   Ranmore Common, Surrey.

   220-acre venture using mix of German varieties and advice from
   Trier. Yet to crop – but England's biggest vineyard.

Ditchling   nr. Hassocks, Sussex.

   5-acre v'yd well reputed for consistency. Good MÜLLER-THURGAU.
   Leased to ROCK LODGE.

Elmham Park   nr. East Dereham, Norfolk.

   6-acre v'yd of a wine-merchant/fruit farmer, planted with MÜLLER-
   THURGAU, Madeleine-Angevine, etc. "Mosel-style" light, dry, flowery
   wines. First vintage 1974. Also a fine dry cider.

Fonthill   Salisbury, Wiltshire.

   9.5 acres, wines made at Lamberhurst, winning medals.

Gamlingay   nr. Sandy, Bedfordshire.

   8½ acres of MÜLLER-THURGAU, Reichensteiner and SCHEUREBE since
   1970.

Hambledon   nr. Petersfield, Hampshire.

   The first modern English v'yd, planted in 1951 on a chalk slope with
   advice from Champagne. Grapes are CHARDONNAY, PINOT NOIR and
   SEYVAL BLANC. Now 15.4 acres. Fairly dry wines.

Harden Farm   Penshurst, Kent.

   18 acres of Schönburger, Bacchus, Reichensteiner, Regner and
   Huxelrebe. Not yet producing.

Headcorn   Kent

   10-acre medal-winning vineyard with SEYVAL BLANC, HUXELREBE, etc.

High Weald Winery   E. Sussex.

   No vines, but an influential wine-maker (proprietor Christopher
   Lindlar) for several small growers.

Lamberhurst Priory   nr. Tunbridge Wells, Kent.

   55 acres, planted 1972. Largely MÜLLER-THURGAU, SEYVAL BLANC, also
   Reichensteiner, Schönburger. Their Huxelrebe Dry 1986 was
   awarded high marks at a recent international tasting. Production
   capacity approx. half a million bottles a year including winemaking
   for several other v'yds. Also makes Horam Manor, 4.4 acres at
   Heathfield, Sussex. A regular prize-winner. Méthode champenoise is
   latest news.

Leeford Vineyards   nr. Battle, Sussex.

   35-acre vineyard producing wines under Saxon Valley label.

Lexham Hall   nr. King's Lynn, Norfolk.

   8-acres, planted 1975. MÜLLER-THURGAU, SCHEUREBE, Reichensteiner
   and Madeleine-Angevine.

Moorlynch   nr. Bridgewater, Somerset.

   11 acres produce award-winning wines from an idyllic farm.

New Hall   nr. Maldon, Essex.

   87 acres of a mixed farm planted with Huxelrebe, MÜLLER-THURGAU
   and PINOT NOIR. Makes award-winning whites. Experimental reds.

Nutbourne Manor   nr. Pulborough, Sussex.

   12.5 acres producing elegant and tasty Schönburger, Bacchus and
   Huxelrebe. Good wines made by HIGH WEALD WINERY. Estate for sale in
   1990.

Penshurst   nr. Tunbridge Wells, Kent.

   12 acres of the usual varieties in production since 1976.

Pilton Manor   nr. Shepton Mallet, Somerset.

   19-acre hillside v'yd, chiefly of MÜLLER-THURGAU and SEYVAL BLANC,
   planted 1966.

Plumpton Agricultural College.   nr. Lewes, Sussex.

   2-acre experimental vineyard at college which runs courses for
   winemakers.

Pulham nr. Norwich, Norfolk.

12.6-acre v'yd planted 1973; principally MÜLLER-THURGAU, Auxerrois and experimental Bacchus. Award-winning wines using the Magdalen label.

Rock Lodge nr. Haywards Heath, Sussex.

3-acre v'yd of MÜLLER-THURGAU and Reichensteiner making dry white since 1970 and méthode champenoise "Imperial". See also DITCHLING.

St George's Waldron, Heathfield, E. Sussex.

15 acres planted 1979. MÜLLER-THURGAU etc. and some GEWÜRZ. Well-publicized young venture has sold wine to Japan, etc.

Sedlescombe Robertsbridge, Sussex.

5.5 acres which claims to be England's first organic vineyard.

Shawsgate ramlingham, Suffolk

17 well-found acres incl. CHARDONNAY. Wins awards.

Staple nr. Canterbury, Kent.

7 acres, mainly MÜLLER-THURGAU. Some Huxelrebe and Reichensteiner. Dry and fruity wines of fine quality.

Tenterden nr. Tenterden, Kent.

16 acres. Planted 1977. Six wines from very dry to sweet, incl. MÜLLER-THURGAU, SEYVAL BLANC, Gutenborner and rosé. Trying oak ageing. To watch.

Thames Valley Twyford, Berkshire

17-acre vineyard of MULLER-THURGAU, PINOT NOIR, Schönburger, etc.

Three Choirs nr. Newent, Gloucestershire.

34 acres of MÜLLER-THURGAU, SEYVAL BLANC, Reichensteiner, etc. Successful wines incl. a late harvest Huxelrebe.

Wellow nr. Romsey, Hampshire.

Ambitious new venture which at 80 acres is England's third-biggest. 12 varieties, incl. CHARDONNAY, predominantly MÜLLER-THURGAU and Bacchus. First (2,000 bottles) vintage 1987. Successful wines include a Late Harvest Huxelrebe. Expects 100 acres to be planted by 1992.

Westbury nr. Reading, Berkshire.

12½ acres of a mixed farm. 11 varieties in commercial quantities since 1975, incl. England's only real PINOT NOIR red. MÜLLER-THURGAU-SEYVAL 1982 awarded gold medal.

Wickham Shedfield, Hampshire.

9.5 acres: has done well in contests.

Wootton nr. Wells, Somerset.

6-acre v'yd of Schönburger, MÜLLER-THURGAU, SEYVAL BLANC, etc., making consistently good, fresh and fruity wines since 1973.

Wraxall nr. Shepton Mallet, Somerset.

4.6 acres of MÜLLER-THURGAU and SEYVAL BLANC. Planted 1974.

The current trend towards "low-alcohol" wines and beers, from which most alcohol has been removed by artificial means, should be a golden opportunity for the producers of wines that are naturally lower in alcohol than the 12 or 13 degrees expected in most table wines. Germany is the prime example. England is another. Their best wines with plenty of fruity acidity do not need high alcohol to make an impact. They are today's logical choice.

Central &
South-East Europe

Brno

MORAVIA   Czechoslovakia

LANGENLOIS   WEINVIERTEL
WACHAU   Vienna   Bratislava   MATRAA

Austria   SOMLÓ
SOPRON   Budapest

BURGENLAND   Hungary
Graz

STYRIA   BALATON

Italy   LUTOMER
Ljubljana   VILLANYI-PÉCS

SLOVENIA   SLAVONIA   VOJVODINA
Trieste   Zagreb

CROATIA

BOSNIA-HERZEGOVINA
Yugoslavia

DALMATIA   Sarajevo

Split

Adriatic Sea   MONTENEG

Dubrovnik

Since the last edition of this book the political context of this map
has changed so radically that we can confidently expect its wine-
growing standards to do the same. Where Bulgaria, Yugoslavia
and to some extent Hungary have been sound basic providers
of low-price wines, their real potential (and that of their
neighbours) may soon emerge. So far, though, it is too soon to
record significant movement – or to foresee its direction.

In this section references are arranged country by country,
with all geographical references back to the map on this page.

Labelling in all the countries involved, except Greece and
Cyprus, is broadly based on the now international pattern of
place-name plus grape-variety. The main grape-varieties are
therefore included alongside areas and other terms in the
alphabetical listings. Quality ratings in this section are given
where experience justifies more than a single, everyday, star.

TOKAY

MOLDAVIA

TRANSYLVANIA

Tirnăve

FOCSANI

Romania

BANAT

DRAGAŞANI

DEALUL MARE

Belgrade

Bucharest

DOBRUJA

R. Danube

SERBIA

SVISHTOV

Varna

PAVLIKENI

Black Sea

SUKHINDOL

KOSOVO

Sofia

Bulgaria

MISKET

Plovdiv

R. Euros

MELNIK

ASENOVGRAD

MACEDONIA

Istanbul

THRACE

Thessaloniki

Greece

Aegean Sea

Turkey

ATTICA

Patras

Athens

SAMOS

IONIA

PELOPONNESE

SANTORINI

RHODES

CRETE

USSR

Austria

Austria has re-emerged, after a difficult period in the '80s, as a vigorous but well-regulated producer of hearty white wines with German-style flavours. New laws passed in 1986 include curbs on yields (Germany please copy) and impose higher levels of ripeness for each category than their German counterparts. Many regional names, introduced under the 1986 law, are still unfamiliar to international consumers.

Recent vintages:

1989 Some weather problems reduced size of crop. Quality fair to good, best in Burgenland & Styria.

1988 Good quantity, some excellent wines.

1987 A third small harvest, but quality is good.

1986 An outstanding vintage in most cases, though small.

1985 A small but excellent-quality harvest.

1984 Good wines for early drinking.

1983 Outstandingly ripe; many sweet wines though some are low in acidity.

Apetlon Burgenland (r.) w. s./sw. or sw. ★→ ★★
> Village of the SEEWINKEL making good whites and some reds on sandy soil, incl. very good sweet wines, esp. Prädikat wines from SEPP HOLD, LENZ MOSER.

Ausbruch Term used for very sweet wines between Beerenauslese and Trockenbeerenauslese (see Germany) in richness.

Baden Vienna (r.) w. dr. or sw. ★→★★★
> Town and wine region s. of VIENNA incl. GUMPOLDSKIRCHEN. Some good lively high-flavoured wines, whites best from ROTGIPFLER and ZIERFÄNDLER grapes.

Blaufränkisch Reputedly the GAMAY grape; gives adequate reds. Kékfrankos in Hungary.

Bouvier Native Austrian grape giving soft but aromatic wine esp. for Beerenauslese and Trockenbeerenauslese.

Burgenland Burgenland r. w. dr. sw. ★→ ★★★
> Region on the Hungarian border with ideal conditions for sweet wines and 45,000 acres. Four wine-regions: NEUSIEDLERSEE (e. of the lake), Neusiedlersee-Hügelland (w. shore and around EISENSTADT) and Mittel-and Südburgenland."Noble rot" occurs regularly and AUSBRUCH, Beerenausleses, etc., are abundant. (See Oggau, Rust, etc.)

Donauland-Carnuntum Unwieldly new name for Danube (Donau) valley wine region incl. KLOSTERNEUBURG.

Dürnstein w. dr. sw. ★★→★★★
> Wine centre of the WACHAU with a famous ruined castle and the important WINZERGENOSSENSCHAFT WACHAU. Some of Austria's best whites, esp. Rheinriesling and GRÜNER VELTLINER.

Eisenstadt Burgenland (r.) w. dr. or sw. ★★→★★★
> Capital of BURGENLAND and historic seat of the ESTERHAZY family.

Esterházy Noble and historic family (patrons of Haydn) whose AUSBRUCH and other BURGENLAND wines are often of superlative quality.

Falkenstein See Weinviertel.

Grinzing Vienna w. ★★ D.Y.A.
> Suburb of VIENNA with often delicious lively HEURIGE wines.

Grüner Veltliner Austria's most characteristic white grape (32% of her white v'yds) making short-lived but at best spicy and flowery, racy and vital wine – ideal HEURIGE, in fact.

Gumpoldskirchen Vienna (r.) w. dr. or sw. ★★→★★★
Pretty resort s. of VIENNA with wines of great character from ROTGIPFLER and ZIERFÄNDLER grapes. See Thermenregion.

Heiligenkreuz, Stift Cistercian Monastery at THALLERN making some of Austria's best wine, particularly RIESLING from a fine steep v'yd: Wiege.

Heurige Means both new wine and the tavern where it is drunk.

Kahlenberg Vienna w. ★★→★★★
Village and v'yd hill n. of VIENNA, famous for HEURIGEN.

Kamptal-Donauland (r.) w. dr. or sw. ★→→★★
Wine region around KREMS and the Kamp valley, a tributary of the Danube (Donau), with pleasant GRÜNER VELTLINER and RIESLING.

Klöch Steiermark (r.) p. w. ★→★★
The chief wine town of Styria, the s.e. province. No famous wines, but several agreeable ones, esp. Traminer.

Klosterneuburg Danube r. w. ★→→★★★
District just n. of VIENNA, with a famous monastery which is a major producer, a wine college and a research station.

Kloster Und New wine college and tasting centre in restored Capuchin monastery at KREMS, run by Erich SALOMAN.

Krems Danube w. ★→→★★
Town and district just e. of the WACHAU with good GRÜNER VELTLINER and Rheinriesling (see Riesling) esp. from Austria's biggest WINZER-GENOSSENSCHAFT.

Langenlois Langenlois r. w. ★→→★★
Chief town of the KAMPTAL with many modest and some good wines, esp. peppery GRÜNER VELTLINER and Rheinriesling (see Riesling) from its loess soil. Reds less interesting.

Lenz Moser Major wine grower. Invented a high vine system amd makes good to excellent wine at Röhrendorf near KREMS, APETLON and elsewhere. Owns the Schlossweingut Malteser Ritterorden (formerly the estate of the Knights of Malta) at MAILBERG. Experiments with CAB SAUV, MERLOT and P NOIR. Took over SIEGENDORF in 1988.

Mailberg Weinviertel (r.) w. ★★
Town of the WEINVIERTEL known for lively light wine.

Mörbisch Burgenland r. w. dr. or sw. ★→ ★★★
Leading wine-village of BURGENLAND. Good sweet wines. Reds and dry whites not inspiring.

Müller-Thurgau Far less interesting than GRÜNER VELTLINER, represents 10% of all Austria's vines.

Muskat-Ottonel The strain of muscat grape grown in e. Europe, incl. Austria. Can be dry and pungent.

Neuberger Popular white grape: pleasant wine in KREMS/LANGENLOIS but soft and coarse in BURGENLAND.

Neusiedlersee A broad shallow lake in flat sandy country on the Hungarian border, creating autumn mists and giving character to the sweet wines of BURGENLAND. Under the new law, centre of two wine regions: see Burgenland.

Niederösterreich Lower Austria: i.e. all the n.e. corner of the country, with 5 wine regions: DONAULAND-CARUNTUM, KAMPTAL-DONAULAND, WACHAU, WEINVIERTEL.

Nussdorf Vienna w. ★★
Suburb of VIENNA with well-known HEURIGEN.

Oggau Burgenland r. w. sw. ★★→ ★★★
One of the wine-centres of BURGENLAND, famous for Beerenausleses (see Germany) and AUSBRUCH.

Portugieser With BLAUFRÄNKISCH, one of the two main red-wine grapes of Austria, giving dark but rather characterless wine.

Retz Weinviertel (r.) w. ★
Wine-centre of the WEINVIERTEL, known for GRÜNER VELTLINER, etc.

Ried Single vineyard: when named on the label it is usually a good one.

Riesling When used alone is German Riesling. Wälschriesling, which is almost always inferior, is labelled as such.

Rotgipfler Good and high-flavoured grape peculiar to BADEN and GUMPOLDS-KIRCHEN. Used with ZIERFÄNDLER to make powerful but lively whites. Very heavy/sweet on its own.

Rust Burgenland (r.) w. dr. or sw. *→→***
Most famous wine centre of BURGENLAND, long and justly famous for its AUSBRUCH, often made of mixed grapes.

St-Laurent Traditional Austrian red grape, faintly muscat-flavoured.

Saloman, Fritz **→****
Top grower of oak-aged RIESLING, WEISSBURGUNDER and Gewürztraminer at Weinkellerei Undhof in the Danube valley near KREMS. Erich Saloman is a partner in the KLOSTER UND wine college.

Schilcher Pleasant sharp rosé, a speciality of STYRIA.

Schloss Grafenegg w. dr./sw. **→****
Famous castle and estate of the Metternich family near KREMS. Good standard whites and excellent Ausleses, some dry (trocken).

Seewinkel "Sea corner": the sandy district around the NEUSIEDLERSEE.

Sepp Hold Well-known BURGENLAND grower and merchant.

Siegendorf, Klosterkeller First-class 60 acre BURGENLAND wine estate experimenting with CAB SAUV and MERLOT.

Sievering Vienna w. **
Picturesque suburb of VIENNA with notable HEURIGEN.

Spätrot Another name for the ZIERFÄNDLER grape.

Spitzenwein Top wines – as opposed to TISCHWEIN: ordinary table wines.

Steiermark (Styria) Province in the s.e., not remarkable for wine but well supplied with it. Three wine regions: Süd (south), Süd-Ost (south-east) and West-Steiermark. Sauvignon Blanc showing promise here. See Klöch.

Stift The word for a monastery. Monasteries have been, and still are, very important in Austria's winemaking, combining tradition and high standards with modern resources.

Südbergenland Wine region in south of Burgenland, away from the lake. Some steep slopes. Grapes include RIESLING and Blauburgunder.

Thallern Vienna (r.) w. dr. or sw. **→****
Village near GUMPOLDSKIRCHEN and trade-name of wines from Stift HEILIGENKREUZ.

Thermenregion New name for region s. of VIENNA, incl. GUMPOLDSKIRCHEN.

Tischwein Everyday wine, as opposed to SPITZENWEIN.

Traiskirchen Vienna (r.) w. **
Village near GUMPOLDSKIRCHEN with similar wine.

Veltliner See Grüner Veltliner.

Vöslau Baden r. (w.) *
Spa town s. of BADEN (and WIEN) known for its reds made of PORTUGIESER and BLAUFRANKISCH: refreshing but no more.

Wachau Wine region on the bank s. of the Danube round DÜRNSTEIN with cliff-like slopes giving some of Austria's best whites, esp. Rheinriesling (see Riesling) and GRÜNER VELTLINER.

Weinviertel "The wine quarter": name given to the huge and productive district between VIENNA and Czech border. Mainly light white wines. Formerly divided into Falkenstein-Matzen (east) and Retz (west).

Wien (Vienna) The capital city, with 1,800 acres of v'yds in its suburbs to supply its cafés and HEURIGEN.

Weissburgunder Alias Pinot Blanc. Increasingly for solid, often dry wines.

Winzergenossenschaft Growers' cooperative.

Zierfändler White grape of high flavour peculiar to the BADEN area. Used in a blend with ROTGIPFLER.

Hungary

The traditional and characteristic firmness and strength of character which used to make Hungarian wine the most exciting of Eastern Europe have been modified by modern ideas. Average quality is still high; whites are generally lively and at least some reds made to last, but much of the drama has gone at least from the standard exported lines. Foreign buyers seem frightened of real character. Visitors to the country will find plenty of excellent wines in the old style. They are distinguished by numbered bottles (and higher prices). Recent changes are sure to let the Hungarians recapture their individuality and regain foreign markets.

Agker The official agricultural export organisation.

Alföld Hungary's Great Plain, producer of much everyday wine and some much better, esp. at Kecskemet, Kiskunhalas, Hajós, Szeged.

Aszú Word meaning "shrivelled" applied to very sweet wines, esp. Tokay (TOKAJI), where the "aszú" is late-picked and "nobly rotten" as in Sauternes. (See p. 49)

Aszú Eszencia Tokaji br. sw. ****** 57 63**
The highest quality of Tokay commercially available: superb amber wine like a cross between Sauternes and sherry.

Badacsony Balaton w. dr. sw. ****→*****
Famous 1,400 ft. hill on the n. shore of Lake BALATON whose basalt soil can give rich high-flavoured white wines, among Hungary's best.

Balatonbogler Balaton r.w.p. ***→****
Progressive cellars with sound modern-style wines, esp. whites.

Balatonfüred Balaton (r.) w. dr. sw. ******
Town on the n. shore of Lake BALATON, centre of the Balatonfüred-Csopak district. Good but softer, less fiery wines.

Balaton Balaton r. w. dr. sw. ***→*****
Hungary's inland sea and Europe's largest lake. Many wines take its name and most are good. The ending "i" (e.g. Balatoni, Egri) is the equivalent of -er in Londoner.

Bikavér Eger r. *****
"Bulls Blood". The historic name of the best-selling red wine of EGER: at best full-bodied and well-balanced, but disconcertingly variable in its export version today.

Csopak Village next to BALATONFÜRED, with similar but generally drier whites, incl. good CHARD, S. BLANC, SZURKEBARAT, etc.

Debrö Mátraalya w. sw. ******
Town of the MATRAALYA famous for its mellow, aromatic and HARSLEVELU.

Eger Eger district r. w. dr. sw. ***→****
Best-known red wine centre of n. Hungary; fine baroque city of cellars full of BIKAVER. Also delicate white LEANYKA (perhaps its best product today) OLASZRIZLING, CHARD and CABERNET.

Eszencia The fabulous quintessence of Tokay (TOKAJI): intensely sweet grape-juice of very low, if any, alcoholic strength, reputed to have miraculous properties. Now almost unobtainable.

Ezerjó The grape grown at MOR to make one of Hungary's best dry white wines: potentially distinguished, fragrant and fine.

Furmint The classic grape of Tokay (TOKAJI), with great flavour and fire, also grown for table wine on Lake BALATON.

Hajós Alföld r. *****
Village in s. Hungary known as a centre for good lively CAB SAUV reds of medium body and ageing potential. Also a good PINOT NOIR.

Hárslevelü The "lime-leaved" grape used at DEBRO and as the second main grape of TOKAJI. Gentle mellow wine.

Hungarovin Wine traders with huge cellars at Budafok near Budapest.

Gyongyos Matraalya (r.) w. ★★
>Northern district offering real promise in dry whites of SZURKEBARAT, CHARDONNAY, MUSKOTALY, etc.

Kadarka The commonest red grape of Hungary, grown in vast quantities for light everyday wine on the plains in the s.; capable (e.g. at SZEKSZARD and VILLANY) of ample flavour and interesting maturity.

Kékfrankos Hungarian for Blaufränkisch; reputedly related to Gamay. Makes good light and full-bodied reds in many areas, esp. at SOPRON on the Austrian border and goes into "Bulls Blood" at EGER.

Kéknyelü High-flavoured white grape making the best and "stiffest" wine of Mt. BADACSONY. It should be fiery and spicy stuff.

Különleges Minöség Special vintage. Highest official quality grading.

Leányka Old Hungarian white grape also grown in Transylvania. Makes admirable pale soft dry wine in many areas.

Mátraalya Wine-district in the foothills of the Mátra range in n. Hungary, incl. DEBRO, GYONGYOS and NAGYREDE.

Mecsekalja District in s. Hungary, known for the good whites of PECS.

Médoc Noir Grape apparently similar to MERLOT, used to make sweet red at VILLANY and in the blend of BIKAVER, at EGER.

Mór North Hungary w. dr. ★★
>Town famous for its fresh dry EZERJO. Now also RIESLING, SAUV. BLANC.

Muskotály Makes light though long-lived dry Muscat wine at Tokay (TOKAJI) and EGER. Very occasionally made ASZU at Tokay.

Nagyburgundi Literally "great burgundy" – an indigenous grape and not P NOIR as sometimes thought. Makes sound solid wine in s. Hungary, esp. round VILLANY and SZEKSZARD.

Olaszrizling The Hungarian name for the Italian, or Welschriesling.

Pécs Mecsek (r.) w. dr. ★ →★★
>Source of agreeable well-balanced (if rather sweet) OLASZRIZLING.

Puttonyos The measure of sweetness in Tokay (TOKAJI). A 7-gal. container from which ASZU is added to SZAMORODNI. One "putt" makes it sweetish; 6 (the maximum) very sweet indeed. Each "putt" is a 20-25 kilo hod of ASZU grapes added to 136 litres of base wine. The minimum now made is 3 putts, the maximum 6.

Siklos Southern district known for its white wines.

Siller Pale red or rosé. Usually made from KADARKA or KEKFRANKOS grapes.

Somló North Hungary w. dr. ★★
>Isolated small v'yd district n. of BALATON making white wines formerly of high repute from FURMINT.

Sopron West Hungary r. ★★
>Little Hungarian enclave s. of the Neusiedlersee (see Austria) specializing in light KEKFRANKOS reds and some Austrian-style sweet wines.

Szamorodni Word meaning "as it comes"; used to describe TOKAJI without the addition of ASZU grapes. Can be dry or (fairly) sweet depending upon the proportion of ASZU grapes naturally present.

Szürkebarát Literally means "grey friar": PINOT GRIS, which makes rich (not nec. sweet) wine in the BADACSONY v'yds and elsewhere.

Szekszárd r. ★★
>District in south-central Hungary. KADARKA red which needs age (say 3-4 years). Also good organic wines.

Tokaji (Tokay) Tokaji w. dr. sw. ★★ →★★★★
>The ASZU is Hungary's famous strong sweet wine, comparable to a maderized Sauternes, from hills in the n.e. close to the Soviet border. See Aszu, Eszencia, Furmint, Puttonyos, Szamorodni.

Villány Siklos r. p. (w.) ★★
>Southernmost town of Hungary and well-known centre of red wine production. Villányi Burgundi is largely KEKFRANKOS and rather good Cabernets Sauvignon & Franc are v. promising. See also Nagyburgundi.

Czechoslovakia

While there is little or no tradition of exporting from this mainly white-wine producing country, there are good wines to be had, especially from Moravia, the central province (capital Brno) and Slovakia (capital Bratislava). Moravian wines are the favourites in Prague.

A short list of the best cellars includes the cooperatives of Znojmo, Blatnice, Hustopeče, Šaldorf and Velké Pavlovice in Moravia and pezinok and Nitra in Slovakia. Best wines are the young Rieslings, Sauvignons, Rülanders (Pinot Gris), Traminers and Grüner Veltliner. 1989 was an outstanding vintage.

Romania

Romania has a long winemaking tradition and good potential for quality, wasted during decades of supplying the Soviet Union with the sweet wine the Russians like. The 1989 Revolution offers hope that a re-born Romania may emerge as a commercial rival to its highly successful neighbour, Bulgaria.

Alba Iulia Town in the TIRNAVE area in Transylvania, known for off-dry whites from Italian RIESLING, FETEASCA and MUSKAT-OTTONEL.

Aligoté The junior white burgundy grape makes pleasantly fresh white wine in Romania.

Babeasca Traditional red grape of the FOCSANI area: agreeably sharp wine tasting slightly of cloves.

Banat The plain on the border with Serbia. Workaday Italian RIESLING and light red CADARCA.

Cabernet Increasingly grown, particularly at DEALUL MARE, to make dark intense wines, though often too sweet for Western palates.

Cadarca Romanian spelling of the Hungarian Kadarka.

Chardonnay Used at MURFATLAR to make sweet dessert wine.

Cotesti Part of the FOCSANI area making reds of PINOT NOIR, MERLOT, etc., and dry whites claimed to resemble Alsace wines.

Cotnari Romania's most famous historical wine but rarely seen: light dessert wine from MOLDAVIA. Rather like very delicate Tokay.

Dealul Mare Important up-to-date v'yd area in the s.e. Carpathian foothills. Red wines from CABERNET, MERLOT, PINOT NOIR, etc.

Dobruja Black Sea region round the port of Costanta. See MURFATLAR.

Dragasani Region on the river Olt s. of the Carpathian Mts. Both traditional and "modern" grapes. Good MUSKAT-OTTONEL.

Feteasca Romanian white grape of mild character, the same as Hungary's Leanyka (and some say Switzerland's Chasselas).

Focsani Important eastern wine region including those of COTESTI, ODOBESTI and NICORESTI.

Grasa A form of the Hungarian Furmint grape grown in Romania and used in, among other wines, COTNARI.

Moldavia The n.e. province, now largely within the USSR.

Murfatlar Big modern v'yds near the Black Sea specializing in sweet wines, incl. CHARDONNAY. Now also dry reds and whites.

Muskat-Ottonel The e. European muscat, a speciality of Romania.

Nicoresti Eastern area of FOCSANI best known for its red BABEASCA.

Odobesti The central part of FOCSANI; white wines of FETEASCA, RIESLING.

Oltenia Wine regions including DRAGASANI. Sometimes also a brand name.

Perla The speciality of TIRNAVE: a pleasant blended semi-sweet white of Italian RIESLING, FETEASCA and MUSKAT-OTTONEL.

Pinot Noir Grown in the south: can surprise with taste and character.

Pitesti Principal town of the Arges region s. of the Carpathian Mtns. Traditionally whites from FETEASCA, TAMIIOASA, RIESLING.

Premiat Reliable range of higher-quality wines for export.

Riesling Italian Riesling. Very widely planted. No exceptional wines.

Sadova Town in the SEGARCEA area exporting a sweetish rosé.

Segarcea S. wine area near the Danube. Rather sweet CABERNET.

Tamiioasa Traditional white grape of no very distinct character.

Tirnave Important Transylvanian wine region, known for its PERLA.

Trakia Export brand. Better judged for Western palates than most.

Valea Calugareasca "The Valley of the Monks", part of the DEALUL MARE v'yd with a well-known research station. CABERNET, MERLOT and PINOT NOIR are generally made into heavy sweetish wines.

Yugoslavia

A well-established supplier of wines of international calibre if not generally exciting quality. Yugoslav "Riesling" was the pioneer, since followed by Cabernet, Pinot Blanc and Traminer, as well as such worthwhile specialities as Zilavka, Plavač and Prokupać. All parts of the country except the central highlands make wine, almost entirely in giant cooperatives. Tourists on the Dalmatian coast and in Macedonia will find more original products – all worth trying.

Amselfelder German marketing name for the Red Burgundac (Spätburgunder or PINOT NOIR) wine of KOSOVO. Disagreeably sweet.

Babic Standard red of DALMATIA, ages better than ordinary PLAVAC.

Banat Sandy north-eastern area, partly in Romania, with up-to-date wineries making adequate RIESLING.

Beli Pinot The PINOT BLANC, a popular grape in SLOVENIA.

Bijelo (Beli) White.

Blatina The red grape and wine of MOSTAR. White ZILAVKA is much better.

Bogdanusa Local white grape of the Dalmatian islands, esp. Hvar and Brac. Pleasant refreshing faintly fragrant wine.

Burgundac Bijeli CHARDONNAY, grown in SLAVONIA and VOJVODINA.

Cabernet Now introduced in many places with usually pleasant, occasionally exciting, results. See Kosovo.

Crno Black – i.e. red wine.

Cvićek Traditional pale red or dark rosé of the Sava valley, SLOVENIA.

Dalmaciajavino Important cooperative based at Split and selling a full range of Dalmation coastal and island wines.

Dalmatia The middle coast of Yugoslavia from Rijeka to Dubrovnik. Has a remarkable variety of wines of character – most of them potent.

Dingac Heavy sweetish red from the local PLAVAC grape, speciality of the mid-Dalmatian coast.

Faros Substantial age-worthy PLAVAC red from the island of Hvar.

Fruska Gora Hills in VOJVODINA, on the Danube n.w. of Belgrade, with modern v'yds and a wide range of wines, incl. rather higher strength Traminer and Sauvignon Blanc.

Grasevina Slovenian for Italian Riesling (also called Wälschriesling, LASKI RIZLING, etc.). The normal Riesling of Yugoslavia.

Grk White grape, speciality of the island of Korcula, giving strong, even sherry-like wine (and also a lighter pale one).

Istria Peninsula in the n. Adriatic, Porec its centre, with a variety of pleasant wines, the MERLOT as good as any.

Jerusalem Yugoslavia's most famous v'yd, at LJUTOMER. Its best wines are late-picked RAJNSKI RIZLING, LASKI RIZLING.

Kadarka The major red grape of Hungary, widely grown in SERBIA.

Kosovo (or Kosmet) Region in the south between SERBIA and Macedonia, with modern v'yds. Source of AMSELFELDER and some lively CABERNET.

Kraski Means grown on the coastal limestone "karst" of SLOVENIA.

Laski Rizling Yet another name for Italian Riesling.

Ljutomer (or Lutomer)-Ormoz Yugoslavia's best known and probably best white-wine district, in n.e SLOVENIA, famous for its LASKI RIZLING: at its best rich and satisfying wine. Export qualities can be variable.

Malvasia White grape giving luscious wine, used in W. SLOVENIA.

Maraština Strong dry white of the Dalmatian islands, best from Cara Smokviča on Hvar.

Maribor Important centre of n. SLOVENIA. White wines, mainly from VINAG, incl. LASKI RIZLING, RIESLING, SAUV BLANC, PINOT BLANC, TRAMINER.

Merlot Grown in SLOVENIA and ISTRIA with reasonable results.

Mostar Islamic-looking little city inland from DALMATIA, making admirable dry white from the ZILAVKA grape. Also BLATINA.

Muskat-Ottonel The East European muscat, grown in VOJVODINA.

Navip The growers' cooperative of SERBIA, with its H.Q. at Belgrade.

Opol Pleasantly light pale red made of PLAVAC grapes round Split and Sibenik in DALMATIA.

Plavać Mali Native red grape of SLOVENIA and DALMATIA; wine of body and strength, can age well. See Dingac, Postup, Opol, etc. Ordinary reds are often called "Plavać". There is also a white Plavać Beli.

Plavina Light red of the DALMATIAN coast round Zadar.

Plovdina Native red grape of Macedonia in the south, giving mild wine. Generally blended with tastier PROKUPAC.

Portugizac Austria's Portugieser: plain red wine.

Pošip Pleasant, not-too-heavy white wine of the Dalmatian islands, notably Korcula.

Postup Sweet and heavy DALMATIAN red from the Peljesać peninsula near Korcula. Highly esteemed locally.

Prokupać Principal red grape of s. SERBIA and Macedonia: 85% of production. Makes dark rosé (RUZICA) and full-bodied red of character. Some of the best comes from ZUPA. PLOVDINA is often added for smoothness.

Prošek The dessert wine of DALMATIA, of stupefying natural strength but variable quality. The best is excellent, but hard to find.

Radgonska Ranina Ranina is Austria's BOUVIER grape (see Austria). Radgona is near MARIBOR. The wine is sweet and carries the trade name TIGROVO MLJEKO (Tiger's Milk).

Rajnski Rizling The Rhine Riesling, rare in Yugoslavia but grown a little in LJUTOMER-ORMOZ.

Refosco Italian grape (see) grown in e. SLOVENIA and ISTRIA as TERAN.

Renski Rizling Alternative spelling for Rhine Riesling.

Riesling Used without qualification formerly meant Italian Riesling. Now legally limited to real Rhine Riesling.

Ruzića Rosé, usually from PROKUPAC. Darker than most; and better.

Serbia The e. state of Yugoslavia, with nearly half the country's v'yds, stretching from VOJVODINA to Macedonia.

Sipon Yugoslav name for FURMINT of Hungary, grown in SLOVENIA.

Slamnak A late-harvest LJUTOMER estate Reisling.

Slavonia Northern Croatia, on the Hungarian border between SLOVENIA and SERBIA. A big producer of standard wines, mainly white, including most "Yugoslav Riesling".

Slovenia The n.w. state, incl. Yugoslavia's most European-style v'yds and wines: LJUTOMER, etc. Slovenija-vino, the sales organization, is Yugoslavia's biggest. Some small producers with good sauvignon etc.

Smederevka Major white grape of SERBIA and KOSOVO. Fresh dry wines.

Teran Stout dark red of ISTRIA. See Refosco.

Tigrovo Mljeko See Radgonska Ranina.

Tocai The PINOT GRIS, making rather heavy white wine in SLOVENIA.

Traminac The TRAMINER. Grown in SLOVENIA and VOJVODINA. Particularly successful in the latter.

Vinag Huge production cellars at MARIBOR.

Vojvodina An autonomous province of n. SERBIA developing substantial v'yds. Wide range of grapes, both European and Balkan.

Vranać Red grape making attractive vigorous wine in Montenegro.

Vugava Rare white variety of Vis in DALMATIA. Linked (at least in legend) with the VIOGNIER of the Rhône valley.

Zilavka The white wine of MOSTAR in Hercegovina. Can be one of Yugoslavia's best: dry, pungent and memorably fruity, with a faint flavour of apricots. Exported samples are disappointing.

Zupa Central SERBIAN district giving its name to
above-average red and rosé (or dark and light red) of PROKUPAC and PLOVDINA: respectively Zupsko Crno and Zupsko Ruzića.

Bulgaria

Bulgaria has, in little more than a decade, become one of the world's top four wine exporters, exporting 85% of production. Enormous new vineyards and industrial-sized wineries have been grafted onto an old, if embattled, wine tradition. The state-run and state-subsidized wineries have learnt a great deal from the New World and offer Cabernet, Chardonnay and other varieties at bargain prices. Controlled appellation ("Controliran") wines, introduced in 1985, are being joined by wood-aged "Reserve" bottlings. A drop in sales to the USSR has led to renewed emphasis on quality wines, somewhat higher prices and a ban on planting outside the 24 Controliran regions. A tasting in London in 1989 demonstrated the ability of top wines to improve for 15-20 years.

Asenovgrad Main MAVRUD-producing cellar on the outskirts of Plovdiv, Bulgaria's second city.

Cabernet The Bordeaux grape is highly successful in n. Bulgaria. Dark, vigorous, fruity and well-balanced wine drinks well young, but top qualities mature well for suprisingly long.

Chardonnay The white burgundy grape is rather less successful. Very dry but full-flavoured wine improves with a year in bottle. Some recent oak-aged examples are developing real quality.

Controliran See introductory note.

Dimiat The common native white grape, grown in the east towards the coast. Agreeable dry white without memorable character.

Euxinograd (Château) Ageing cellar on the coast, part of the ex-King's palace. Wines reserved for State functions and top restaurants.

Fetiaska The same grape as Romania's Feteasca and Hungary's Leanyka. Pleasant pale wine, best a trifle sweet, sold as Donau Perle.

Gamza Good red grape, Hungary's Kadarka. Aged examples, esp. from PAVLIKENI, can be delicious.

Han Krum The most modern white-wine plant, near Varna in the east, esp. for oak-aged CHARDONNAY.

Iskra The national brand of sparkling wine, normally sweet but of fair quality. Red, white or rosé.

Kadarka Grape (also found in Hungary) and a popular brand of GAMZA red from n. Bulgaria.

Karlovo Town in central Bulgaria famous for the "Valley of Roses" and its very pleasant white MISKET.

Khan Krum see Han Krum

Lozitza "Controliran" CABERNET from the north; more "elegant" than most.

Mavrud Grape variety and darkly plummy red from s. Bulgaria, esp. ASENOVGRAD. Can mature 20 years. Traditionally considered the country's best.

Melnik City of the extreme s.e. and its highly prized grape. Such concentrated red wine that locals say it can be carried in a handkerchief. Needs at least 5 years and lasts for 15.

Merlot Soft red grape variety grown mainly in Haskovo in the south.

Misket Muscat-flavoured local grape used for sweet whites.

Muscat Ottonel Normal muscat grape, grown in eastern Bulgaria for medium-sweet, fruity whites.

Novi Pazar Controlled appellation CHARDONNAY winery near VARNA. Finer wines than VARNA.

Novo Selo "Controliran" red MISKET from the north.

Orjahoviza Major south area for "Controliran" CABERNET/MERLOT. Rich savoury red best at 4-5 years. Recent RESERVE CABERNET releases have been good, especially '80, '84.

Pamid The light soft everyday red of the south-west and north-west.

Pavlikeni Northern wine town with a prestigious estate specializing in GAMZA and CABERNET of high quality.

Pleven Northern cellar important for PAMID, GAMZA and CABERNET. Also Bulgaria's wine research station.

Plovdiv Southern wine town and region, source of good CABERNET.

Provadya East of SHUMEN, near the coast, another centre for good white wines, especially dry CHARDONNAY.

Rcatziteli One of Russia's favourite white grapes for strong, sweet wine. Produces bulk dry or medium whites in n.e. Bulgaria.

Reserve Used on labels of selected and oak-aged "controliran" wines.

Riesling Normally refers to Italian Riesling. Some Rhine Riesling is grown and is now made into Germanic-style whites.

Sauvignon Blanc Grown in eastern Bulgaria, recently released as dry white wine on export markets.

Shumen Eastern Bulgaria's largest white wine-producing cellar specializing in dry wines. Also makes rather good brandy.

Sonnenkuste Brand of medium-sweet white sold in Germany.

Suhindol PAVLIKENI's neighbour, site of Bulgaria's first cooperative (1909). Good cellar for GAMZA, CABERNET and PAMID.

Sungarlare E. town giving its name to a dry "controliran" MISKET.

Svishtov CABERNET-producing winery by the Danube in the north. A front-runner in Bulgaria's controlled appellation wines.

Sylvaner Some pleasant dry Sylvaner is exported as "Klosterkeller".

Tamianka Sweet white; sweeter than HEMUS.

Targovichte Independent (non-VINPROM) white wine cellar near SHUMEN that concentrates on medium and sweet wines.

Tirnovo Strong sweet dessert red wine.

Varna Major coastal appellation for CHARDONNAY.

Vinimpex The "State Commercial Enterprise for Export and Import of Wines and Spirits".

Vinprom State body controlling all 145 cooperative cellars and responsible for dramatic quality improvements over last decade. Owns 10% of the country's vineyards and 3 research institutes.

Greece

Despite Greece's entry into the EEC, disappointingly little has happened to modernize a wine industry that has been up a backwater for two thousand years. The pace of change is far faster in, say, Portugal (also a recent EEC member) and in Bulgaria to the north. A new EEC-style system of 29 appellations is now in place in Greece and much is spoken of the hopeful future for Greek wines. So far evidence is scarce. Athenian waiters try to sell over-priced brands and look snooty when you ask for Retsina (which is almost always the best value). But look for local wines in the country, esp. in the north.

Achaia-Clauss The best-known Greek wine merchant, with cellars at Patras, n. PELOPONNESE, makers of DEMESTICA, etc.

Agioritikos Mount Athos, the monastic peninsula in Chalkidiki. Source of CABERNET and other grapes for TSANTALI. Brand name of a good dry rosé.

Aminteion (Appellation) Crisp red or rosé from the mountains of Macedonia.

Attica Region round Athens, the chief source of RETSINA.

Boutari Merchants and makers with high standards in Macedonian and other wines, esp. NAOUSSA. Grand Réserve is the best wine.

Calliga Modern winery with 800 acres on CEPHALONIA. ROBOLA white and reds from indigenous grapes are adequately made but grossly over-dressed.

Cambas, Andrew Important Athenian wine-growers and merchants.

Carras, John Hotelier at Sithonia, Chalkidiki, n. Greece, died 1989, leaving an estate producing interesting red and white wines under the names Château Carras, Porto Carras and COTES DU MELITON. Ch Carras is a Bordeaux-style barrel-aged red, worth 2-4 yrs in bottle.

Castel Danielis One of best brands of dry red wine, from ACHAIA-CLAUSS.

Cephalonia (Kephalonia) Ionian (western) island with good white ROBOLA and red Thymiatiko. Also MAVRODAPHNE. See Gentilini, Calliga.

Corfu Adriatic island with wines scarcely worthy of it. Ropa is the traditional red.

Côtes du Meliton (Appellation) Thracian red, white and rosé of fair quality, made by CARRAS.

Courtakis, D. Athenian merchant with good dark NEMEAN red.

Crete Island with the name for some of Greece's better red wine. Appellations are: Archanes, Daphnes, Peza and Sitia. But Cretan white can also be suprisingly good.

Demestica A reliable brand of dry red and white from ACHAIA-CLAUSS.

Gamalafka Speciality of Mykonos. Alarmingly like sherry vinegar.

Gentilini New ('84) up-market white from CEPHALONIA, a Robola blend, soft and appealing. Now a v. promising oak-aged version. To watch.

Goumenissa (Appellation) Good-quality, oak-aged mid-weight red from BOUTARI.

Hymettus Standard brand of red and dry white without resin.

Kokkineli The rosé version of RETSINA: like the white. Drink cold.

Lac des Roches Sound, blended Dodecanese white from BOUTARI.

Lindos Name for the higher quality of RHODES wine, whether from Lindos itself or not. Acceptable; no more.

Malvasia The famous grape is said to originate from Monemvasia in the S. PELOPONNESE. See Rhodes.

Mantinia (Appellation) A fresh white from the PELOPONNESE, by CAMBAS.

Mavro "Black" – the word for dark (usually sweet) red wine.

Mavrodaphne (Appellation) Literally "black laurel": dark sweet concentrated red; a speciality of the Patras region, n. PELOPONNESE.

Mavroudi (Appellation) The red wine of Delphi and the n. shore of the Gulf of Corinth: dark and plummy.

Metsovo (Appellation) CABERNET red from Epirus in the north.

Minos Popular Cretan brand; the Castello red is best.

Naoussa (Appellation) Above-average strong dry red from Macedonia in the north, esp. from BOUTARI and TSANTALI.

Nemea (Appellation) Town in the e. PELOPONNESE famous for its lion (a victim of Hercules) and its fittingly forceful MAVRO.

Patras (Appellation) Important wine town on the Gulf of Corinth.

Peloponnese The south landmass of mainland Greece, with a half of the whole country's vineyards incl. NEMEA, PATRAS etc.

Pendeli Reliable dry red from ATTICA, grown and bottled by CAMBAS.

Retsina White wine with Aleppo pine resin added, tasting of turpentine and oddly appropriate with Greek food. The speciality of ATTICA.

Rhodes Easternmost Greek island. Its sweet MALVASIAS are its best wines. LINDOS is a brand name for tolerable table wines.

Robola or Rombola (Appellation) The fashionable dry white of Cephalonia; island off the Gulf of Corinth. Can be a pleasant soft wine of some character.

Samos (Appellation) Island off the Turkish coast with a reputation for its sweet pale-golden muscat. The normal quality is nothing much.

Santorini Dramatic volcanic island north of Crete, making sweet Vinsanto from sun-dried grapes, and dry white Thira. Unrealized potential here.

Tsantali Producers at Agios Pavlos with a wide range of table wines, including Macedonian Cabernet, wine from the monks of Mt. Athos, NAOUSSA and Muscat from PATRAS. "Cava" is a blend.

Verdea The dry white of Zakinthos, the island just west of the PELOPONNESE. The red is Byzantis.

Xynomavro The best of many indigenous Greek red grapes, basis for NAOUSSA and other northern wines.

Cyprus

A well-established exporter of strong wines of reasonable quality, best known for low-price Cyprus sherry, though old Commandaria, a treacly dessert wine, is the island's finest product. Until recently only traditional grape varieties of limited potential were available; now better kinds are beginning to improve standards, but regrettably slowly.

Afames Village at the foot of Mt. Olympus, giving its name to one of the better red (MAVRON) wines from SODAP.

Aphrodite Full-bodied medium-dry white from KEO, named after the Greek goddess of love.

Arsinöe Dry white wine from SODAP, named after an unfortunate female whom Aphrodite turned to stone.

Bellapais Fizzy medium-sweet white from KEO named after the famous abbey near Kyrenia. Essential refreshment for holidaymakers.

Commandaria Good-quality brown dessert wine made since ancient times in the hills north of LIMASSOL, named after a crusading order of knights. The best (sold as "100 yrs old") is superb, of incredible sweetness. Most is standard Communion wine.

Domaine d'Ahera Modern-style lighter red from KEO.

Emva Cream Best-selling sweet sherry from Etko, a HAGGIPAVLU subsidiary.

Etko See Haggipavlu.

Haggipavlu Well-known wine-merchant at LIMASSOL. Trades as Etko.

Keo One of the biggest and most go-ahead firms at LIMASSOL.

Khalokhorio Principal COMMANDARIA village, growing only XYNISTERI.

Kokkineli Rosé: the name is related to "cochineal".

Kolossi RedÅ and white table wines from SODAP.

Limassol "The Bordeaux of Cyprus". The wine-port in the south.

Loel Major producer. Amathus and Kykko brands, Command Cyprus sherry and good Negro red.

Mavron The black grape of Cyprus (and Greece) and its dark wine.

Mosaic KEO's brand of Cyprus sherries. Includes a fine dry wine.

Othello A good standard dry red: solid, satisfying wine from KEO.

Palomino Soft dry white made of this (sherry) grape by LOEL. Very drinkable ice-cold.

Pitsilia Region south of Mt. Olympus producing the best white and COMMANDARIA wines.

Rosella Brand of strong medium-sweet rosé.

St Panteleimon Brand of strong sweet white from Keo.

Semeli Good traditional red from HAGGIPAVLU.

Sherry Cyprus makes a full range of sherry-style wines, the best (particularly the dry) of very good quality.

SODAP Major wine cooperative at LIMASSOL.

Xynisteri The native white grape of Cyprus.

Zoopiyi Principal COMMANDARIA village, growing MAVRON grapes.

Asia & North Africa

Algeria The massive v'yds of Algeria have dwindled in the last decade from 860,000 acres to well under 500,000. Red, rosé and white wines of some quality are still made in the coastal hills of Tlemcen, Mascara, Haut-Dahra, Zaccar and Ain-Bessem. Most goes for blending (much of it to the USSR).

China Germans and Russians started making wine on the Shantung (now Shandong) peninsula in the early 1900s. Since 1980 a modern industry, initiated by Rémy Martin, has produced the adequate white Dynasty and Tsingtao wines, and new more sophisticated plantings of better varieties in Shandong and Tianjin, further north, promise more interest in the future. Basic table wines are made of the local Dragon Eye and Muscat Hamburg grapes (esp. in Tianjin). In Quingdao Italian Riesling has been followed by Chardonnay and the Hua Dong winery started experimental plantings of many varieties in 1985. Events in 1989 have delayed further progress.

India In 1985 a Franco-Indian firm launched a Chardonnay-based sparkling wine, Omar Khayyam, made at Narayangoan, near Poona, s.e. of Bombay. Plans are to export up to 2m. bottles and to add still wines of Chardonnay and Cabernet. Omar Khayyam sets an astonishing standard.

Israel Israeli wine, since the industry was re-established by a Rothschild in the 1880s, has been primarily of Kosher interest until recently, when CABERNET, SAUVIGNON BLANC, SEMILLON, PETITE SIRAH and GRENACHE of fair quality have been introduced. Carmel is the principal brand. Since 1986 Yarden wines from the Golan Heights has set a higher standard, esp. for oak-aged SAUV BLANC and Gamla Cabernet.

Japan Japan has a small wine industry in Yamanashi Prefecture, w. of Tokyo. Most of the production here is blended with imports from S America, E Europe, etc. Premium wines of SEMILLON, CHARDONNAY, CABERNET and the local white grape, Koshu, are light but can be good, though expensive. Château Lumière leads the way with high-quality

CHARD, CABERNET etc. Perhaps the most interesting (and expensive) is Suntory's Sauternes-like Château Lion. The main producers are Suntory, Mercian, Mann's. In 1985 tainted Austrian wine was discovered being sold as Japanese by a major company. Regrettably, Japanese labelling laws are so lax that misrepresentation of imported wines as "Japanese" has been the rule rather than the exception. There are increasing signs of more honourable conduct but still much confusing labelling.

Lebanon The small Lebanese wine industry, based on Ksara in the Bekaa valley n.e. of Beirut, continues against all odds to make red wine of real vigour and quality. Château Musar ✱✱✱ produces splendid matured reds, largely of CABERNET SAUVIGNON, a full-blooded white, suprisingly capable of ageing 10-15 years, and recently a lighter red "Tradition", which is 75% Cinsaut, 25% Cabernet Sauvignon.

Morocco Morocco today makes North Africa's best wine from v'yds along the Atlantic coast and round Meknes. In ten years the v'yds have declined from 190,000 to 54,000 acres. Tarik and Sidi Brahim are two drinkable reds. Vin Gris is the best bet for hot-day refreshment.

Tunisia Tunisia now has 75,000 acres compared with 120,000 ten years ago. Her speciality is sweet muscat, but reasonable reds and rosés come from Carthage, Mornag and Cap Bon.

Turkey Most of Turkey's huge v'yds produce table grapes. But her wines, from Thrace, Anatolia and the Aegean, are remarkably good. Trakya (Thrace) white and Buzbag (Anatolian) red are the well-known standards of the State wineries. Doluca and Kavaklidere are private firms of good quality. Villa Doluca red from Thrace is very well made. Buzbag is a (sometimes rough and ready) bargain.

USSR With over 3 million acres of v'yds the USSR is the world's fourth-biggest wine-producer – almost entirely for home consumption. Ukraine (incl. the Crimea) is the biggest v'yd republic, followed by Moldavia, the Russian Republic and Georgia. The Soviet consumer has a sweet tooth, for both table and dessert wines. Of the latter the best come from the Crimea. In 1990 Sotheby's auction house sold wines from the Tsar's private Crimean cellars at Massandra and revealed their splendid quality. Moldavia and Ukraine use the same grapes as Romania, plus CABERNET, RIESLING, PINOT GRIS, etc. The Russian Republic makes the best Rieslings (Arbau, Beshtau, Anapa) and sweet sparkling Tsimlanskoye "Champanski". Georgia uses antique methods to make extremely tannic wines for local consumption, and (relatively) modern methods to make blended products for export (e.g. Tsinandali, Mukuzani). Kakhetià (e. Georgia) is historically famous for both reds and whites of withering tannin content. Imeteria (w. Georgia) makes milder, highly original wines. When the equipment (e.g. good bottles) becomes available Georgia will be a hit on the export market. Georgian sparkling is extremely cheap and drinkable.

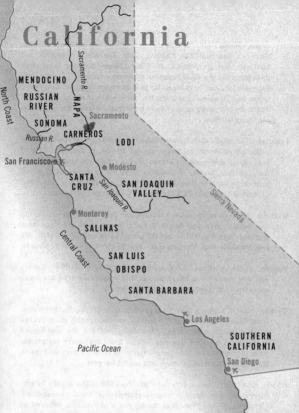

California

California has made wine for 150 years, but her modern wine industry has grown from scratch in scarcely more than 25. In the past 15 it has challenged the world with good-quality cheap wines and a growing number of luxury wines of brilliant quality. The industry is still expanding and altering at a frenied pace. Many of the wineries listed here have little track record. Quality ratings must often therefore be tentative. This edition records some 250 of the nearly 600 wineries now operating. Brevity is not dismissive; it is intended to be practical. Vintage dates given (usually for Chardonnay and Cabernet) reflect the probable maturity of wines kept in e.g. reasonable restaurant conditions. It is certain that some considerably older bottles kept in ideal cellars will still be excellent. Chardonnays can sometimes mature for 10 years with ease, Cabernets for 20.

Appellation areas are an important recent fact of life in California. They are being registered thick and fast; the current total is more than 30, with five in the Napa Valley alone and four more proposed. It is still too soon to use them as a useful guide to style. Listed below are the broad regions usually referred to.

Grape varieties combined with brand-names are the key to California wine. Since grapes in California play many new roles they are listed separately over.

Principal vineyard areas

Amador County in the Sierra foothills e. of Sacramento. Grows very good Zinfandel, esp. in Shenandoah Valley.

Central Coast A long sweep of coast with increasing though scattered wine activity, from San Francisco Bay s. to Santa Barbara.

Central Coast/Santa Barbara Santa Maria valley is dominant, esp. for v.g. Chardonnay. The smaller Santa Ynez valley also has cool foggy conditions for white wines.

Central Coast/Santa Cruz Mts. Wineries (though few vineyards) are scattered round the Santa Cruz Mts. s. of San Francisco Bay, from Saratoga down to the HECKER PASS.

Central Coast/Hecker Pass Pass through the Santa Cruz Mts. s. of San Francisco Bay with a cluster of small old-style wineries.

Central Coast/Salinas Valley/Monterey The Salinas Valley runs inland s.e. from Monterey. After frenzied expansion in the '70s, many vines were removed. What are left make wines of great character.

Central Coast/San Luis Obispo Edna Valley just s. of San Luis Obispo (1,000 acres) and new more scattered v'yds nr. Paso Robles (5,000 acres).

Livermore Valley e. of San Francisco Bay long famous for white wines but now largely built over.

Lodi Town and district at the n. end of the San Joaquin Valley, its hot climate modified by a westerly air-stream.

Mendocino Northernmost coastal wine country; a varied climate coolest in Anderson Valley nr. the coast, warm around Ukiah inland.

Napa The Napa valley, n. of San Francisco Bay, long established as a top-quality wine area. Coolest at southern end (Los Carneros).

San Joaquin Valley The great central valley of California, fertile and hot, the source of most of the jug wines and dessert wines in the State.

Sonoma County n. of San Francisco Bay, between Napa and the sea. Most v'yds are in the north (see below). A few, historically important, are in the Valley of the Moon in the south. Vineyards extend south into Los Carneros. (See also Napa.)

Sonoma/Alexander Valley/Russian River Top-quality area from Alexander Valley (n. of Napa Valley) towards the sea (Russian River). Incl. Dry Creek Valley.

Temecula (Rancho California) New small area in s. California, 25 miles inland, halfway between San Diego and Riverside.

California has adopted the world's repertoire of "classic" grapes: for notes on these see pp. 6–9. Grapes specific to California include:

Carmine, Carnelian, Centurion, Ruby Cabernet are university-bred hybrids of Cabernet, Carignan and Grenache intended to add Cabernet class to humble wines. Rarely if ever seen as "varietals".

Gamay Beaujolais not true Gamay but a Pinot Noir clone.

Gray Riesling not Riesling, makes full-bodied but standard white.

Johannisberg Riesling real (also called White) Riesling.

Petite Sirah no relation to Syrah, a synonym for the obscure French Durif.

Symphony A recent muscat-based hybrid from U.C. Davis for sweet and sparkling wines. Planted in Sonoma and San Joaquin.

Zinfandel California's own red, open to many interpretations from light-weight and fruity to galumphing. The current fad is for white or "blush" Zin. The red is capable of ageing to high quality.

Recent vintages

The Californian climate is far from being as consistent as its reputation. Although on the whole the grapes ripen regularly, they are subject to severe spring frosts in many areas, sometimes a wet harvest-time and sometimes drought.

Wines from the San Joaquin Valley tend to be most consistent year by year. The vintage date on these, where there is one, is more important for telling the age of the wine than its character.

Vineyards in the Central Coast are widely scattered; there is little pattern. The Napa and Sonoma valleys are the areas where comment can usefully be made on the last dozen or more vintages of the top varietal wines: Cabernet Sauvignon and Chardonnay. Almost all Chardonnays can be considered "ready" at 2 years, though the best can develop for up to 10 years.

	Chardonnay	Cabernet Sauvignon
1989	Some rain damage, but many will be v.g.	Long cool ripening season; some v.g. results.
1988	Excellent overall	Most are more charming than solid.
1987	Ideal weather: very good wines.	Considered extremely promising.
1986	Cool season; fine wines.	Good, but not as good as '85.
1985	Big crop, good acidity, excellent and maturing well.	Coolish ripening season. Excellent balance; some great wines.
1984	Now fully mature. Drink up.	Exceptional; very ripe and fragrant. Will improve for years.
1983	Drink up.	Similar to '80 but maturing faster.
1982	Sound, agreeable; drink up	Many outstanding; now mostly mature.
1981	Good if not too strong. Drink up.	Should be drunk soon.
1980	Should have been drunk.	Excellent, but drink soon.
1979	Excellent; drink up.	Rain; generally light. Drink up.
1978	Very good but drink up.	Excellent. Generally ready.
1977	Generally excellent. Drink up.	Attractive; fully mature. Drink up.
1976	Should have been drunk.	Small crop but splendid. Mature.
1975	Very good; getting old.	Delicate: charming. Mature.
1974	Should have been drunk.	Difficult: but many superb. Mature.
1973	Very good, but drink up.	Big and good; drink up.
1970	Should have been drunk.	One of the best ever. Mature.

California wineries

Acacia Napa. ★★★ CH 84 85 86 87 88 PN 80 81 82 83 84 85 86
Carneros winery, now owned by CHALONE, specializing in CHARDONNAY and P NOIR. Both are fulfilling initial high promise.

Adelaida Cellars Central Coast/San Luis Obispo. ★★
Skilful maker of soft CHARD and supple CAB at Paso Robles.

Alderbrook Sonoma. ★★ CH 86 87 88
Young ('82) winery using owner-grown and other grapes to make full-flavoured whites. CHARD, SAUV BLANC and SEMILLON all good.

Alexander Valley Vineyards Alexander Valley. ★★→★★★ CH 85 86 87 88 CS 81 82 83 84 85 86 Small winery best known for well-balanced CHARD and RIESLING CABERNET also v. well made.

Almaden San Joaquin. ★
Famous pioneer name bought in '87 by Heublein; now everyday brand operated from Madera.

S. Anderson Vineyard Napa. ★★→★★★ CH 85 86 87
Young winery with extensive caves. Good CHARDONNAY and recently good sparkling wine.

Arrowood Sonoma.
1990 debut by CH, ST JEAN's winemaker with his own winery (at Glen Ellen). Chardonnay ('86) and Cabernet ('85).

Au Bon Climat Santa Barbara.
Small specialist winery becoming established with the Burgundy varieties: P NOIR and CHARD.

Balverne Sonoma/Russian River. ★★ CHARD, S.B. CAB
Small winery near Windsor, started in '80 with fine CHARD, SAUV BLANC.
CAB SAUV is above average. New managers in 1988.

Beaulieu Napa. ★★★ CS 74 76 77 78 79 80 81 82 83 84 85 86 87
Justly famous long-established medium-size growers and makers of
esp. CABERNET. Top wine: De Latour Private Reserve Cabernet.
Crackerjack SAUV BLANC. Now owned by Grand Metropolitan. Beautour
CAB SAUV is value ('86).

Bel Arbors A second label of FETZER.

Belvedere Sonoma ★★ CAB, CHARD.

Beringer Napa. ★★→★★★ CS 85 86 87 88 CS 80 81 82 83 84 85 86
Century-old winery now restored to the front rank by owners Nestlé.
Increasingly fine wines incl. esp. CHARD (excellent Private Reserve),
CABERNET (ditto) and "Nightingale", induced-botrytis dessert wine. 2nd
label: Napa Ridge.

Benziger see Glen Ellen

Black Mountain Sonoma. ★★ CHARD, SAUV BL, P.Sirah, ZIN (2nd label:
J.W. Morris)

Boeger El Dorado. ★★ CS 79 80 81 82 83 84 85 86 87
Small winery in Sierra foothills. Good ZIN, too.

Bonny Doon Vineyard Central Coast/Santa Cruz Mtns. ★★ CH 86 87
Small winery (since '81) with original ideas about Rhône grapes, incl.
Syrah, Grenache, and even the white Roussanne and Marsanne.
(E.g. Le Cigare Volant; Grenache spiced with Mourvèdre: 84 85 86.)

Bouchaine Napa/Carneros. ★★→★★★ CH 84 85 86 PN 85 86
Young firm in old Carneros barn started with Acacia-style oaky PINOT
NOIR. Now similar v.g. CHARDONNAY and SAUV BLANC.

Brander Central Coast/Santa Barbara. ★★
Small new winery specializes in excellent SAUVIGNON BLANC of Santa
Ynez Valley grapes. Now also hitting high notes with CAB FRANC and
MERLOT labelled "Bouchet" (84 85 86).

Bruce, David Central Coast. ★★ CS 83 84 85 86 87
Small luxury winery with heavy-weight wines. To watch.

Buena Vista Sonoma. ★★ CH 83 84 85 86 87 CS 83 84 85
Historic pioneer winery with German owners and very sound recent
record esp. in whites (CHARD, RIESLING, FUME BLANC). Good value CAB.

Burgess Cellars Napa ★★ CH 85 86 87 88 CS 80 81 82 83 84 85 86 Z 81 82 83
84 85 86 87 Small hillside winery, in former Souverain cellars,
making good CABERNET, very good ZIN, and CHARD.

B.V. Abbreviation of BEAULIEU VINEYARDS used on their labels.

Bynum, Davis Sonoma. ★★ CH 85 86 CS 82 83 84 85 86
Well-established maker of standard varieties, w. of Healdsburg. Esp.
GEWÜRZ, CHARD, P NOIR.

Byron Vineyards Santa Barbara. ★★★ CH 85 86 87 88 CS 85 86 87
Long-time Zaca Mesa winemaker Ken Brown sold his own Santa
Maria Valley winery to Robert Mondavi in 1989. P NOIR memorable.

Cain Cellars Napa ★★ CH 85 86 87 CS 84 85
Young (1984) winery draws on estate v'yd on Spring Mountain for
ambitious Bordeaux-blend Cain Five. Also CAB SAUV, CHARDONNAY.

Cakebread Napa. ★★★ CH 85 86 87 88 CS 80 81 82 83 84 85 86
Started 1973. Increasing reputation, esp. for SAUVIGNON BLANC and
CABERNET (79 N.B.); also CHARDONNAY.

Calera Monterey-San Benito. ★★→★★★ PN 80 81 82 83 84 85 86 CH 85 86
87 1975 winery ambitious and often successful with PINOT NOIR.

Callaway S. California. ★★ CH 85 86 87 88
Mid-sized winery in new territory at TEMECULA owned by Allied-Hiram
Walker. Sound whites.

Cambria Santa Barbara Chardonnay specialist.

Carmenet Sonoma. ★★→★★★ CS 83 84 85
Where CHALONE emulates Burgundy, the same owners have chased

Bordeaux here since '82 with SAUV BL. from Sonoma, and v.ripe CAB/ MERLOT from high above Sonoma town. Also "Gavilan" FRENCH COLOMBARD from Napa and CHARD from Carneros.

Carneros Creek Napa. ✦✦✦ CH 85 86 87 88 CS 74 77 80 81 82 83 84 85
The first winery in the cool Carneros area between Napa and the Bay. Good P NOIR, CHARDONNAY and CABERNET. Good-value MERLOT.

Caymus Napa. ✦✦✦ →✦✦✦✦ CS 76 77 78 79 80 81 82 83 84 85 86 Outwardly modest small winery at Rutherford with v. high standards, esp. for notably complex CAB and ZIN; also WHITE P NOIR, SAUV BLANC, occasionally CAB FRANC. Second label: Liberty School (value).

Chalk Hill Sonoma/Russian River. ✦✦ CH 85 86 87 88 CS 83 84 85
Considerable vineyards in Chalk Hill near Windsor. High standards.

Chalone Central Coast/Salinas. ✦✦✦✦ CH 80 81 82 83 84 85 86 87 88 PN 80 81 82 83 84 85 86 Unique small hilltop v'yd/winery at the Pinnacles. French-style CHARDONNAY and PINOT NOIR of super quality. Also excellent PINOT BLANC. See also Acacia, Carmenet. In 1989 traded shares with Domaine Barons de (Lafite) Rothschild.

Chappellet Napa. ✦✦✦ CH 81 83 84 85 86 87 CS 74 75 76 78 79 80 81 82 83 84 85 86 Luxury winery and beautiful amphitheatrical hillside v'yd. Excellent very long-lived CABERNET, CHARDONNAY and RIESLING; very good dry CHENIN BLANC.

Château Montelena Napa. ✦✦✦ CH 85 86 87 CS 75 77 78 79 80 81 82 83 84 85 Small 1969 winery making very good distinctive CHARDONNAY and very tannic CABERNET SAUVIGNON.

Chateau Potelle Napa French-owned; Cab, Chard.

Château St-Jean Sonoma. ✦✦✦ CH 85 86 87
Impressive winery specializing in whites from individual v'yds, incl. CHARD, P BLANC and esp. late harvest RIES. Also fine sparkling wine and bargain "Vin Blanc". Owned by Suntory. Reds to come.

Château Souverain Alexander Valley. ✦✦ CH 85 86 CS 78 79 80 81 82 83 84 85 Luxurious mid-sized winery with a record of competent wines, bought by BERINGER in 1986. Carneros Reserve CHARD is fine value.

Chimney Rock Napa Stags' Leap area Cab, Chard.

Christian Brothers Napa and San Joaquin. ✦→✦✦✦ CH 87 88 CS 84 85 86 For long the biggest Napa winery, run by a religious order; bought in 1989 by Heublein, Inc. Sound and improving CABERNET (since 84), attractive CHARD, useful FUME BLANC, sweet white Ch La Salle, very good brandy and ZIN "port".

Cline Cellars Contra Costa A "Rhône Ranger"; grows Mouvédre, etc.

Clos du Bois Sonoma. ✦✦ →✦✦✦ CH 85 86 87 88 CS 78 79 80 81 82 83 84 85 86 Healdsburg winery with v'yds in Dry Creek and Alexander Valleys. V.g. GEWÜRZ, P NOIR, MERLOT, CHARD, SAUV BLANC. Named-v'yd wines outstanding. Now owned by Allied-Hiram Walker.

Clos du Val Napa. ✦✦✦ CH 85 86 87 88 CS 77 78 79 80 81 82 83 84 85 86 French-run. V.g. bold ZIN, fine CAB, MERLOT, CHARD and SEM.

Clos Pegase Napa. ✦✦✦
Amazing post-modernist building near STERLING. Wines steadily improving; esp. v.good CHARD. CABERNET also promises well.

Concannon Livermore. Table. ✦✦ CH 86 CS 85
Substantial winery first famous for whites; reds now prominent. Owned by winemaker Sergio Traverso and Deinhards of Germany.

Congress Springs Santa Clara/Santa Cruz. ✦✦ CH 84 85 86
Tiny winery above Saratoga with substantial reputation. Well-made whites, e.g. SAUV BLANC, CHARD and esp. PINOT BLANC. Also CAB FRANC.

Conn Creek Napa. ✦✦→✦✦✦ CH 85 86 87 CS 78 79 80 81 82 83 84 85 86 Winery built on Silverado Trail in 1979 has built a solid following. Now owned by Ch Ste Michelle of Washington. Best known for CAB.

Cooks "Cooks Champagne" – See Guild.

Corbett Canyon Central Coast/San Luis Obispo. ★★ ᴄʜ 84 85 86 87
Edna Valley winery makes small lots of Reserve and sizeable amounts of good value " Coastal Classics", all varietal.

Culbertson Temecula. ★★
Young sparkling-wine specialist using local grapes of an improbable region with medal-winning results.

Cuvaison Napa. ★★→★★★ ᴄʜ 83 85 86 87 88 ᴄs 78 79 80 81 82 83 84 85 86
Small winery with expert new direction. Formerly austere ᴄᴀʙᴇʀɴᴇᴛ and ᴄʜᴀʀᴅᴏɴɴᴀʏ now more approachable; ᴄʜᴀʀᴅ from own Carneros v'yd is tops. Now ᴍᴇʀʟᴏᴛ too.

Dehlinger Sonoma. ★★→ ★★★ ᴄʜ 85 86 87 ᴘɴ 79 80 81 82 83 84 85 86 86 87 Small winery and v'yd w. of Santa Rosa. Since 1976 ᴄʜᴀʀᴅᴏɴɴᴀʏ, ᴄᴀʙᴇʀɴᴇᴛ and since '79 ᴘ ɴᴏɪʀ all extremely well made.

DeLoach Vineyards Sonoma. ★★★ ᴄʜ 85 86 87 88 ᴘɴ 80 81 82 83 84 85 86 Russian River winery founded 1975 for ᴄʜᴀʀᴅᴏɴɴᴀʏ, ɢᴇᴡᴜʀᴢ, ᴘ ɴᴏɪʀ. Also good ᴢɪɴ (v.g. white ᴢɪɴ), and ᴄᴀʙʏ ʙʟᴀɴᴄ.

Delorimier Sonoma small estate: ᴄʜᴀʀᴅ, ᴄᴀʙ blend, ᴄᴇᴍ-sᴀᴜᴠ. blend.

De Moor Napa. ★★ ᴄᴀʙ, ᴄʜᴀʀᴅ, ᴢɪɴ.

Diamond Creek Napa. ★★★ ᴄs 74 75 76 78 79 80 81 82 83 84 85 86 87
Small winery since the 60s with austere, long-ageing ᴄᴀʙᴇʀɴᴇᴛ from hills w. of Calistoga, e.g. "Volcanic Hill", "Gravelly Meadow".

Domaine Carneros Napa.
Taittinger's highly visible cellar in Carneros is the newest sparkling producer with roots in Champagne. First wines due in 1990.

Domaine Chandon Napa. ★★★
Californian outpost of Moët & Chandon Champagne. Launched 1976. Promise is being fulfilled. First Reserve wine (released in 1985) was a showstopper. So was second. Shadow Creek now its non-Napa label.

Domaine Laurier Sonoma. ★★★ ᴄʜ 83 84 85 86 87 ᴄs 78 79 80 81 82 83 84 85 86 Small winery started with beautifully structured wines, esp. ᴄᴀʙᴇʀɴᴇᴛ and ᴄᴀᴜᴠ ʙʟᴀɴᴄ, using the new appellation Green Valley. New owners (also run ʟʏᴇᴛʜ) have hired Merry Edwards to make wine. To watch.

Domaine Mumm Napa. (★★)
Seagram-owned. Sparkling-wine house near Rutherford. First wine released '86, promising, and promises kept: v. crisp and fine.

Domaine Napa Napa. French/New Zealand venture. ᴄᴀʙ, ᴄʜᴀʀᴅ.

Dominus Napa. (★★★★) 83 84 85 86
First fruits (1984 vintage released '88) of partnership ("John Daniel Society") between inheritors of ex-Inglenook v'yd n. of Yountville and Christian Moueix of Pomerol. B'x-style Cabernets-Merlot blend shows immense promise. Winery building by I.M.Pei.

Dry Creek Sonoma. ★★★ ᴄʜ 85 87 88 ᴄs 82 83 84 85 86
Small winery with high ideals, making old-fashioned dry wines, esp. whites, incl. ᴄʜᴀʀᴅᴏɴɴᴀʏ, ᴄʜᴇɴɪɴ ʙʟᴀɴᴄ and ꜰᴜᴍᴇ ʙʟᴀɴᴄ and outstanding ᴄᴀʙ sᴀᴜᴠ. Cabernet Franc on its way.

Duckhorn Vineyards Napa. ★★→★★★ ᴍ 82 83 84 85 86 87 ᴄs 80 81 82 83 84 85 86 Small winery on Silverado Trail best known for reds, esp. v.g. ᴍᴇʀʟᴏᴛ. Also sᴀᴜᴠɪɢɴᴏɴ ʙʟᴀɴᴄ.

Dunn Vineyards Napa. (★★★) ᴄs 81 82 83 84 85 86
Randall Dunn (ex-Caymus) now makes small lots of dark, stern Howell Mountain ᴄᴀʙᴇʀɴᴇᴛ sᴀᴜᴠɪɢɴᴏɴ in his own winery.

Durney Vineyard Central Coast/Monterey. ★★ ᴄs 79 80 81 82 83 84 85 86 Well-established source of robust ᴄᴀʙᴇʀɴᴇᴛ. Also ᴄʜᴇɴɪɴ ʙʟ, ʀɪᴇsʟɪɴɢ.

Eberle Winery Central Coast/San Luis Obispo. ★★
Most stylish and consistent ᴄᴀʙ producer in Paso Robles area since '79. Also ᴄʜᴀʀᴅ.

Edna Valley Vineyard Central Coast/San Luis Obispo. ★★→★★★ ᴄʜ 85 86 87 88 Joint venture of grape-grower with ᴄʜᴀʟᴏɴᴇ winemakers. Fat ᴄʜᴀʀᴅᴏɴɴᴀʏ full of character.

Estancia See Franciscan.

Far Niente Napa. ★★★ CH **85 86 87** CS **84 85** 86
Founded 1885; reactivated in 1979. (Very) full-flavoured CHARDONNAY first; now similar CABERNET.

Ferrari-Carano Sonoma. ★★★ CH **85 86 87 88**
New (1985), family-owned major player with 1,000 acres of v'yd land in ALEXANDER, Dry Creek, Knights Valley. CHARD SAUV BL. well received. CAB SAUV, MERLOT in the works.

Fetzer Mendocino. ★★→★★★ CH **85 86 87 88** CS **81 82 83 84** 85
Rapidly expanding winery with interesting reliable wines, at several price levels, esp. CHARD and CAB. Also FUME BLANC, RIES and strong dark ZIN. A byword for value, esp. in Barrel Select range.

Ficklin San Joaquin. ★★★
Family firm making California's best "port": "Tinta" and vintage.

Field Stone Sonoma (Alex Valley). Petite Sirah, CAB, Rosé, etc.

Firestone Central Coast/Santa Barbara. ★★★ CH **85 86 87** CS **81 82 83 84** 85 86 Ambitious 1973 winery n. of Santa Barbara. Cool conditions are producing full spectrum of unusual, gentle wines incl. delicious RIESLING, GEWÜRTZ, MERLOT. J.Carey is subsidiary for stylish SAUV BL, CAB.

Fisher Sonoma/Napa. ★★
Small mountain estate nr. Calistoga for v.g "coach" CAB and CHARD.

Flora Springs Wine Co. Napa. ★★ CH **85 86 87** CS **81 82 83 84 85**
Old stone cellar in St-Helena reopened 1979. CHARDONNAY and SAUV BLANC are v. successful, CABERNET coming nicely. Also good MERITAGE blend: Trilogy.

Folie à Deux Napa. ★★ CH **81 83 84 85** CS 86
Tiny producer of impeccable Chardonnays, v. good CHENIN BL, CAB, from bought-in grapes.

Foppiano Sonoma. ★★
Old winery at Healdsburg with estate varieties incl. FUME BLANC, CAB, PETITE SIRAH. Reserve CHARD and CAB are labelled Fox Mountain. Second label, Riverside Farms, has good value ZIN.

Forman Napa
Tiny prestigious winery for CHARD and CAB, just opened by the winemaker who brought STERLING its fame.

Franciscan Vineyard Napa. ★★ CH **85 86 87 88** CS **80 81 82 83 84** 85
Rapidly expanding winery with v'yds in Napa, Alex Valley and Monterey. Good ZIN, CAB, CHARD and RIES. Wines from own SONOMA and Monterey v'yds are labelled "Estancia" (value).

Franzia San Joaquin. ★
Large old winery with well-distributed brands. Various labels, but all say "made and bottled in Ripon".

Freemark Abbey Napa. ★★★★ CH **83 84 85** 86 **87** CS **74 75 76 77 78 79 80 81 82 83 84 85** Small connoisseur's winery with high reputation for CABERNET, CHARDONNAY and RIESLING (esp. late-harvest "Edelwein"). Top CAB is "Bosché" (**74 75 78 79 80'** 81 82 83 84 85. Also "Sycamore" CAB and now exceptional Carpy Ranch CHARD.

Frog's Leap Napa. ★★
Little St Helena winery as charming as its name. Now CAB SAUV and CHARD outclass the original SAUV BL and ZIN.

Gainey Vineyard Santa Barbara ★★ CHARD, CAB, SAUV BL.

Gallo, E. & J. San Joaquin. ★→★★ CH **85 86 87 88** CS **78 80 81 82** ZIN **81 83**
The world's biggest winery, pioneer in both quantity and quality. Family owned. Hearty Burgundy and Chablis Blanc set national standards. Vintage-dated CAB has won wide approval. Drink it fairly young. Varietals come from the company's huge SONOMA v'yds. Also "André" fizz and many lines.

Gan Eden Sonoma. (★★) CH **86 87 88** CS 86 87
Kosher producer of serious CHARD, CAB SAUV has won wide critical acclaim in each vintage since 1985.

Gauer Estate Sonoma. New and v.g. CHARD, CAB.

Geyser Peak Sonoma. ★★
Old winery revived by Schlitz Brewery then sold to local grower Henry Trione. Wines are increasingly from his 700 acres. Penfolds of Australia bought half-share in '89.

Giumarra San Joaquin. ★★ "Burgundy", "Chablis" and CAB, CHARD.

Glen Ellen Sonoma. ★★→★★★ CH 85 86 87 CS 83 84 85 86
Family team making restrained elegant wines from own-grown and other Sonoma grapes under Benziger of Glen Ellen label. SAUV BLANC, CHARD and CABERNET. "Proprietor's Reserve" indicates bought-in everyday wines, despite its name.

Gloria Ferrer Sonoma. ★★
Big sparkling winery launched in '85 by FREIXENET of Spain. An impressive start.

Grand Cru Sonoma. ★★ CH 87 88 CS 80 81 82 83 84 85 86
Small 1971 winery now concentrating on CHARD and CAB S. and continuing tradition of good GEWÜRZ, CHENIN and SAUV. BL.

Green and Red Napa ★★ Tiny winery; vigorous ZIN.

Greenwood Ridge Mendocino RIESLING specialist.

Grgich Hills Cellars Napa. ★★★ CH 83 84 85 86 87 Z 77 78 79 80 81 82 83 84 85 86 Grgich (formerly of Ch Montelena) is winemaker, Hills grows the grapes – esp. CHARDONNAY and RIESLING. Lively wines include high-strength ZINFANDEL and (since '85) CABERNET.

Groth Vineyards Napa. (★★) CH 87 CS 84 85 86
Estate at Oakville is challenging leaders with polished, subtle CAB SAUV. Also CHARD.

Guenoc Vineyards Lake County. ★★ CH 85 86 87
Ambitious vineyard/winery venture originally owned by Lillie Langtry just beyond the Napa county line. SAUV. BLANC, ZIN and PETITE SIRAH are esp. appealing.

Guild San Joaquin. ★
Big growers' cooperative. B. Cribari is table wine label, "Cooks American Champagne" a runaway success.

Gundlach-Bundschu Sonoma. ★★ CH 85 86 87 88 CS 79 80 81 82 83 84 85 86 Very old small family winery revived by the new generation. Excellent very flavoury CABERNET, MERLOT, ZIN and good whites: CHARDONNAY, GEWÜRZ, RIESLING.

Hacienda Sonoma. ★★ CH 85 86 CS 79 81 84 85 86
Small winery at Sonoma specializing in high-quality CHARDONNAY and GEWÜRZ. CABERNET has steadied recently. Also P. NOIR.

Handley Cellars Mendocino. (★★)
Small family-owned Anderson Valley cellar specializes in impressive sparkler, CHARDONNAY. Also refreshing Brightlighter (Gewürz-based).

Hanzell Sonoma. ★★★ CH 83 84 85 86 87 PN 83 84 85 86
Small winery whose (late) founder revolutionized Californian CHARDONNAYS in the '50s. CHARD and P NOIR are both huge wines. CABERNET first released in 1986.

Haywood Vineyard Sonoma. ★★ CH 85 86 CS 83 84 85 86
Small new estate on hills above SEBASTIANI. First wines were lovely fruity CHARDONNAY and RIESLING and gutsy ZIN. Now CABERNET.

Heitz Napa. ★★★★ CH 83 84 85 86 87 CS 76 77 78 79 80 81 82 83 84 85
An inspired individual winemaker who has set standards for the whole industry. His CABERNETS (esp. "Martha's Vineyard" and "Bella Oaks") are as dark, deep and emphatic as ever. But Chard and other wines can be eccentric or worse. Added substantial new v'yds in 1984 and 1989.

Hess Collection, The Napa.
Swiss art-collector's extravaganza est. '83 in old Mont la Salle (Christian Brothers) winery. CHARD and CAB from mountain v'yd estate.

Hill, William Winery Napa. ★★→★★★ CH 85 86 87 CS 80 81 82 83 84 85 86 87 Huge new plantings in the Mayacamas Mts. and a new winery have yielded very emphatic (but well-received) wines.

Hop Kiln Sonoma/Russian River. ★★ CH 83 87 88
Small winery. Individual, tasty PETITE SIRAH, ZIN, GEWÜRZ.

Husch Vineyards Mendocino. ★★ CHARD, P.NOIR, GEWÜRZ, CAB, SAUV. BL.

Inglenook Napa. ★★→★★★ CH 85 86 87 88 CS 76 77 78 79 80 81 82 83 84 85 One of the great old Napa wineries much changed by current owners Grand Metropolitan. Inglenook Napa Valley is Napa label, with two qualities: "Cask" (Reserve) and Estate, now joined (since '83) by hugely tannic "Reunion". CAB SAUV, MERLOT, CHARD and SAUV BLANC are v. well made. PETITE SIRAH is tasty. (Inglenook Navalle are low-cost Central Valley wines, only nominally related.)

Iron Horse Vineyards Sonoma. ★★★ CH 85 86 87 88 CS 79 80 81 82 83 84 85 Stylish Russian River property with CHARDONNAY, CABERNET, P NOIR and SAUV BLANC of vivid flavours. Sparkling IRON HORSE is v. dry and fine. Tin Pony is second label.

Jekel Vineyards Central Coast/Monterey. ★★→★★★ CH 85 86 87 CS 81 82 83 84 85 86 Well-made RIESLING, CHARDONNAY, and CABERNET have rich resounding flavours. Wines (esp. whites) mature fast but tastily.

Jepson Vineyards Mendocino. (★★)
A Chicago industrialist owns 100 acres of CHARD, SAUV BLANC near Ukiah. They produce varietals, a sparkler, and a little pot-still brandy.

J. Lohr Central Coast. ★★
Substantial winery in San José and Paso Robles with its own v'yds in SALINAS Clarksburg, San Luis Obispo, Napa. Reliable RIESLING, CABERNET rosé and CHENIN BLANC.

Johnson-Turnbull Napa. ★★ CS 80 81 82 83 84 85 86
Very small new estate producing balanced and distinguished, not overweight, CABERNETS from next door to MONDAVI.

Johnson's of Alexander Valley Sonoma. ★★ CAB S, CHARD, P.NOIR etc.

Jordan Sonoma. ★★★ CH 85 86 87 CS 78 79 80 81 82 83 84 85 86
Extravagant winery. CABERNET modelled on Bordeaux, smooth CHARDONNAY. Highly polished wines to please sophisticates.

Karly Amador. ★★ Stylish producer of esp. ZIN from Sierra foothills.

Keenan, Robert Napa. ★★ CH 85 86 CS 83 84 85 86
V'yds on Spring Mountain started with over-strong and tannic wines. More polite recent style is winning approval.

Kendall-Jackson Lake County. ★★→★★★ CH 85 86 87 88 CS 84 85 86
Dynamically expanding maker of good uncomplicated CHARD, RIES, SAUV BLANC, CABERNET. ZIN a speciality. V.g. Syrah in 86.

Kenwood Vineyards Sonoma. ★★★→★★★★ CH 85 86 87 CS 78 79 80 81 82 83 84 85 86 Growing producer of steadily stylish reds, esp. CABERNET and ZIN also v.g. SAUV BLANC, good CHARD and CHENIN.

Kistler Vineyards Sonoma. ★★ CH 85 86 87 88 CS 80 81 82 83 84 85 86
Young small winery in hills. First CHARDONNAY was overwhelming; recent wines show more restraint. Now also CAB and P NOIR

Konocti Cellars Lake County ★★
Mid-sized cooperative winery in remote north, half-owned by John PARDUCCI. RIESLING, Fumé Blanc, CAB SAUV are consistently attractive.

Korbel Sonoma ★★
Long-established sparkling wine specialists. "Natural" and "Brut" are among California's best standard "champagnes". Also brandy.

Kornell, Hanns Napa. ★★
Independent-minded sparkling wine house using RIES to make full-flavoured dry Sehr Trocken. Now also a sp. CHARD.

Krug, Charles Napa. ★→★★★ CS 74 77 78 79 80 81 82 83 84 CH 86 87 88
Historic old winery with generally sound wines. Good CABERNET (incl. releases of mature vintages), sweet CHENIN BLANC **and very sweet Muscat Canelli. C.K. Mondavi is the jug-wine brand.**

La Crema Sonoma. ★★ CH 85 86 87 88 PN 79 80 81 82 83 84 85 86 87
Founded 1979 at Petaluma; moved 1990 to Russian River Valley. CHARD now more restrained than formerly; P.NOIR impressive.

Lakespring Napa ★★ MERLOT, CAB., CHARD., SAUV. BL.

Lambert Bridge Sonoma. ★★ CS 80 81 82 83 84 85
Small 1975 winery nr. Healdsburg. CHARD less oaky than formerly; CABERNET austere, needs ageing.

Landmark Sonoma. ★★ CH 83 84 85 86
Young winery at Kenwood; sound CHARD. Signs of class. 2nd label: Cypress Lane.

Laurel Glen Sonoma. ★★★ CS 81 82 83 84 85 86 87
Splendid '81 CABERNET was first wine of tiny winery at Glen Ellen. More recent wines look very good.

Lazy Creek Mendocino. CHARD, good dry GEWÜRZ.

Leeward Winery Central Coast/Ventura. ★★ CH 85 86 87 88 CS 83 84 85 86
CHARDONNAY from Monterey and San Luis Obispo grapes started this new venture near Santa Barbara well in 1980.

Long Vineyards Napa. ★★ CH 85 86 87 CS 79 80 81 82 83 84 85
Tiny winery in eastern hills nr. CHAPPELLET. First good CHARDONNAY and late-harvest RIESLING, now CABERNET.

Lyeth Vineyard Sonoma. ★★ 84 85
New winery with ambitions for Bordeaux-style red and white. Red is 78% CAB SAUV, 12% MERLOT, etc. – and promising.

Lytton Springs Sonoma. ★★ Z 83 84 85 86 87
Small specialist in Russian River ZIN; thick, heady, tannic.

Madrona El Dorado. ★★
Winery with loftiest v'yd in Sierra Foothills and impressive CHARD.

Maison Deutz Sonoma. ★★★
New sp. winery with Champagne parentage. Promising first wines.

Mark West Sonoma. ★★→★★★ CH 85 86 87 88 PN 79 80 81 82 83 84 85 86 Young winery in cool sub-region. Very satisfactory GEWÜRZ, CHARDONNAY. Now P NOIR and sparkling Blanc de Noirs.

Markham Napa. ★★ CS 78 79 80 81 82 83 84 85 CH 85 86 87 88
1979 winery with 300 acres. CAB very sound, not thrilling. Good bone dry CHENIN BLANC. CHARD gaining a reputation. Now Japanese owned.

Martin Bros Central Coast/San Luis Obispo. ★★
Excellently crisp CHENIN BL. and CHARD. The small family winery aims to justify Nebbiolo vines in Paso Robles.

Martini, Louis Napa. ★★→ ★★★ CS 78 79 80 81 82 83 84 85 86 Z 78 79 80 81 82 83 84 85 86 Large but individual winery with very high standards at every level. CABERNET "Vineyard Selection" one of California's best. BARBERA, MERLOT, PETITE SIRAH, P NOIR, ZIN, GEWÜRZ and Moscato Amabile are all well made. Also now good CHARD from Carneros and Russian River. Second label: "Glen Oaks".

Masson, Vineyards Central Coast. ★→★★
Famous old name sold by Seagram's in '87, moved to Monterey. New owners seem to have raised their sights.

Matanzas Creek Sonoma. ★★ CH 85 86 87 88 M 79 80 81 82 83 84 85 86
Young winery now on track with well-balanced CHARD, SAUV BL, and MERLOT.

Mayacamas Napa. ★★★ CH 85 86 87 CS 76 77 78 79 80 81 82 83 84 85
First-rate very small v'yd and winery offering CABERNET, monster CHARD recently civilised, also SAUV BLANC and ZIN (sometimes).

McDowell Valley Vineyards Mendocino. ★★ CS 83 84 85 86
Big new development using old-established v'yd to make wide range. To watch, esp. for ZIN and real SYRAH.

Meridian Central Coast/San Luis Obispo.
Charles Ortman wine-maker and BERINGER/Nestlé investment in former Estrella River winery. 700 acres of CHARD and CAB nr, Paso Robles. First vintage '88.

Meritage Term for reds and whites using Bordeaux grape varieties.

Merry Vintners Sonoma. (★★)

Merry Edwards (ex-MOUNT EDEN, MATANZAS CREEK) made her name with CHARDONNAYS (regular, reserve), but is branching out into P NOIR.

Milano Mendocino ★★ CHARD. (CAB).

Mill Creek Sonoma. ★★ CAB, CHARD, MERLOT, SAUV. BL.

Mirassou Central Coast. ★★

Dynamic mid-sized growers and makers, the fifth generation of the family. Pioneers in SALINAS v'yds. Sound chard, cab (esp Harvest Reserve) GEWÜRZ and very pleasant sparkling.

Mondavi, Robert Napa. ★★ →★★★★ CH 85 86 87 88 CS 74 75 76 77 78 79 80 81 82 83 84 85 86 Winery with a brilliant quarter-century record of innovation in styles, equipment and technique. Famous successes incl. CABERNET, SAUV BLANC (sold as Fumé Blanc), CHARDONNAY, and even PINOT NOIR. "Reserves" are marvellous – regularly among California's best wines. Also V. useful table wines. See also Opus One.

Monterey Peninsula Central Coast/Salinas. ★★ CH 85 86 87 CS 80 81 82 83 84 Very small winery near Carmel making chunky v. long-living ZINFANDEL and CABERNET from SALINAS and other grapes.

Monterey Vineyard Central Coast/Salinas. ★★

The first big modern winery of SALINAS, opened 1974. Now owned by Seagrams. Good ZIN, GEWÜRZ and SYLVANER and fruity feather-weight GAMAY BEAUJOLAIS. "Classic Red" is value.

Monteviña Amador. ★★ CS 80 81 82 83 84 85 z 80 81 82 83 84 85 86 87 Pioneer winery in revitalized area: Shenandoah Valley, Amador County, in the Sierra foothills. ZINFANDEL, BARBERA and SAUVIGNON BLANC are achieving balance. Now owned by SUTTER HOME.

Monticello Cellars Napa. ★★★ CH 85 86 87 CS 80 81 82 83 84 85 86 Ultra-modern new winery near TREFETHEN. Outstanding GEWÜRZ (now v. limited) first caught the eye. Now v.g. CHARDONNAY, fine tannic CABERNET.

Mont St John Napa ★★ Old Napa family. Wide range.

Morgan Central Coast/Salinas.★★→★★★ CH 82 83 84 85 86 87 88 Ex-JEKEL winemaker now making his own v.g. CHARD.

Mount Eden Vineyards Central Coast. ★★ CH 84 85 86 87 CS 84 85 Company owning a major share of what were MARTIN RAY vineyards. Expensive wines.

Mount Veeder Napa. ★★ CS 74 75 77 78 79 80 81 82 83 84 86 Ambitious little 1973 winery now owned by FRANCISCAN. High prices but good CABERNET.

Chateau Napa-Beaucanon Napa. New, French-owned, CHARD, CAB, CHENIN, MERLOT.

Navarro Vineyards Mendocino. ★★

Grower of first-rate CHARD, P NOIR, outstanding GEWÜRZ and RIESLING in cool Anderson Valley.

Newton Vineyards Napa. ★★★ CH 85 86 87 88 CS 84 85 86 Luxurious estate. Big oak-scent CAB SAUV, MERLOT, CHARD, SAUV BL.

Opus One Napa. ★★★★ CS 79 80 81 82 83 84 85 86 Not a winery but a wine; the joint venture of Robert Mondavi and the late Baron Philippe de Rothschild. So far, in effect, a Mondavi Reserve of Reserves at a far-fetched price, however good. Spectacular new winery marks the accession of Baron Philippe's daughter, Baroness Philippine.

Parducci Mendocino. ★★ →★★★ CH 85 86 87 88 CS 78 79 81 82 83 84 85 86 Well-established mid-sized winery with v'yds in several locations. Good sturdy reds: CABERNET (and an excellent Cab/ Merlot blend), PETITE SYRAH, ZIN, "Burgundy". Also pleasant CHENIN BLANC and FRENCH COLOMBARD. N.B. The no-oak CHARD.

Pecota, Robert Napa ★★ CAB, SAUV. BL, CHARD, Gamay.

Pedroncelli Sonoma/Russian River. ★★→★★★ CH 85 86 87 88 CS 78 81 82 83 84 85 86 Long-established family business with recent reputation for well-above-average ZIN and CHARDONNAY, all growing more stylish with practice.

Pepi, Robert Napa. ★★→★★★ CH 83 84 85 86 CS 82 83 Young stone hilltop winery between Oakville and Yountville launched well as a SAUVIGNON BLANC specialist; now makes very fine CHARD.

Phelps, Joseph Napa. ★★★→★★★★ CH 80 81 83 84 85 86 87 CS 74 75 76 77 78 79 80 81 82 83 84 85 De-luxe mid-size winery and v'yd with impeccable standards. Very good CHARDONNAY, CABERNET, SYRAH. The "Reserve" wine, "Insignia", has been over-tannic at times. Late harvest RIESLING exceptional. Whites age v. well, too. (e.g. '80 GEWÜRZ perfection in '88.)

Pine Ridge Napa. ★★ CH 85 86 87 CS 79 80 81 82 83 84 85 86 Small winery near STAG'S LEAP has made constantly stylish CHARD, MERLOT and CAB. Also mild but fresh, off-dry CHENIN BLANC.

Piper-Sonoma Sonoma. ★★★ A venture of Piper-Heidsieck of Champagne which released its first (very good) sparkling cuvée in 1980. It benefits from bottle-age.

Preston Sonoma. ★★ CS 83 84 Tiny winery with very high standards in Dry Creek Valley, Healdsburg, esp. for SAUV BLANC, ZIN and now blended SIRAH-SYRAH.

Quady Winery Central Valley. ★★ Imaginative dessert wines from Madera since '75. Celebrated orangey "Essencia"; "Elysium" from Black Muscat.

Quail Ridge Napa. ★★ CH 84 85 86 87 Small specialist in barrel-fermented CHARD. Also CAB. Good, if pricey. Owned by the CHRISTIAN BROTHERS.

Quivira Sonoma. ★★ Young ('86) winery with fine SAUV BL. and ZIN from Dry Creek Valley, recently CAB S and a ZIN-SYRAH blend, Regnum.

Rafanelli, A. Sonoma. ★★ Tiny cellar specializing in outstanding ZIN; also CABERNET.

Ravenswood Sonoma. Small winery; growing quality reputation, esp. for ZIN and CAB.

Raymond Vineyards Napa. ★★★ CH 85 86 87 88 CS 78 80 81 82 83 84 85 86 Expanding 1974 winery near St. Helena with experienced owners. CHARD, RIESLING and CABERNET all excellent.

Ridge Central Coast/Santa Cruz Mts. ★★★★ CS 78 80 81 82 83 84 85 86 Small winery of highest repute among connoisseurs for concentrated reds needing long maturing in bottle. Notable CAB and ZIN from named v'yds; esp. Monte Bello and York Creek, Napa.

Roederer USA Mendocino. ★★★ The Anderson Valley branch of the Reims Champagne house. First wine, released in 1988 is impressive.

Rombauer Vineyards Napa. ★★ CH 85 86 87 CS 84 85 86 Young ('80) small winery buying Napa grapes for impressive CHARD and CAB SAUV.

Roudon-Smith Santa Clara/Santa Cruz. ★★→ ★★★ CH 85 86 87 CS 78 79 81 82 83 84 85 86 Small winery offering stylish CHARD and CAB.

Round Hill Napa. ★★→★★★ CH 85 86 87 88 CS 80 81 82 83 84 85 86 87 Consistent good value, esp. GEWÜRZ and FUME BLANC, from big new winery in St Helena. Rutherford Ranch is label for best wines.

Rutherford Hill Napa. ★★★ CH 83 84 85 86 87 CS 80 81 82 83 84 85 Larger stable-mate of FREEMARK ABBEY. Good GEWÜRZ. Excellent CHARD, MERLOT and CABERNET.

Rutherford Ranch See Round Hill.

Rutherford Vintners, Inc. Napa. ★★ CH 85 86 87 CS 78 79 80 81 82 83 84 Small winery started in 1977 by Bernard Skoda. "Chateau Rutherford" is "Reserve" label.

St Andrews Napa. ★★ CH **83 84 85 86** CS 83 84 85

Small CHARDONNAY estate on Silverado Trail near Napa city. Steadily excellent wine.

St Clement Napa. ★★→★★★ CH **85 86 87 88** CS **78 80 81 82 83 84** 85

Small production. Good CABERNET, powerful CHARD and delicious SAUVIGNON BLANC (worth ageing).

St Francis Sonoma. ★→★★ CH **83 84 85 86 87 88**

Young small winery is using excellent CHARD, CABERNET, GEWÜRZ, MERLOT grapes. Wines are settling down very well.

Saintsbury Napa. **★★★** CH **83 84 85 86 87 88** PN **81 82 83 84 85 86**

Young winery using Carneros grapes to make perhaps the best P NOIR and CHARD of this region.

Sanford Santa Barbara. ★★★ CH **84 85 86 87 88** PN **81 84 85**

New winery started with striking 1982 SAUV BLANC and CHARDONNAY in the toast and oak school. P NOIR is beautifully made; also P Noir Blanc.

San Martin Central Coast. ★★ CH **85 86 87**

Restructured old company using Salinas and San Luis Obispo grapes to make correct varietals. Also pioneers in "soft" (low-alcohol) wines.

Santa Barbara Winery Santa Barbara. ★★

One-time jug-wine producer showing ever greater turns of speed, esp. with estate CHARD.

Santa Cruz Mountain V'yd. Central Coast. ★★ CS 78 79 **80 81 82** 83 PN 79 **80 81 82 83 84 85 86** Small winery in the hills with hopes for fine PINOT NOIR, but problems with overbearing alcohol. Now CABERNET too.

Santa Cruz Valley Winery Sta Barbara. ★★ SAUV. BL., CHARD.

Santino Amador.

New Sierra foothills pioneer: Sangiovese and other Italian varieties as well as v.g. ZINS.

Scharffenberger Mendocino. ★★

The major pioneer of champagne method sparkling Mendocino, now owned by Champagne Pommery. Move planned from Ukiah to Anderson Valley.

Schramsberg Napa. ★★★★

A dedicated specialist using historic old cellars to make California's best "champagne", incl. splendid "Reserves". "Blanc de Noirs" is outstanding, deserves 2-10 years' ageing.

Schug Cellars Napa. ★★ CH **83 84 85 86 87** PN **80 81 82 83 84 85** 86

New (1982) enterprise of PHELPS' ex-winemaker. Very tough PINOT NOIR at outset; recently moderated. Also dense dry CHARD.

Sebastiani Sonoma. ★→★★★ CS **78 80 81 82 83 84 85 86**

Substantial and distinguished old family firm with robust appetizing wines, incl. BARBERA. Eye of the Swan is seductive "blush". Top wines have SONOMA appellation. Keep under observation.

Seghesio Sonoma. ★

Old Healdsburg bulk producer offers notable value in P NOIR and ZIN.

Sequoia Grove Napa. ★★★ CH **85 86 87** CS 83 **84 85** 86

Small winery nr. Oakville. CHARD since '79 has been well-balanced. CAB SAUV (Napa and Alexander Valleys) is tannic and meant to age.

Shadow Creek See Domaine Chandon.

Shafer Vineyards Napa. ★★→★★★ CH **81 83 84 85** 86 87 CS **80 81 82 83 84 85** 86 Young winery and vineyard near STAG'S LEAP is making polished CHARDONNAY and very stylish CABERNET and MERLOT.

Shaw, Charles F., Vineyards and Winery Napa. ★★ CH **85 86 87**

St Helena specialist in GAMAY light red, has added CHARD, SAUV BLANC.

Sierra Vista El Dorado. ★★

Steady producer of CHARD, CAB SAUV, ZIN; more recently SYRAH from Sierra Foothills v'yds.

Silver Oak Napa. **★★** →★★★ CS **78 79 80 81 82 83 84** 85

Small 1972 winery succeeding with oaky CABERNETS, incl. v. expensive "Bonny's Vineyard".

Silverado Vineyards Napa. ★★★ CH 84 85 86 87 88 CS 83 84 85 86
Showy hilltop winery east of Yountville. Early CHARD and SAUV BLANC made news. Now CAB is even better. The owner is Mrs. Walt Disney, which suggests adequate capital.

Simi Alexander Valley. ★★★ CH 83 84 85 86 87 CS 78 79 80 81 82 83 84 85 Restored historic winery with expert direction of Zelma Long. Some of America's best, most lively CHARDONNAY, delicate CABERNET and (since '82) splendid SAUV BLANC. Also good CHENIN BLANC, irresistible rosé.

Smith & Hook Central Coast/Monterey. ★★ CS 80 81 82 83 84 85
Specialist entirely dedicated to CAB SAUV from Salinas Valley w. hills.

Smith-Madrone Napa. ★★ RIESLING, CHARD, CAB.

Sonoma-Cutrer Vineyards, Inc. Sonoma. ★★★★ CH 81 82 83 84 85 86 87 Perhaps the ultimate (so far) in specialist estates, using new techniques to display the characters individual v'yds give to CHARDS (as in Burgundy). So far Les Pierres v'yd is No. 1.

Spottswoode Napa. ★★→★★★★ S.B. 85 86 87 88
From a v'yd right at St Helena town, small lots of increasingly subtle, stylish SAUV BLANC, CAB SAUV.

Spring Mountain Napa. ★★ CH 85 86 87 CS 75 78 81 82 83 84 85
Renovated small 19th-century property with winery noted for good CHARD, SAUV and CAB. Has been coasting recently.

Stag's Leap Wine Cellars Napa. ★★★→★★★★ CH 83 84 85 86 87 CS 74 75 78 79 80 81 82 83 84 85 86 Celebrated small v'yd and cellar with the highest standards. Excellent CABERNET and MERLOT, fresh GAMAY, fine CHARD. Top CAB is "Cask 23": 74 77 78' 79 83 84 85

Sterling Napa. ★★★ CH 83 84 85 86 87 88 CS 82 83 84 85 86
Extremely proficient (also scenic) winery owned by Seagrams. Strong, tart SAUVIGNON BLANC and CHARDONNAY; oaky CABERNET and MERLOT. Also "Three Palms" red from '85.

Stonegate Napa ★★ Estate CHARD, SAUV. BL., CAB, MERLOT.

Stony Hill Napa. ★★★★ CH 74 75 76 77 78 79 80 81 82 83 84 85 86 87
Many of California's very best whites have come from this minute winery over 30 years. Owner Fred McCrea died in 1977; his widow Eleanor carries on. Stony Hill CHARDONNAY, GEWÜRZ and RIESLING are all delicate and fine. CHARD recently weightier.

Stratford Napa. ★★ CH 84 85 86 87 CS 83 84 85
First wine ('82) was an impressive blended CHARD. New winery nr. Rutherford to provide more; also good SAUV BL. (from '85), CAB SAUV, MERLOT.

Strong, Rodney, Vineyards Sonoma/Russian River. ★★ →★★★ CH 85 86 87 88 CS 78 79 80 81 82 83 84 85 Formerly called Sonoma Vineyards. Well regarded, esp. for CHARD. Range includes single-v'yd wines, esp. Alexander's Crown CABERNET.

Sutter Home Napa. ★ Z 80 81 82 83 84 85 86
Small winery revived and hugely expanded on the success of its sweet, pink "white" ZINFANDEL. (1m. cases a year.)

Swan, J. Sonoma. ★★ Z 74 76 77 78 80 81 82 83 84 85 PN 85
Joe Swan died 1989. His son-in-law continues with ZIN, CHARD, P NOIR.

Taft Street Sonoma ★★→★★★ CH 85 86 87 88
After muddling along, the winery hit impressive stride with Russian River CHARDS and good SAUV. BL.

Trefethen Napa. ★★→★★★★ CH 81 82 83 84 85 86 87 88 CS 74 75 76 77 78 79 80 81 82 83 84 85 86 Much-respected family-owned winery in Napa's finest old wooden building. Very good dry RIESLING, CABERNET, P NOIR. Tense CHARDONNAY for ageing and a notable low-price blend, Eshcol. Late-released "Library" wines demonstrate ageing potential.

Tudal Napa. ★★ CS 79 80 82 83 84 85
Small estate winery since '79 just n. of St Helena. Excellent dark age-worthy CABERNET.

Tulocay Napa. ★★ CH **83 84 85 86 87** 88 CS **80 81 82 83 84 85** 86 87
Tiny young winery at Napa City. PINOT NOIR and CABERNET can be really accomplished.

Ventana Central Coast/Monterey. ★★ CH **83 84 85 86 87** 88
New in '78 with flavoury CHARDONNAY, SAUV BL., RIESLING etc.

Viansa Sonoma. New Vickie and Sam SEBASTIANI venture. CHARD, CAB, SAUV BL.

Vichon Winery Napa. ★★→★★★ CH **85 86 87** 88 CS **77 78 79 80 81 82** 83 **84** 85 86 Founded 1980; original and ambitious. Fine CHARDONNAY and blended (50/50) SAUVIGNON/SEMILLON "Chevrignon Blanc". Now v. promising CABS. Bought (1985) by Robert MONDAVI.

Villa Mount Eden Napa. ★★ CH **85 86 87** 88 CS **77 78 79 80 81 82** 83 **84** 85
Small Oakville estate has made excellent dry CH BLANC, good CHARD, outstanding CAB. Bought (1986) by CH STE MICHELLE of Washington.

Weibel Central Coast and Mendocino ★→★★
Veteran mid-sized winery giving value in its class. Specialist in own-label sparkling wines.

Wente Livermore and Central Coast. ★→★★★ CH **84 85 86** 87 **88**
Important and historic specialists in whites. Fourth-generation Wentes are as dynamic as ever, CHARD, SAUV BLANC and RIESLING are all successful. Arroyo Seco Chard is v.g. Now also good CABERNET, fruity ZIN, and sparkling.

Whitehall Lane Napa. ★★
Small St Helena producer to follow for fresh and lively P NOIR.

White Oak Sonoma. (★★)
Small Healdsburg winery using Alexander Valley CHARD, SAUV BLANC, CHENIN BLANC for rich, ripe wines. Now CABERNET.

Wild Horse Winery San Luis Obispo. ★★
Small, young winery near Paso Robles draws on local Santa Barbara v'yds. Impressive P NOIR.

William Wheeler Winery Sonoma. ★★ CH **85 86 87** 88 CS **82 83 84**
Young Dry Creek Valley family firm. Big CAB, good SAUV BLANC, CHARD to watch with interest.

Zaca Mesa Central Coast/Santa Barbara. ★★ CH **84 85 86 87** 88 CS **80 81 82** 83 84 85 86 Santa Ynez Valley pioneer with good CHARD and RIESLING now scaling the heights with P NOIR.

Z D Wines Napa. ★★★ CH **83 85 86 87** CS **79 80 81 82** 83 84 85
Very small winery (moved from Sonoma to Rutherford) with a name for powerful PINOT NOIR and CHARDONNAY.

The Pacific North-West

There are now over 16,000 acres of vines and over 100 wineries in the States of Washington, Oregon and Idaho.

Oregon's vines lie mainly in the cool-temperate Willamette and warmer Umpqua valleys between the Coast and Cascades ranges. Those of Washington and Idaho are mainly east of the Cascades in the semi-arid Yakima Valley and Columbia basin, with hot days and cold nights. Most Oregon-grown wines are consequently more delicate, Washington's more intensive in flavour. Individual wineries, with some notable exceptions, can be hard to characterize. In Oregon most are small and have yet to establish a steady track-record. Vintages are also as uneven as in e.g. Burgundy, whose Pinot Noir is Oregon's most talked-about grape. Drouhin of Burgundy has encouraged the talk by buying land. Yet whites remain in the majority, and serious over-supply continues to threaten the finances of the industry in the north-west. Its excellent Riesling is sadly out of fashion (and is consequently a first-rate bargain).

Adelsheim Vineyard Willamette, Oregon.
> Small winery: good P NOIR, oaky CHARDONNAY, fresh PINOT GRIS.

Alpine Vineyards Willamette, Oregon.
> Young small estate winery with high spots, incl. P NOIR, RIESLING.

Arbor Crest Spokane, Washington.
> Expanding and encouraging young winery. Early CHARD and SAUV BLANC v.g. Reds also promising, if unpredictable.

Bethel Heights nr. Salem, Oregon.
> Much praised start-up, esp. for PINOT NOIR ('85). Owned by Bonny Doon (see California).

Château Benoit Oregon.
> Sound producer of MÜLLER-THURGAU, CHARD, and P NOIR has acquired a winemaker from Chablis and is launching sparkling.

Château Ste Chapelle Caldwell, Idaho.
> The first Idaho winery, near Boise. Early CHARD and RIESLING had intense flavours but beautiful balance. Now well settled in.

Château Ste Michelle Seattle, Columbia and Yakima valleys, Washington.
> The largest north-west winery (550,000 cases), though now operating separately from COLUMBIA CREST. Wineries at Grandview and Woodin-ville offer wide range incl. v.g. CABERNET, SEMILLON, CHARDONNAY, MERLOT and sparkling. Second label: Farron Ridge.

Columbia Cellars (formerly Associated Vintners) Washington.
> A Washington pioneer and still a leader, at Redmond, nr. Seattle. CABERNET, RIESLING, dry spicy GEWÜRZ and esp. SEMILLON have all been successful. Good value. Now good CHARDONNAY.

Columbia Crest Washington.
> Label used by CHATEAU STE MICHELLE for wines from River Run, the group's big new Columbia Valley winery. Good delicately fruity CHARD.

Covey Run (formerly Quail Run) Yakima, Washington.
> Admirable whites incl. ALIGOTE; reds are strong in alcohol and flavour.

Elk Cove Vineyards Willamette, Oregon.
> Very small but well established (1977) winery. Good CHARDONNAY and RIESLING from named v'yds. PINOT NOIR less consistent.

The Eyrie Vineyards Willamette, Oregon.
> Pioneer (1965) winery with Burgundian convictions. Oregon's most famous and consistently good P NOIR, and v. oaky CHARD. Also Pinots Gris and Meunier and dry Muscat.

Hogue Cellars   Yakima Valley, Washington.

Expanding young winery outstanding for off-dry whites, esp. RIESLING, CHENIN BLANC, SAUV BLANC, and bold CHARD. Since '83 really stylish CAB, MERLOT. The leader in the region.

Kiona Vineyards   Yakima Valley, Washington.

Small cellar and v'yd nr. Benton City attracting attention with RIESLING, and CHARD.

Knudsen Erath   Willamette, Oregon.

Oregon's second-biggest winery with good-value PINOT NOIR, esp. Vintage Select. Austere CHARDONNAY. But wobbly recently.

F. W. Langguth Winery   Yakima Valley, Washington.

German Mosel-maker succeeded with German-style RIESLINGS, esp. late harvest, now a second label owned by SNOQUALMIE.

Latah Creek   Spokane, Washington.

Recent source of fruity, off-dry whites, esp. CHENIN BL., RIES, SAUV BL.

Leonetti   Walla Walla, Washington

Harmonious and refined Cabernet/Merlot at steep prices.

Mercer Ranch   Columbia Valley, Washington.

Young winery has made some outstanding CABERNET and (unusually) Lemberger from established v'yds.

Neuharth   Western Washington

Olympic Peninsula winery uses grapes from eastern state, esp for suppley attractive Cab.

Oak Knoll   Willamette, Oregon.

Developed from a fruit-wine maker but emerging as one of Oregon's most skilful, esp. with P Noir.

Preston Wine Cellars   Yakima Valley, Washington.

Early winery with broad range of sound to very good wines.

Rex Hill   Yamhill City, Oregon.

Well-financed assault on top levels of P NOIR from individual v'yds, incl. Reserve wines. Also RIES. Fine new winery.

Saddle Mountain   Second label for SNOQUALMIE.

Shafer Vineyard Cellars   Willamette, Oregon.

Small meticulous P NOIR specialist. White P NOIR may be Oregon's best; CHARD almost certainly is.

Snoqualmie   Yakima Valley, Washington.

Off to new start in 1988 after complete financial reorganization. Whites (Chard, Sémillon, Chenin) are already performing very well. High hopes for reds.

Sokol Blosser Vineyards   Willamette, Oregon.

Largest Oregon winery with wide range, incl. CHARD (esp. "Yamhill County"), SAUV BLANC, MERLOT and RIESLING. P NOIR is best effort.

Staton Hills   Yakima Valley, Washington.

Reliable, occasionally excellent source of easy, not very dry whites.

Stewart Vineyards   Yakima Valley, Washington.

New estate nr. Sunnyside. Early whites v. impressive.

Paul Thomas   Seattle, Washington.

Former fruit winery nr. Seattle now making v.g SAUV BLANC, RIESLING and CHARDONNAY. Reds hold promise.

Tualatin Vineyards   Willamette, Oregon.

Third-largest Oregon winery, now weaned from Washington to home-grown grapes. Wine style is a trifle eccentric. Mainly whites with emphasis on CHARD, P NOIR (red and white).

Tyee   Cornwallis, Oregon Newcomer with v. well-made Gewürz, Chard.

Woodward Canyon   Walla Walla, Washington.

New district, small cellar with ultra-bold "buttered toast" Chard and similarly emphatic reds.

Yamhill Valley   Oregon.

First wines, made at SOKOL BLOSSER, were good. Own v'yds may confirm prospects.

The North & East

New York State and its neighbours Ohio and Ontario have traditionally made their wine from grapes of native American ancestry. American grapes have a flavour known as "foxy"; a taste acquired by many easterners. Fashion has moved in favour of hybrids between these and European grapes with less, or no, foxiness, and is now rapidly turning towards fully European varieties. Recent European-style wines both from old vineyards and areas such as Long Island have turned old ideas on their heads. Chardonnays and Rieslings can both be excellent. The entries below include both wineries and grape varieties.

Andres Canada's second-largest wine-producer, with wineries in Ontario and British Columbia.

Aurora One of the best white French-American hybrid grapes, the most widely planted in New York. Good for sparkling wine.

Baco Noir One of the better red French-American hybrid grapes. High acidity but good clean dark wine.

Banfi 55-acre CHARDONNAY v'yd at Old Brookville, Long Island, released its first wine in 1986. First impressions v. favourable.

Benmarl Highly regarded and expanding v'yd and winery at Marlboro on the Hudson River. Wines are mainly from French-American hybrids (e.g. Seyval Blanc), but CHARD can be splendid.

Bridgehampton Wine Co. Tiny winery on Long Island. RIESLING and CHARD.

Brights Canada's biggest winery, in Ontario, now tending towards French-American hybrids and experiments with European vines. Their BACO NOIR is a sound red, CHARDONNAY is steely, ALIGOTE pleasant. Now also in British Columbia.

Bully Hill FINGER LAKES winery founded 1970, using both American and hybrid grapes to make varietal wines.

Byrd Vineyards Maryland Winery with CABERNET intended for ageing.

Canandaigua Wine Co. Major traditional eastern winemaker ("the nation's third largest"). Bought WIDMERS in 1986. Also in California.

Catawba One of the first American vine-grapes, still the second most widely grown. Pale red and foxy flavoured.

Château des Charmes Smaller Ontario winery, doing well with CHARD, P NOIR, GAMAY, RIESLING.

Château Gai Big Canadian (Ontario) winery making European and hybrid wines, incl. v. light CHARD, GAMAY, MERLOT.

Chautauqua The biggest grape-growing district in the east, along the s. shore of Lake Erie from New York to Ohio. 20,000 acres.

Chelois Popular red hybrid. Dry wine with some richness, slighlty foxy.

Delaware Old American white-wine grape making pleasant, slightly foxy dry wines. Used in "champagne" and for still wine.

De Chaunac A good red French-American hybrid grape, popular in Canada as well as New York. Full-bodied dark wine.

Finger Lakes Century-old wine district in upper New York State, best-known for its "champagne". The centre is Hammondsport.

Firelands CABERNET from Isle St George in Lake Erie, Ohio.

Finger Lakes Wine Cellars Young winery. Good CHARD, and (esp.) RIES.

Fournier, Charles Brand-name now v. remote from the late President of Gold Seal, who with Dr FRANK introduced Vinifera vines to New York.

Frank, Dr Konstantin (Vinifera Wine Cellars) Small but influential winery. Dr Frank was a pioneer in growing European wines, incl. Riesling, Chard and Pinot Noir, in the FINGER LAKES. Some excellent wines.

Glenora Wine Cellars Recent FINGER LAKES winery. Very successful RIES and CHARD.

Gold Seal Formerly one of New York's biggest and best wineries, bought recently by TAYLORS who closed it down but still produce Charles Fournier "champagne" under the Gold Seal label.

Great Western The brand name of the PLEASANT VALLEY WINE CO'S "champagne", one of New York's sound traditional wines.

Hargrave Vineyard Trend-setting winery planting extensively on North Fork of Long Island, N.Y. Well established with CHARDONNAY and PINOT NOIR.

Heron Hill Vineyards Small FINGER LAKES estate with good RIES, CHARD, etc.

Inniskillin Leading quality Canadian winery at Niagara. European and hybrid wines, incl. good MARECHAL FOCH, also CHARDONNAY.

Phylloxera is an insect that lives on the roots of the vine. Its arrival in Europe from North America in the 1860s was an international catastrophe. It destroyed almost every vineyard on the Continent before it was discovered that the native American vine is immune to its attacks. The remedy was (and still is) to graft European vines on to American rootstocks. Virtually all Europe's vineyards are so grafted today. Whether their produce is just as good as the wine of pre-phylloxera days is a favourite debate among old-school wine-lovers.

Johnson Estate One of the best makers of French-American hybrid whites. CHAUTAUQUA region.

Lenz Small property on North Fork of Long Island. V.g Merlot.

Maréchal Foch Useful red French hybrid between PINOT NOIR and GAMAY.

Marrko Small Ohio winery with buttery CHARD.

New Land Promising new FINGER LAKES winery. Rielsing, Chard, P. Noir, Merlot.

Niagara Old American white grape used for sweet wine. Very foxy.

Pindar Vineyards Substantial young company on North Fork, Long Island. RIESLING has been successful.

Pleasant Valley Wine Co. Famous old winery at Hammondsport, FINGER LAKES, owned by TAYLOR'S, producing GREAT WESTERN wines.

Ravat Vignoles (Ravat 51) French-American hybrid grape of intense flavour and high acidity often made in "Late Harvest" style.

Seibel Celebrated French grape hybridist. Many successful French-American crosses originally known by numbers, since christened as AURORA, DE CHAUNAC, CHELOIS.

Seyve-Villard Another well-known French hybridist. His best-known cross, no. 5276, known as Seyval Blanc, is the most successful variety of its kind, making clean, aromatic wine with good acidity.

Six Mile Creek NEW FINGER LAKES winery. Interesting dry RIESLING.

Taylor's The biggest wine-company of the E. States, based in the FINGER LAKES. Brands incl. GREAT WESTERN and lake country. Most vines are American. Also in California. Changed hands in 1987.

Treleaven Promising new FINGER LAKES winery. RIESLING outstanding, Chard in "French" style.

Wagner Vineyards Excellent CHARD incl. the "barrel-fermented", also GEWÜRZ, AURORA from the FINGER LAKES.

Widmers Major FINGER LAKES winery selling native American varietal wines: DELAWARE, NIAGARA, etc. Now also good RIESLING.

Wiemer, Herman J. Creative and daring German FINGER LAKES winemaker. Fine RIESLINGS incl. a v.g. sparkling version, and Late Harvest; ferments v.g. CHARDONNAY in oak.

Woodbury Vineyards CHAUTAUQUA estate for CHARD, RIES and some P NOIR.

Texas

In the past few years a brand-new Texan wine industry has sprung noisily to life. It already seems past the experimental stage, with some very passable wines, though such a short track-record can only confirm the state's potential. The biggest winery is Ste Genevieve, at Fort Stockton, with French financial and technical involvement. Wines include SAUV BLANC, CHENIN BLANC, FRENCH COLOMBARD. With 450 growers and 25 wineries now active, the state's wines have begun to show some form. Llano Estacado, with 220 acres near Lubbock, has been the consistent leader to date. Nearby and much smaller is Pheasant Ridge, which has made good CHARDONNAY and SEMILLON. Fall Creek, 80 miles n. of Austin, has become a name to watch, esp. for its v.g. CARNELIAN, the first Texan red to excite interest. Pressing these front-runners are Oberhellman, Taysha (esp. for GEWÜRZTRAMINER) and Slaughter-Leftwich. Total production is a relatively minute 220,000 cases per year, but growing swiftly.

Missouri

Has a small but long-established wine industry at Augusta, where Mount Pleasant Vineyards makes some very good white, esp. from Seyval Blanc. Their high acidity gives them the capacity to age remarkably: five years is not too long.

Virginia

Early successes with lean-bodied, fresh-flavoured CHARDONNAYS and RIESLINGS have given growers in Virginia the self-confidence to push into new territories with a broader range of European grape varieties. CHARDONNAY and RIESLING remain the most popular varieties in most of the state, with Barboursville Vineyards, Meredyth Vineyards and Prince Michael trading the honours. North, around Charlottesville, Bordeaux red varieties are the focal point; Montdomaine Cellars at Monticello appear to be showing the way with creditable '84 and '86 Cabernets.

Maryland

Maryland has long been known for its Boordy vineyards, pioneers with such French-American hybrids as Seyval Blanc. Now bottled "sur lie", like Muscadet, this is very attractive. Experiments with French varieties are encouraging.

South America

Argentina

Argentina has the world's fifth largest wine production, most of it gratefully and uncritically consumed within S. America. But things are stirring. The country's crop of gold medals at Vinexpo Bordeaux '89 surprised everyone. The quality vineyards (all irrigated) are concentrated in Mendoza province in the Andean foothills at about 2,000 feet. San Rapheal, south of Mendoza city, is centre of a slightly cooler area. Salta, to the north, and Rio Negro, to the south, also produce interesting wines.

Bianchi, Bodegas Well-known premium wine producer at San Rafael owned by Seagrams. "Don Valentin" CABERNET and Bianchi Borgoña are best-sellers. "Particular" is their top CABERNET.

Canale, Bodegas Premier Rio Negro winery : CABERNET and SEMILLON both won Bordeaux gold medals.

Crillon, Bodegas Owned by Seagram's, only for tank-method sp. wines.

Esmeralda Producers of a good CAB and CHARD, St Felician, at Mendoza.

Etchart Salta winery making typical aromatic but dry Torrontes white (gold medal Bd'x, '87) and sound range of reds in Salta and Mendoza.

Flichman, Bodegas Old Mendoza firm now owned by a bank. Top "Caballero de la Cepa" white and red, plus SYRAH, MERLOT and sp.

Goyenechea, Bodegas Basque family firm in San Rafael making old-style wines, including Aberdeen Angus red.

La Rural, Bodegas ("San Filipe") Family-run winery at Coquimbito (Mendoza) making some of Argentina's best RIESLING and GEWÜRZ whites and some good reds. Also a charming wine museum.

Lopez, Bodegas Family firm best known for their "Château Montchenot" red and white and "Château Vieux" CABERNET.

Luigi Bosca, Bodegas Small Mendoza winery with excellent MALBEC and SAUVIGNON BLANC.

Martins Recent excellent MALBEC from MENDOZA.

Nacari, Bodegas Small La Rioja cooperative. Its Torrontés white won a gold medal and Oscar at Vinexpo, Bordeaux '87.

Norton, Bodegas Old firm, originally English. Reds (esp. Malbec) are best. "Perdriel" is their premium brand. Also good sparkling wines.

Orfila, José Long-established bodega at St Martin, Mendoza. Top wines: Cautivo CAB and white Extra Dry (P BLANC).

Peñaflor Argentina's biggest wine company, reputedly the world's third-largest. Bulk wines, but also some of Argentina's finest premium wines, incl. Trapiche (esp. "Medalla"), Andean Vineyards and Fond de Cave CHARDONNAY and CABERNET. A sherry, Tio Quinto, is exported.

H. Piper Sparkling wine made under licence from Piper-Heidsieck.

Proviar, Bodega Producers of "Baron B" and "M. Chandon" sparkling wine under MOET & CHANDON supervision. Also still reds and whites including v.g. Castel Chandon, less exciting Kleinburg, Wunderwein (whites), smooth Comte de Valmont, Beltour and Clos du Moulin reds.

Roblevina Winery in S Mendoza. Cab took 1989 Vinexpo Bordeaux Oscar.

Santa Ana, Bodegas Small, old-established family firm at Guaymallen, Mendoza. Wide range includes good Syrah Val Semina and sparkling.

San Telmo Modern winery with a Californian air and outstanding fresh, full-flavoured CHARD, MERLOT, CAB and esp. MALBEC.

Suter, Bodegas Swiss-founded firm owned by Seagram's making best-selling "Etiquetta Marron" white and good "Etiquetta Blanca" red.

Toso, Pascual Old Mendoza winery at San José, making one of Argentina's best reds, Cabernet Toso. Also RIES and sparkling wines.

Weinert, Bodegas Small winery. Tough old-fashioned reds led by good CAB/MERLOT/MALBEC "Cavas de Weinert" and promising SAUV BLANC.

Chile

Natural conditions are ideal for wine-growing in central Chile, just south of Santiago. But political conditions have been difficult for decades, and the country's full potential has only really started to be explored in the past five years. Chilean Cabernets lead the way with original flavours that will one day lead to worldwide renown. Other varieties now show equal promise. New oak barrels are starting to revolutionize standards.

Canepa, José Chile's most modern big bodega, handling wine from several areas. Very good frank and fruity CABERNET from Lontué, Curico, 100 miles south; recently particularly good CHARD, RIESLING and SAUV BLANC. Top wines from Domaine Caperana.

Concha y Toro The biggest and most outward-looking wine firm, with several bodegas and 2,500 acres in the Maipo valley. Remarkable dark and deep CABERNET, MERLOT, Verdot. Brands are Santa Cruz. Marques de Casa Concha, Casillero del Diablo. CHARDONNAY and SAUV BLANC are now well established. The new top wine is Don Melchor CAB.

Cousiño Macul Distinguished and beautiful old estate near Santiago. Very dry SEMILLON and CHARD. Don Luis light red, Don Matias dark and tannic are good CABS. Antiguas Reservas ('82) is top export CAB.

Errazuriz Panquehue Historic firm in Aconcagua valley, n. of Santiago, making very rich full-bodied wines, esp. CAB Don Maximiano ('84).

Los Robles Label of cooperative of Curico. Wines incl Cabernet ('82) and Merlot ('85).

Los Vascos Family estate in Colchagua Prov. 400 acres making some of Chile's best CAB ('85 '86) influenced by Bd'x and California. Also stylish SAUV/SEM. Made headlines in '88 by link with Lafite-Rothschild.

Santa Carolina Architecturally splendid old Santiago bodega with old-style "Reserva de Familia" and better "Ochagavia" wines.

San Pedro Long established at Lontué, Curico. The second-biggest exporter, with a range of good wines. Gatto Negro and Gatto Blanco are biggest sellers. Llave de Oro is the middle range and Castillo de Molina is top. Also "blush" Amigo. Santa Helena is associated.

Santa Rita Long-established bodega in the Maipo valley s. of Santiago. Medalla Real CABERNET ('84) and Reserva '86 have a high reputation.

Saint Morillon Lontüne bodega with Sauv. Blanc, Chard, Cab, and Cab Reserva ('85), co-owned with Bodegas Valdivieso.

Torres, Miguel Enterprise of Catalan family firm (see Spain) at Lontüé sets a modern pace. Good SAUV BLANC ("Bellaterra" is oak-aged) and CHARD, v.g. RIESLING. CAB is made more "elegantly" and ages well.

Undurraga Famous family business; one of the first to export to the USA. Wines in both old and modern styles: good clean SAUVIGNON BLANC and oaky yellow "Viejo Roble".

Viña Caliterra Joint venture of Errazuriz Panquehue and Franciscan of California. Good-value Chard, Cabernet ('86).

Viña Carmen A second bodega of SANTA RITA.

Viña Linderos Small family winery in the Maipo valley exports good full-bodied CABERNET which gains from bottle-age.

Viña Montes New high-quality bodega with v.g. Montes Cabernet '87.

Viña Portal del Alto Small new bodega with excellent Cab/Merlot blend.

Brazil International investments, esp. in the Rio Grande du Sud, are starting much talk. Exports are beginning.

Mexico The oldest American wine industry has upgraded quality. Good wines are made in Baja California (Bodegas Santo Tomas) and at Aguascalientes.

Peru Viña Tacama has exported some Sauvignon Blanc and sparkling wine of very promising quality.

Australia

N.S.W.

It is little more than 20 years since new technology revolutionized Australia's 150-year-old wine industry, making table wines of top quality possible. Old-style Australian wines were thick-set and burly Shiraz reds or Semillon or Riesling whites grown in warm to hot regions. A progressive shift to cooler areas, to new wood fermentation and maturation, with Cabernet, Pinot Noir, Chardonnay and Sauvignon Blanc at the forefront, has seen a radical change in style which has by no means run its course. Nonetheless, extract and alcohol levels continue to be high and the best wines still have great character and the ability to age splendidly.

Exports have assumed great importance for Australia, increasing from 8 million to 40 million litres in five years. Today Australia's best wines are to be found in London and New York. But it is not easy to keep tabs on them. There are now almost 600 wineries in commercial production. Labels are becoming less garrulous (but less informative) as Australian consumers become more sophisticated. Such information as they give can be relied on, while prizes in shows (which are highly competitive) mean a great deal. In a country lacking any formal grades of quality the buyer needs all the help he can get.

Wine areas

The vintages here are those rated as good or excellent for the reds of the areas in question. Excellent recent vintages are marked with an accent.

Adelaide Hills (Sth Aust) **84′** 85 86′ 88
    Spearheaded by PETALUMA: numerous new v'yds at very cool 1500ft sites in Mt Lofty ranges coming into production.

Adelaide Plains (Sth Aust) 82 84′ 86′ 87 88′
    Small area immediately n. of Adelaide formerly known as Angle Vale. Wineries incl. Anglesey, Lauriston, PRIMO ESTATE.

Barossa (Sth Aust) 66 76 80 82 84′ 86′ 87 88

Australia's most important winery (though not v'yd) area, processing grapes from diverse sources (local, to MURRAY VALLEY, through to high-quality cool regions from adjacent hills to far-distant COONAWARRA) to make equally diverse styles.

Bendigo/Ballarat (Vic.) 73 75 80′ 82′ 84 87 88

Widespread small v'yds, some of extreme quality, re-creating the glories of the last century. 14 wineries incl. CH LE AMON, BALGOWNIE, Heathcote Winery and Passing Clouds.

Canberra District (ACT) 16 wineries now sell cellar door to local and tourist trade. Quality is variable, as is style.

Clare Watervale (Sth Aust) 71′ 75′ 80′ 82 84′ 85 86′ 87

Small high-quality area 90 miles n. of Adelaide best known for RIESLING; also planted with SHIRAZ and CABERNET. 20 wineries spill over into new adjacent sub-district of Polish Hill River.

Coonawarra (Sth Aust) 66 71 76′ 79 80′ 82′ 84′ 86′ 87 88

Southernmost and greatest v'yd of state, long famous for well-balanced reds, recently successful with RIESLING, CHARDONNAY. Numerous more recent arrivals incl. Hollicks; Haselgrove, Penley Estate, Zema Estate.

Geelong (Vic.) 80′ 82′ 84 85 86 88

Once famous area destroyed by phylloxera, re-established mid-60s. Very cool, dry climate produces firm table wines from premium varieties. Names incl. BANNOCKBURN, IDYLL.

Goulburn Valley (Vic.) 68 71′ 76 80′ 82 85 86 88

A mixture of old (e.g. CH TAHBILK) and new (e.g. MITCHELTON) wineries in temperate region; full flavoured table wines.

Granite Belt (Qld.) 85 87′ 88

Rapidly developing high altitude and (relatively) cool region just n. of N.S.W. border with 13 wineries; spicy Shiraz and rich SEM/CHARD are district specialities.

Great Western (Vic.) 78 80′ 82′ 84′ 85 86 88

Temperate region in central w. of state. High quality table and sparkling wines. Now 8 wineries, 6 of recent origin.

Hunter Valley (N.S.W.) 66′ 67 73 75′ 79′ 82 83 85 86′ 87

The great name in N.S.W. Broad soft earthy SHIRAZ reds and SEMILLON whites with a style of their own. Now also CABERNET and CHARDONNAY. Many changes in identity.

Margaret River (W. Aust) 73′ 76 79′ 81 82′ 85′ 86′ 87

New cool coastal area producing superbly elegant wines, 174 miles s. of Perth. 27 operating wineries; others planned.

Mornington Peninsula (Vic.) 84′ 86′ 87 88

21 commercial wineries on dolls-house scale making exciting wines in new cool coastal area 25 miles s. of Melbourne. Total plantings of 350 acres. Wineries incl. ELGEE PARK, Merricks.

Mount Barker/Frankland River (W. Aust) 80 81′ 83 85 86 87 89

Promising new far-flung cool area in extreme south of state; GOUNDREY and PLANTAGENET are the two biggest and best wineries.

Mudgee (N.S.W.) 74 75 78 79 83 84′ 86 87

Small isolated area 168 miles n.w. of Sydney. Big reds of colour and flavour and full CHARDONNAYS from 23 wineries.

Murray Valley (Sth Aust, Vic. & N.S.W.) NV

Important irrigated v'yds near Swan Hill, Mildura (N.S.W. and Vic.), Renmark, Berri, Loxton, Waikerie and Morgan (S.A.). Principally "cask" table wines. 40% of total Australian wine production.

N.E. Victoria 66′ 70′ 75′ 80′ 82′ 86′ 87 88

Historic area incl. Rutherglen, Corowa, Wangaratta. Heavy reds and magnificent sweet dessert wines. 22 wineries.

Padthaway   80 82' 84 85 86' 87 88

Large new v'yd area (no wineries) developed by big companies as an overspill of adjacent COONAWARRA. **Cool climate: good commercial reds and better whites** and CHARD/PINOT NOIR sparkling wines.

Perth Hills   (W.A.). Fledgling area 19 miles e. of Perth with 8 wineries and a larger number of growers on mild hillside sites.

Pyrenees   (Vic.) 82 84 85 86 87 88

Central Vic. region with seven wineries producing rich minty reds and one or two interesting whites, esp. FUMÉ BLANC.

Riverina   (N.S.W.) NV

Large volume producer centred around Griffith; good-quality "cask" wines esp. whites and great botrytized Semillon.

Southern Vales   (Sth Aust) 71' 77 80' 82' 84 85 86' 87 88

Covers energetic McLaren Vale/Reynella regions on s. outskirts of Adelaide. Big styles now being rapidly improved; promising CHARD.

Swan Valley   (W. Aust) 75' 78' 81' 82' 84' 85' 86 88 89'

The birthplace of wine in the west, on the n. outskirts of Perth. Hot climate makes strong low-acid table, good dessert wines. Declining in importance viticulturally.

Tasmania   82' 84' 86 87 88'

16 vineyards now offer wine for commercial sale, producing over 200,000 litres. Great potential for CHARD and P NOIR.

Upper Hunter   (N.S.W.) 75' 79' 80' 81' 83' 85' 86' 87

Est. early 60s; with irrigated vines produce mainly white wines, lighter and quicker-developing than Hunter whites. Often good value.

Yarra Valley ("Lilydale")   76' 78' 80' 81 82' 84' 85 86' 88'

Historic wine area near Melbourne fallen into disuse, now being rapidly redeveloped by enthusiasts with 31 small wineries. A superb viticultural area with noble varieties only, and almost 2,000 acres.

Wineries

Allandale   Hunter Valley. Table ★→★★

Small winery without v'yds buying selected local grapes. Quality variable; can be good; esp. CHARD.

Allanmere   Hunter Valley. Table ★★→★★★

Small winery run by expatriate English doctor making excellent SEM, CHARD and smooth reds.

All Saints   N.E. Vic. Full range ★→★★

Once famous old family winery, being revived by new owners.

Angove's   Riverland. Table and dessert ★→★★★

Family business in Adelaide and Renmark in the Murray Valley. Notable value in CAB and esp. CHARD and other whites.

Arrowfield   Upper Hunter. Table ★★

Substantial vineyard, on irrigated land. Light CABERNET, succulent "Reserve" CHARD; also "wooded" SEM. Acquired 1989 by former retailer Andrew Simon and banker Nick Whitlam.

Bailey's   N.E. Vic. Table and dessert ★★→★★★★

Rich old-fashioned reds of great character, esp. Bundarra Hermitage, and magnificent dessert MUSCAT and TOKAY.

Balgownie   Bendigo/Ballarat. Table ★★★

Specialist in fine reds, particularly straight CAB. Also occasional exceptional CHARD. Now owned by MILDARA.

Bannockburn   Geelong Table ★★★

Intense, complex CHARD and P NOIR using Burgundian techniques.

Basedow   Barossa Valley. Table ★★→★★★

Small to medium winery buying grapes for reliably good range of red and white; SEMILLON White Burgundy esp. good.

Berri-Renmano Coop   Riverland. Full range ★→★★★

Aust's largest cooperative winery following recent merger with Renmano, selling mostly to other companies. Now developing own brands on local and export markets. (See Renmano.)

Best's Great Western. Full range ★★ →★★★
Conservative old family winery at Great Western with good mid-weight reds and improving CHARD.

Blass, Wolf (Bilyara) Barossa. Table and sp. ★★★
Wolf Blass is the ebullient German winemaker. Dazzling labels and extraordinary wine-show successes, with mastery of blending varieties, areas and lashings of new oak. Not to be missed.

Bowen Estate Coonawarra. Table ★★★
Small winery; intense but not heavy CAB, and spicy SHIRAZ.

Brand Coonawarra. Table ★★→★★★
Family estate. Fine, bold and stylish CAB and SHIRAZ under the Laira label. A few quality blemishes in late 70s/early 80s, now rectified.

Brokenwood Hunter Valley. Table ★★★
Exciting quality of CAB and SHIRAZ since 1973; new winery 1983 added high quality CHARD and SEM.

Brown Brothers Milawa. Full range ★→★★★
Old family firm with new ideas, wide and reliable range of rather delicate varietal wines, many from cool mountain districts. CHARD and dry white MUSCAT outstanding.

Buring, Leo Barossa. Full range ★★→ ★★★
"Château Leonay", old white-wine specialists, now owned by LINDE-MAN. Steady "Reserve Bin" Rhine Riesling, great with age.

Campbells of Rutherglen N.E. Vic. Full range ★★
Impressive lively whites, smooth reds plus good dessert wines.

Cape Clairault Margaret River, W.A. Table ★★
Progressive producer of SEM, SAUV BL. and CAB in reasonable quantity and with promise of better things to come.

Cape Mentelle Margaret River. Table ★★→★★★★
Idiosyncratic robust CAB departs from district style and can be magnificent; also ZINFANDEL and v. popular SEM. Also Cloudy Bay, N.Z.

Capel Vale S.W. Western Aust. ★★★
Outstanding range of whites, incl. RIESLING and GEWÜRZ. New v.g. CAB.

Cassegrain Hastings Valley, N.S.W. Table ★★→★★★
New winery on N.S.W. coast taking grapes both from local plantings and from Hunter Valley. CHARD can be outstanding.

Chambers' Rosewood N.E. Vic. Full range ★★→★★★
Good cheap table and great dessert wines, esp. TOKAY.

Château Le Amon Bendigo. Table ★★★
Very stylish minty CAB and peppery SHIRAZ.

Château Hornsby Alice Springs, N. Territory. ★→★★
A charming aberration. Full-flavoured clean reds from the Bush.

Château Rémy Great Western/Avoca. Sp. and table ★★
Owned by Rémy Martin. Trebbiano/CHARD blend surprisingly success-ful. Also good "Blue Pyrenees" reds.

Château Tahbilk Goulburn Valley. Table ★★→★★★
Beautiful and historic family-owned estate making long-lived CAB, SHIRAZ, Rhine Riesling and Marsanne. "Private Bins" are outstanding.

Coldstream Hills Yarra Valley, Vic. Table ★★★→★★★★
Yarra's second largest winery, built 1987 by wine critic James Halliday. International acclaim for prize-winning P NOIR, and v.g. CHARD.

Conti, Paul Swan Valley. Table ★★
Elegant Hermitage, also fine CHARD and other estate whites.

Craigmoor Mudgee. Table and port ★★
Oldest district winery now part of ORLANDO group and making good CHARD and SEM, the two blended, and CAB/SHIRAZ.

Cullens Willyabrup Margaret River. Table ★★★
Butch but kindly CAB/MERLOT, pungent SAUV BLANC and bold "wooded" CHARD are all real characters.

d'Arenberg S. Vales. Table and dessert ★→★★
Old-style family outfit with strapping rustic reds and RIESLING.

De Bortoli Griffith, N.S.W. ★→★★★

Irrigation-area winery. Standard reds and whites but magnificent sweet "botrytized" Sauternes-style SEM.

Delatite Central Vic. Table ★★★

Rosalind Ritchie makes appropriately willowy and feminine RIESLING, GEWURZ, P NOIR and CAB from this very cool mountainside v'yd.

Diamond Valley Yarra Valley, Vic. Table ★★→ ★★★

Producer of outstanding P NOIR in significant quantities; other wines good rather than great.

Domaine Chandon Yarra Valley, Vic. Sp.

The showpiece of the Yarra Valley. Substantial production from grapes grown in all the cooler parts of Australia, with strong direction from owner Moët & Chandon. Early indications of exciting, perhaps exceptional, quality.

Drayton's Bellevue Hunter Valley, N.S.W. Table ★★

Traditional Hermitage and SEM; occasionally good CHARD; recent quality improving after lapse.

Dromana Estate Mornington Peninsular. Table ★★★

Largest and best producer in district. Great skill in making glorious CAB, P NOIR and CHARD. Schinus Molle second label.

Eaglehawk Clare Watervale. Full range. ★→★★

Formerly QUELLTALER. Old winery known for good "Granfiesta" sherry. Recently good Rhine Riesling and SEMILLON. Owned by WOLF BLASS.

Elgee Park Mornington Pensinsular. Table ★★★

Substantial modern winery on longest-established v'yd producing good CAB/MERLOT, CHARD, RIESLING and a hatful of VIOGNIER.

Enterprise Wines Clare Valley. Table ★★★

Tim Knappstein, an exceptionally gifted winemaker, produces Rhine Riesling. FUME BLANC, GEWÜRZ and CABERNET. Now part of WOLF BLASS.

Evans and Tate Swan Valley. Table ★★→★★★

Fine elegant reds from the Margaret River Redbrook and Swan Valley Gnangara v'yds. Good SEM too.

Evans Family Hunter Valley, N.S.W. ★★★

Excellent CHARD, fermented in new oak, from small v'yd owned by family of Len Evans and made at ROTHBURY ESTATE.

Forest Hills Mount Barker, W.A. Table ★★→★★★

Pioneer v'yd in region, with wines made under contract at PLANTAGENET. RIESLING, CHARD and CAB can be and usually are excellent.

Giaconda Central Vic. Table. ★★★

Very small but ultra-fashionable winery near Beechworth producing eagerly sought CHARD and P NOIR.

Goundrey Wines Great Southern, W. Aus. Table ★★★

Recent expansion and quality upgrade. Now in first rank with esp. good CAB and wooded whites.

Hardy's S. Vales, Barossa, Keppoch, etc. Full range ★→★★★

Famous family-run company using and blending wines from several areas. Top wines are "Collection" series and Australia's greatest vintage ports. Hardy's bought HOUGHTON and REYNELLA and, most recently, STANLEY. Reynella's beautifully restored buildings are now group headquarters.

Heathcote Bendigo. Table ★★→★★★

Stylish producer of eclectic range of white and red varietals, showing abundant flavour and technical perfection.

Heemskerk Tasmania. Table ★★★

Most successful commercial operation in Tasmania. Herby CAB; promising CHARD. Also P NOIR and RIESLING. Recent partnership with Louis Roederer plans high class sparkling wine in years to come.

Henschke Barossa. Table ★★★ →★★★★

Family business known for sterling SHIRAZ and v.g. CAB. New high-country v'yds on Adelaide Hills add excitement.

Hickinbotham Winemakers Mornington Peninsula. Table ★★→★★★
  Innovative winemaking by Hickinbotham family (since 1980) has produced fascinating styles from grapes grown in many regions.

Hollick Coonawarra. Table ★★★
  Ian and Wendy Hollick won instant stardom with trophy-winning '84 CAB; also v.g. CHARD and RIES from small winery.

Houghton Swan Valley, W.A. Full range ★→★★★
  The most famous old winery of W.A. Soft, ripe White Burgundy is top wine; also excellent CAB, VERDELHO, etc. See Hardy's.

Hungerford Hill Hunter Valley and Coonawarra. Table ★→★★
  Medium-sized winery producing good varietals esp. RIESLING and CABERNET from COONAWARRA.

Huntington Estate Mudgee. Table ★★→★★★
  Small winery; the best in Mudgee. Fine CABERNETS and clean SEMILLON and CHARDONNAY. Invariably under-priced.

Idyll Geelong. Vic. Table ★★★
  Small winery with GEWÜRZ and v.g. CAB in very individual style.

Jeffrey Grosset Clare. Table ★★→★★★
  Exceedingly elegant RIESLING, CHARD and CABERNET made in consistent style by fastidious young winemaker.

Kaiser Stuhl Barossa. Full range ★→★★★
  Now part of PENFOLDS; huge winery takes fruit from diverse sources. "Green Label" RIESLING can be excellent. So can Red Ribbon reds.

Katnook Estate Coonawarra. Table ★★★
  Excellent pricey CAB and CHARD; also SAUV BL, P NOIR, RIES.

Krondorf Wines Barossa Valley. Table ★★→ ★★★
  Acquired by MILDARA in 1986, but quality and brand image will be preserved. "Show Reserve" wines are best.

Lake's Folly Hunter Valley. Table ★★★★
  The work of an inspired surgeon from Sydney. CABERNET and new barrels make fine complex reds. Also exciting CHARD.

Lark Hill Canberra District ★★→★★★
  Best and most consistent producer with RIESLING esp. attractive.

Leeuwin Estate Margaret River. Table ★★→★★★★
  Lavishly equipped estate leading W. Australia with superb (and very expensive) CHARD; developing fine P. NOIR, RIES, and CAB.

Lilydale Vineyards Yarra Valley. Table ★★★
  Foremost producer of CHARD using sophisticated techniques; also scented GEWÜRZ and crisp RIESLING. CAB and P NOIR recent additions.

Lehmann Wines, Peter Barossa Valley. Table ★★→ ★★★
  Defender of the Barossa faith, Lehmann makes vast quantities of wine, mostly sold in bulk, and v.g. special cuvées under his own label.

Leconfield Coonawarra. Table ★★→★★★
  Coonawarra CABERNET of great style. RIESLING improving.

Lindeman Orig. Hunter, now everywhere. Full range ★→★★★
  One of the oldest firms, now a giant owned by PENFOLDS. Owns BURINGS in BAROSSA and Rouge Homme in COONAWARRA, and important v'yds at PADTHAWAY: outstanding CHARD and COONAWARRA reds. Pioneered new styles, yet still make fat old-style "Hunters". Bin-number "classics" can be v. good.

McWilliams Hunter Valley and Riverina. Full range ★→ ★★★
  Famous family of Hunter winemakers at Mount Pleasant (HERMITAGE and SEMILLON). Pioneers in RIVERINA with noble varieties, incl. CABERNET and sweet white "Lexia". Quality showing marked improvement.

Marsh Estate Hunter Valley. Table ★★→★★★
  Substantial producer of good SEM, SHIRAZ and CAB of growing quality.

Mildara Coonawarra. Murray Valley. Full range ★→★★★
  Sherry and brandy specialists at Mildura on the Murray River also making fine CABERNET and RIESLING at COONAWARRA. Now own BALGOWNIE, KRONDORF and YELLOWGLEN.

Mitchells Clare Valley. Table ***

Small family winery, excellent RIESLING and CABERNET.

Mitchelton Goulbourn Valley, Vic. Table ***

Big modern winery. A wide range incl. v.g. wood-matured Marsanne, CAB and second label Thomas Mitchell offering esp. good value.

Montrose Mudgee, N.S.W. Table ** →***

Recent winemaking and marketing initiatives have had much success; superb CHARD, interesting BARBERA and NEBBIOLO; now part of the ORLANDO group.

Moorilla Estate Tasmania. Table ***

Senior winery on outskirts of Hobart on Derwent River producing superb P NOIR, v.g. CHARD. Botrytis RIESLING in tiny quantities.

Morris N.E. Vic. Table and dessert ** →****

Old winery at Rutherglen making Australia's greatest dessert muscats and tokays; also recently v.g. low-price table wines.

Moss Wood Margaret River. Table ****

Best Margaret River winery (with only 29 acres). CABERNET SAUVIGNON, P NOIR, CHARD all with rich fruit flavours not unlike best Californians.

Mount Langi Ghiran Great Western, Vic. Table **→ ***

Producer of superb rich peppery Rhône-like SHIRAZ, v.g. CAB and less exhilarating RIESLING.

Mount Mary Yarra Valley, Vic. Table ***

Dr. John Middleton is a perfectionist with tiny amounts of suave CHARD, P NOIR and (best of all) CAB SAUV/CAB FRANC/MERLOT.

Murray Robson Wines Hunter Valley. Table **

The reincarnation of Murray Robson with a deliberately similar label; the wines are made at Richmond Grove under Robson's direction.

Oakridge Yarra Valley. Red Table **→***

Cabernet specialist, albeit in small quantities. 87 88 disappointing.

Orlando (Gramp's) Barossa Valley. Full range **→ ***

Great pioneering company, bought by management 1988 but now part owned by Pernod Ricard. Full range from good standard Jacob's Creek Claret to excellent COONAWARRA CAB. William Jacob is low-price line. See also Wyndham Estate.

Penfold's Orig. Adelaide, now everywhere. Full range *→****

Ubiquitous and excellent company: in BAROSSA, RIVERINA, COONAWARRA, CLARE VALLEY, etc. In 1990 bought LINDEMAN's. Grange Hermitage (**78 80** 82′) is ****, St Henri Claret some way behind. Bin-numbered wines are usually outstanding. "Grandfather Port" is sensational. New: "Magill Estate" (**84** 85) from old Grange v'yd and "Clare Estate" from Clare v'yd.

Petaluma Adelaide Hills. ****

A rocket-like success in '80s with CAB, CHARD and RIESLING, now at new winery in ADELAIDE HILLS using COONAWARRA and CLARE grapes. Bollinger now part owner, with ambitious sparkling wine v'yds and facilities in ADELAIDE HILLS. V.g. sparkling wine, called "Croser" (after the boss, Brian C.), since '85.

Petersons Hunter Valley. Table **→***

For a time the most accomplished small Hunter winery, with exceptional CHARD and v.g. SEM: recently a little wobbly.

Piper's Brook Tasmania. Table ***

Cool-area pioneer with very good RIESLING, P NOIR, superb CHARD from Tamar Valley near Launceston. Lovely labels.

Pirramimma S. Vales, S.A. Full range. *→***

Big supply of good standard; reds best.

Plantagenet Mount Barker, W. A. Full range **→***

The region's largest producer with a wide range of varieties, esp. rich CHARD, SHIRAZ and vibrant, potent CAB.

Quelltaler See Eaglehawk.

Redman Coonawarra. Red Table ★—→★★

The most famous old name in COONAWARRA make two wines (Claret, CABERNET). Recent quality disappointing.

Renmano Murray Valley, S.A. Full range. ★→ ★★

Huge coop (see Berri-Renmano). "Chairman's Selections" v.g. value. Exceedingly voluptuous CHARD.

Reynella S. Vales, S.A. Full range ★★—→★★★

Historic red wine specialists s. of Adelaide. Rich CAB (partly COONAWARRA), Claret and excellent "port". See Hardy's.

Rockford Barossa Valley, S.A. Table ★★

Small producer, but a wide range of thoroughly individual styles often made from grapes grown on very old low-yielding v'yds.

Rosemount Upper Hunter and Coonawarra. Table ★—→★★★

Rich, unctuous HUNTER "Show" CHARD is an international smash. This and COONAWARRA CHARD lead the wide range.

Rothbury Estate Hunter Valley. Table ★★—→ ★★★

Important syndicate-owned estate. Traditional HUNTER "Hermitage" and long-lived SEMILLON: "Black Label" best. Rich flavoured buttery CHARDONNAY (from Cowra) is especially good.

S. Smith & Sons Barossa. Full range ★→ ★★★

Big old family firm with considerable verve, using computers, juice evaluation, etc., to produce full spectrum of high-quality wines, incl. "Hill-Smith Estate". "Heggies Vineyard" is best.

St Huberts Yarra Valley. Vic. Table ★★—→★★★

Erratic, much sought-after CABERNET; recent change in winemaking has improved consistency for this largest YARRA winery.

St Leonards N.E. Vic. Full range ★★

Excellent varieties sold only at cellar door and mailing list, incl. exotics, e.g. Fetyaska and Orange Muscat.

St Matthias Tamar Valley, Tas. Table ★★

Has joined the "big three" Tasmania wineries almost overnight; superbly situated v'yd and cellar-door sales on banks of Tamar estuary. Wines made under contract at HEEMSKERK.

Saltram Barossa. Full range ★—→★★★

Seagram-owned winery making wines of variable quality. "Pinnacle Selection" best wines; also Mamre Brook.

Sandalford Swan Valley. Table ★

Fine old winery with contrasting styles of red and white varietals from Swan and Margaret rivers. Wonderful old Verdelho.

Saxonvale Hunter Valley. Table ★★

Medium-sized operation now making good early-maturing SEMILLON and CHARDONNAY. Also good soft CABERNET, SHIRAZ.

Seaview S. Vales, S.A. ★★

Brand name owned by PENFOLD's used for good value CAB, CHARD and sparkling.

Seppelt Barossa, Great Western, Keppoch, etc. Full range ★—→★★★

Far-flung producers of Australia's most popular "champagne" (Gt. Western Brut), good dessert wines, the reliable Moyston claret and some very good private bin wines, incl. CHARD, from Gt. Western and Drumborg in Victoria, and PADTHAWAY and BAROSSA in South Australia. Top sp. is called "Salinger".

Seville Estate Yarra Valley. Table ★★—→★★★

Tiny winery with CHARD, very late-picked RIES, SHIRAZ, P NOIR and v.g. CAB.

Stanley Clare Valley. Full range ★—→ ★★★

Important medium-size quality winery purchased by HARDY late 1987. Good RHINE RIESLING, SEM, CHARD and Cabernet/Malbec blends under Leasingham Domaine label.

Stanton & Killeen N.E. Vic. Table and dessert ★★

Small old family firm. Rich muscats, also strong Moodemere reds.

Taltarni   Great Western/Avoca. Table ★★★

Dominique Portet, brother of Bernard (Clos du Val, Napa), son of André (ex-Ch Lafite), produces huge but balanced reds, good SAUV BLANC and adequate sparkling wines.

Tarrawarra   Yarra Valley. Table ★★

Multi-million dollar investment making limited quantities of idiosyncratic and expensive CHARD, with P NOIR now available.

Taylors Wines   Clare Valley. Table ★→★★

Large wine-producing unit making range of inexpensive table wines.

Tisdall Wines   Goulburn Valley. Table ★★→★★★

Substantial winery in the Echuca area, making local ("Rosbercon") wines plus finer material from central ranges (Mount Helen CABERNET, CHARDONNAY, RHINE RIESLING).

Tollana   Barossa, S.A. Full Range ★★→★★★

Old company once famous for brandy, has latterly made some quite fine CABERNET and RHINE RIESLING. Acquired by PENFOLD's 1987.

Tulloch   Hunter Valley, N.S.W. Table ★→★★

An old name at Pokolbin, with dry reds, CHARD and VERDELHO, now part of PENFOLDS group, but a shadow of its former self.

Tyrrell   Hunter Valley, N.S.W. Table ★★→ ★★★

Some of the best traditional Hunter wines, Hermitage and SEMILLON. Also big rich "Vat 47" CHARDONNAY, delicate P NOIR and v.g. sp.

Vasse Felix   Margaret River. Table ★★→★★★

The pioneer of the Margaret River. Elegant CABERNETS notable for mid-weight balance, bought by Robert Holmes à Court 1987.

Virgin Hills   Bendigo/Ballarat. Table ★★★★

Tiny supplies of one blended (CAB/SHIRAZ/MALBEC) red of legendary style and balance.

Westfield   Swan Valley. Table ★→ ★★

John Kosovich's CAB, CHARD and VERDELHO show particular finesse for a hot climate. Also good "port".

Wirra Wirra   S. Vales, S.A. Table ★★→★★★

Under PETALUMA influence high quality, beautifully packaged whites and reds have made a big impact.

Woodleys   Barossa, S.A. Table ★★

Well-known for low-price Queen Adelaide label. "Reference" CAB is best wine. Acquired by SEPPELT in 1985.

Wyndham Estate   Branxton, N.S.W. Full range ★ →★★

Aggressive large Hunter and Mudgee group with Richmond Grove, Hunter Estate, Hollydene, Saxonvale, Montrose and Craigmoor as its brands. Acquired by ORLANDO early 1990.

Wynn   Coonawarra, S. Vales. Table ★★→★★★

Since its acquisition by PENFOLD's in 1985 has produced even better wines; RIES, CHARD, SHIRAZ and CAB all very good, esp. JOHN RIDDOCH CAB.

Yalumba   See S. Smith & Sons.

Yarra Burn   Yarra Valley. Table ★→★★★

Substantial boutique producing wines of variable quality and style. Sometimes excellent P NOIR and CAB.

Yarra Yering   Yarra Valley. Table ★★★→★★★★

One of the best Lilydale boutique wineries. Esp. racy powerful P NOIR, deep CABERNET (Dry Red No.1) and SHIRAZ (Dry Red No.2).

Yarrinya Estate   Yarra Valley. Table ★★→★★★

Purchased by de Bortoli in 1987 and being aggressively expanded; now has largest plantings (tho' not all in bearing) in the Yarra Valley.

Yellowglen   Bendigo/Ballarat. Sparkling ★→★★

High-flying sparkling winemaker acquired by MILDARA. Sales are more impressive than quality.

Yeringberg   Yarra Valley. Table ★★★

Historic estate now again producing v. high-quality CHARD, CAB, P NOIR, in minute quantities.

New Zealand

Over the last decade New Zealand has made an international impact with white table wines of startling quality, well able to compete with those of Australia or California. It is now regarded as the foremost cool-climate viticultural region among the world's newer wine countries.

White grapes predominate. Müller-Thurgau is the most planted variety, but is being rapidly overtaken by varieties in demand overseas, Sauvignon Blanc, Chardonnay and Riesling in whites, and Cabernet Sauvignon and Merlot for reds. Booming exports have led to acute shortage of supply, particularly for Sauvignon Blanc and Chardonnay.

New vineyards areas opening up in Martinborough (North Island, north of the capital city, Wellington), and Canterbury and Central Otago, in South Island. NZ now boasts the world's southernmost (Otago) and easternmost (East Cape) vineyards.

Intensity of fruit and varietal character, and crisp acidity, are the hallmarks of New Zealand wines. No region on earth can match the pungency of its best Sauvignon Blanc. Barrel fermentation and/or ageing are adding to the complexity and interest of its wines. The principal areas and producers are:

Auckland Largest city in NZ, location of head offices of major wineries, plus largest number of medium and small wineries in outskirts.

Babich Henderson, nr. Auckland.
Old Dalmatian family firm of some size, highly respected in NZ for consistent quality and value. Also using grapes from GISBORNE and HAWKES BAY. Good CHARDS (esp. "Irongate"), SAUV BL, SEMILLON/CHARD, GEWÜRZ, CAB SAUV and CAB/MERLOT. Pinot Noir not so good.

Brajkovich See Kumeu River

Brookfields Meeanee, Hawkes Bay.
Small volume winery, newcomer to export. Noted for SAUV BL, CHARD and CAB.

Cape Mentelle Renwick, Marlborough.
Offshoot of W. Australia winery, better known by its NZ brand name, "Cloudy Bay" after nearby coastal feature. Excellent initial SAUV BL now joined by outstanding CHARD.

Cellier Le Brun Renwick, nr. Blenheim.
Small winery established by son of Champagne family, producing méthode champenoise, with v.g. Blancs de Blancs.

Cloudy Bay The top name for SAUV BLANC and CHARDONNAY ('88 is sumptuous). Richly subtle excellent whites. MERLOT ('87) needs more body and richness.

Collard Henderson, nr. Auckland.
Small family winery using grapes from several areas, CHARD, SAUV BL, dry CHENIN BL and CAB/MERLOT.

Cooks Wineries at Te Kauwhata, s. of Auckland and in Hawkes Bay. Large company now merged with Corbans and former McWilliams, using grapes from GISBORNE and HAWKES BAY. Steadily good record with CHARD, GEWÜRZ, CHENIN BL and CAB SAUV, now producing fresh, nettly SAUV BL, also late picked MÜLLER-THURGAU.

Cooper's Creek Huapai Valley, n.w. of Auckland.
Small winery augmenting own grapes with GISBORNE and HAWKES BAY fruit. Exporting good CHARD, SAUV BL, RIES, GEWÜRZ and popular blends Coopers Dry (White) and Coopers Red.

Corbans Henderson, nr. Auckland.

Old-established firm with wineries at GISBORNE and HAWKES BAY. Now incorporating Cooks and McWilliams, and second largest in NZ. New premium brand, "Stoneleigh" CHARD (over-oaked in '88; Riesling '89 is excellent), from vineyards in Marlborough producing v.g SAUV BL, CHARD, RIES and CAB SAUV. Wide range of sound wines under Corban label. Additional premium wines under affiliate label Robard & Butler.

De Redcliffe Mangatawhiri, s.e. of Auckland.

Small progressive winery with associated resort "Hotel du Vin"; producing good CHARD, SEMILLON and CAB/MERLOT.

Delegat's Henderson, nr. Auckland.

Medium-sized family winery, using grapes from GISBORNE and HAWKES BAY for good CHARD, SAUV BL and CAB SAUV, plus impressive Auslese RIESLING. '88 Hawkes Bay Chard is exceptionally aromatic on the palate. CABERNET Reserve '87 is v.g.

Esk Valley Bayview, Hawkes Bay.

Former large family concern, now merged with VILLA MARIA/VIDAL group, concentrating on small range of premium whites and reds incl. v.g. dry Chenin Blanc '89 and one of NZ's best Cabernets '88.

Giesen Burnham, s. of Christchurch, Canterbury, South Island.

Small winery established by immigrant German family, using own v'yd and some MARLBOROUGH grapes. Good CHARD, SAUV BL, RIES and reds.

Gisborne Site of three large wineries, MONTANA, CORBANS and PENFOLD'S, and centre of large viticultural area incl. MATAWHERO and TOLAGA BAY. Good area for MÜLLER-THURGAU, CHARD, SEMILLON and GEWÜRZ.

Goldwater Waiheke Island in Hauraki Gulf, nr. Auckland.

Small vineyard at sea edge, known best for CAB/MERLOT and SAUV BL.

Hawkes Bay Large viticultural region on e. coast of North Island, s. of GISBORNE, known for high-quality grapes, esp. CHARD and CAB SAUV.

Hunters Marlborough.

Small, progressive winery using only MARLBOROUGH grapes. Highly reputed for outstanding SAUV BL (and oaky "Fumé" style), and CHARD. ('89 needs 2-3 years in bottle). Riesling since '89.

Kumeu River Kumeu, n.w. of Auckland.

Premium label of small San Marino family winery, establishing reputation for SAUV FUME, CHARD, CAB/MERLOT and light fruity CAB FRANC under Brajkovich family crest label.

Lincoln Vineyards Henderson, nr. Auckland.

Medium-sized family winery now producing varietals esp. CHARD, CHENIN BLANC and CABERNET. ('88 shows real promise).

Marlborough Leading export wine region, at north end of South Island, on stony plain formed by Wairau River. Well suited to white varieties CHARD, SAUV BL and RIESLING, but also good CAB SAUV and promising PINOT NOIR. Potential here for v.g. sparkling.

Martinborough New smallish appellation in s. Wairarapa, North Island (n. of Wellington). Stony soils, similar to MARLBOROUGH.

Martinborough Vineyards Martinborough.

Largest of the small operations in the area. Awards already for CHARD, "Fumé" SAUV BL and PINOT NOIR.

Matawhero nr. Gisborne.

Small winery with established name for GEWÜRZ, CHARD and SAUV BL.

Matua Valley n.w. of Auckland.

Medium-sized family winery, pioneer with new varieties. Own grapes supplemented by HAWKES BAY and GISBORNE. Well known for Judd Chard (Gisborne), intense, unwooded SAUV BL and oaky Reserve, unique PINOT NOIR/BLANC and good CAB SAUV, MERLOT and late-harvest Muscat.

Millton nr. Gisborne.

Small new producer using organic cultivation methods. Good SAUV BL/SEMILLON blend, CHARD and RIESLING (both dry and late harvest). Splendid barrel-fermented Chenin Blanc '87 like a v. fine Anjou.

Mission Greenmeadows, Hawkes Bay.

The oldest continuing winemaking establishment in NZ, founded by French missionaries and still operated by Society of Mary. Good SEMILLON/SAUV BL blend and CAB/MERLOT.

Montana Auckland.

Largest winemaking enterprise in NZ, with wineries in GISBORNE and MARLBOROUGH and now incorporating PENFOLDS NZ operations. Pioneered viticulture in MARLBOROUGH, but draws grapes also from GISBORNE and HAWKES BAY. Marlborough labels incl. SAUV BL, CHARD, RIESLING, CAB SAUV and PINOT NOIR. Gisborne CHARD also sound wine and big seller. Success with "Lindauer" méthode champenoise has led to licensing agreement with Champagne DEUTZ.

Morton Estate Katikati, nr. Tauranga. e. coast North Island.

Expanding new winery with high reputation for CHARD from HAWKES BAY (esp. premium black label), full-bodied SAUV BL, and CAB SAUV. Recently released its first (v.g.) méthode champenoise.

Ngatarawa nr. Hastings, Hawkes Bay.

Boutique winery in old stables of established HAWKES BAY family. Good CHARD, SAUV BL and CAB/MERLOT under "Glazebrook" family name label.

Nobilo Huapai Valley, n.w. of Auckland.

NZ's largest family-owned winery, with own grapes plus fruit from GISBORNE, HAWKES BAY, MARTINBOROUGH and MARLBOROUGH. Good CHARD (esp. from Gisborne), pungent SAUV BL, SEMILLON, and long established reputation for age-worthy reds, CAB SAUV and PINOT NOIR. Associate label, "Classic Hills". "Concept One" is Huapai Cab and Pinotage.

Penfolds See Montana.

Robard & Butler See Corbans.

St Nesbit Karaka, nr. Papakura, s. of Auckland.

Expanding boutique winery: single red wine blended from CAB SAUV, CAB FRANC and MERLOT, well made and matured in barriques.

Selak's Kumeu, n.w. of Auckland.

Small family firm with good export reputation for fresh, sharpish SAUV BL, SAUV BL/SEMILLON blend (in "Fumé" style), CHARD and CAB SAUV. ("Founders" label for top wines of two last-named).

Stoneleigh See Corbans.

Stonyridge Waiheke Island, nr. Auckland.

Boutique winery concentrating on two reds in Bordeaux style; LAROSE exceptional, AIRFIELD v.g.

Te Mata Havelock North, Hawkes Bay.

Oldest winery premises in continuous operation, now restored and producing good CHARD and SAUV BL from nearby vineyards, plus excellent "Coleraine" CAB/MERLOT from proprietor's home vineyard.

Vidal Hastings, Hawkes Bay.

Atmospheric old winery now merged with Villa Maria (see below). Good HAWKES BAY CHARD, SAUV BL, CAB SAUV and NOIR. Cab/Merlot '87 is v.g.

Villa Maria Mangere, outskirts s. Auckland.

Large company, now incorporating VIDAL and ESK VALLEY. Uses grapes from Ihumatao (nr. Auckland airport), GISBORNE and HAWKES BAY. Full range of wines, with emphasis on barrel-fermented CHARD, SAUV BL (and wooded "Fumé" variation), GEWÜRZ, CAB SAUV and CAB/MERLOT.

Weingut Seifried Upper Moutere, nr. Nelson, South Island.

Small winery started by Austrian immigrant. Good CHARD, SAUV BL, RIESLING (in dry and late-harvest styles) and PINOT NOIR.

South Africa

Quality in S. Africa's table wines began around 1970 when vineyard owners began to plant Cabernet Sauvignon, followed by better white varieties. The success of small new wineries in the 1980s has encouraged others to buy oak barrels from France. Cellarmasters are now showing more care in harvesting and cellar treatment and standards are rising steadily.

Allesverloren ★★
Estate in MALMESBURY with 395 acres of v'yds, well known for "port", and now also specializing in powerful reds from CABERNET and Tinta Barocca.

Alphen ★
Gilbey's brand name for wines from STELLENBOSCH area.

Alto ★★
STELLENBOSCH estate of 247 acres high on a hill, known for massive-bodied CAB and a good SHIRAZ/CAB/MERLOT blend: Alto Rouge.

Altydgedacht ★★
Durbanville area. Bottles good CAB and other wines since '85.

Backsberg ★★ →★★★
A prize-winning 395-acre estate at PAARL with notably good white wines (incl. CHARD) and medium bodied CABERNET and SHIRAZ.

Bellingham ★★→★★★
Top brand name of Union Wine Co. Reliable reds and whites, esp. CABERNET. Johannisberger is top-selling blend.

Bergkelder Big wine concern at STELLENBOSCH, member of the OUDE MEESTER group, making and distributing many brands (FLEUR DU CAP, GRÜNBERGER) and estate wines.

Bertrams ★★
Gilbey's brand of good varietal reds, plus a B'x-style blend: "Robert Fuller."

Blaauwklippen ★★→★★★
Estate S. of STELLENBOSCH producing some of S. Africa's very best reds, CAB, P NOIR and ZIN, and good RHINE RIES, and SAUV BLANC.

Boberg Controlled region of origin for fortified wines consisting of the districts of PAARL and TULBAGH.

Boplass ★★
New winery at Calitzdorp. Early success with Tinta Barocca port-style.

Boschendal ★★★
Vast (617-acre) estate in PAARL area on an old fruit farm. Emphasis on white wines, Blanc de Noir and sparkling "Brut".

Breede River Valley Fortified and white wine region east of Drakenstein Mtns.

Buitenverwachting ★★★
Exceptional v'yds plus bought grapes produce notable SAUVIGNON BLANC and Blanc Fumé. Good RHINE RIESLING and claret blend.

Cabernet The great Bordeaux grape, particularly successful in the COASTAL REGION. Sturdy, long-ageing wines. Use of new oak from about '82 has made great improvement.

Cape Independent Winemakers Guild Young group of winemakers in the vanguard of quality and without direct links to the major wholesalers. Holds an annual auction of progressive-style wines.

Cavendish Cape ★★
Range of remarkably good sherries from the K.W.V.

Chardonnay Classic white variety, fairly new in S. Africa due to official restrictions. Recent release of good vines has resulted in leap in quality and number: now 40 on the market. Great expectations.

Chenin Blanc Work-horse grape of the Cape; one vine in three. Adaptable and sometimes very good. Alias STEEN. K.W.V. makes a very good example at a bargain price.

Cinsaut The principal bulk-producing French red grape in S. Africa; formerly known as Hermitage. Very seldom seen with varietal label.

Coastal Region Demarcated wine region, includes PAARL, STELLENBOSCH, Durbanville, SWARTLAND, TULBAGH.

Colombard The "French Colombard" of California. High acidity and fruity flavour add interest to blended whites.

Constantia Once the world's most famous Muscat wine, from the Cape. Now the southernmost district of origin.

Delaire Vineyards New 90-acre estate at Helshoogte, STELLENBOSCH.

Delheim ★★★
Winery at Driesprong in one of the highest areas of STELLENBOSCH. Delicate STEEN and GEWÜRZ whites; impressive reds: CABERNET, PINOTAGE, SHIRAZ. Grande Reserve (CAB SAUV, CAB FRANC, MERLOT) is top class.

Douglas Green of Paarl ★★
Merchants buying wine for own-label blends.

Drostdy ★★
Quality range of sherries from BERGKELDER.

De Wetshof ★★★
Pioneering estate in ROBERTSON district. CHARDONNAY, SAUVIGNON BLANC, RHINE RIESLING.

Edelkeur ★★★★
Excellent intensely sweet white made with nobly rotten (p. 49) grapes by NEDERBURG.

Estate wine Strictly controlled term applying only to registered estates making wines from grapes grown on the same property.

Fleur du Cap ★★
Popular and well-made range of wines from the BERGKELDER. Good CAB; interesting SAUV BL.

Gewürztraminer The famous spicy grape of Alsace, best at NEDERBURG, SIMONSIG and (for drier style) STELLENRYCK. Naturally low acidity makes this variety difficult to handle at the Cape.

Glen Carlou ★★
Promising new winery at Klapmuts, PAARL. Good early CHARD, MERLOT.

Graca ★
S.F.W. popular white blend in Portuguese-style bottle.

Grand Cru (or Premier Grand Cru) Term for a totally dry white, with no quality implications. Generally to be avoided.

Groot Constantia ★★★
Historic estate, now government owned, near Cape Town. Source of superlative muscat wine in the early 19th century. Now making wide range of wines, esp. good RHINE RIESLING, GEWÜRZ.

Grünberger ★
BERGKELDER brand using STEEN to make range of dry and semi-sweet white wines.

Hamilton Russell ★★★
Young but already renowned estate in cool coastal valley. Among leaders with P NOIR, CHARDONNAY and SAUV BLANC.

Hanepoot Local name for the sweet Muscat of Alexandria grape.

Hartenberg ★★
Stellenbosch estate producing fine CABERNET and SHIRAZ. Previously known as (Gilbey's) Montague.

Haute Provence ★
New Franschoek estate with interesting SAUV BLANC.

Hazendal ★★
Family estate in W. STELLENBOSCH specializing in semi-sweet STEEN, marketed by the BERGKELDER.

Kanonkop ★★★

> Outstanding estate in n. STELLENBOSCH. Stylish full-bodied CAB and PINOTAGE. Paul Sauer Fleur is a Bordeaux-style blend.

Klein Constantia ★★★→★★★★

> S. Africa's new star. No expense spared in vineyard or cellar. First Chardonnay in '88 extremely fine; '88 Cabernet will be when released in '92. Top class SAUV BLANC and RIESLING.

Koopmanskloof ★★

> STELLENBOSCH estate making good dry Chenin Blanc-based blend "Blanc de Marbonne" from SAUV BLANC plus SEMILLON.

K.W.V. The Kooperatieve Wijnbouwers Vereniging, S. Africa's national wine cooperative created 60 years ago to absorb surpluses. Vast premises in PAARL making range of good wines, esp. sherries.

La Bri ★★

> Whites made in Franschoek coop cellar from SAUV BL, RHINE RIES and SEMILLON. Sauvignon de la Bri is best.

Laborie ★★

> K.W.V.-owned showpiece estate on Paarl Mtn. Blended white and red.

Landgoed South African for estate; a word which appears on estate-wine labels and official seals.

Landskroon ★★

> Family estate owned by Paul and Hugo de Villiers. Good dry reds esp. SHIRAZ, CABERNET, CAB FRANC.

Late Harvest Term for a mildly sweet wine. "Special Late Harvest" must be naturally sweet (no added concentrate). "Noble Late Harvest" is the highest quality level of all.

La Motte ★★

> Rupert family's new Franschoek estate. Rather oaky reds and whites.

Lemberg ★★

> Tiny estate in TULBAGH, making full-bodied, wood-aged Harsleveld and SAUV BLANC. Growing reputation.

Lievland ★★

> Promising estate with attractive reds and medal-winning RIESLING.

L'Ormarins ★★★

> Rupert family estate at Franschoek. Good SAUV BLANC; now stylish CAB.

Le Bonheur ★★★

> STELLENBOSCH estate producing only three wines: CAB, unoaked BLANC FUME and CHARDONNAY.

J.C. Le Roux ★★

> Old brand revived as BERGKELDER's sparkling wine house. SAUV BLANC (Charmat) and P NOIR (méthode champenoise). Also CHARDONNAY.

Meerendal ★★

> Estate near Durbanville producing traditional robust reds (esp. SHIRAZ and PINOTAGE) marketed by the BERGKELDER.

Meerlust ★★★

> Beautiful old family estate s. of STELLENBOSCH making outstanding CAB, Rubicon (Médoc-style blend), MERLOT and P NOIR. CHARD in the pipeline.

Middelsvlei ★★

> BERGKELDER STELLENBOSCH estate with good Pinotage, lately CABERNET.

Monis ★→★★★

> Well-known wine concern of PAARL, with fine "Vintage Port".

Muratie ★

> Ancient estate in STELLENBOSCH, best known for its port. Recently sold; bright future expected.

Nederburg ★★★→★★★★

> The most famous wine farm in modern S. Africa, operated by the STELLENBOSCH FARMERS' WINERY. Its annual auction is a major event. Pioneer in modern cellar practice and with fine CABERNET, "Private Bin" blends, EDELKEUR and GEWÜRZ. Also good sparkling wines and Paarl RIESLINGS. New winemaker recently.

SOUTH AFRICA/Kan-Ste

Neethlingshof ★★
　　Major German investment employing Gunter Brozel (ex-NEDERBURG) as winemaker. Real promise with (so far) GEWURZ and CABERNET.

Neil Ellis Vineyards ★★→★★★
　　Wines made in central cellar from grapes grown in widely differing areas. Very fine SAUV BLANC, CAB.

Overgaauw ★→★★★
　　Estate w. of STELLENBOSCH making good CHARDONNAY, very good CABERNET, and Tria Corda, a CABERNET/MERLOT blend.

Paarl　South Africa's wine capital, 30 miles n.e. of Cape Town, and the surrounding demarcated district, among the best in the country, particularly for white wine and sherry.

Pierre Jourdan ★★★
　　Impressive méthode champenoise made from CHARD and P NOIR.

Pinot noir　Like counterparts in California and Australia, Cape producers struggle to get complexity of flavour. Best are HAMILTON RUSSELL, BLAAUWKLIPPEN, MEERLUST, RUSTENBERG.

Pinotage　S. African red grape, a cross between P NOIR and CINSAUT, useful for high yields and hardiness. Wine is never quite first-class.

Premier Grand Cru　See Grand Cru.

Rhine Riesling　Produces full-flavoured dry and off-dry wines. Generally needs two years or more of bottle age. See Weisser Riesling.

Riesling　South African Riesling (actually Crouchen Blanc) is very different from RHINE RIESLING, providing neutral, easy drinking wines.

Rietvallei ★★
　　ROBERTSON estate producing excellent fortified Muscadel.

Robertson　Small demarcated district e. of the Cape and inland. Mainly dessert wines (notably Muscat), but red and white table wines are on the increase. Includes Bonnievale. Irrigated vineyards.

Roodeberg　★★
　　Good-value brand of blended red from the K.W.V.

Rozendel ★★★
　　STELLENBOSCH (Jonkershoek) winery with good CAB/MERLOT blend.

Rustenberg　★★★
　　Effectively, if not officially, an estate red wine from just n.e. of STELLENBOSCH. Excellent B'x-style Rustenberg, good CAB/CINSAUT "Dry Red" and outstanding CABERNET. Now also CHARD and v.g. PINOT NOIR.

Sauvignon Blanc　Adapting well to warm conditions. Widely grown and marketed in both "wooded" and "unwooded" styles.

Schoongezicht ★★★
　　Beautiful old STELLENBOSCH estate producing top-class wines made Bunder the RUSTENBERG label.

Simonsig ★★★
　　Estate owned by F.J. Malan, pioneering estate producer. Produces a wide range, incl. GEWÜRZ, Vin Fumé (wood-matured dry white) v.g. CHARDONNAY and a méthode champenoise.

Simonsvlei　One of S. Africa's best-known cooperative cellars, just outside PAARL. A prize-winner with PINOTAGE.

Spier ★★
　　Estate of five farms w. of STELLENBOSCH producing reds and whites. COLOMBARD and PINOTAGE are best.

Steen　South Africa's commonest white grape, said to be a clone of the CHENIN BLANC. It gives strong, tasty and lively wine, sweet or dry, normally better than S. African RIESLING.

Stein　Name often used for commercial blends of semi-sweet white wine. Not necessarily to be despised.

Stellenbosch　Town and demarcated district 30 miles e. of Cape Town, extending to the ocean at False Bay. The heart of the wine industry, with all three of the largest companies. Most of the best estates, esp. for red wine, are in the mountain foothills of the region.

Stellenbosch Farmers' Winery (S.F.W.) South Africa's biggest winery (after the K.W.V.) with several ranges of wines, incl. NEDERBURG and ZONNEBLOEM. Wide range of mid-and low-priced wines.

Stellenryck ★★★
Top-quality BERGKELDER range, RHINE RIESLING, Fumé Blanc, CABERNET and GEWÜRZ.

Tassenberg ★
Popular and good-value red known to thousands as Tassies.

Thelema ★★
Promising winery in STELLENBOSCH (Banghoek). CAB, CHARD, SAUV BLANC.

Theuniskraal ★★
Well-known TULBAGH estate specializing in white wines, esp. RIESLING, GEWÜRZTRAMINER. No longer a leader.

Tulbagh Demarcated district n. of PAARL best known for the white wines of THEUNISKRAAL and TWEE JONGEGEZELLEN, and the dessert wines from Drostdy. See also Boberg.

Twee Jongegezellen ★★
Estate at TULBAGH. One of the great pioneers which revolutionized S. African wine in the 1950s, still in the family of its 18th-century founder. Mainly white wines, incl. "Schanderl" and "T.J. 39". New sparkling wine may herald revival.

Uiterwyk ★★
Old estate w. of STELLENBOSCH. Good CAB SAUV and pleasant whites.

Uitkyk ★★
Old estate (400 acres) at STELLENBOSCH famous for Carlonet (big gutsy CAB) and Carlsheim (chiefly SAUV BLANC) white.

Vergenoegd ★★→★★★
Old family estate in S. STELLENBOSCH supplying high-quality sherry to the K.W.V. and offering deeply flavoured CABERNET and excellent SHIRAZ under the estate label. Not as good as before.

Villiera ★★★
Paarl estate with Tradition top class méthode champenoise. Winner of 1988 Gault et Millau Paris Olympiad with RHINE RIESLING. Fine CAB and CAB/MERLOT blend called Cru Monro.

Vriesenhof ★★★
Small-scale winery with vines high on Stellenbosch mountain slope. Highly rated CAB and CHARD and CAB/MERLOT blend.

Warwick ★★
New STELLENBOSCH estate. CABERNET and v.g. Médoc-style blend.

Weisser Riesling Alias Rhine Riesling. Producing good wines in S. Africa. They need time to mature and are not really appreciated.

Welgemeend ★★★
Boutique PAARL estate producing Médoc-style blends, delicate CABERNET and Amadé, a Grenache, SHIRAZ and PINOTAGE blend.

Weltevrede ★→★★
Progressive ROBERTSON estate. Blended white and fortified wines.

Wine of Origin The S. African equivalent of appellation contrôlée. Demarcated regions are described on these pages.

Worcester Demarcated wine district round the Breede and Hex river valleys, e. of PAARL. Many cooperative cellars make mainly dessert wines, brandy and dry whites.

Zandvliet ★★
Estate in the ROBERTSON area making a fine light SHIRAZ.

Zevenwacht ★★★
Large Stellenbosch Estate with wines only available through shareholders and restaurants. CAB SAUV is impressive.

Zonnebloem ★★
Good-quality brand of CABERNET, RIESLING, PINOTAGE, SAUV BLANC and SHIRAZ from the STELLENBOSCH FARMERS' WINERY. Much improved quality recently.

A few words about words

In the shorthand essential for this little book (and sometimes in bigger books as well) wines are often described by adjectives that can seem irrelevant, inane – or just silly. What do "fat", "round", "full", "lean" and so on mean, when used about wine? Some of the more irritatingly vague are expanded in this list:

Attack	The first impression of the wine in your mouth. It should "strike" positively, if not necessarily with force. Without attack it is feeble or too bland.
Attractive	Means "I like it, anyway". A slight put-down for expensive wines; encouragement for juniors. At least refreshing.
Big	Concerns the whole flavour, including the alcohol content. Sometimes implies clumsiness, the opposite of elegance. Generally positive, but big is easy in California and less usual in, say, Bordeaux. So the context matters.
Charming	Rather patronizing when said of wines that should have more impressive qualities. Implies lightness, possibly slight sweetness. A standard comment on Loire wines.
Crisp	With pronounced but pleasing acidity; fresh and eager.
Deep/depth	This wine is worth tasting with attention. There is more to it than the first impression; it fills your mouth with developing flavours as though it had an extra dimension. (Deep colour simply means hard to see through.) All really fine wines have depth.
Easy	Used in the sense of "easy come, easy go". An easy wine makes no demand on your palate (or intellect). The implication is that it drinks smoothly, doesn't need maturing, and all you remember is a pleasant drink.
Elegant	A professional taster's favourite term when he is stuck to describe a wine whose proportions (of strength, flavour, aroma), whose attack, middle and finish, whose texture and all its qualities call for comparison with other forms of natural beauty.
Fat	With flavour and texture that fills your mouth, but without aggression. Obviously inappropriate in e.g. a light Moselle, but what you pay your money for in Sauternes.
Finish	See Length.
Firm	Flavour that strikes the palate fairly hard, with fairly high acidity or tannic astringency giving the impression that the wine is in youthful vigour and will age to gentler things. An excellent quality with high-flavoured foods, and almost always positive.
Flesh	Refers to both substance and texture. A fleshy wine is fatter than a "meaty" wine, more unctuous if less vigorous. The term is often used of good Pomerols, whose texture is notably smooth.
Flowery	Often used as though synonymous with fruity, but really means floral, like the fragrance of flowers. Roses, violets, etc., are sometimes specified.
Fresh	Implies a good degree of fruity acidity, even a little nip of sharpness, as well as the zip and zing of youth. All young whites should be fresh: the alternative is flatness, staleness . . . ugh.
Fruity	Used for almost any quality, but really refers to the body and richness of wine made from good ripe grapes. A fruity aroma is not the same as a flavoury one. Fruitiness usually implies at least a slight degree of sweetness. Attempts at specifying *which* fruit the wine resembles can be helpful. E.g. grapefruit, lemon, plum, lychee.

Full	Interchangeable with full-bodied. Lots of "vinosity" or wineyness: the mouth-filling flavours of alcohol and "extract" (all the flavouring components) combined.
Hollow	Lacking a satisfying middle flavour. Something seems to be missing between first flavour and last. A characteristic of wines from greedy proprietors who let their vines produce too many grapes. A v. hollow wine is "empty".
Lean	A bit more flesh would be an improvement. Lack of mouth-filling flavours: often astringent as well. But occasionally a term of appreciation of a distinct and enjoyable style.
Length	The flavours and aromas that linger after swallowing. In principle the greater the length the better the wine. One second of flavour after swallowing = one "caudalie". Ten caudalies is good; 20 terrific.
Light	With relatively little alcohol and body, as in most German wines. A very desirable quality in the right wines.
Meaty	Savoury in effect with enough substance to chew. The inference is lean meat; leaner than in "fleshy".
Oaky	Smelling or tasting of fresh-sawn oak; e.g. a new barrel.
Plump	The diminutive of fat, implying a degree of charm as well.
Rich	Not necessarily sweet, but giving an opulent impression.
Robust	In good heart, vigorous, and on a fairly big scale.
Rough	Flavour and texture give no pleasure. Acidity and/or tannin are dominant and coarse.
Round	Almost the same as fat, but with more approval.
Structure	The "plan" of the flavour, as it were. The French word "carpentry" relates it to the architecture of a roof, where the forces at work are expressed in beams. By analogy a wine needs a beam for breadth, another for length, a firm "backbone" or king-post, etc. Without structure wine is bland, dull, and won't last.
Stylish	Style is bold and definite; wears its cap on its ear.
Supple	Often used of young red wines which might be expected to be more aggressive. More lively than an "easy" wine, with implications of good quality.
Well-balanced	Contains all the desirable elements (acid, alcohol, flavours, etc) in appropriate and pleasing proportions.

A few words about labels

The American public has become so accustomed to warning labels on all sorts of products and in all sorts of places that it takes them for granted. Perhaps it holds the view that stating the obvious (which most of them do) is harmless enough. But there are some who challenge the right of the Surgeon General to warn wine-drinkers, on every wine-label in America, that "consumption of alcoholic beverages ... may cause health problems." It is almost impossible to think of any human activity which does not answer this description. So what is the objection? The objection is that the Bureau of Alcohol, Tobacco and Firearms, the label-regulating agency, vetoes any additional wording that suggests there may be a less negative point of view. A California wine-merchant, Kermit Lynch, proposed a one-line quote from Thomas Jefferson, the notorious hell-raiser who drafted the Declaration of Independence and served two terms as third President of the United States. Jefferson strongly believed in wine as the beverage of moderation and the only antidote to the hard liquor that was the curse of the young Union. Lynch's label was rejected by the BATF because, as he said, "they have decided that we can't read what Thomas Jefferson has to say about wine because we might think that Jefferson was right".   *Source: The Wine Spectator*

What to drink in an ideal word

Wines at their peak in 1991

Red Bordeaux:
Top growths of 1984, 1981, 1979, 1976, 1975, 1970, 1966, 1962, 1961
Other Crus Classés of 1986 (St-Emilion/Pomerol), 1984, 1982 (St-Emilion/Pomerol), 1981, 1979, 1978, 1975, 1970, 1966, 1961
Petits châteaux of 1987, 1986, 1985, 1983, 1982, 1981, 1979, 1978

Red Burgundy
Top growths of 1984, 1982, 1980, 1979, 1978, 1976, 1971, 1969, 1966, 1964
Premiers Crus of 1985, 1983, 1982, 1980, 1979, 1978, 1976, 1971 . . .
Village wines of 1988, 1987, 1986, 1985, 1983

White Burgundy
Top growths of 1987, 1985, 1984, 1983, 1982, 1981, 1979, 1978 . . .
Premiers Crus of 1986, 1985, 1983, 1981, 1978 . . .
Village wines of 1988, 1987, 1986, 1985, 1984

Sauternes
Top growths of 1984, 1982, 1981, 1980, 1979, 1978, 1976, 1975, 1971, 1970, 1967 . . .
Other wines of 1986, 1985, 1983, 1982, 1981, 1980, 1979, 1978, 1976, 1975 . . .

Sweet Loire wines
Top growths of (Anjou/Vouvray) 1985, 1982, 1981, 1979, 1978, 1976, 1975, 1973, 1971, 1969, 1964 . . . and (dry) Muscadet 1988.

Alsace
Grands Crus and late-harvest wines of 1987, 1986, 1985, 1983, 1981, 1979, 1978, 1976 . . .
Standard wines of 1989, 1988, 1987, 1986, 1985, 1983 . . .

Rhône
Hermitage/top Northern Rhône reds of 1986, 1985, 1984, 1982, 1980, 1979, 1978, 1971, 1970
Châteauneuf-du-Pape of 1985, 1984, 1983, 1982, 1981, 1980, 1979, 1978

German wines
Great sweet wines of 1985, 1983, 1976, 1975, 1971 . . .
Ausleses of 1985, 1983, 1981, 1979, 1976 . . .
Spätleses of 1986, 1985, 1983, 1979, 1976 . . .
Kabinett and QbA wines of 1988, 1987, 1986, 1985, 1984, 1983 . . .

California
Top Cabernets, Pinot Noirs, Zinfandels of 1985, 1984, 1983, 1982, 1980, 1979, 1978, 1975, 1974
Most Cabernets etc. of 1988, 1987, 1986, 1985, 1984 . . .
Top Chardonnays of 1987, 1986, 1985, 1984 . . .
Most Chardonnays of 1988, 1987, 1986, 1985 . . .

Vintage Port
1975, 1970, 1966, 1963, 1960 . . .

Quick reference vintage charts for France and Germany

These charts give a picture of the range of qualities made in the principal areas (every year has its relative successes and failures) and a guide to whether the wine is ready to drink or should be kept.

ı drink now	_ needs keeping	✓ can be drunk with pleasure now, but the better wines will continue to improve
0 no good	10 the best	

FRANCE	RED BORDEAUX		WHITE BORDEAUX	
	MÉDOC/GRAVES	POM ST-EM	SAUTERNES & SW.	GRAVES & DRY
89	8-10 _	7-10 _	7-10 _	6-8 ↙
88	7-9 ◢	7-10 ◢	6-10 _	7-9 ↙
87	3-6 _	3-6	2-5 _	7-10 ↙
86	6-9 ◢	5-7 ↙	7-10 ◢	7-9 ✓
85	6-8 ✓	7-9 ✓	6-8 ✓	5-8 ✓
84	4-7 ↙	2-5 ↙	4-7 ↙	5-7 ✓
83	6-9 ↙	6-9 ↙	6-10 ✓	7-9 ı
82	8-10 ↙	7-9 ✓	3-7 ✓	7-8 ı
81	5-8 ı	6-9 ı	5-8 ✓	7-8 ı
80	4-7 ✓	3-5 ✓	5-9 ✓	5-7 ı
79	5-8 L	5-7 ✓	6-8 ✓	4-6 ı
78	6-9 ı	6-8 ı	4-6 ı	7-9 ı
77	3-5 ı	2-5 ✓	2-4 ✓	6-7 ı
76	6-8 ✓	7-8 ✓	7-9 ✓	4-8 ı
75	7-9 ı	8-9 ı	8-10 ı	8-10 ı
74	4-6 ı	3-5 ı	0 ı	4-6 ı
73	5-7 ı	5-7 ı	0-4 ı	7-8 ı
72	2-5 ı	2-4 ı	2-4 ı	4-5 ı
71	5-8 ✓	6-8 ✓	8-9 ı	8-9 ı

FRANCE	RED BURGUNDY		WHITE BURGUNDY	
	CÔTE D'OR	CÔTE D'OR	CHABLIS	ALSACE
89	6-9 _	6-9 _	7-10 ↙	8-10 ↙
88	7-10 _	7-9 _	7-9 ✓	6-9 ı
87	6-8 ↙	4-7 ↙	5-7 ✓	7-8 ✓
86	5-8 ◢	7-10 ↙	7-9 ↙	7-8 ↙
85	7-10 ı	5-8 ı	6-9 ı	7-10 ı
84	3-6 ✓	4-7 ✓	4-7 ✓	4-6 ✓
83	5-9 ı	6-9 ı	7-9 ✓	8-10 ı
82	4-7 ı	6-8 ı	6-7 ✓	6-8 ı
81	3-6 ı	4-8 ı	6-9 ✓	7-8 ı
80	4-7 ı	4-6 ı	5-7 ı	3-5 ı
79	5-6 ✓	6-8 ı	6-8 ✓	7-8 ı
78	8-10 ı	7-9 ı	7-10 ı	6-8 ı
77	2-4 ✓	4-6 ı	5 ı	3-5 ✓

Beaujolais: 89 was excellent, 88 was good, 87 rather better. Mâcon-Villages (white) 88, 87, 86, are good now. **Loire:** Sweet Anjou and Touraine. Best recent vintages: 89, 88, 85, 84, 83, 82, 79, 78, 76. **Upper Loire:** Sancerre and Pouilly-Fumé 89, 88, 86 are good now. **Muscadet:** D.Y.A. (89 v.g.)

FRANCE	RHÔNE	GERMANY	RHINE	MOSELLE
89	6-9 ◢	89	7-10 _	8-10 _
88	7-9 ✓	88	6-8 ✓	7-9 ✓
87	3-6 ↙	87	4-7 ✓	5-7 ✓
86	5-8 ↙	86	4-8 ↙	5-8 ↙
85	6-8 ✓	85	6-8 ✓	6-9 ✓
84	5-7 ↙	84	4-6 ✓	4-6 ✓
83	6-9 ✓	83	6-9 ı	7-10 ı
82	5-8 ✓	82	4-6 ✓	4-7 ✓
81	5-7 L	81	5-8 ı	4-8 ı
80	6-8 ✓	80	4-7 ı	3-7 ı
79	6-7 ↙	79	6-8 ı	6-8 ı
78	8-10 ı	78	5-7 ı	4-7 ı
77	4-6 ı	77	5-7 ✓	4-6 ✓
76	6-9 ı	76	9-10 ı	9-10 ı

yr + D = when drunk.